TORTS

SIXTH EDITION

STEVEN L. EMANUEL

Founder and Editor-in-Chief, the *CrunchTime* series,
Emanuel Law Outlines, and *Emanuel Bar Review*

Harvard Law School, J.D. 1976
Member (Ret.) NY, CT, MD and VA bars

The Emanuel *CrunchTime*® Series

ASPEN
PUBLISHING

To contact Customer Service, e-mail customer.service@aspenpublishing.com, call 1-800-950-5259, or mail correspondence to:

Aspen Publishing
Attn: Order Department
1 Wall Street
Burlington, MA 01803

Printed in the United States of America.

1 2 3 4 5 6 7 8 9 0

ISBN 978-1-5438-0747-9

SUSTAINABLE FORESTRY INITIATIVE Certified Sourcing
www.forests.org
SFI-00756

About Aspen Publishing

Aspen Publishing is a leading provider of educational content and digital learning solutions to law schools in the U.S. and around the world. Aspen provides best-in-class solutions for legal education through authoritative textbooks, written by renowned authors, and breakthrough products such as Connected eBooks, Connected Quizzing, and PracticePerfect.

The Aspen Casebook Series (famously known among law faculty and students as the "red and black" casebooks) encompasses hundreds of highly regarded textbooks in more than eighty disciplines, from large enrollment courses, such as Torts and Contracts to emerging electives such as Sustainability and the Law of Policing. Study aids such as the *Examples & Explanations* and the *Emanuel Law Outlines* series, both highly popular collections, help law students master complex subject matter.

Major products, programs, and initiatives include:

- **Connected eBooks** are enhanced digital textbooks and study aids that come with a suite of online content and learning tools designed to maximize student success. Designed in collaboration with hundreds of faculty and students, the Connected eBook is a significant leap forward in the legal education learning tools available to students.
- **Connected Quizzing** is an easy-to-use formative assessment tool that tests law students' understanding and provides timely feedback to improve learning outcomes. Delivered through CasebookConnect.com, the learning platform already used by students to access their Aspen casebooks, Connected Quizzing is simple to implement and integrates seamlessly with law school course curricula.
- **PracticePerfect** is a visually engaging, interactive study aid to explain commonly encountered legal doctrines through easy-to-understand animated videos, illustrative examples, and numerous practice questions. Developed by a team of experts, PracticePerfect is the ideal study companion for today's law students.
- The **Aspen Learning Library** enables law schools to provide their students with access to the most popular study aids on the market across all of their courses. Available through an annual subscription, the online library consists of study aids in e-book, audio, and video formats with full text search, note-taking, and highlighting capabilities.
- Aspen's **Digital Bookshelf** is an institutional-level online education bookshelf, consolidating everything students and professors need to ensure success. This program ensures that every student has access to affordable course materials from day one.
- **Leading Edge** is a community centered on thinking differently about legal education and putting those thoughts into actionable strategies. At the core of the program is the Leading Edge Conference, an annual gathering of legal education thought leaders looking to to pool ideas and identify promising directions of exploration.

TABLE OF CONTENTS

Preface

Thank you for buying this book.

The *CrunchTime* Series is intended for people who want Emanuel quality, but don't have the time or money to buy and use the full-length *Emanuel Law Outline* on a subject. We've designed the Series to be used in the last few weeks (or even less) before your final exams.

This book includes the following features, some of which have been extracted from the corresponding *Emanuel Law Outline*:

- ***Flow Charts*** — We've reduced most principles of *Torts* to a series of 15 Flow Charts, not published in the full-length Emanuel or elsewhere. We think these will be especially useful on open-book exams. A list of all the Flow Charts is printed on p. 2.
- ***Capsule Summary*** — This is a 128-page summary of the subject. We've carefully crafted it to cover the things you're most likely to be asked on an exam. The Capsule Summary starts on p. 61.
- ***Exam Tips*** — We've compiled these by reviewing dozens of actual past essay and multiple-choice questions asked in past law school and bar exams, and extracting the issues and "tricks" that surface most often on exams. The Exam Tips start on p. 193.
- ***Short-Answer*** questions — These questions are generally in a Yes/No format, with a "mini-essay" explaining each one. They've been adapted from our *Law in a Flash* Series. The questions start on p. 291.
- ***Multiple-Choice*** questions — These are in a Multistate-Bar-Exam style, and were adapted from a book we publish called the *Finz Multistate Method*. They start on p. 317.
- ***Essay*** questions — These questions are actual ones asked on law school exams. They start on p. 343.

Good luck in your Torts course. If you'd like any other Aspen publication, you can find it at your bookstore or at www.AspenPublishing.com. If you'd like to contact me, you can email me at semanuel@westnet.com.

Steve Emanuel
Larchmont, NY
September 2024

FLOW CHARTS

TABLE OF CONTENTS to FLOW CHARTS

Fig.

Note: The cross-references in the Flow Charts' footnotes (e.g., "See Ch. 6(V)(B)") are to the full-length *Emanuel Law Outlines: Torts,* Eleventh Edition, 2024.

Figure 1

Analyzing Any Torts Question

This multi-page flowchart allows you to do a first-level analysis of practically any set of facts, and determine which tort(s) P has a good chance of establishing. Generally, the chart does not cover defenses except in the footnotes. When the chart says, in a circle, that the facts "probably" establish some particular tort, this usually means that the facts establish a prima facie case for that tort, but that D may still have an affirmative defense.

In most instances, where there is a series of requirements for a tort, to save space only the "yes" branch (i.e., a requirement is satisfied) is shown; if the appropriate answer on your facts is "no," you should assume that the tort in question does not apply. (Example: In #1 below, if the answer to "Did D intentionally bring about..." is no, the tort cannot be battery.)

The numbers 1-29 down the left-hand side of the page generally each refer to a separate tort (except within negligence, where some of the numbered items are defenses or special doctrines, rather than independent torts).

I. Intentional Torts

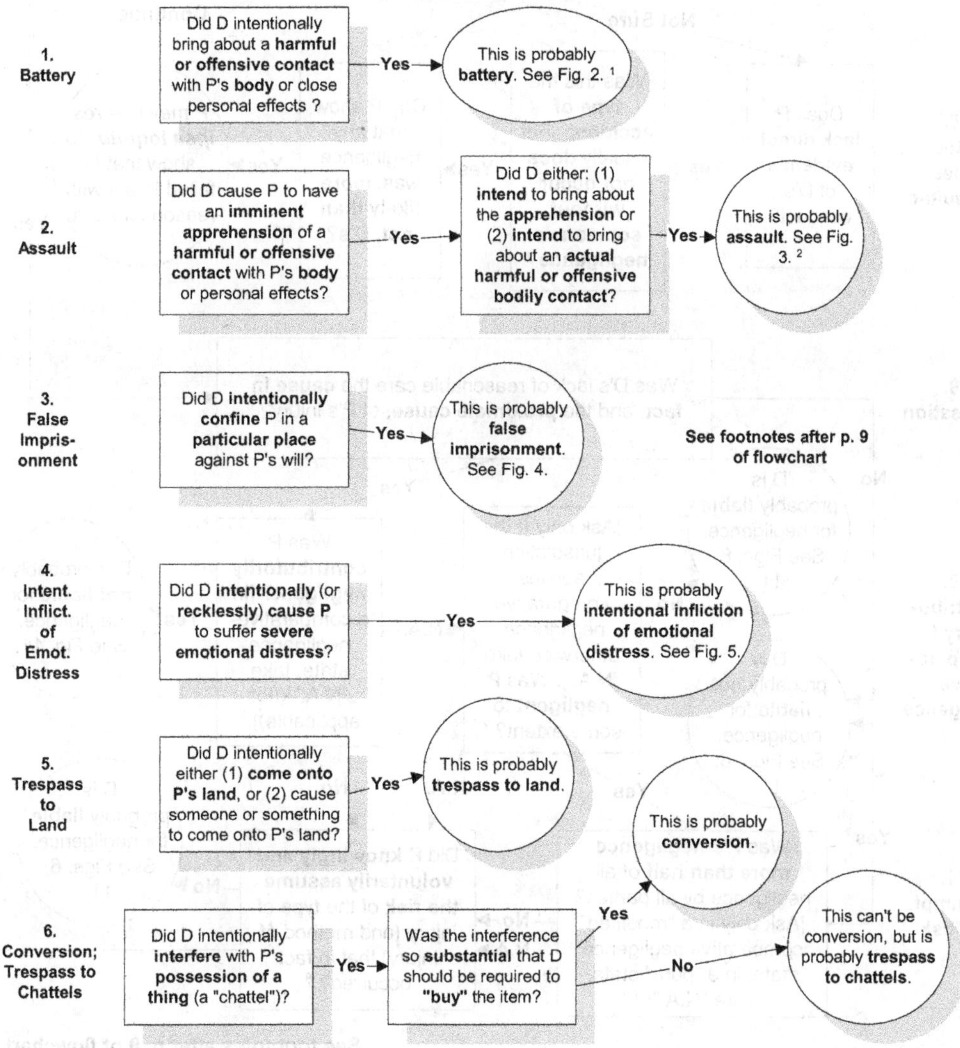

Figure 1 (p. 2)

Analyzing Any Torts Question

II. Negligence

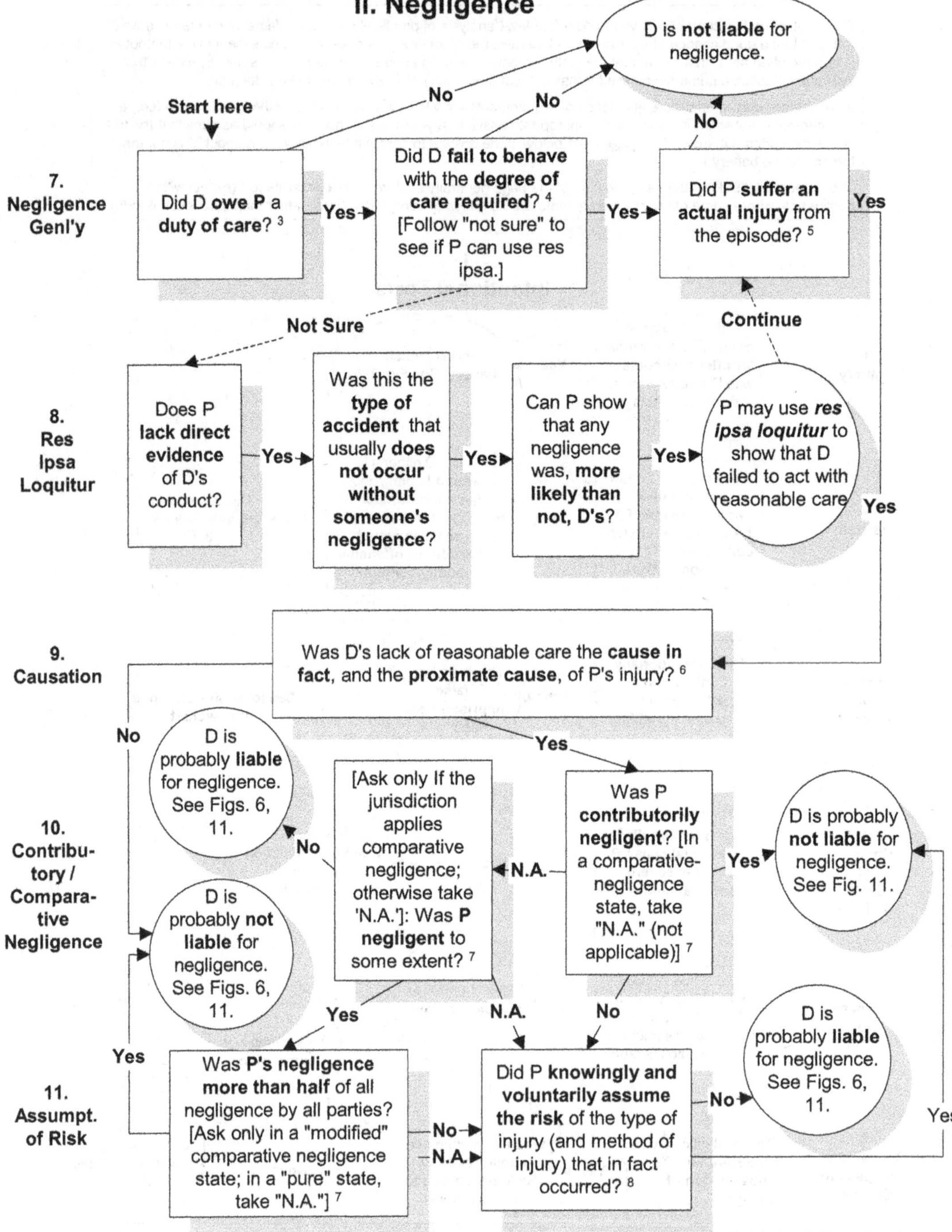

See footnotes after p. 9 of flowchart

Figure 1 (p. 3)

Analyzing Any Torts Question

III. Vicarious Liability

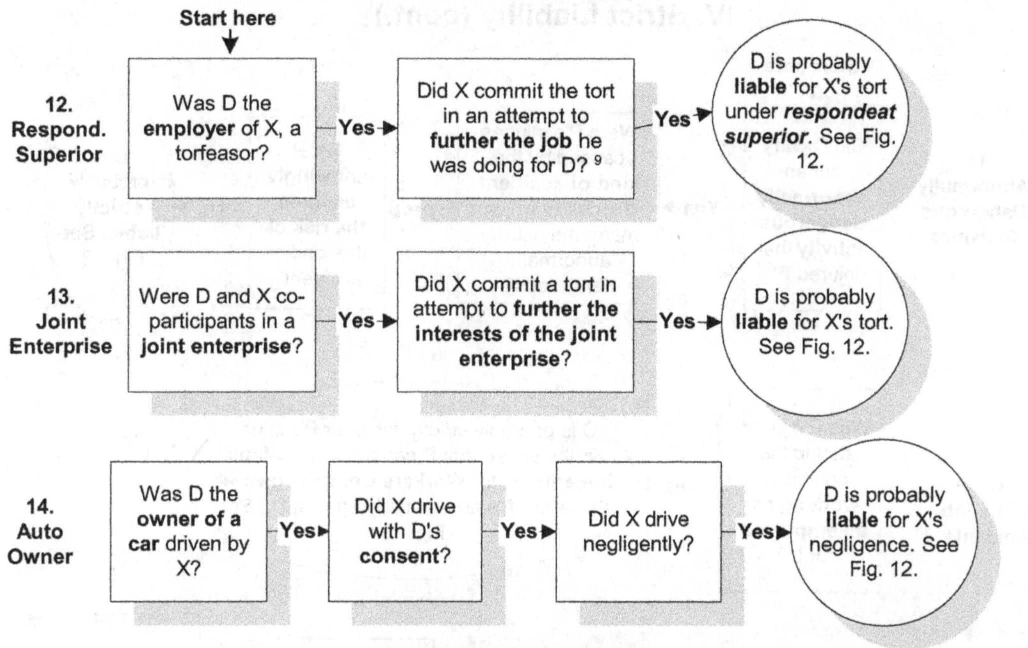

IV. Strict Liability

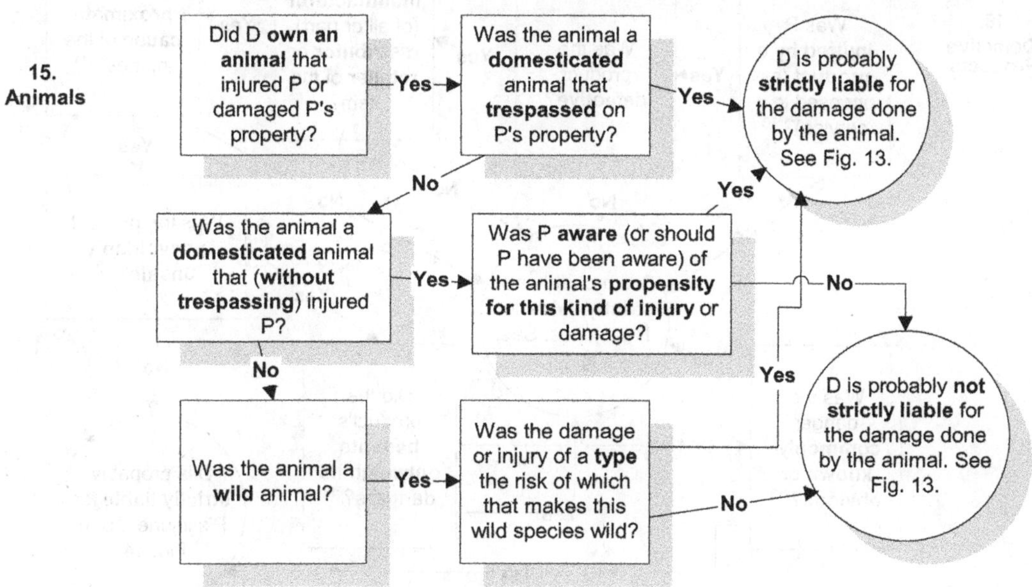

See footnotes after p. 9 of flowchart

Figure 1 (p. 4)

Analyzing Any Torts Question

IV. Strict Liability (cont.)

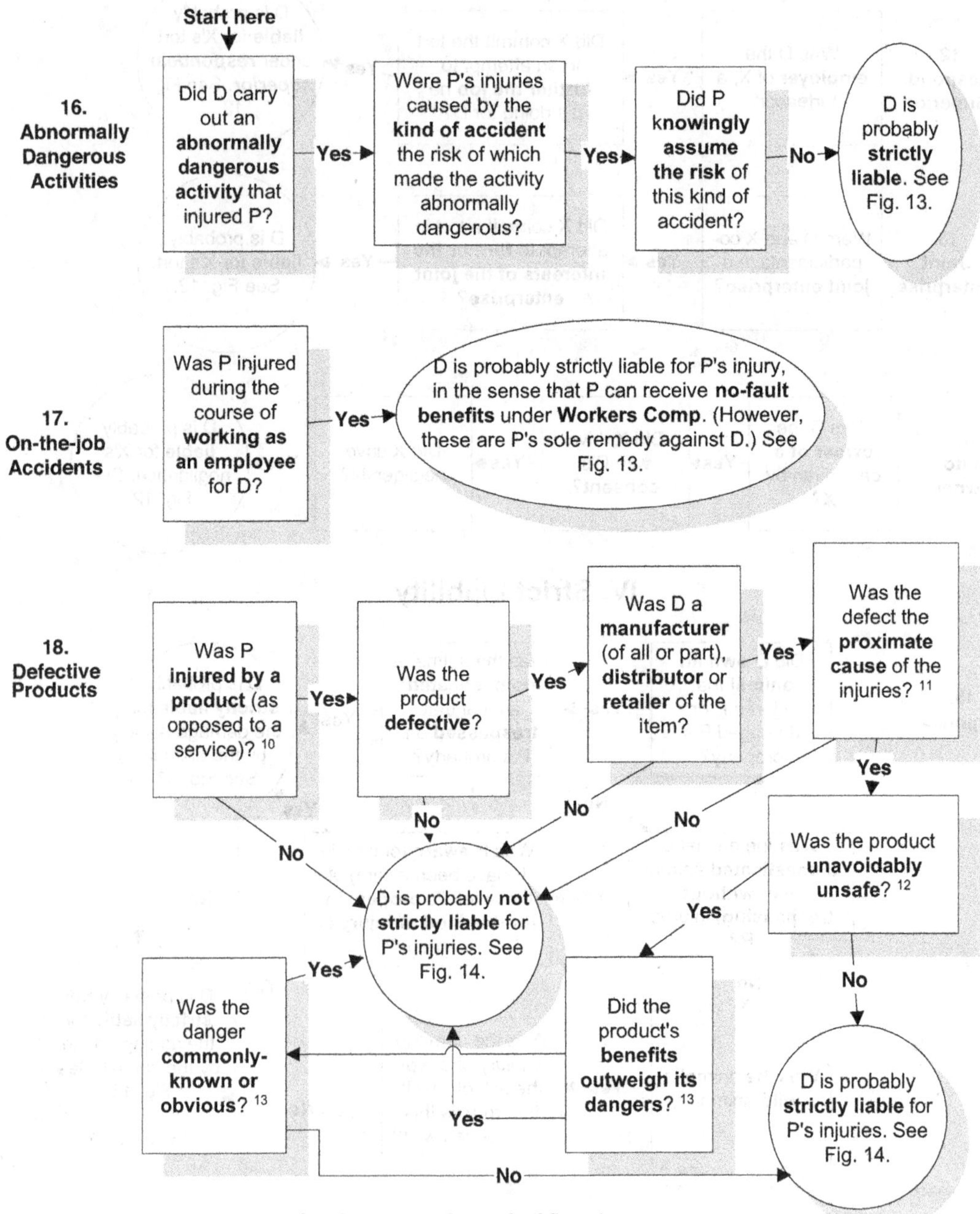

See footnotes after p. 9 of flowchart

Figure 1 (p. 5)

Analyzing Any Torts Question

V. Nuisance

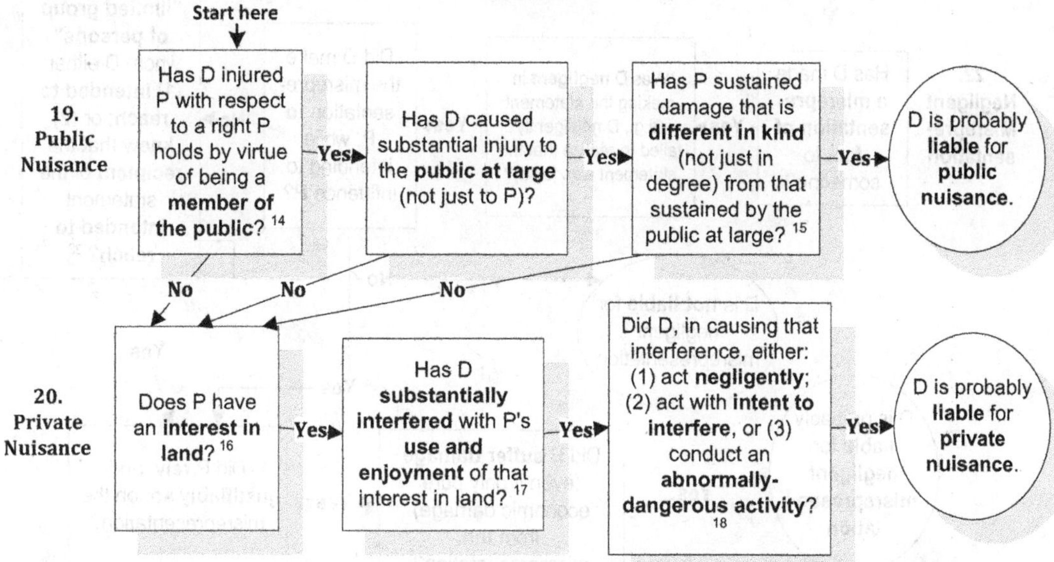

VI. Misrepresentation

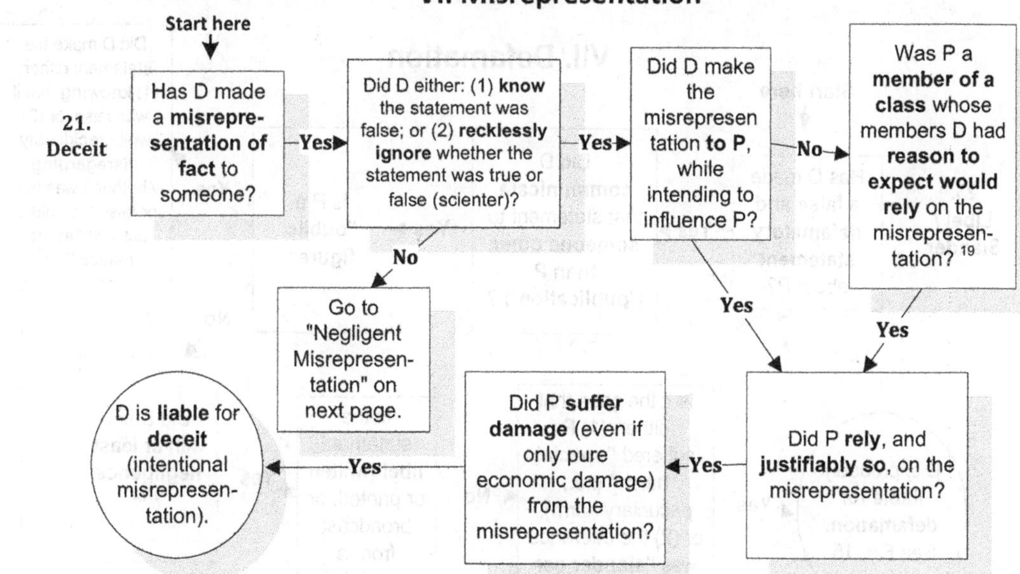

See footnotes after p. 9 of flowchart

Figure 1 (p. 6)

Analyzing Any Torts Question

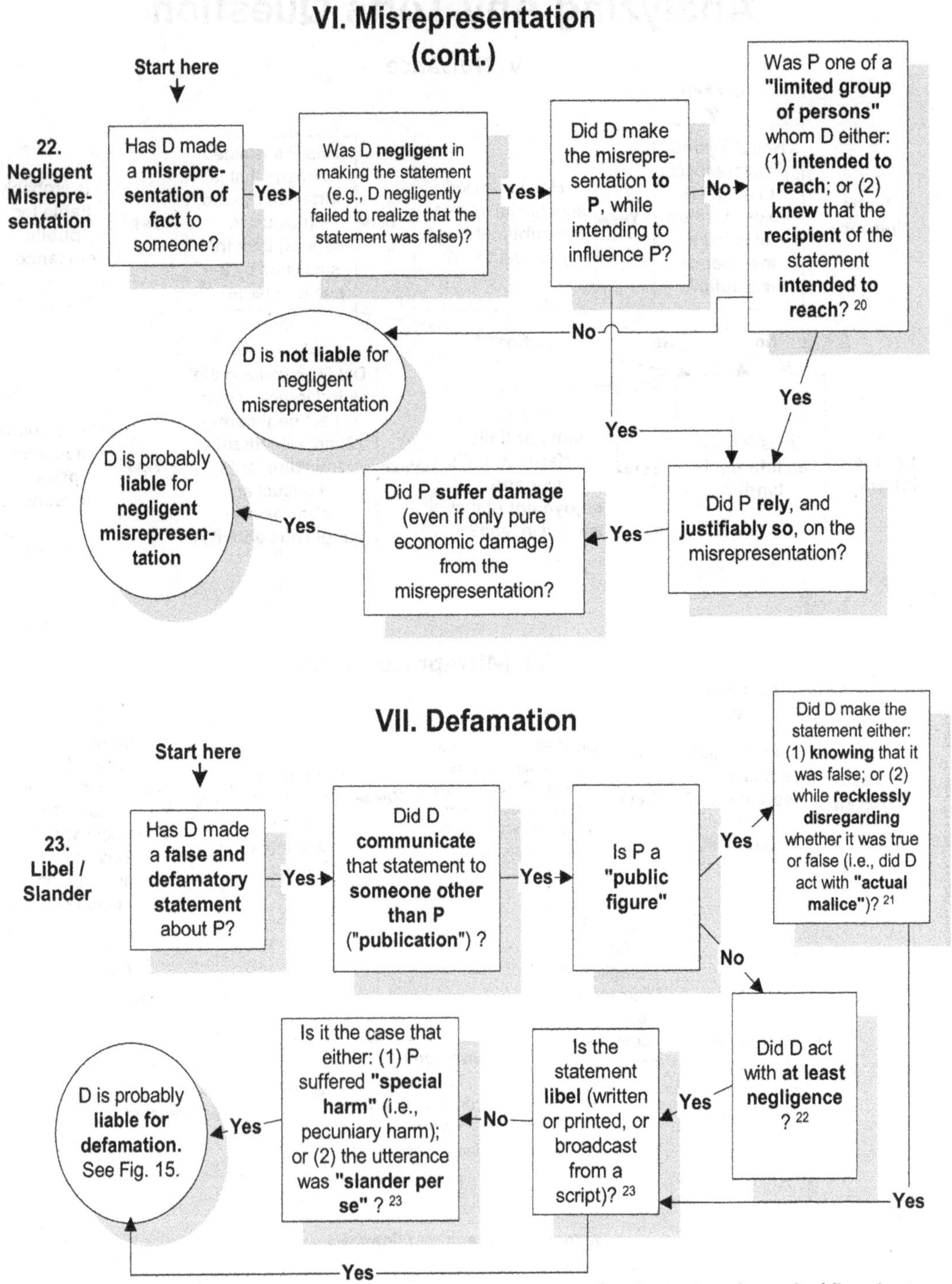

See footnotes after p. 9 of flowchart

Figure 1 (p. 7)

Analyzing Any Torts Question

VIII. Invasion of Privacy

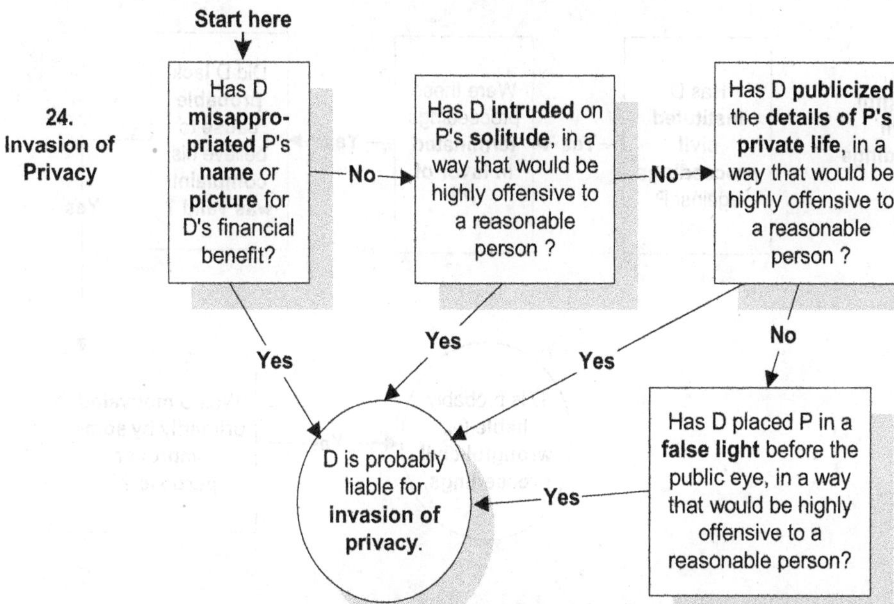

IX. Misuse of Legal Procedures

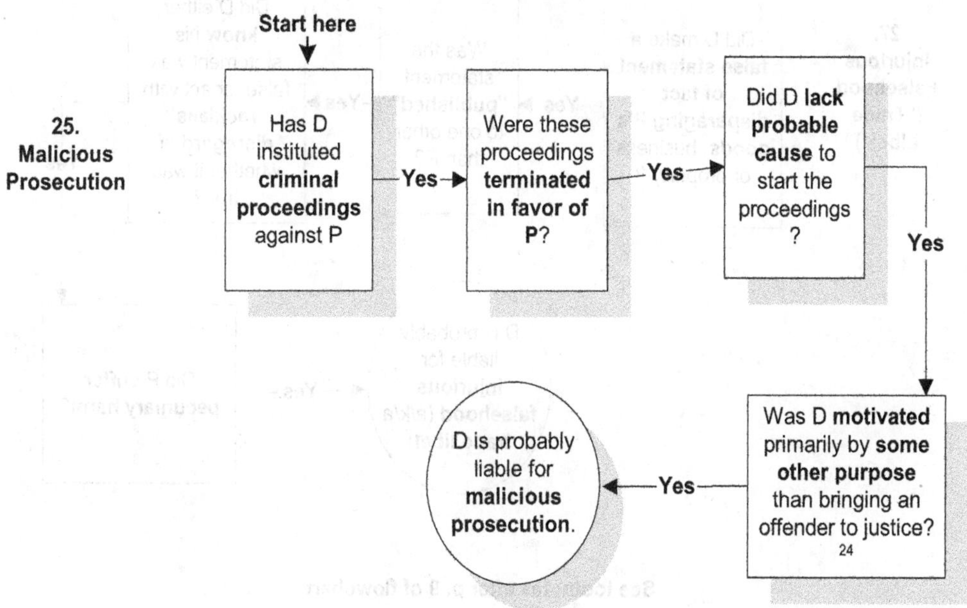

See footnotes after p. 9 of flowchart

Figure 1 (p. 8)

Analyzing Any Torts Question

IX. Misuse of Legal Procedures (cont.)

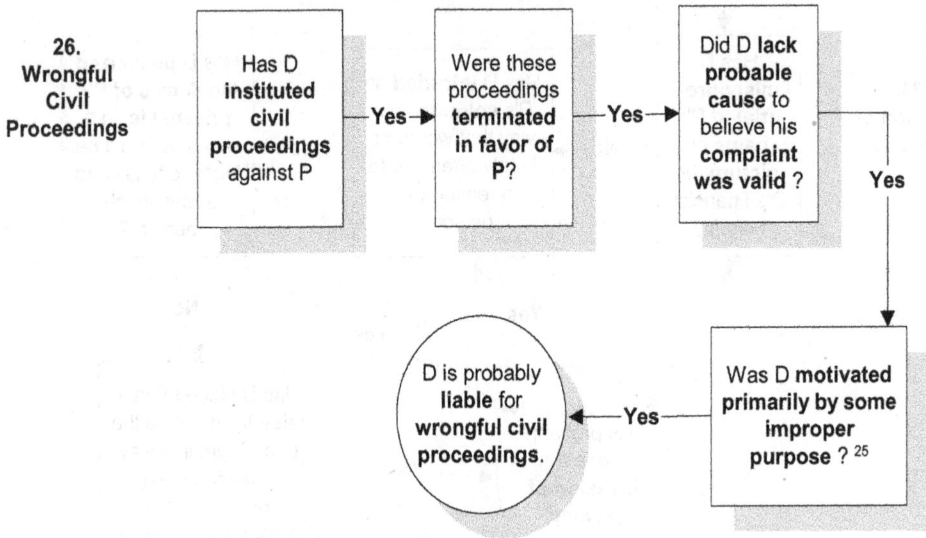

X. Interference with Advantageous Relations

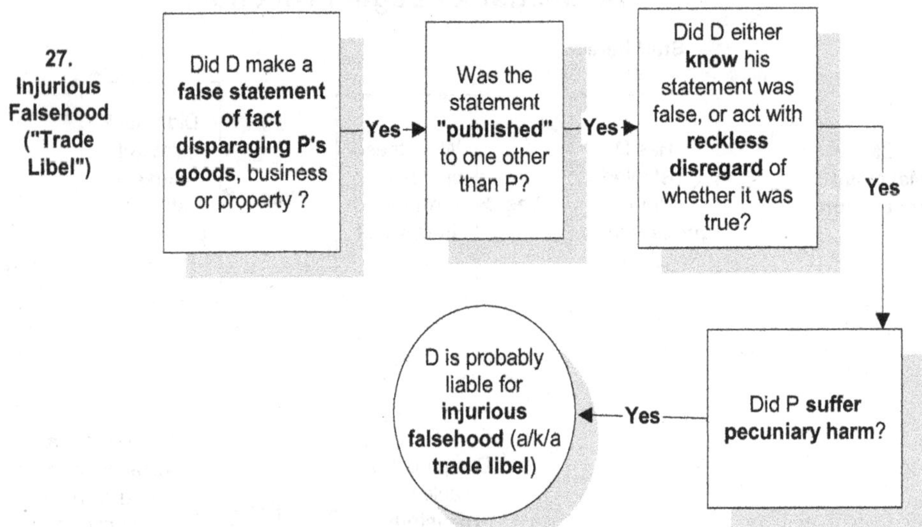

See footnotes after p. 9 of flowchart

Figure 1 (p. 9)

Analyzing Any Torts Question

X. Interference with Advantageous Relations (cont.)

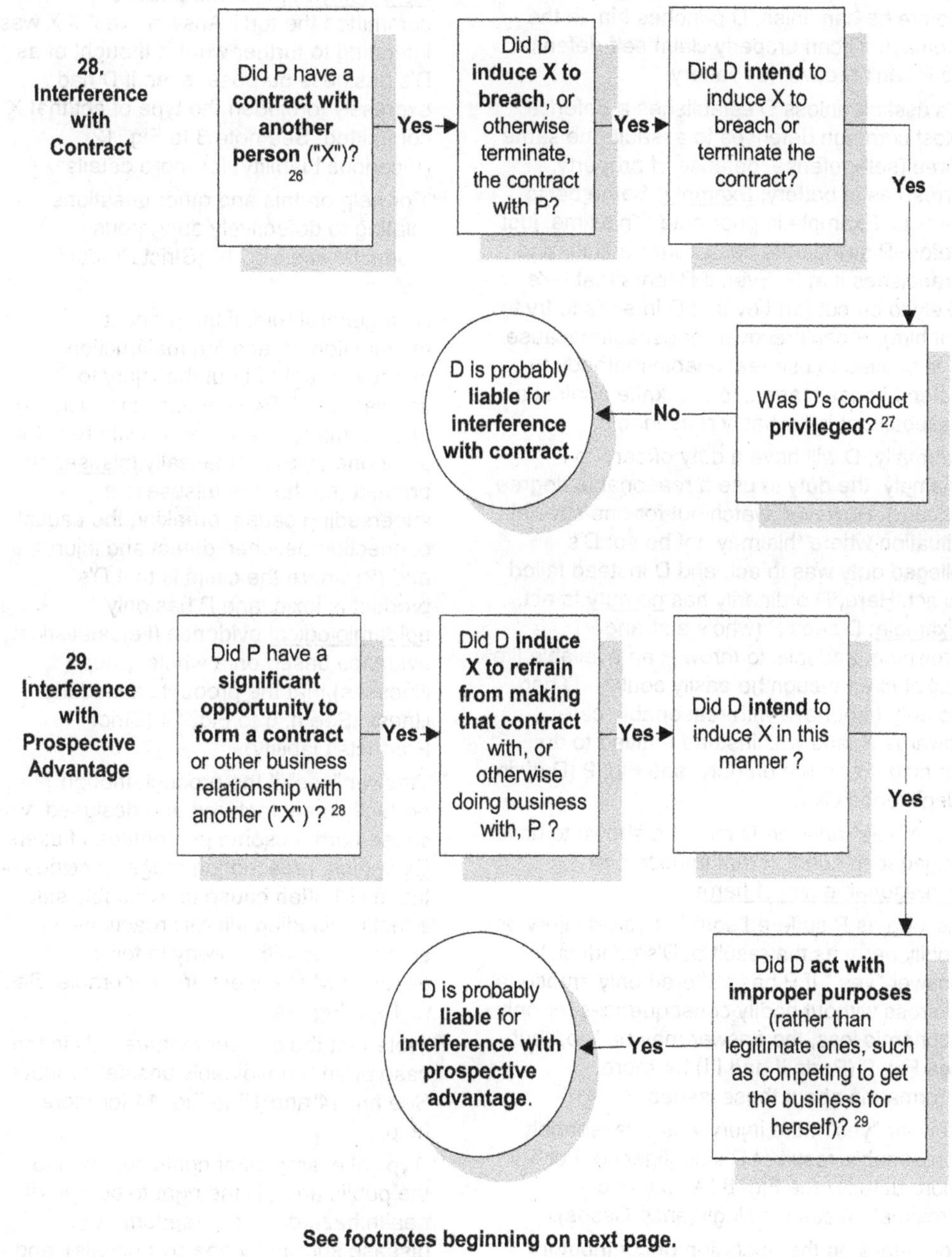

See footnotes beginning on next page.

Notes to Figure 1 (Analyzing Any Torts Question)

1 It's battery unless D establishes a defense. Most common defenses to battery: self-defense, defense of property, arrest. Example: D shouts an insult at P. P takes a baseball bat and is about to swing it at D. Before he can finish, D punches him in the stomach. D can properly claim self-defense, so P can't recover for battery.

2 It's assault unless D establishes a defense. Most common defenses to assault: the same three (self-defense, defense of property, arrest) as in battery. Example: Same basic facts as Example in prior note. This time, just before P swings the bat, D pulls a knife and brandishes it at P. Even if P fears that he's likely to be cut (and even if D intends to try to cut him), P can't recover for assault because D is entitled to use reasonable methods to defend himself, and use of a knife against a baseball bat is probably reasonable.

3 Normally, D will have a duty of care to P (namely, the duty to use a reasonable degree of care). However, watch out for one special situation where this may not be so: D's alleged duty was to act, and D instead failed to act. Here, D ordinarily has no duty to act. Example: D sees P (who's a stranger) drowning, and fails to throw P an available life jacket even though he easily could -- D had no duty to behave with reasonable care towards P, and was instead entitled to do nothing. For more on duty, see Fig. 9 (Duty in Negligence Cases).

4 For a "yes" answer, D must be shown to have engaged in conduct that imposed an unreasonable risk of harm on P.

5 As long as P suffered some physical injury or bodily harm as the result of D's conduct, answer "yes." If P has suffered only emotional distress without bodily consequences, or only economic loss, the answer may be "no," but see Fig. 9 (Parts II and III) for more information about these issues.

6 Answer "yes" if the injury was a reasonably foreseeable result of D's negligence. For more details, see Fig. 8 (Actual and Proximate Cause in Negligence Cases).

7 For details on the operation of contributory and comparative negligence, see Fig. 11 (Major Defenses in Negligence Cases), part I.

8 For details on the assumption of risk defense, see Fig. 11 (Major Defenses in Negligence Cases), part II.

9 That is, was X acting within the "scope of his employment" at the time he committed the tort? Answer "yes" if X was intending to further what X thought of as D's business purpose, even if D had expressly forbidden the type of act that X committed. See note 3 to Fig. 12 (Vicarious Liability) for more details.

10 For help on this and other questions relating to defectively dangerous products, see Fig. 14 (Strict Products Liability).

11 As a general rule, if the product malfunctioned, and the malfunction directly brought about the injury to P, answer "yes." Two contexts in which the answer may be "no" are: (1) where P (or someone else) dramatically misused the product (so that the misuse is a superseding cause, breaking the causal connection between defect and injury); and (2) where the claim is that D's product is toxic, and P has only epidemiological evidence (i.e., statistical evidence based on a whole group's illnesses) that the product caused the illness. See n. 6 to Fig. 14 (Strict Products Liability).

12 Answer "yes" if the product, though perfectly manufactured and designed, will cause harm in some percentage of users. Examples: prescription drugs, vaccines -- these will often cause unavoidable side effects, including allergic reactions, in some users, with no way to tell in advance which users are vulnerable. See n. 13 to Fig. 14.

13 Note that the answer matters only in the case of an "unavoidably unsafe" product. See nn. 14 and 15 to Fig. 14 for more help.

14 Typical examples of rights common to the public are: (1) the right to be free of health hazards (e.g., freedom from disease spread by nearby animals); and (2) the right to be free of crime or

Notes (p. 2) to Figure 1 (Analyzing Any Torts Question)

physical-safety risk (e.g., freedom from shootings and fights that frequently occur outside a nearby bar).

Example of right not common to public: L rents T an asbestos-riddled apartment, without disclosing this. T can't sue D (the original installer of the asbestos) in nuisance, because T's injuries are not common to the public, and are instead attributable to T's occupancy of particular premises.

[15] Example: D's oil tanker spills massive amounts of oil on a coastal area where the Ps, commercial fisherman, earn their living. The oil kills most fish. The Ps can probably recover for public nuisance, since their damage (direct loss of the thing they harvest for a living) is different in kind from the loss suffered by other nearby members of the public. But a hotel owner 100 miles inland, whose business suffered from a drop in regional tourism because of the spill, might be found not to have the requisite "different in kind" damages.

[16] The interest in land doesn't have to be a fee simple. A tenant's interest will suffice. So will the interest of a family member living on the land, if someone else in the household holds the fee simple or the lease. But P must have, or live with someone who has, *some* interest in land. Example: On the facts of the prior example, the fishermen couldn't recover in private nuisance, because their interest in being able to fish was not tied in to any interest in land.

[17] Example: P, a homeowner, lives next door to D, an electric utility. D repeatedly burns dirty coal, as a result of which ashes and noxious fumes come onto P's property. This will probably be a substantial interference with P's use and enjoyment of his property, entitling P to recover for private nuisance.

[18] Notice that there is no strict liability for private nuisance -- P must show either that D either acted intentionally/negligently, or that the activity was ultra-hazardous. Thus on the prior example, if D unintentionally and non-negligently spewed the ashes onto P's property on a single occasion, that would not suffice. (But if D continued to operate the plant in this way after being notified by P of the problem, then D would be held to have known with substantial certainty that the interference was occurring, making D's continuing conduct a form of intentional intereference, even if D didn't actively "desire" to interfere with P's use/ enjoyment.)

[19] Example: D applies for a home equity loan from X, a mortgage company. On the application, D falsely (and knowingly) says that he has no debts. In fact, D is up to his eyeballs in debts that he can't pay. Assume that at the time of the application, D should be aware (but isn't) that if X makes the loan, X will immediately resell the loan to some other financial institution. X makes the loan, then immediately resells it to P, another finance company, which relies on the statements made on D's application to X. D will be liable to P for deceit, because P was a member of a class (all people who would consider buying the loan in reliance on D's application statements) that D knew, or had reason to know, would rely on the statement's truth.

[20] Notice that this class is narrower than the class who can be plaintiffs in a deceit (intentional misrepresentation) action. Here, D must either intend to reach the limited group of which P is a part, or know that the person to whom D made the statement intends to reach such a group. So there's no liability if D merely negligently fails to realize that the recipient will repeat the statement to a class of which P is a part. Example: On the facts of the prior example, assume that D's misstatement about his debts is inadvertent but negligent. Assume that D negligently fails to realize that X (the mortgage company) may pass D's application on to some other buyer, who will rely on the application's correctness.

Notes (p. 3) to Figure 1 (Analyzing Any Torts Question)

If that other buyer, P, sues D for negligent misrepresentation, P will not win, because P did not fall within the requisite limited class.

[21] This is the *N.Y. Times v. Sullivan* "actual malice" standard, which is required by the First Amendment's protection of free speech and a free press. Notice that the actual malice standard applies only where P is a public figure (because only then does D have such a strong public

interest in being able to comment about P that this outweighs P's interest in being able to recover for, say, negligent defamations).

[22] In other words, the states are not free to allow P to recover for an incorrect, but non-negligent, misstatement that defames D. Example: D, a newspaper, reproduces a police blotter entry that says that local resident "John Doolittle" was arrested for burglary the prior night. In fact, the person arrested was James Doolittle, John's brother. P (John Dolittle) sues D for libel. D shows that it asked the police dept. to confirm the accuracy of the blotter entry before printing it, and the police said the item was accurate. (Assume that attempt at verification is enough that D cannot be said to have behaved negligently in running the item.) As a constitutional matter, P cannot win -- even though P is not a public figure, the states are prevented from allowing P to recover for a non-negligent defamation.

[23] Notice that the distinction between libel and its oral counterpart, slander, matters only with respect to the requirement of "special harm." That is, if the case involves slander, P will have to show that he suffered pecuniary harm unless the utterance was "slander per se." (Slander per se consists of statements that P: (i) committed a crime, (ii) has a loathsome disease; (iii) is unfit in his business or profession, or (iv) has committed sexual misconduct.) By contrast, there is no requirement of "special harm" if the statement is libel.

[24] Example: P bounces a $100 check to D, a merchant who has sold P goods. D is aware of facts indicating that P thought that he had sufficient funds in the account. D nonetheless tells P that he'll prosecute unless P pays D $2,000 plus the $100 check amount, to compensate D for his inconvenience. P offers to make up the $100 plus pay a $10 bad-check fee, but refuses to pay more. D rejects the offer, and convinces the D.A. to institute bad-check charges against P. P is acquitted when he shows that he thought there were sufficient funds. P then sues D for malicious prosecution. If P can show that D was primarily motivated by a desire to collect the original debt plus extra funds (not the desire to bring an offender to justice), P will be entitled to recover.

[25] Example: D falsely claims, in a civil tort suit, that D was injured when he choked on a screw found in a hamburger served at P's restaurant. D recognizes that P will probably correctly deduce that D's claim is invalid (the alleged episode was wholly fabricated). D's principal motive is to settle the case for a small sum, less than the costs to P of defending and dealing with bad publicity. P instead litigates the civil suit, wins, then sues D for wrongful civil proceedings. D was primarily motivated by an improper purpose (extorting a settlement based on a fraudulent complaint). Therefore, P can recover.

[26] Courts are split about whether Interference with Contract can apply where the contract is terminable at will. The modern (and 2d Restatement) view is that the tort can apply even to an at-will contract.

[27] There is no bright-line rule separating privileged behavior from non-privileged. D's desire to get the business for himself is generally not, by itself, privileged. On the other hand, D's pursuit of ostensibly socially-worthwhile goals is privileged. Example: D, a community activist, urges Wal-Mart to terminate a contract with P, a clothing manufacturer, on the grounds that P uses foreign sweat-shops that don't pay a living wage. Wal-Mart agrees and terminates, even though P is not violating the laws of the nation where its factories are located. If D sues P for interference

Notes (p. 4) to
Figure 1 (Analyzing Any Torts Question)

with contract, D will probably win on the grounds that her conduct was privileged, since she was urging the contracting party to behave in a more socially-responsible manner.

[28] Interference with Prospective Advantage (as distinguished from Interference with Contract) applies where P did not yet have an actual contract or business relationship with X at the time of D's action.

[29] Example: P and D are each competing to get a large contract supplying a certain type of merchandise to X, a large store chain. P correctly tells X that D is having financial problems, and says that X might therefore risk not getting the contracted-for deliveries if X chooses D. Relying on what P says, X chooses P rather than D. A court would probably hold that D acted with a proper purpose (competing to get the business for herself), in which case P could not recover against D for Interference with ProspectiveAdvantage.

(Notice, however, that if X had an actual existing contract with P, and D's truthful statement about P's financial difficulties induced X to terminate and give the business to D, D probably would be liable if D's purpose was to get the business. The presence of a privilege to compete is precisely what distinguishes Interference with Prospective Advangtage from Interference with Contract.)

Figure 2
Battery

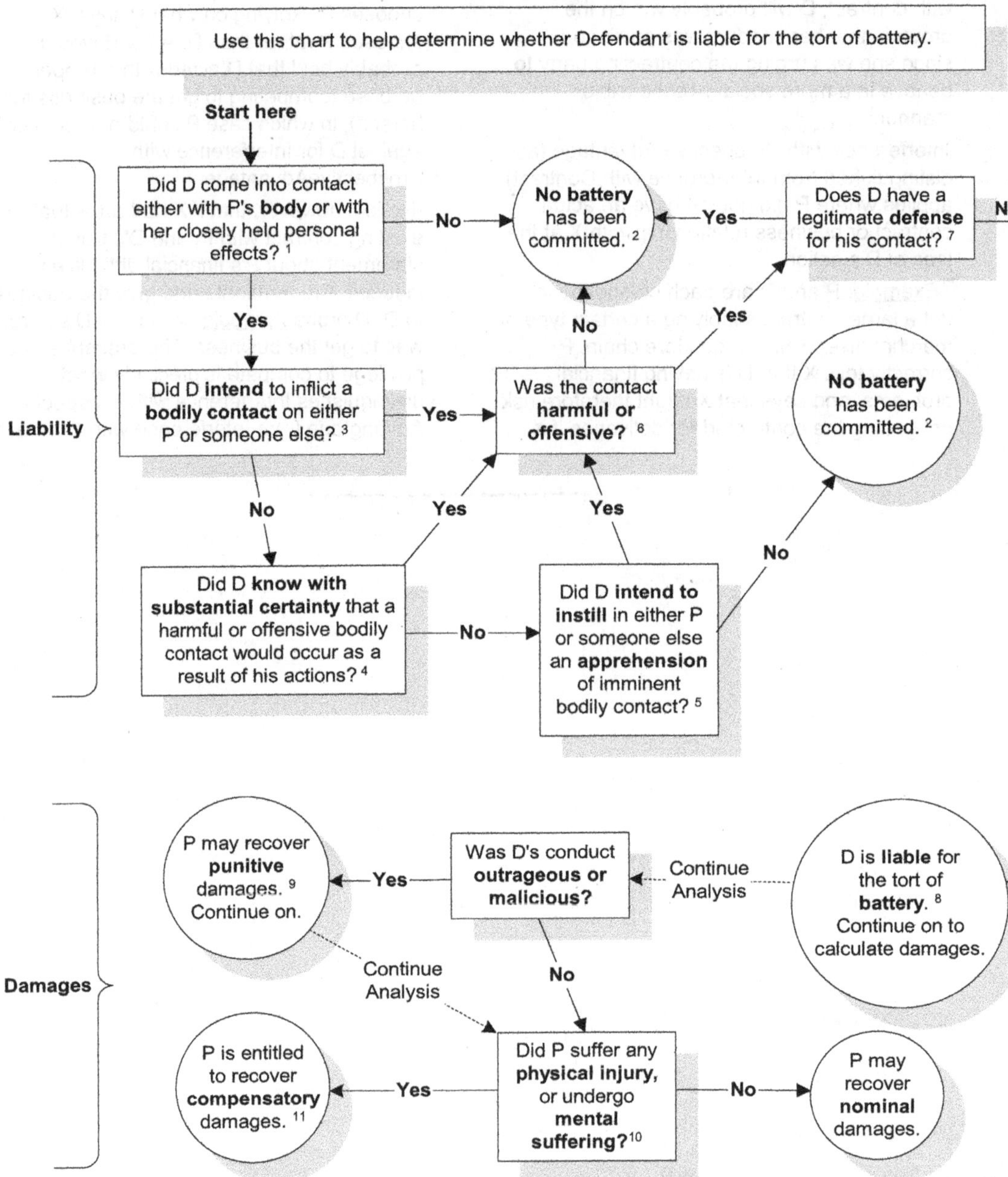

See footnotes on next page

Notes to Figure 2 (Battery)

[1] The tort of battery extends beyond actual bodily contact. It includes contact with the plaintiff's clothing, with something she is holding, or with anything else closely associated with her body. Ch. 2 (IV)(D). For the sake of simplicity, we will refer to all of these types of contacts as "bodily contact" in the rest of this flow chart. Note that the contact can be either direct or indirect. For example, D can touch P himself (direct contact), or he can cause P to be touched indirectly, such as by ordering a dog to attack, by using a stun gun, or by throwing a rock at her. D need not even be present when the contact occurs, as long as he intended for the contact to happen. Ch. 2 (IV)(D)(1).

[2] Although no battery has been committed, your inquiry should not end here. Be sure to check out any other torts that may be implicated by the facts. Be especially on the lookout for Assault (Fig. 3) and Negligence (Fig. 6).

[3] If D thinks that the contact will not be harmful or offensive, but he's wrong about that, the intent requirement is satisfied.

Also, under the doctrine of "transferred intent," the requisite intent will be found where D intended to inflict a bodily contact on someone other than P, but actually inflicted it upon P. Ch. 2 (I)(D).

If D intentionally exceeds the scope of P's consent, this will be battery too. (Example: P gives D, a surgeon, permission to operate on P's toe and D also operates on P's ankle.)

[4] This is a subjective test: D must have believed that the bodily contact was almost certain to occur. Rest. 2d, §8A; Ch. 2 (I)(B).

[5] Example: D swings his fist near P's nose, intending to make P think he'll be hit, but not intending to actually hit him. D has the requisite intent for battery (and if by accident he hits P, he'll be liable for battery).

Also, under the doctrine of "transferred intent," the requisite intent will be found where D intended to instill in someone other than P an apprehension of bodily contact, but actually instilled it in P. Ch. 2 (I)(D).

[6] "Harmful" contact causes pain or bodily damage; "offensive" contact is contact that is damaging to a "reasonable sense of dignity." Ch. 2 (IV)(B). Offensive contact is judged objectively: if an ordinary person would not be offended by the contact, it does not rise to the level of offensive even if P was actually offended. Ch. 2 (IV)(C).

[7] Most-common defenses: consent, self-defense, defense of property, recapture of chattel, arrest.

[8] Check to see if D is also liable for assault. If P saw in advance what was about to happen, there is an assault just before the battery.

[9] Rest. 2d, §908; Ch. 2 (II)(A)(2).

[10] Plaintiffs can recover compensatory damages for emotional pain, suffering, or embarrassment, even if they suffer no physical harm. Ch. 2 (IV)(G)(1).

[11] D will be liable for both foreseeable and unforeseeable consequences of the contact (the "eggshell skull" principle). Ch. 2 (IV)(F).

Figure 3
Assault

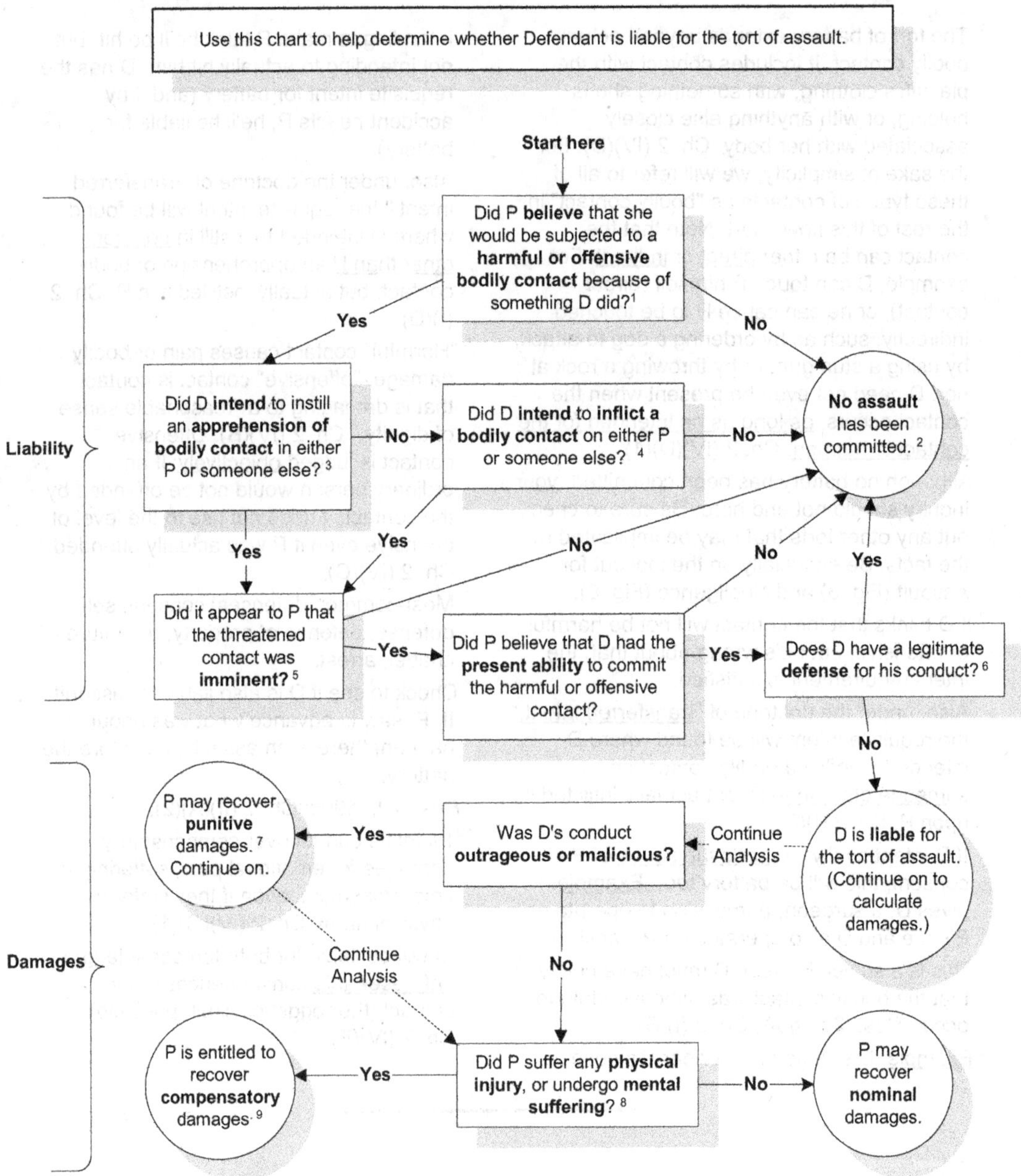

See footnotes on next page

Notes to Figure 3 (Assault)

[1] Words alone cannot constitute an assault, so your answer to this question should be "no" if D made verbal threats without any other overt act. But if D did make an overt act together with the words -- such as shaking a fist while uttering the words -- this can constitute assault.

"Harmful" contact causes pain or bodily damage; "offensive" contact is contact that is damaging to a "reasonable sense of dignity." Ch. 2 (IV)(B).

P must have had an apprehension that she herself would be subjected to the bodily contact. If the apprehension was of contact to a third person, your answer to the question should be "no." If that's the case, however, be sure to check out whether D committed the tort of intentional infliction of emotional distress. Ch. 2 (V)(H).

[2] Be sure to check out any other torts that may be implicated by the facts, including Assault (Fig. 3) and Negligence (Fig. 6).

[3] See Rest. 2d, §21(1)(a) and (b). Under the doctrine of "transferred intent," the requisite intent will be found where D intended to instill in someone other than P a fear of bodily contact, but actually instilled it in P. Ch. 2 (V)(B)(4).

[4] This question reflects the fact that "intent to commit a battery" is one of the ways to satisfy the mental-state requirement for assault. Example: D swings his fist at P's nose, intending to hit P by suprise (so that P won't see what's coming). P sees the swing coming, and ducks, but for an instant thinks he may be hit. D satisfies the mental-state requirement for assault, because he intended to inflict a bodily contact on P.

The intended contact can be either direct or indirect. For example, D could have intended to touch P himself (direct contact), or he could have intended to touch P indirectly, such as by ordering a dog to attack, by using a stun gun, or by throwing a rock at him. Ch. 2 (IV)(D)(1). Also, under the doctrine of "transferred intent," the requisite intent will be found where D intended to inflict a bodily contact (directly or indirectly) on someone other than P. Ch. 2 (V)(B)(4).

[5] While there is no exact definition of "imminent," most cases hold that the threat must be of contact that would have occurred within moments of the threat itself (i.e., "I'm going to punch you in the face if you don't give me your purse"). Threats of non-imminent future harm cannot constitute assaults, but they may constitute the tort of intentional infliction of emotional distress. Ch. 2 (V)(D).

[6] Most-common defenses: consent, self-defense, defense of property, recapture of chattels, arrest.

[7] Rest. 2d, §908; Ch. 2 (II)(A)(2).

[8] Plaintiffs can recover compensatory damages for emotional pain, suffering, or embarrassment, even if they sufer no physical harm. Indeed, mental-suffering damages unaccompanied by physical injury are very common in assault cases. Ch. 2 (V)(M)(2).

[9] D will be liable for both foreseeable and unforeseeable consequences of the assault. Example: P runs away in fear, and trips and breaks her leg. D will be liable for this physical injury. Same result if the fear causes P to have a heart attack. Ch. 2 (V)(M)(2).

Figure 4

False Imprisonment

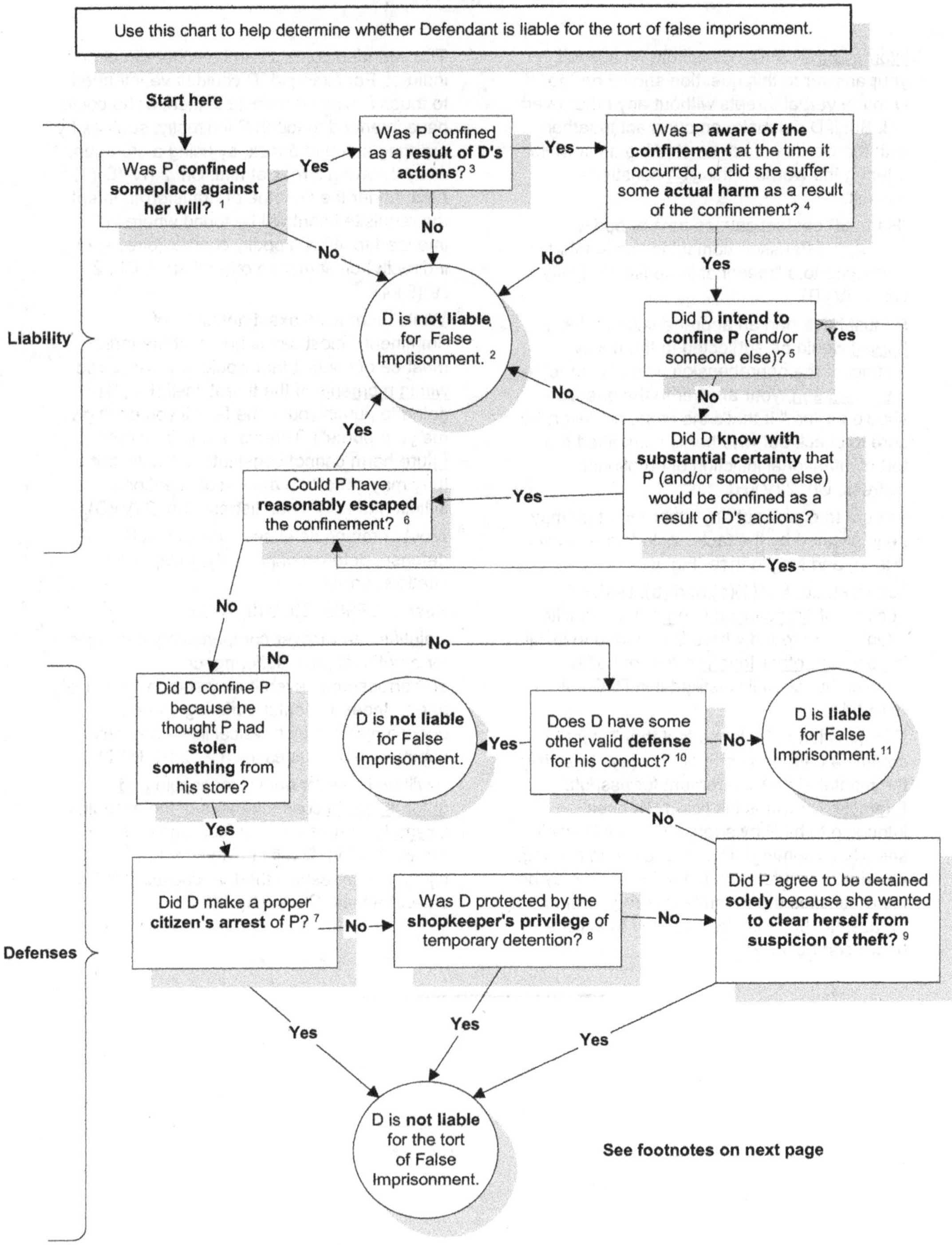

See footnotes on next page

Notes to
Figure 4 (False Imprisonment)

[1] Confinement requires that P be kept within certain physical boundaries. Merely blocking P's way if P can turn around and go back the other way does not count. Nor does preventing P from entering a place she has a right to be. Rest. 2d, §36(2); Ch. 2 (VI)(D).

[2] Be sure to check out any other torts that may be implicated by the facts, including negligence (Fig. 6).

[3] Answer "yes" to this question not just if D physically confined P by force, but also if D kept P in a specific place by threatening -- either explicity or implicitly -- to use force, under circumstances in which a reasonable person in P's position would have yielded. Ch. 2 (VI)(F). The threats can be of harm to P, to a third person, or to P's property. (Example: D grabs P's shopping bag or purse to prevent her from leaving D's store; this is potentially false imprisonment). However, the threats must be of imminent harm, not future harm.

Note: If D confined P with purely verbal commands (e.g., "Don't leave.") that were unaccompanied by threats of force (and unaccompanied by assertions of legal authority), you should answer "no" to this question. Ch. 2 (VI)(F)(1)(b).

[4] Most courts have held that P must be aware of the confinement while she is suffering it. But the Second Restatement says that it's enough that P either: (1) was aware of the confinement; or (2) was unaware, but suffered actual harm as a result of the confinement. Rest. 2d, §42; Ch. 2 (VI)(H).

[5] If the confinement was unintentional (Example: D is a security guard who locks a store without realizing that P is inside), the requisite intent does not exist.

Also, under the doctrine of "transferred intent," the requisite intent will be found where D intended to confine someone other than P, but actually (or in addition) confined P. Ch. 2 (VI)(C).

[6] If P could reasonably have escaped the confinement, there is no false imprisonment. A means of escape is unreasonable if it would pose a physical danger to P, harm her clothing, be "offensive" to her "reasonable sense of decency or personal dignity," or pose a danger to a third person. Rest. 2d, §36, Comment a; Ch. 2 (V)(E)(1). Also, P must have known about the avenue of escape for it to be considered "reasonable."

[7] If P actually committed the suspected theft, and P's conduct is a felony in the jurisdiction, most states say a citizen may make an arrest. However, if the theft did not in fact happen (or wasn't committed by P), you must answer "no" even if D reasonably suspected that P had stolen. Ch. 4 (IX)(B)(2)(a).

[8] Some but not all states give a merchant a privilege (as a method of recovering stolen goods) to detain a suspected shoplifter pending investigation of whether the theft occurred. Where the privilege exists the following rules apply: (1) the shopkeeper's suspicions must be reasonable; (2) the investigation must be brief (10-15 min. or less); and (3) the shopkeeper may not purport to "arrest" the suspect or try to obtain a confession. Ch. 4 (VI)(C). However, the privilege is not lost even if the merchant's suspicions prove incorrect.

[9] When a suspected shoplifter submits to a search, or to be briefly detained for questioning, D will not be liable for fale imprisonment if P's sole motive for submitting to the confinement was to clear herself. If, however, she submitted at least in part because of a threat of implied force, D may be liable and you should answer "no" to this question. Ch. 2 (VI)(F)(1)(a).

[10] The defenses relating to investigation of shoplifting have already been covered in this chart; other defenses might include: assertion of legal authority and arrest (e.g., police mistakenly but reasonably arrest and confine P); consent (e.g., D reasonably believes P has consented to play a bondage game); and self-defense (e.g., D, a home owner, locks P in a closet while mistakenly believing that P is a burglar).

[11] You should also examine the appropriate measure of damages. Generally, P can recover for mental damages (even in the absence of physical harm), and nominal damages if there is no suffering or physical harm. Ch. 2 (VI)(I).

Figure 5

Intentional Infliction of Emotional Distress

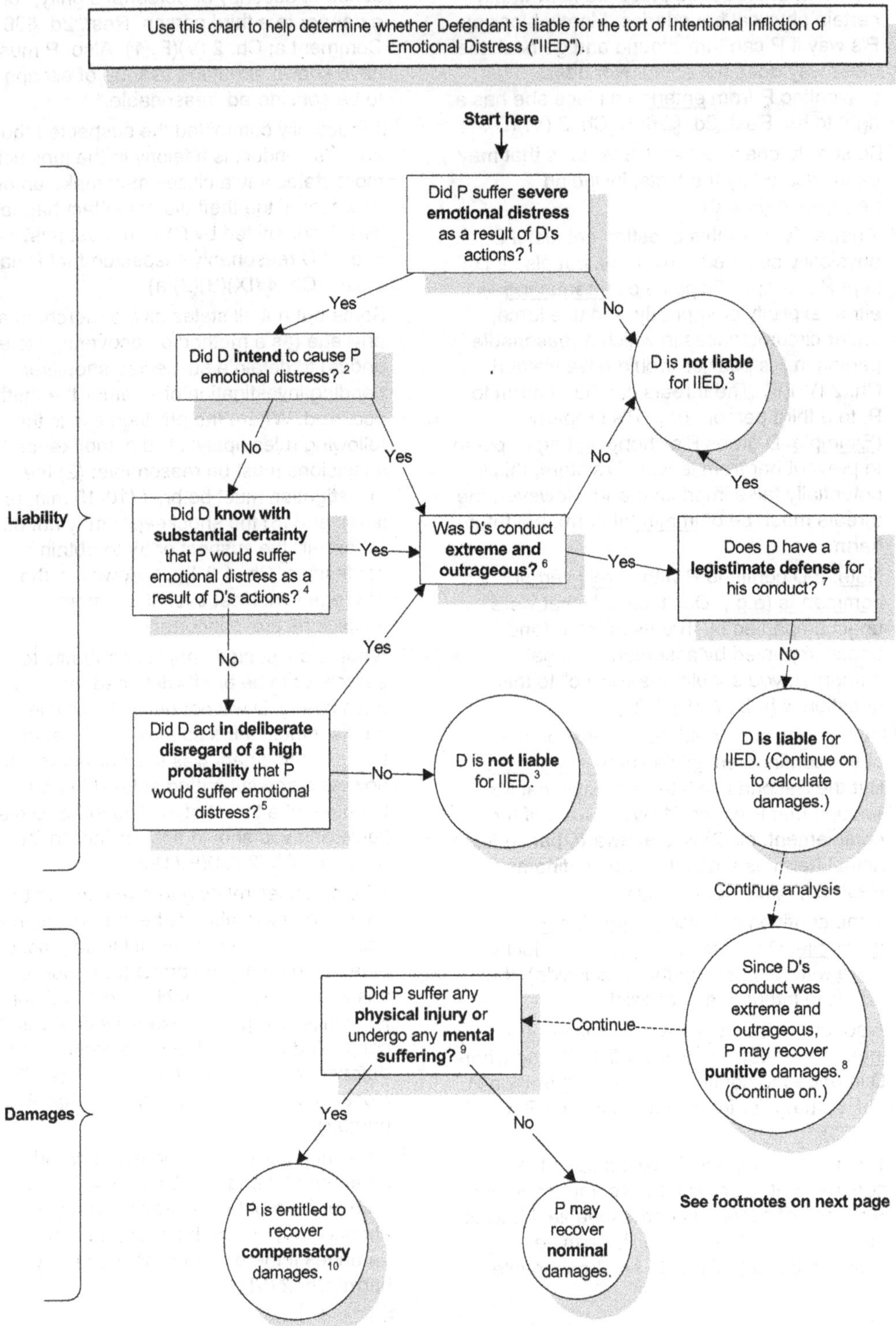

See footnotes on next page

Notes to Figure 5 (Intentional Infliction of Emotional Distress)

[1] According to most courts, a "yes" answer here requires that P have sought medical aid (for example, consulting with a therapist). However, P does not have to prove that he suffered physical consequences from the distress. Ch. 2 (VII)(D).

[2] The doctrine of "transferred intent" has limited application to the tort of Intentional Infliction of Emotional Distress. If D's conduct was not directed at P, most courts (and the Second Restatement) would agree that you can nonetheless answer "yes" to this question if: (1) D directed his actions at a member of P's immediate family (call her X); and (2) P was present at the time (e.g., D was beating X, P's father, while P was forced to watch). The Second Restatement extends the notion of transferred intent further, to cover situations where X is not a family member of P, if P suffers "bodily harm" from the distress. Rest. 2d, §46(2); Ch. 2 (VII)(E).

[3] But check for other torts that may have occurred. In particular, check to make sure that there has not been: (1) assault (where D's conduct intentionally or recklessly put P in fear of imminent bodily harm); or (2) negligent infliction of emotional distress (allowable only where the distress produces bodily harm). As to (2), see Fig. 9 (Duty in Negligence Cases).

[4] If D's conduct was directed at someone other than P, the transferred-intent analysis is the same as in footnote 2. (E.g, if D knew with substantial certainty that he would cause severe distress to X, he's liable to P, X's immediate family member, who was present at the event).

[5] This box covers the situation in which D behaves "recklessly" with respect to the risk of causing severe distress. In order for you to answer "yes," D must have taken a grossly unreasonable risk that his conduct would cause emotional distress, and must have known of (and disregarded) this risk. It's not enough that D negligently ran the risk of causing the distress. Ch. 2 (VII)(B).

[6] According to the Second Restatement, the conduct must be "so outrageous in character, and so extreme in degree, as to go beyond all possible bounds of decency, and to be regarded as atrocious, and utterly intolerable in a civilized community." Rest. 2d. §46, Comment d; Ch. 2 (VII)(C)(1). D's conduct will typically be viewed in light of how a reasonable person would have reacted, unless P is very young, retarded, or senile, or D specifically knew that P was extra sensitive.

In addition, D will be held to a stricter standard of conduct if he is (or pretends to be) a police officer, of if he is an employee of a public utility, a common carrier, or a hotel. When that's the case, insulting words alone may give rise to an action for IIED. Otherwise, insulting words alone rarely qualify as "outrageous."

[7] For instance, D may be able to assert self-defense, or the defense of assertion of legal rights. (Example: D is a landlord who threatens to evict P and her children while knowing they are destitute, if they don't immediately pay 6 months back rent. D's conduct is heartless, but he is entitled to exercise -- and to threaten to exercise -- his legal rights. Rest. 2d §46, Illustr. 46.)

[8] Rest. 2d, §908; Ch. 2 (II)(A)(2).

[9] Plaintiffs can recover compensatory damages for emotional pain, suffering, or embarrassment, even if they suffer no physical harm. Ch. 2 (IV)(G)(1). (But as noted in fn. 2 supra, if P is a witness to conduct against a third person, X, who is not P's immediate family member, even liberal courts won't allow P to recover unless P suffers bodily harm from the distress.)

[9] D will be liable for both foreseeable *and* unforeseeable consequences of his actions. Ch. 2 (IV)(F).

Figure 6

Negligence in General

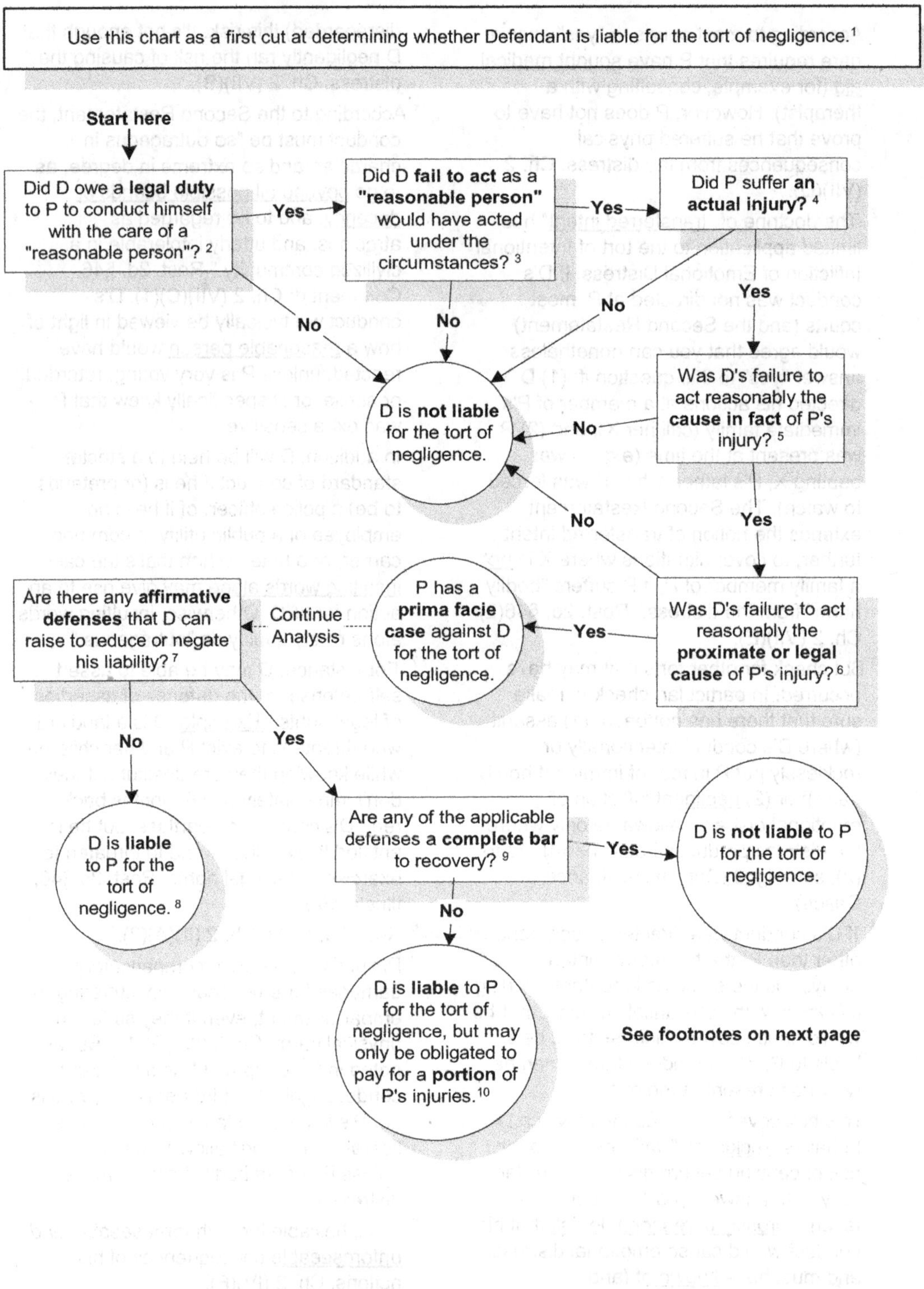

See footnotes on next page

Notes to
Figure 6 (Negligence in General)

1 Figures 7 (*Res Ipsa Loquitur* in Negligence Cases), 8 (Actual and Proximate Cause in Negligence Cases), 9 (Duty in Negligence Cases), 10 (Damages in Negligence Cases) and 11 (Major Defenses in Negligence Cases) each treats certain aspects of negligence in greater detail.

2 In the usual case where D commits an affirmative act, and that act causes physical injury to P, you can safely answer "yes" to this question. You have to worry that the proper answer may be "no" in 3 basic kinds of situations: (1) D's alleged negligence consists of a failure to act rather than an affirmative action; (2) D's act caused P emotional distress but no physical injuries; and (3) D's act caused P economic loss but no physical injuries. Some commentators describe situations (2) and (3) as involving a "lack of duty," although it may be better to think of them as involving types of damages that can't be recovered. In any event, each of these three special situations is covered in Fig. 9, Duty in Negligence Cases.

3 For a "yes," the plaintiff must show that D's conduct imposed an unreasonable risk of harm on P. Rest. 2d, §282; Ch. 5 (III)(A). For more help in answering this question, refer to Fig. 7 *(Res Ipsa Loquitur* in Negligence Cases).

4 If P suffered some physical injury or bodily harm from D's conduct, answer "yes." (Any emotional distress or economic loss can then be "tacked on" to the award for physical injury.)

If P has not suffered any physical injury or bodily harm, there are a number of difficult questions you'll have to answer (e.g., Can P recover for purely emotional damages? Can P recover for purely economic injury?). These questions are dealt with in Fig. 9 (Duty in Negligence Cases).

5 Answer "yes" if, but for D's negligence, P's injuries would not have occurred. If you are having trouble answering this question, refer to the flow chart on Actual and Proximate Cause (Fig. 8).

6 Answer "yes" if the injury was a reasonably foreseeable result of D's negligence. If you are having trouble answering this question, refer to the flow chart on Actual and Proximate Cause (Fig. 8).

7 Refer to the flow chart on Major Defenses in Negligence Cases (Fig. 11). The most common defenses you need to check are: (1) contributory/comparative negligence; and (2) assumption of risk.

8 Refer to the flow chart on Damages in Negligence Actions (Fig. 10) to calculate any damages.

9 For example, contributory negligence and assumption of risk are generally a complete bar to recovery (but comparative negligence is not).

10 The defense of comparative negligence, for example, may not relieve defendant of liability, but may reduce the amount of that liability. Refer to the flow chart on Damages in Negligence Actions (Fig. 10) to calculate any damages.

Figure 7

Res Ipsa Loquitur in Negligence Cases

Res ipsa loquitur means "the thing speaks for itself." Plaintiff can use this doctrine to create an inference that defendant was probably negligent based upon the fact of the accident itself, even though she has no direct evidence of what defendant actually did. Use the following chart to see if the plaintiff in your set of facts can take advantage of this doctrine.

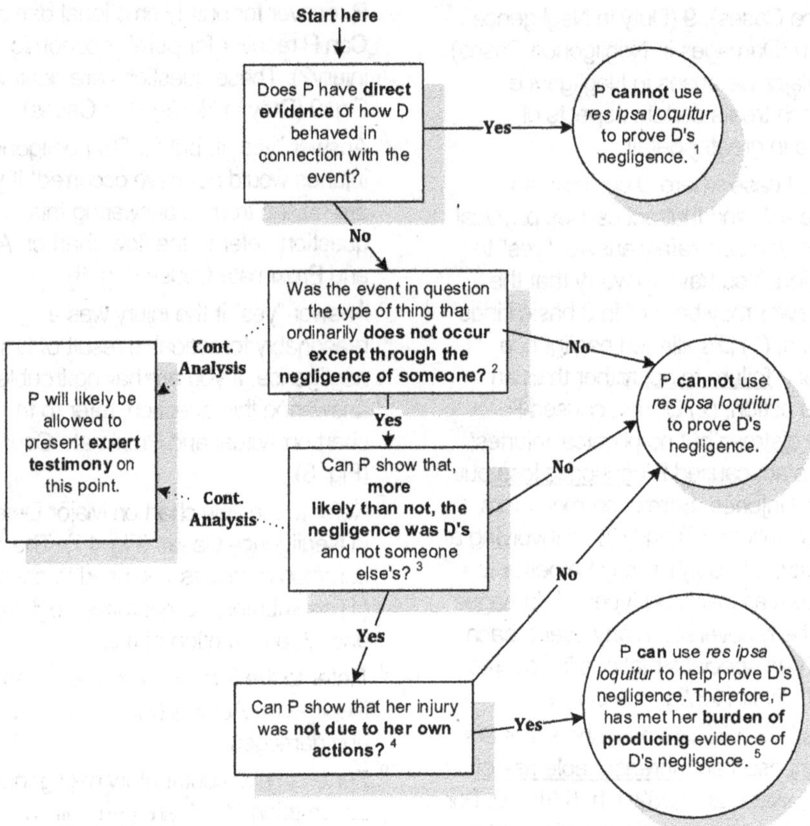

Footnotes:

[1] *Res ipsa loquitur* is only used as an indirect means of inferring that D was probably negligent. P cannot take advantage of it if she knows -- and can directly prove -- the details of D's conduct. Ch. 5 (X)(C).

[2] P does not have to show there were no other possible causes of the accident. She must merely show a more-than-fifty-percent probability that the accident was caused by someone's negligence. Rest. 2d, §328D, Comments e and f; Ch. 5 (X)(D)(3).

[3] In older cases, plaintiff had to show that the instrumentality which caused the harm was under the exclusive control of the defendant. The modern view eases plaintiff's burden somewhat: she must now merely produce evidence showing the negligent act was more likely the fault of the defendant than of anyone else. Ch. 5 (X)(E).

[4] If P's own actions (contributorily negligent or not) are shown to have helped bring about the accident, and if those actions make it less than probable that D was negligent, the doctrine cannot be applied, and you should answer "no". But if P's actions (including contributory negligence) do not materially lessen the probability that D was *also* negligent, the doctrine can be applied, and you should answer "yes". (The contributory negligence or comparative negligence may then be a full or partial defense -- but this happens *after* application of the doctrine.)

[5] In other words, just by qualifying for *res ipsa*, P is entitled to go to the jury on the question of whether D was negligent.

Figure 8

Actual and Proximate Cause In Negligence Cases

Once P has established that D acted negligently, P must then show that D's behavior "caused" his injury. To do so, P must prove that D's conduct was both: (1) the "actual" cause (or "cause in fact") of the injury, and (2) the "proximate" (or "legal") cause. This chart will help you decide whether plaintiff can meet this two-pronged burden. *Do not use this chart unless you've first established that D behaved (or at least may have behaved) negligently.*

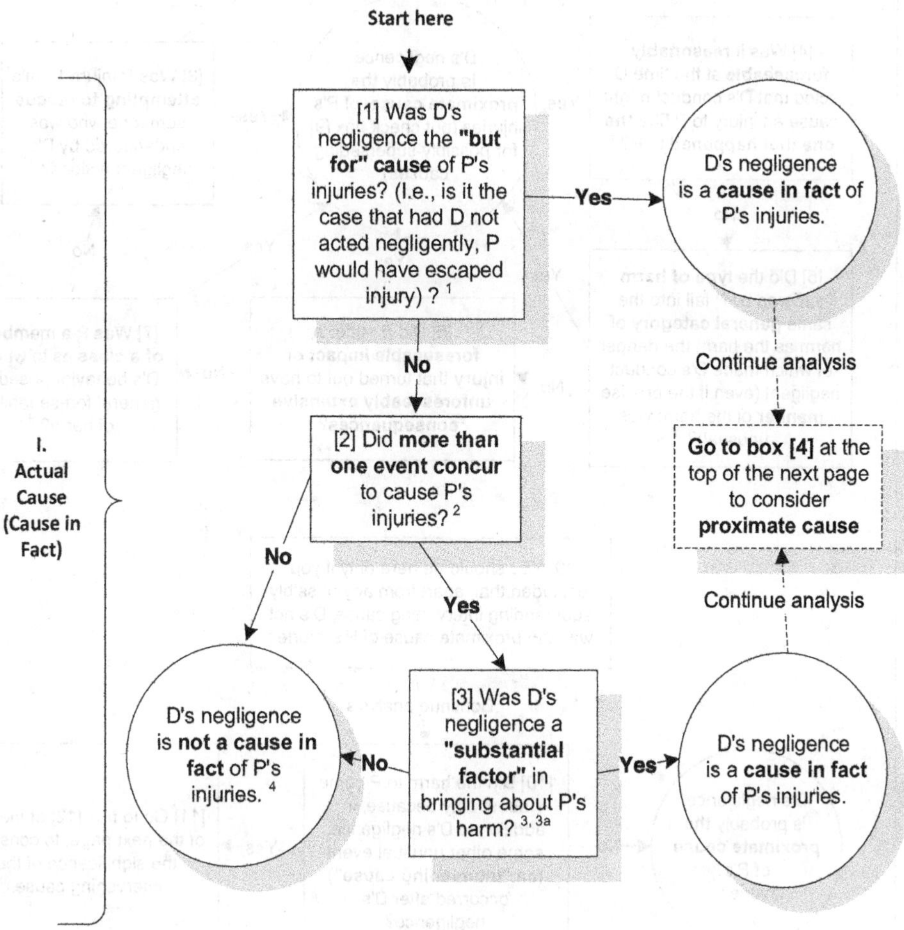

See footnotes after p. 3 of flowchart

Figure 8 (p. 2)
Actual and Proximate Cause In Negligence Cases

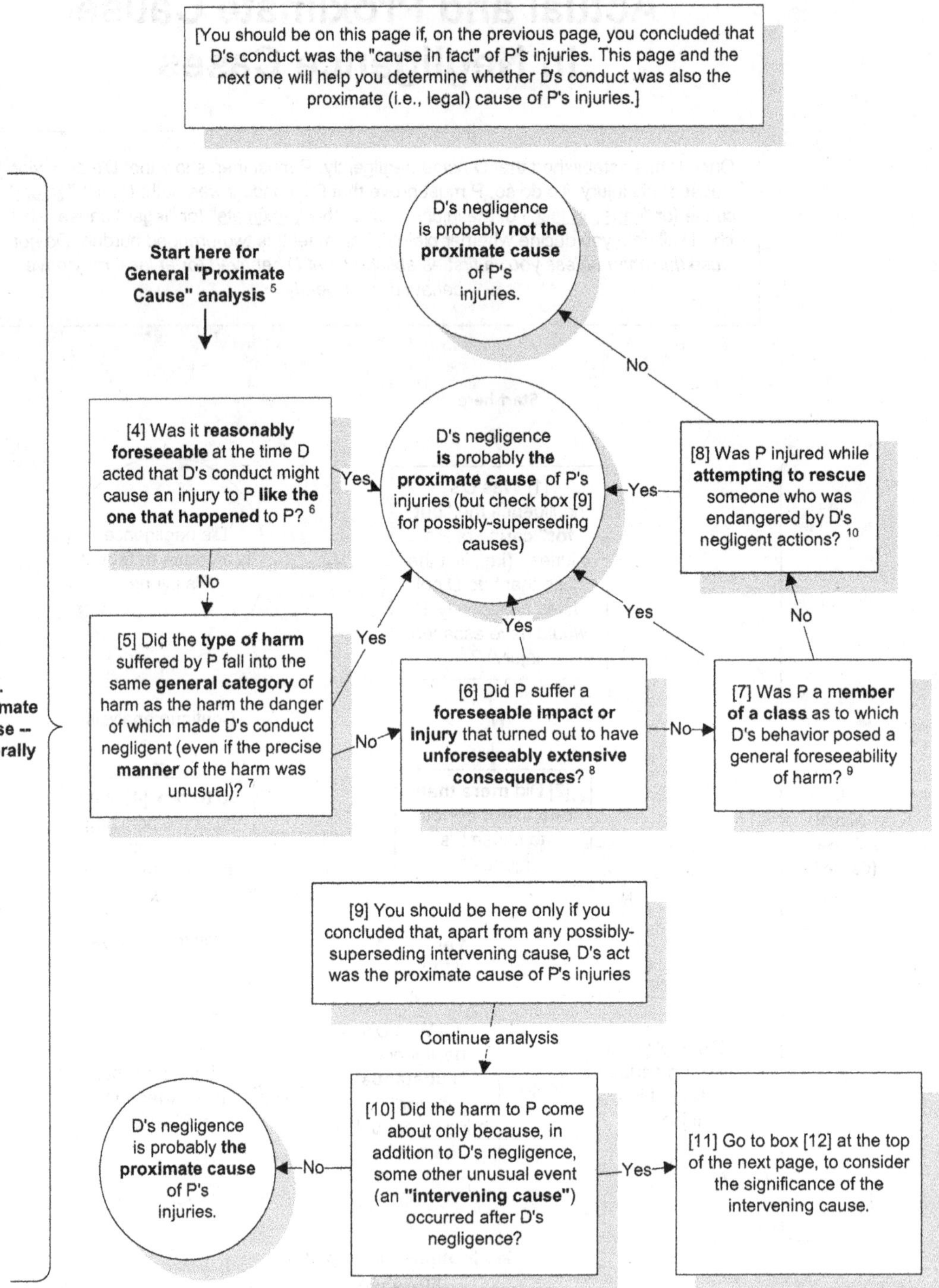

See footnotes after p. 3 of flowchart

Figure 8 (p. 3)

Actual and Proximate Cause In Negligence Cases

[You should be here if (and only if) you concluded that some sort of "intervening cause" occurred after D's negligence. This page will help you figure out whether the intervening cause should be viewed as "superseding," in which case D's negligence won't be treated as the proximate cause of P's injury.]

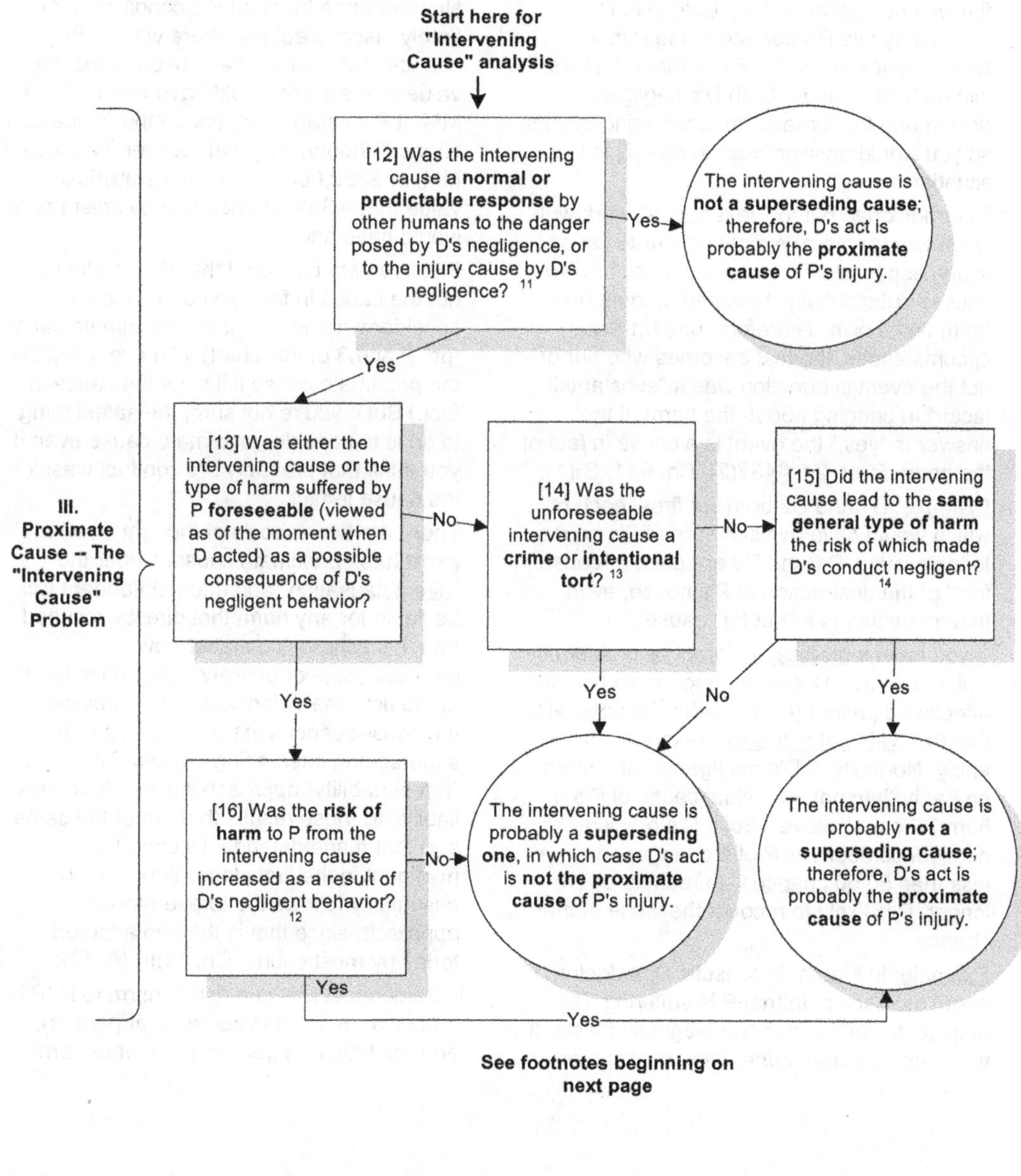

See footnotes beginning on next page

Notes to Figure 8
(Actual and Proximate Cause in Negligence Cases)

1 Where D's act is a "but for" cause of P's injuries, D's act is automatically a "cause in fact" of those injuries. Rest. 2d, §432; Ch. 6 (I)(A)(1). Note that P need only prove by a preponderance of the evidence that the injury would not have occurred but for D's act. Ch. 6 (I)(C).

2 A concurring "event" can include an act of God (e.g., a flood or tornado), an act by a negligent defendant, or an act of unknown origin (e.g., a fire with no known cause). Example: D negligently hits P's car, stranding P in a remote roadway. While P is stranded, she's injured by a tornado. Both D's negligent driving and the tornado are concurring events, so you would answer "yes" to box [2] in this situation.

3 The traditional "but for" test doesn't work well when two (or more) events concur to cause injury, especially if each of them could have caused substantially the same amount of harm on its own. Therefore, under these circumstances, the test becomes whether or not the event in question was a "substantial factor" in bringing about the harm. If the answer is "yes," the event is a cause in fact of the harm. Rest. 2d, §432(2); Ch. 6 (1)(B)(1).

Example: D1 and D2 both set fires, each of which would have by itself burned P's house to the ground. D1 and D2 are each a "cause in fact" of the destruction of P's house, even though neither is a "but for" cause.

3a If you have a medical malpractice problem in which a doctor, D, fails to diagnose a disease affecting a patient (P), consider the possibility that the "value of a chance" doctrine may apply. Normally, if D's negligence isn't more probably than not the actual cause of P's harm, P can't recover. But if D's medical negligence deprives P of a chance -- even a less than 50/50 chance -- to recover or live longer, P is likely to recover the value of that chance.

Example: In March, P consults D, a doctor, about stomach pain that P is suffering. D negligently fails to perform diagnostic tests. If the tests had been done, they would have shown that P had early-stage stomach cancer; treatment at that point would have given P a 35% chance of a complete cure (but a 65% chance that he would die very soon). By December, another doctor discovers that P's cancer is very advanced, and he dies soon thereafter.

P's estate should be able to recover the "value of the chance" that had D not been negligent, P would have been cured. Now, assume that had P's condition been timely discovered, and there was a 100% chance that P would have been cured, the value of P's claim would have been, say, $1 MM. If P's estate recovers on the "value of a chance" theory, it should recover 35% x $1 MM, or $350,000 -- that's the statistical value that a 35% chance of a complete cure would have had.

4 If you're very confident that D's conduct was not the cause in fact, you don't need to consider whether it was the proximate cause (pp. 2 and 3 of this chart). (An event can't be the proximate cause if it's not the cause in fact.) But if you're not sure, the safest thing to do is to consider proximate cause even if you think that probably D's conduct wasn't the cause in fact.

5 There are two schools of thought on what constitutes proximate cause. Under the "direct causation" approach, defendant will be liable for any harm that directly resulted from his actions, no matter how unforeseeable or unlikely it may have been at the time the defendant acted, provided the consequences are not due in part to superseding intervening causes. The "foreseeability" approach limits defendant's liability to those results that are of the same sort that made defendant's conduct negligent in the first place. This flow chart essentially follows the foreseeability approach, since that is the one adopted today by most courts. Ch. 6 (III) (A) (2).

6 If D's conduct posed a risk of harm to P (P in particular, not just to some other person), and the type and general manner of harm

Notes (p. 2) to Figure 8
(Actual and Proximate Cause in Negligence Cases)

that ensued were the type the risk of which made D's conduct negligent, answer "yes" to the question in box [4]. Often, you'll answer "yes" to this question. But there are two main types of situations where you should answer "no" to box [4]:

(1) First, there's the situation where D's conduct poses an unreasonable risk of harm to P, but rather than the type of harm and manner of harm that was reasonably foreseeable, some other type of harm (or harm occurring in some other manner) befalls P through a fluke. Example: D is a shipowner. Through D's employees' negligence, a small amount of oil escapes from D's ship while it's docked at P's wharf. The oil makes the wharf slightly slippery, but does not pose any other likely danger. Then, through an unrelated fluke, one of P's workers drops (non-negligently) some hot metal that causes the oil to combust, burning down the wharf. Here, the type and manner of harm are so different from the harm (slippery wharf on which people might fall) the risk of which made the spillage negligent, that the answer to box [6] should be "no." [*Wagon Mound No. 1*]

(2) Then, there's the situation in which D acts negligently with respect to one potential plaintiff, but a different person (who was not apparently significantly at risk) is injured through a fluke of circumstances. This latter situation is termed the "unforeseeable plaintiff" problem. Example: D, running on a train platform, pushes X, who (unbeknownst to D) is carrying fireworks. The fireworks drop and explode. The explosion makes scales at the other end of the platform fall, hitting P. Since D's act (viewed from D's perspective) did not pose any measurable risk to P, you would answer "no" to box [4]. [*Palsgraf v. Long Isl. R.R.*]

Both examples in this footnote would not only yield "no" answers to the question in box [4], but would also result in "no" answers for boxes [5] through [8], so that D's negligence would end up not being the proximate cause of the harm.

[7] Example: D hands a loaded gun to X, a 6-year-old child. X drops the gun. When the gun hits the ground, instead of hitting the carpet it freakishly hits a toy truck, causing it to go off and injure P, a bystander. The specific risk that makes giving a gun to a child most dangerous is the risk that the child will intentionally fire the gun. But the general category of harm that makes giving a gun to a child dangerous is that the gun will somehow go off (whether intentionally fired or not) and hit someone. The harm suffered here by P falls within this general category of harm. Therefore, the answer to the question in box [5] is "yes," and D's negligence will be treated as the proximate cause of P's harm. Rest. 2d, §281, Illustr. 3; Ch. 6 (III)(D)(4).

[8] Virtually all courts agree that the defendant "takes his plaintiff as he finds him." Defendant will be liable for even unforeseen consequences arising out of a negligent infliction of physical injury. Example: D negligently bumps into P, and P falls down. The impact would not have knocked down most people in P's position, and even if it did, most wouldn't be seriously injured. However, P suffers a fractured hip from the fall, because she has unusually weak bones. D will be liable for the broken hip, because: (1) his negligence foreseeably caused an impact; and (2) D is responsible for the unforeseeably great consquences of that impact. Ch. 6 (III)(D)(1)(a).

[9] Example: D, a pharmaceutical manufacturer, negligently allows a small amount of poisonous mercury to get into one dose of D's drug, "Painkill." Randomly, that particular bottle is purchased by X and then given by X to P, who takes it and dies. Even though there was no way in advance to know which particular person would end up with the poisonous dosage (or, indeed, whether anyone would), P was a member of a class (Painkill users) as to which D's behavior posed a general foreseeability of harm. Therefore, D's negligence is the proximate cause of P's harm. Ch. 6 (V)(D)(5).

[10] P's rescue action could conceivably be seen as a superseding intervening act (see p. 3 of the chart) that might otherwise limit D's liability. However, courts generally *do* impose liability for injuries to rescuers, under the theory

Notes (p. 3) to Figure 8
(Actual and Proximate Cause in Negligence Cases)

that a rescue attempt itself is a foreseeable consequence of D's danger-producing conduct. Ch. 6 (IV)(D)(1). (But if P's rescue attempt is performed in a grossly careless manner, then D will *not* be liable for any resulting injuries. *Id.*)

[11] Examples include intervening causes that are a response to the danger or harm caused by defendant, such as cases of attempted escape from harm, rescue, and attempted medical treatment. These intervening acts will only be deemed superseding causes (thus relieving defendant of liability for the resulting harm) if the actions were performed with gross negligence or were totally bizarre in nature. Ch. 6 (IV)(D)(1)(b)(ii).

[12] Example of "yes" answer: D is a tavern owner who serves X, a patron, too much to drink. X drives away from the bar and then negligently crashes into P, injuring him. X's accident is an intervening cause, but the risk of that intervening cause was increased as a result of D's negligence in serving X too much alcohol. Therefore, most states would hold that D is a proximate cause of P's injuries (and that the accident was not a superseding cause). Ch. 6 (IV)(C)(4)(a) and (b).

Example of "no" answer: D negligently drives his car into a collision with P, who is on his way to catch a plane. Because the collision takes 20 minutes to resolve, P misses his scheduled flight. He then has to take the next flight, which crashes, killing him. The risk of P's dying in a plane crash was not increased by D's negligent driving (since no scheduled plane trip, viewed in advance, is materially more likely to crash than any other). Therefore, the plane crash will be viewed as a superseding intervening cause, which will prevent D's negligence from being the proximate cause of P's death.

[13] Example: D negligently collides, at very slow speed, with P's car. The car seems to drive fine, so P drives it 500 miles, then briefly stops at a convenience store. While in the store, P is accosted by X, who tries to rob and assault her. P pulls away, runs to her car and tries to start it. However, due to hidden damage from the collision, the car won't start. The delay allows X to reach into P's car, pull her out, and complete the assault. Because it was not foreseeable to one in D's position that a slight collision might lead to the type of risk from an assailant that materialized (and because the assault was itself an unforeseeable intervening cause), the assault will be superseding, and will prevent D's negligence from being the proximate cause of P's injuries.

[14] For a discussion of when a harm is of the same general type as the harm the risk of which made D's conduct negligent, see box [5] and footnote 7 above.

Figure 9

Duty in Negligence Cases

Defendant cannot be liable to plaintiff for negligence unless she owed him a duty of care, and then violated that duty. In most tort cases, the duty involves behaving toward the plaintiff with the degree of care that a reasonable person would exercise under like circumstances. However, there are 3 special situations in which a duty of care might not arise: (1) where D's alleged negligence arises from D's **failure to act**; (2) where P claims that D's actions caused P **mental suffering**; and (3) where P claims that D's actions caused P **intangible economic harm**. This flow chart helps you analyze these three special cases.

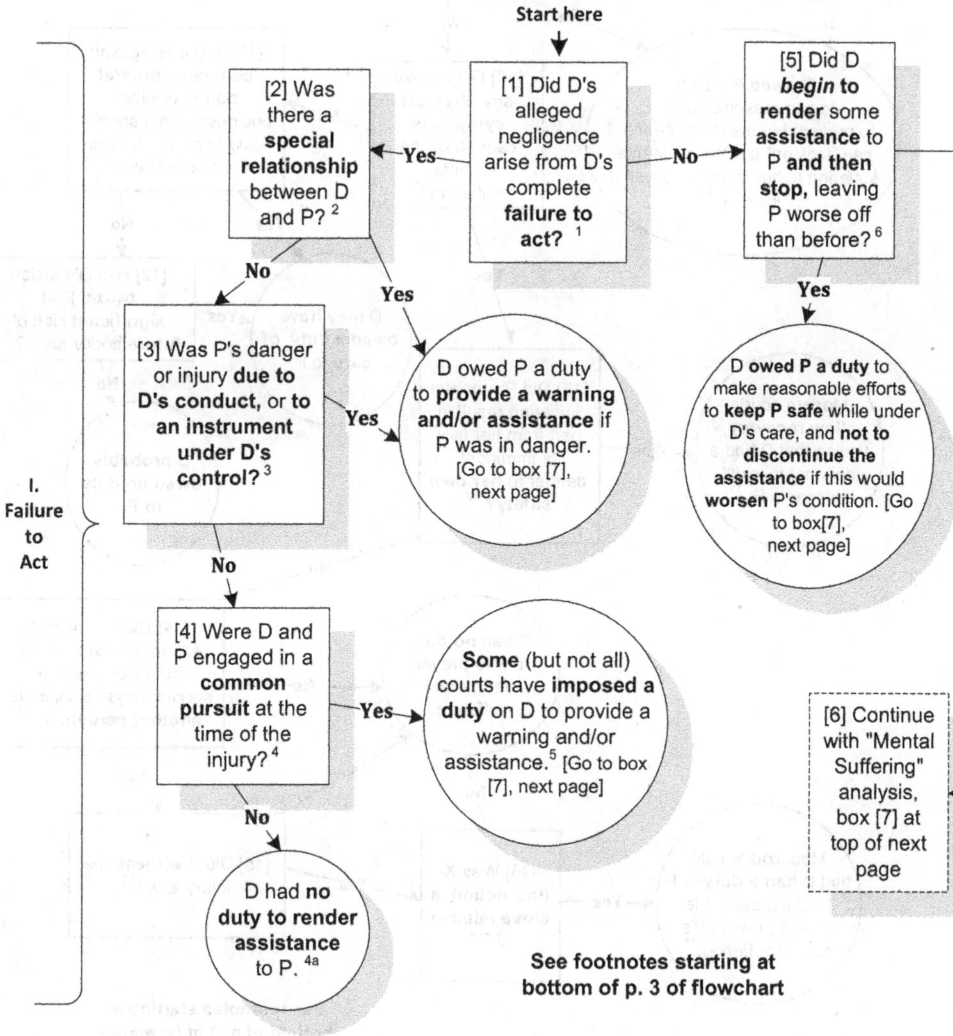

See footnotes starting at bottom of p. 3 of flowchart

Figure 9 (p. 2)

Duty in Negligence Cases

[If P is claiming damages for **mental suffering**, this page will help you figure out whether D owed P a duty to avoid bringing about such suffering. You should use this page no matter what result you reached on the prior page of this chart. Also, you should go on to the next page no matter what you conclude on this page.]

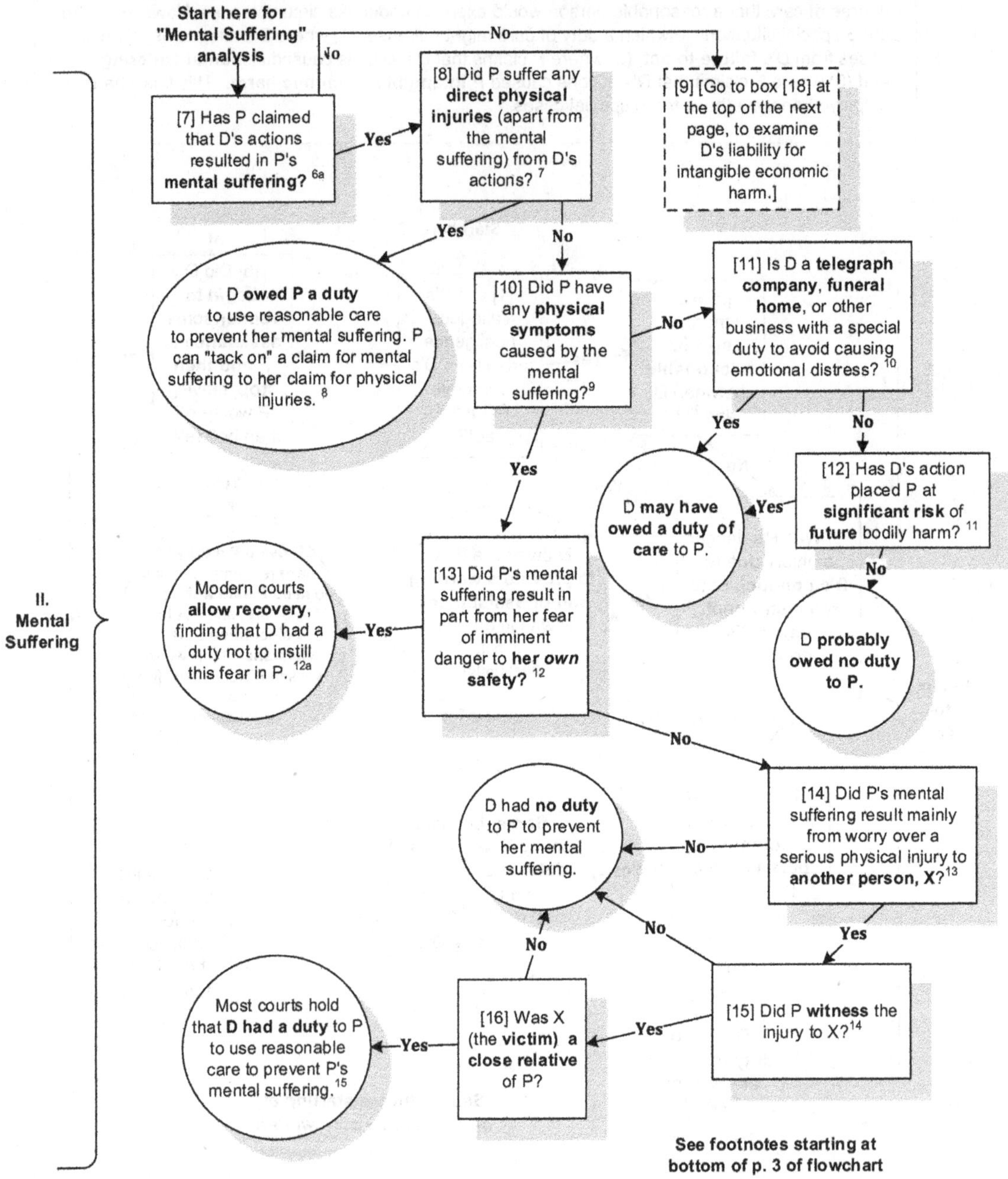

See footnotes starting at bottom of p. 3 of flowchart

Figure 9 (p. 3)

Duty in Negligence Cases

[If P is claiming damages for **intangible economic harm**, this page will help you figure out whether D owed P a duty to avoid bringing about such harm. You should use this page no matter what result you reached on the two prior pages of this chart.]

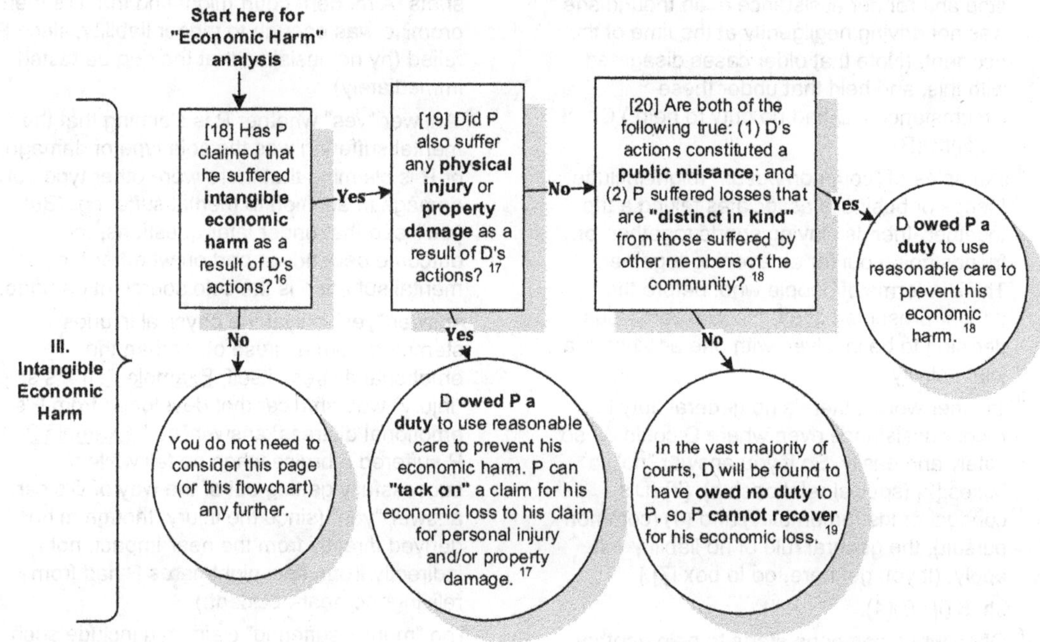

Footnotes:

[1] This question refers to the crucial distinction between <u>misfeasance</u> and <u>nonfeasance</u>. Most negligence scenarios involve misfeasance: D acts in some affirmative way that harms or endangers P. In nonfeasance, D does nothing at all, and it is her failure to act that, P says, created or exacerbated P's harm. Nonfeasance typically comes into play in failure-to-rescue scenarios. Ch. 8 (II)(A)(1). <u>Example</u>: D is walking by a public lake, and sees P (a stranger) drowning. D could easily throw a nearby life-preserver to P, but doesn't do so because D is lazy. On this scenario, you would answer "yes" to box [3] (D's alleged negligence arose from D's failure to act). Then, you'd answer "no" to the questions in boxes [3] and [4], and you'd conclude that D had no duty to render assistance to P.

[2] Here are the main "special relationships" that would dictate a "yes" answer to box [2]: a passenger and a common carrier (e.g., plane, train or bus); a guest and an innkeeper; a business visitor and someone who maintains business premises; an employee and employer; a student and a school; a tenant and a landlord. While the general rule (explained in note 1 above) is that mere bystanders have no duty to rescue plaintiff, courts have held otherwise where D and P had any of these special relationship to each other. In these situations, courts have held that D owes P a duty to furnish warnings and/or assistance if P is injured or in danger. Ch. 8 (II)(B).

Notes (Cont.) to Figure 9 (Duty in Negligence Cases)

[3] Under the modern view, you should answer "yes" to this question even if the actions by D that created the danger to P were totally non-negligent. For example, if D is a driver who has the right of way and P is a pedestrian who suddenly darts out and is hit by D, D must still stop and render assistance even though she was not driving negligently at the time of the accident. (Note that older cases disagreed with this, and held that under these circumstances, D had no duty to help.) Ch. 8 (II)(B)(3)(B).

[4] Examples of "common pusuit" might include friends or business associates taking a trip together, friends playing sports together, or friends going out for an evening together. Think in terms of people who, before the danger presented itself, made a conscious decision to be involved with one another in a joint activity.

[4a] In other words, there's no general duty to render assistance even where D could do so safely and easily. So if you answer "no" to boxes [2] (special relationship), [3] (D's conduct or instrumentality) and (4) (common pursuit), the general rule of no liability will apply. (If you get here, go to box [7].)

[5] Ch. 8 (II)(B)(4).

[6] Often when someone starts to help another, this help dissuades others from rendering aid. For this reason, those who start to render aid have a duty not to make matters worse for the plaintiff. This is sometimes called the "assumption of duty" rationale. Ch. 8 (II)(B)(5).

Example 1: D, an employer, requires P, a job applicant, to take a medical exam. Held, once D assumed a duty to examine P, D had a duty not to perform the exam negligently.

Example 2: D, a railroad, has for a long time always posted a guard to warn cars that are about to cross the tracks that a train is approaching. On one day, D's guard doesn't give the signal, and P, a motorist, is hit by an oncoming car. Probably D is liable, since it has instituted a practice of warnings on which P has relied.

An open question is whether D's mere promise to render aid (where D never actually begins to perform) can trigger this exception. The modern trend seems to be to allow liability if P shows he relied to his detriment on the promise. Ch. 8 (II)(B)(6)(b). Example: P is bitten by D's dog. D promises to keep the dog locked up so it can later be tested for rabies. D then doesn't do so, and the dog runs away. P has to presume that the dog was infected, and has to undergo painful rabies shots. A modern court might find that D's mere promise was enough to trigger liability, since P relied (by not insisting that the dog be tested immediately).

[6a] Answer "yes" whether P is claiming that the mental suffering was the sole type of damage, or P is claiming that there were other types of damage in addition to mental suffering. (But you'll see that under later questions, the outcome depends in part on whether the mental suffering is the sole source of damage.)

[7] Answer "yes" only if the physical injuries stemmed from a cause other than the emotional distress itself. Example 1: If P's sole "injury" was an ulcer that developed from P's emotional distress, answer "no." Example 2: If P suffered a bruise when he fell while successfully getting out of the way of D's car, answer "yes" (since the injury, though minor, derived directly from the near-impact, not indirectly from, say, nightmares P had from reliving the near-accident.)

[8] The "mental suffering" claim can include such items as pain and suffering from the injury, fright at the time of the injury, and ongoing anxiety or humiliation as a result of the injury (e.g., nightmares from reliving the accident). Ch. 8 (IV)(A)(1).

[9] Examples: P suffers a miscarriage; P develops an ulcer; P suffers nightmares and insomnia. (In all these cases, P will have to show that more probably than not, the symptom was caused by the emotional distress that was in turn caused by D's negligence.)

Note that in recent years, a few states have abandoned the requirement of physical symptoms if there is other credible evidence to show plaintiff was actually distressed. In such a state, you can always answer "yes" to box [10].

[10] Example 1: D is a telegraph company that negligently mis-transmits a telegram to P -- D's operator types "Your son is dead" when the telegram should read "Your son is not dead."

Notes (Cont.) to
Figure 9 (Duty in Negligence Cases)

Example 2: D is a funeral home that conducts a wake for P's husband but negligently puts the corpse of a stranger, not P's husband, in the open casket.

[11] Example: D negligently designs a pregnancy-inducing drug, Pregnisone, and sells some to X. X then gives birth to a child, P. P growsup. Statistics show that P has a much higher than average chance of getting uterine cancerin the future that people whose mothers didn't take Pregnisone. Courts are split about whether P can recover for the distress of worrying about her increased cancer risk. Ch. 8 (IV)(H)(2)-(4).

[12] This includes situations where P did not suffer any direct impact -- as long as P's suffering is a not-bizarre result of the fact that P at one point feared for her safety, no impact is required for a "yes" answer.

Example: D negligently drives onto the sidewalk near P, a pedestrian. P sees the accident about to happen, throws herself out of the way, and is not physically hurt at the time. However, P has recurring nightmares in which she relieves the near-accident, and suffers extreme insomnia on account of them. On these facts, answer "yes" (so that, in the next circle, you'll conclude that P can recover even though P never suffered an impact or any direct physical injuries).

[13] Rest. 3d. (Phys. & Emot. Hm.) §47; Ch. 8 (IV)(D). As the idea is often put, P must have been in the "zone of danger" (i.e., have reasonably feared for her own physical safety) in order to recover, assuming there was no physical impact on other persons.

[14] Example: P is standing on the sidewalk, watching her 4-year-old child, X, play at the side of the road. D comes along driving negligently fast. As P watches, X is struck by D's vehicle. (Assume that P never fears for her own safety). You should answer "yes" to this question.

In order for you to answer "yes," P must have perceived the injury at the time it occurred. Watching it through a window is OK. However, if P did not arrive at the scene until a minute after the accident, you shouldanswer "no" (even though P then saw X lying injured on the ground), since P didn't perceivethe injury "contemporaneously" with its occurrence.

[15] See Ch. 8 (IV).

[16] Intangible economic harm is economic loss as opposed to either personal injuries or property damage. Examples: (1) P's restaurant operates at a loss for a day because D, the power company, negligently fails to provide electricity, and P incurs overhead expense without being able to make any sales. (2) Same facts, but P's restaurant merely breaks even for a day (and thus loses the profits it would have made) because of D's failure to provide electricity.

[17] Example of a "yes" answer: Same facts as the two examples in note 16. However, in addition to the "pure" economic loss (lost business profits), P also suffers out-of-pocket loss when frozen meats he holds for resale in its freezer spoil due to the lack of power. Because this spoiled meat constitutes property damage, answer "yes" (so that P can tack on his lost- profits claim to the property-damage claim).

[18] Example (both conditions true): Biz, a retail store, is the only business on an island, and all customers arrive by crossing a publicly-owned bridge to the island. (There are no residents on the island.) Barge, a ship piloted negligently, runs into the bridge, putting it out of action for 4 weeks. Biz has to close and suffers $10,000 in lost profits during the 4 weeks. A court would probably hold that both conditions are true: (1) Barge, by damaging the bridge, has probably interfered with a "right common to the general public" (the main ingredient of a public nuisance); and (2) As the only business on the island, Biz has probably suffered harm that is "different in kind" from that suffered by all others who were affected (none of whom lives or owns a business on the island). If the court so held, you would answer "yes" to this question, and the court would find that Barge is liable to Biz for a negligent breach of the duty of care that Barge owed to Biz (i.e., Biz would recover in a private action for public nuisance).

[19] Example (at least one condition not true): Same facts as prior Example, except that now Biz is one of 30 businesses on the island, all of which have to close for 4 weeks. A court would likely find that the second condition above (D suffers harm "different in kind" from all others) is not satisfied. If so, Biz would not be allowed to recover in nuisance, because Barge would be found not to have violated any duty of care owed to Biz.

Figure 10

Damages in Negligence Cases

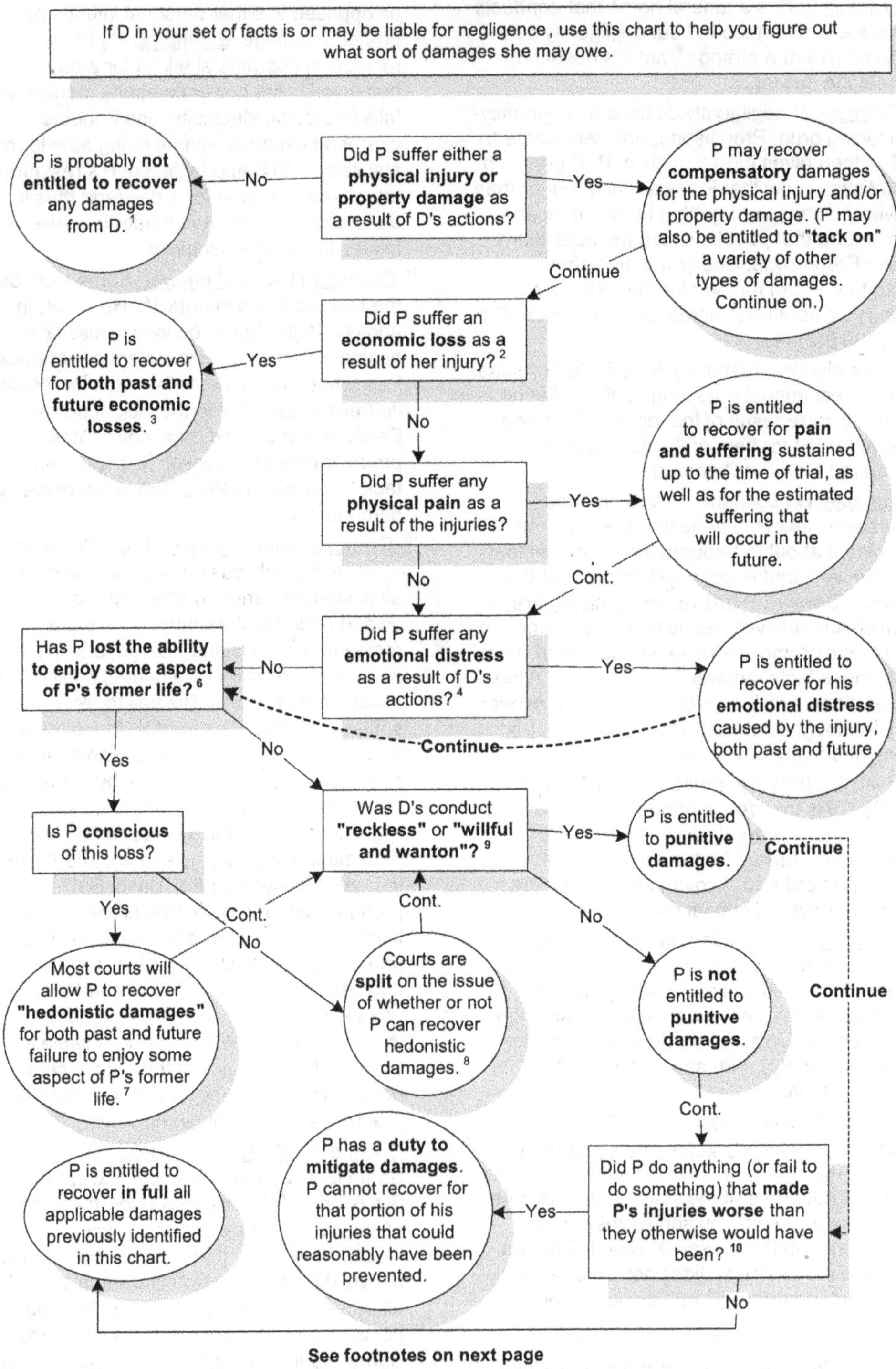

See footnotes on next page

Notes to
Figure 10 (Damages in Negligence Cases)

[1] Unlike intentional torts, nominal damages are not allowed in negligence actions. Therefore, P must generally have suffered some actual injury in order to recover from D. Rest. 2d, §907, Comment a; Ch. 10 (I)(A).

We put the word "probably" in the circle because of the possibility that in certain (probably rare) circumstances, a court might allow P to recover for emotional distress or economic loss even in the absence of direct physical injury or property damage. See pages 2 and 3 of Figure 9 (Duty in Negligence Cases) for an analysis of when this might happen.

[2] Economic loss damages can include the following: medical expenses, lost earnings or profits, and the cost of any labor required to do the things P can no longer do herself, such as housekeeping. Note that under the common-law "collateral source rule," P is entitled to recover from D even for economic losses for which she is reimbursed by a third party. (The rule is still in force in about half the states; the others have abolished it by statute.) The rule typically comes into play with medical expenses that are reimbursed by P's insurance company, or benefits P receives from social welfare programs. Ch. 10 (I)(E).

[3] With respect to future damages, P need only show the approximate amount of damages she will "more likely than not" sustain, including lost earnings and future medical expenses. Rest. 2d, §10; Ch. 10 (I)(C). For future damages designed to compensate for economic loss, courts generally instruct the jury to award only the net present value of the loss, to offset any windfall to P. Ch. 10 (I)(C)(3).

[4] Emotional distress can include any or all of the following: fright and shock at the time of the injury, humiliation due to disfigurement or disability, depression about no longer being able to lead one's previous lifestyle, and anxiety about the future (such as fears about the accident's impact on P's unborn child). I(A)(2)(c).

[6] Examples: The ability to play a specific sport or musical instrument; the ability to have or enjoy sex.

[7] Most courts allow hedonistic damages as an item distinct from pain and suffering damages. Some courts, however, insist that hedonistic damages are merely an aspect of pain and suffering, and therefore combine the two.

[8] The issue arises where the injury is so severe that it leaves P either in a coma or with such extensive brain damage that P is not even aware of his injury or his loss of function. Ch. 10 (I)(B)(2).

[9] In other words, did D disregard what he knew to be a substantial risk of injury to P or others? This is a tougher standard to meet than one merely requiring that D have been "inattentive."

[10] Usually, the measures in questions are ones P should have taken after the accident, most commonly seeking adequate medical care. In other words, P is required to use reasonable care and effort after the accident to mitigate her damages.

Some courts also impose a duty-to-mitigate with respect to safety measures that a reasonable person would have taken before the accident. Examples: Some courts say that a person who fails to wear a seatbelt while driving a car, or a helmet while riding a bike or motorcyle, may not recover for injuries that would not have occurred had the belt/helmet been used. Ch. 10 (I)(F).

Note that in this box, we're not talking about things that would have prevented the accident entirely -- those are handled in Fig. 11, in the discussion of the contributory and comparative negligence defenses. Here, we're concerned with actions/inactions that make a given accident worse.

Figure 11

Major Defenses in Negligence Cases

The most important defenses in negligence cases are: (1) **contributory negligence** or **comparative negligence** (depending upon the jurisdiction), and (2) **assumption of risk.** Use this chart to see if any of these defenses might apply to your facts.

I. Contributory/Comparative Negligence

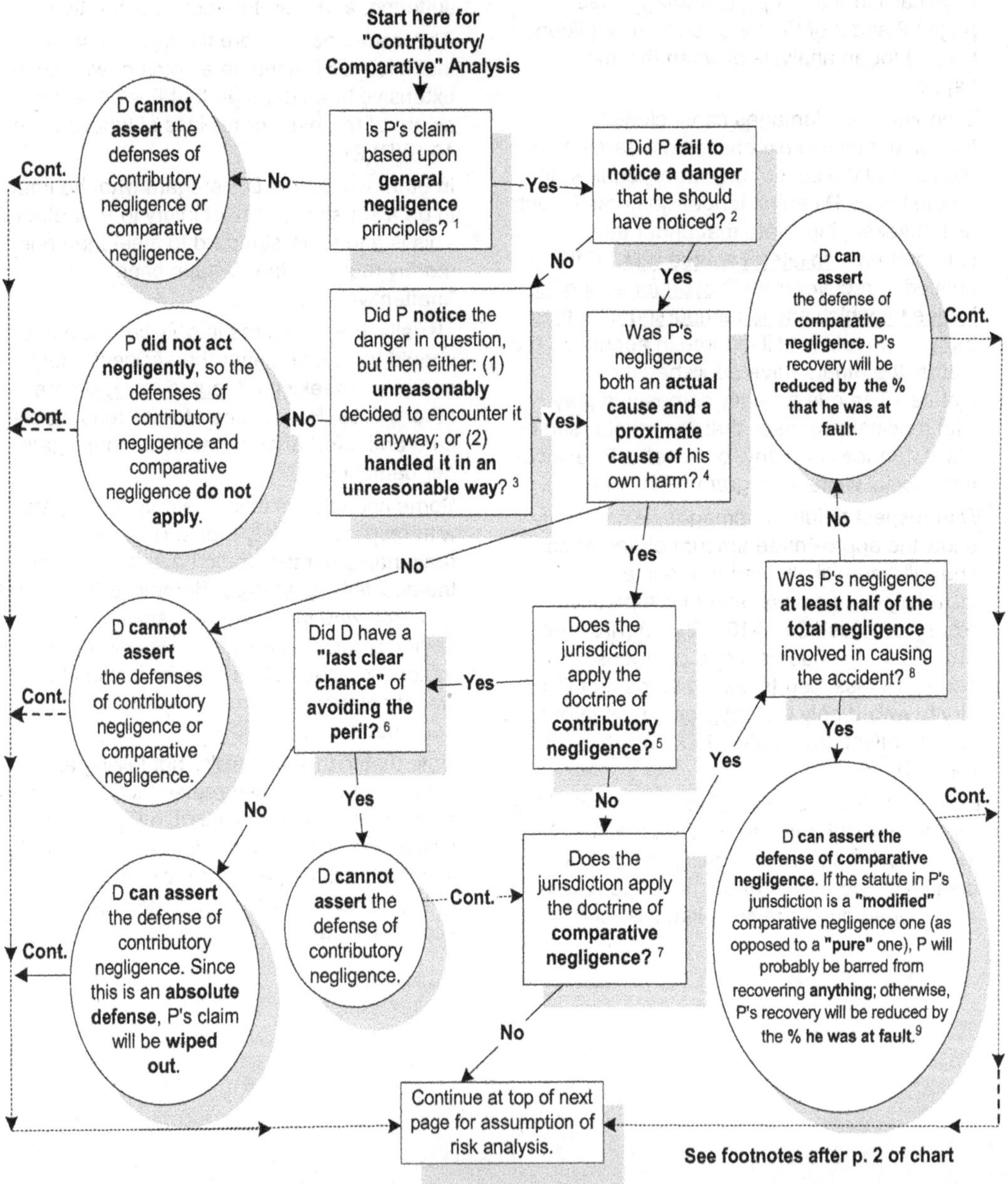

See footnotes after p. 2 of chart

Figure 11 (p. 2)

Major Defenses in Negligence Cases

II. Assumption of Risk

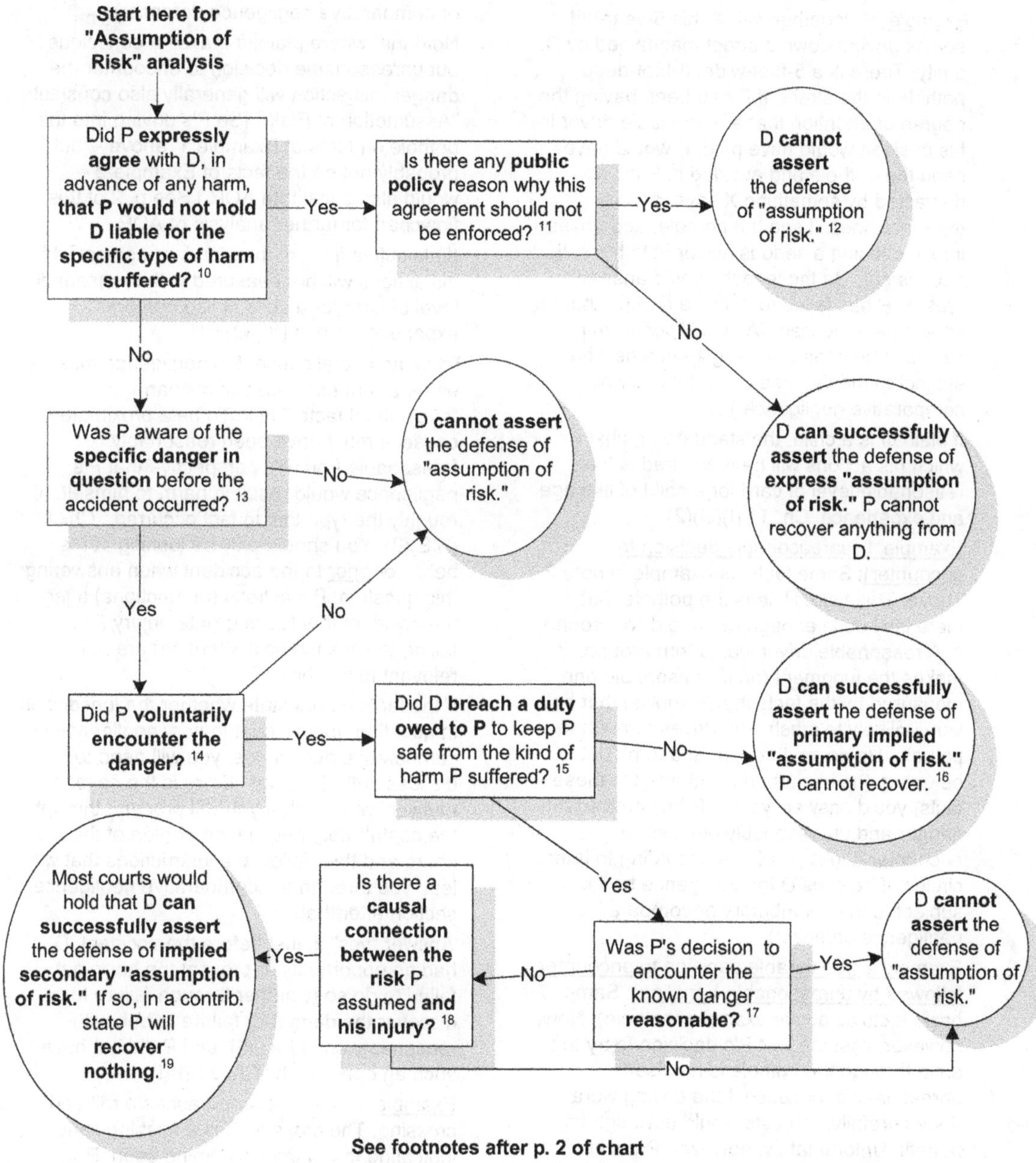

See footnotes after p. 2 of chart

Notes to
Figure 11 (Major Defenses in Negligence Cases)

1 Answer "no" if the claim is based upon an intentional tort, or if defendant's conduct was "willful and wanton" or "reckless," or if defendant has been found strictly liable for his actions. Answer "yes" if the claim is based upon a statutory violation (negligence per se).

2 Example: P, together with X, his 5-year-old son, is driving down a street maintained by D, a city. There is a 5-foot-wide, 3-foot-deep pothole in the street. If P had been paying the degree of attention that a reasonable driver in his position would have paid, P would have seen the pothole and avoided it. P is distracted by something X says, and he therefore doesn't see the pothole, and drives into it, causing a serious accident to himself and his car. On these facts, you'd answer "yes" -- P has failed to notice a danger that he should have noticed. (As you'll see from later circles, if he sues D for negligence he'll be subject to the defense of contributory or comparative negligence.)

If plaintiff is a child, the standard against which his actions will be measured is the reasonable level of care for a child of like age and experience. Ch. 11 (I)(D)(2).

3 Example 1 (unreasonable decision to encounter): Same facts as example in note 2 above. This time, P sees the pothole, but there isn't quite enough room to drive around it. A reasonable driver would turn around. P makes the judgment (an unreasonable one, measured by the facts that P knows) that he's very unlikely to crash if he drives through the pothole. He drives through, and turns out to be wrong (he has a bad accident). On these facts, you'd answer "yes" -- P has noticed the danger and unreasonably decided to encounter it. (As you'll see according to later circles, if he sues D for negligence he'll be subject to the contributory or comparative negligence defense.)

Example 2 (reasonable decision to encounter, followed by unreasonable handling): Same basic facts as above example (pothole). Now, however, assume that P's decision to try to drive through the pothole is not itself unreasonable, because if the driving were done carefully, its costs would outweigh its benefit. Unfortunately, however, P drives unreasonably fast through the pothole, and has an accident. Again, you'd answer "yes" on these facts -- P has reasonably encountered a known danger, but done so in an unreasonable way. (Again, you'll see that according to later circles, if he sues D for negligence he'll be subject to the contributory or comparative negligence defense.)

Note that where plaintiff makes a conscious but unreasonable decision to encounter the danger, his action will generally also constitute "Assumption of Risk." (So P's driving into the pothole on facts of Example 1 above -- but probably not on the facts of Example 2 -- would also constitute AOR.) See p. 2 of this flowchart for further analysis of AOR.

If plaintiff is a child, the standard against which his actions will be measured is the reasonable level of care for a child of like age and experience. Ch. 11 (I)(D)(2).

4 To be an actual cause, P's negligence must be either a "but for" cause of his harm, or a "substantial factor" in it. To be a proximate cause, it must have been reasonably foreseeable from P's perspective that P's negligence would result in harm to himself, of roughly the type that in fact occurred. Ch. 11 (I)(E)(3). You should only be looking at P's behavior prior to the accident when answering this question. P's actions (or inactions) after the accident that led to greater injury (i.e., failing to seek medical attention) are not relevant to this box.

5 If the facts do not state whether the jurisdiction in question applies contributory negligence or comparative negligence, you will need to discuss both doctrines. If this is the case, answer "yes" so that you will proceed through the contributory negligence portion of the chart, and then follow the instructions that will lead you through the comparative negligence section after that.

6 Answer "yes" if, just before the accident, D had an opportunity to prevent the harm but failed to do so (whether through failure to discover the danger or failure to behave reasonably once he did), and P did not have such an opportunity. Ch. 11 (I)(I).

Example: P, a driver, approaches a railroad crossing. The crossing has a flashing light indicating that a train is coming soon. P

Notes (p. 2) to Figure 11 (Major Defenses in Negligence Cases)

unreasonably believes that she has more than enough time to get across the tracks. While she is crossing the tracks, her car stalls. As she sits there on the tracks unable to re-start the car, a train owned by D comes along. Due to the D's engineer's inattentiveness, the engineer does not notice P on the tracks, and fails to stop, crashing into P and killing her. Had the engineer paid attention, there would have been time to brake and avoid the crash. You'd answer "yes" on these facts, because D had a "last clear chance" to avoid the accident. Therefore, the effect of P's contributory negligence will be wiped out, and P can recover.

7 If you know for a fact that plaintiff's jurisdiction applies contributory negligence, your answer will be "no" (since comparative and contributory negligence can't co-exist.) If the facts don't state whether contributory or comparative negligence applies (virtually all states have one or the other), you should discuss each possibility in your answer.

8 Compute a fraction by putting plaintiff's negligence in the numerator and the negligence of all parties (all plaintiffs and all defendants) in the denominator. Example: P sues D1 and D2 for a single accident. A jury finds that P was 40% at fault, D1 35% and D2 25%. You would find that P's negligence did not account for 50% or more of the total negligence, so you'd answer "no". (That way, in later circles you'd conclude that P can recover at least something, even if the jurisdiction has a modified rather than pure comparative negligence statute.) You'd reach this result even though P was more negligent than any other single party.

9 If the facts do not state whether the jurisdiction is a "modified" one or a "pure" one, be sure to discuss both. Under a "pure" comparative negligence statute, plaintiff can recover a portion of his damages even if his own fault accounted for more than half of all negligence by all parties. In a jurisdiction with a "modified" comparative negligence statute, a plaintiff whose fault amounts to at least either 50% or 51% (depending on the statute) of the total negligence by all parties cannot recover anything. Most states today employ some sort of modified comparative negligence. Ch. 11 (II)(D).

Note that even where comparative negligence would otherwise apply, if the defendant had a "last clear chance" to avoid the accident, some (but not all) courts will apply the Lost Clear Chance doctrine to wipe out comparative negligence and restore plaintiff's full recovery. See note 6 for a review of the LCC doctrine.

10 Example: D runs a sky-diving school. Before P is allowed to take a course, P is required to sign a document prepared by D stating that if P is killed or maimed (even if due to D's negligence) P and his estate will not be permitted to recover damages. On these facts, you'd answer "yes." (Then, you'd see below that the agreement would probably be enforced, as long as D's conduct wasn't grossly negligent or intentionally tortious.)

11 Many factors come into play when a court decides whether to strike down on public policy grounds an agreement that imposes on a willing participant the risks of an activity. For example, agreements will not be enforced if the parties had dramatically unequal bargaining power (e.g., D is a unique provider of a service and forces P to waive liability in order to receive the service, or D is a common carrier, public utility, or other quasi-monopoly or regulated industry and P is a consumer). As another example, P's advance agreement to waive D's liability will generally not be enforced if D's actions turn out to be "willful and wanton" or grossly negligent, or if they constitute intentionally tortious activity.

On the other hand, an agreement likely will be enforced if D in good faith attempted to set in advance various damage-recovery caps, and allowed P to pay a graduated fee based on the size of cap elected by P. (Example: D is a trucker and P is a customer. For the lowest fee, D requires P to agree to waive any tort damages for damage to the parcel. But P is allowed to pay a higher fee to be eligible for a higher damage cap. The court will probably enforce this agreement.) Even in this "higher fee for a higher damage cap" scenario, however, public policy may dictate that D not be allowed to escape liability for personal

Notes (p. 3) to Figure 11 (Major Defenses in Negligence Cases)

injuries to a consumer. (Example: If D is a surgeon and P a patient, D probably can't enforce a contractual waiver of damages for malpractice merely because she gives P the right to pay a higher amount to be eligible for damages.) Ch. 11 (III)(C)(1).

[12] Example: On the facts of the Example in note 10 (the skydiver), the agreement would probably be enforced to exclude recovery for D's ordinary negligence, since the agreement probably doesn't fall into any exception to the general enforceability of such liability-waiving agreements. (For instance, there's probably no inequality of bargaining power, as long as other schools were available at least some of which didn't require the waiver.) On the other hand, if D's conduct was grossly negligent or intentionally tortious, the agreement probably wouldn't be enforced.

[13] Plaintiff must actually have known of the danger in order for your answer to be "yes." The fact that a reasonable person in plaintiff's position would have known of the danger is irrelevant -- if plaintiff himself didn't know, answer "no." Example: P agrees to have D, a plastic surgeon, use general anesthetic before performing a face lift on P. Assume that a reasonable person in P's position would know that in a tiny percentage of cases, people have a fatal allergic reaction to general anesthesia, but that P in fact has no such knowledge (and D gives her no warning). P dies from a very unusual allergic reaction. On these facts, you'd answer "no" -- P will not be treated as being aware of the danger. (Therefore, as you'll see in the next circle, D can't assert the assumption-of-risk defense.)

Also, be sure that the danger that plaintiff knew of was the same one that caused the harm. Otherwise, there is no causal link between the risk plaintiff assumed and the harm suffered. Ch. 11 (III)(D)(2)(b).

[14] If plaintiff is forced to encounter the danger under duress, your answer should be "no." If there was a plausibly-suitable alternative that plaintiff could have chosen but declined to do so, answer "yes."

Example 1 (voluntary encountering of danger): D, a city, performs roadwork that requires D to dig a large 1-foot-deep temporary hole in the roadway. P approaches by car, and sees a large sign warning about the hole. Assuming that P had the option to turn around and take a different road, P's decision to drive through the hole will be treated as voluntary, so you'd answer "yes."

Example 2 (involuntary encountering): Same facts as above. Now, however, the hole is on the only road leading to P's house. Therefore, unless P is prepared to park his car overnight in the middle of the road, he has no choice but to try to drive through the hole. Here, you'd answer "no" -- P has not voluntarily encountered the danger.

[15] There are many situations in which defendant owes no duty to plaintiff.

Example: D owns a professional baseball stadium, and posts a sign warning spectators of the risk of foul balls. D will not be liable to someone who is hit by a foul ball in the bleachers, because a court would almost certainly hold that D did not owe P a duty to protect bleacher-dwellers from fouls.

On the other hand, in many types of situations, defendant *does* owe plaintiff a duty to keep plaintiff free from the harm that plaintiff ends up suffering. Example: D is a cosmetic surgeon. Before she does a facelift on P, she has P sign a form listing various risks from surgery, and acknowledging that D has warned P about these risks. One of the stated risks is that P will have an allergic reaction to the general anesthesia. D fails to ask P whether she's ever in fact had an allergic reaction to general anesthesia. Had D asked this question, P would have answered yes, and D wouldn't have done the procedure. P has a fatal reaction. A court would probably hold that notwithstanding the warning to P, a surgeon has an affirmative obligation to find out about a patient's past allergic reactions; if so, you'd answer "yes," D had a duty to ask P about allergies. (Then, at least if P was reasonable in taking the risk, D would not be allowed to assert the defense of primary implied assumption of risk.)

[16] Where defendant never owed any duty to plaintiff in the first place, "primary" assumption of risk occurs.

[17] Example (reasonable encounter): Same basic facts as Example 1 in note 14. This time,

Notes (p.4) to
Figure 11 (Major Defenses in Negligence Cases)

however, assume that P is rushing his seriously-ill child to the hospital. P could turn around and take a different road, but this would add 10 minutes to the trip, minutes that might well significantly worsen the child's condition. On these facts, you'd answer "yes" -- P's decision to encounter the danger by driving through the hole was reasonable. (Then, you'd conclude in the next circle that D can't assert the assumption-of-risk defense.)

Example (unreasonable encounter): Same facts as above Example. Now, however, assume that P is going by himself to a movie, and taking a different route would cause him to miss the first 5 minutes. Almost certainly, you'd answer "no", that P's decision to drive through the hole was not reasonable in the circumstances. (Then, you'd conclude in a later circle that D can successfully assert the implied secondary assumption-of-risk defense.)

[18] In order for defendant to assert the defense of "assumption of risk," there must be a causal connection between the risk assumed and the harm. Example: P unreasonably accepts a ride with X, a driver who P knows is drunk. During the trip, D, a truckdriver, crashes into the car as a result of D's negligence (and through no fault of X). There is no causal connection between the risk P assumed and the harm P suffered. Therefore, assumption of risk will be held not to apply, and P can recover against D.

[19] "Secondary" assumption of risk occurs where defendant has a duty of care to plaintiff, but what would otherwise be a breach of that duty is avoided because plaintiff knew of the danger and voluntarily -- and unreasonably -- subjected himself to the danger.

Note that in states that have comparative negligence, secondary assumption of risk cannot be asserted as a separate defense at all. Ch. 11 (III)(F)(1)(c).

Example: D, who is slightly drunk, offers P a ride home. P realizes that D is slightly drunk, but nonetheless decides voluntarily (and unreasonably, let's assume) to accept the ride. D crashes on the way home, injuring P. In a contributory-negligence state, P's knowing and voluntary acceptance of the ride from a drunk driver would be secondary assumption of risk, and P would be completely blocked from recovery. But in a comparative negligence state, the doctrine of secondary assumption of risk can't apply as a separate defense. Instead, P's unreasonableness in accepting the ride is estimated as a percentage of the total negligence of all parties, and will reduce but not eliminate P's recovery. (This conclusion assumes that either the state has pure comparative negligence, or that [in the event it has modified comparative negligence] P's negligence is less than 50% of the total negligence.)

Figure 12

Vicarious Liability

Under the doctrine of Vicarious Liability, the tortious acts of one can be imputed to another. When this is the case, both are jointly and severally liable to the plaintiff for any damages. There are three main theories under which vicarious liability may be imposed: (1) **respondeat superior** (where an employer may be liable for the torts of the employee); (2) **joint enterprise**; and (3) **auto owner** liability. Use this chart to see if, in addition to the actual tortfeasor, someone else may be liable for the damages in question under any of the three theories

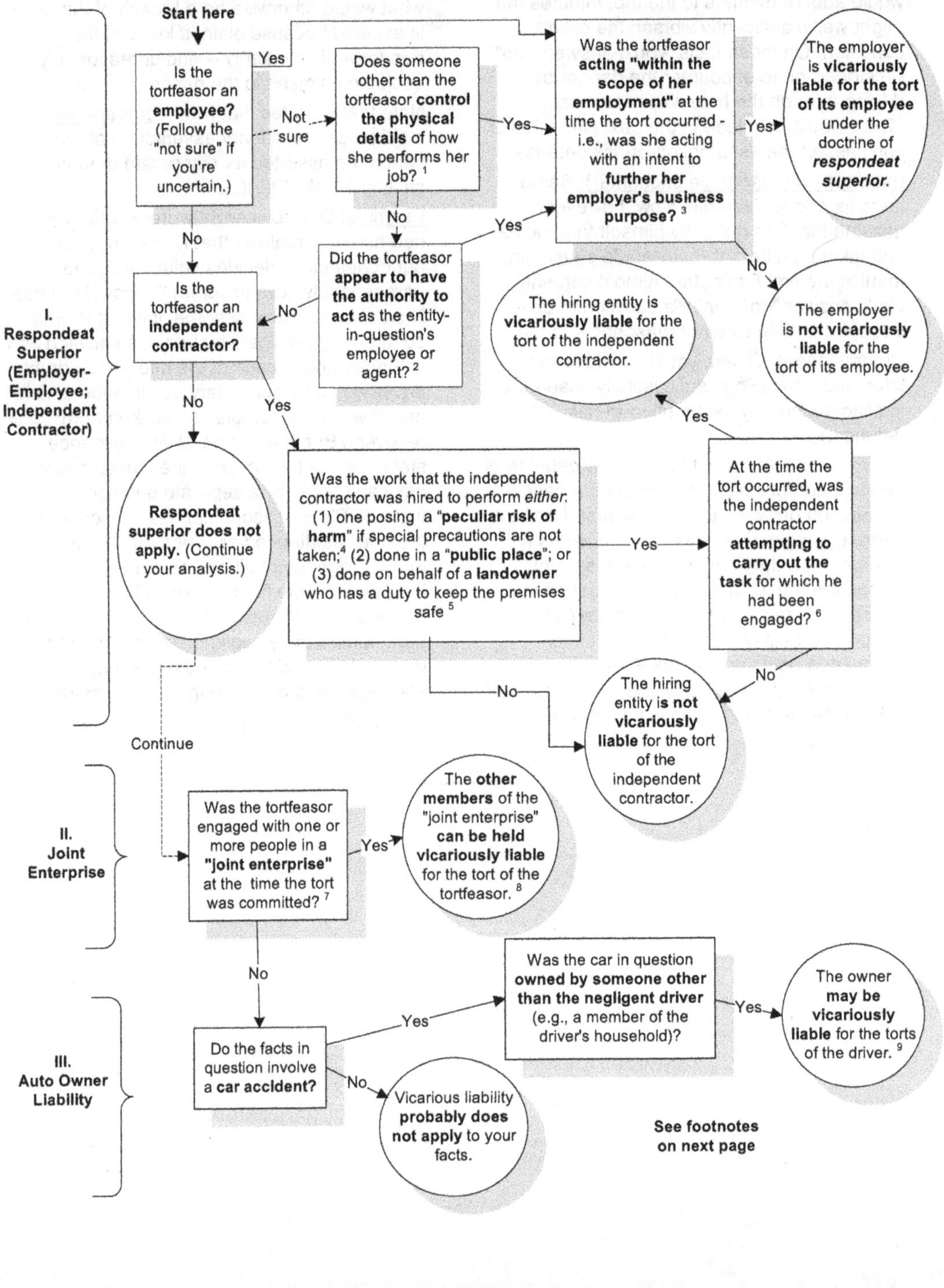

Notes to
Figure 12 (Vicarious Liability)

[1] This question will help you determine whether the tortfeasor in question is an employee or an independent contractor. How the parties label their relationship is less important than how the tortfeasor actually performs her duties. If she is given only general goals and directives for her work, but is responsible for coming up with her own work schedule and providing her own equipment and supplies, she is most likely an independent contractor. Conversely, if someone else dictates where and when she must work, and provides her with most of the tools she needs to get her work done, she is most likely an employee. Use the following test (from Prosser): A person is an employee when "in the eyes of the community, he would be regarded as a part of the employer's own working staff." Ch. 12 (II)(B)(1).

Example 1: X, a truck driver, drives a truck that's owned by D (a trucking company). X has to work regular hours assigned by D, but gets paid based on how many miles he drives, not hourly. He has to take the trips assigned by D. On these facts, X is an employee, because D closely controls the physical details of how X does his job. (Therefore, as later circles show, D will be liable under *respondeat superior* for torts committed by D in the furtherance of his job.)

Example 2: Again (as in the prior example), X is a truck driver. But this time, he drives a truck that he owns. 90% of his driving is done for D (a trucking company), but he's free to accept loads from other companies. He can accept or decline each load, and works his own schedule. As in the prior example, he's paid by the mile. On these facts, X is probably an independent contractor, because D has much less control over the physical details of how X does his job. (Therefore, as later circles show, *respondeat superior* won't apply, and D will be liable for torts committed by X only if the tort was committed during the performance of a task for D that was non-delegable or inherently dangerous. So unless X was, say, carrying a highly-dangerous load such as toxic chemicals, D won't be liable.)

[2] Under the doctrine of "apparent authority," a tortfeasor will be considered an employee even though she is really an independent contractor if, in the eyes of the public, she appears to be working for, and under the direction of, another person or entity.

Example: X, a doctor, is engaged by D, a hospital, to work in D's emergency room. (Assume that the private relationship between X and D is an independent-contractor relationship.) X commits malpractice on P. A court might well hold that X should be treated as if he had been an employee of D, not an independent contractor, because so far as the public at large (including emergency-room patients) could see, X worked for the hospital. (In that event, D would be liable for X's malpractice.) Ch. 12 (II)(B)(1)(c).

[3] You should answer "yes" to this question even if the means the tortfeasor chose were indirect, unwise, or specifically forbidden by the employer, so long as the tortfeasor thought she was carrying out some aspect of her job.

Most courts hold that commuting to or from work does not fall within the scope of employment.

Where an employee has made a short trip or detour for personal purposes (called a "frolic and detour") while on a business trip, the traditional view was that the employee was not acting within the scope of her employment while headed to the detour, but that she *was* acting within the scope of her employment as soon as she started heading back to the path of her original purpose. But the modern view is that the employee is acting within the scope of her employment as long as the deviation is one that was "reasonably foreseeable." Quick side trips generally fall into this category, but major detours do not. Ch. 12 (II)(C)(1) and (2).

A common question is whether the employer is liable for intentional torts committed by the employer. The answer is yes, if the tort was committed in an attempt (even a misguided one) by the employer to further the employer's business purposes.

Example: X is a debt collector employed by D, a collection agency. X threatens P with a beating if P does not immediately back his back debts. Even though X's threats constitute

Notes (p. 2) to Figure 12 (Vicarious Liability)

an intentional tort (assault), and even if D specifically forbade X from making such threats, D will be liable, because the threat was made as part of an attempt by X to do his job (collect debts).

[4] Example: D, a city, hires E, an electrician, to repair a high-voltage transformer in a city-owned parking lot. P gets electrocuted due to E's negligence in doing the work. On these facts, you'd answer "yes," because the work posed a peculiar risk of harm if done without reasonable precautions. (Therefore, D had a non-delegable duty, and would vicariously liable for E's negligence, as a later circle shows.) Ch. 12 (III)(B)(2).

[5] Example: D, a retail store owner, wants to build a new display case. D hires K, a contractor, to build the case. K negligently fails to use proper support, and the case falls on P, a customer. On these facts, you'd answer "yes," because D had a non-delegable duty as landowner to keep the premises safe for customers. (Therefore, as a later circle shows, D would be vicariously liable for K's negligence.)

[6] The test for "attempting to carry out the task" is essentially the same as that for "acting within the scope of the employment" in the employer-employee context. See note 3 for further discussion of that test.

[7] There are four requirements for a "joint enterprise." They are: (1) an agreement, express or implied, between the members; (2) a common purpose to be carried out by the members; (3) a common pecuniary interest in that purpose; and (4) an equal right to control the enterprise. Rest. 2d, §491; Ch. 12 (IV)(B).

Mere social trips are not considered joint enterprises. However, where parties to a trip (whether business or social) agree to share expenses, that's usually enough to tip the trip over into a joint enterprise.

Example 1: X and D agree to go on a hunting trip, on which they will evenly split the driving (and all expenses). While driving to the destination, X negligently hits P, a pedestrian. On these facts, you'd probably answer "yes," that this was a joint enterprise, because all of the above four requirements seem to be met. In that case, D can be held vicariously liable for X's negligence.

Example 2: Same basic facts as above example. Now, however, assume that X is driving his own car and is paying all expenses; D is simply keeping X company on the trip (even though they'll both be hunting). Probably you'd answer "no," there's no joint enterprise. In that event, D wouldn't be liable for X's negligence while driving.

[8] This assumes that the tortfeasor was advancing the purposes of the joint enterprise when the negligence occurred. Example: On the facts of the Example 1 in note 7 (hunting trip), D is liable for X's negligence because at the time of the accident, X was advancing their joint enterprise, the hunting trip. On other other hand, suppose that during the course of the trip, after the two had checked into a hotel, X drove (with D still in the car) to get cigarettes, which only X desired. If X drove negligently at that point, there would probably be no joint-enterprise liability, because X was not advancing the purposes of the joint enterprise at the moment of the accident.

[9] Some states have "Automobile Consent" statutes that make the owner liable for torts committed in the car by anyone who used the car with the owner's consent.

Even if the state in question does not have such a statute, the court may still hold the owner liable under the "Family Purpose" doctrine. Under this doctrine, a car owner who lets members of her household drive her car for their own personal use will be vicariously liable for any torts they commit with the car. Ch. 12 (V)(A) and (B).

Figure 13

Strict Liability

This chart will help you determine whether D should be held strictly liable for damages he caused. The main scenarios in which strict liability (i.e., liability without regard to D's fault or his mental state) may apply are: (1) injuries caused by **animals under D's control**; (2) injuries caused by **abnormally dangerous activities**; (3) injuries **sustained by an employee** of D; and (4) injuries caused by a **dangerously defective product.**

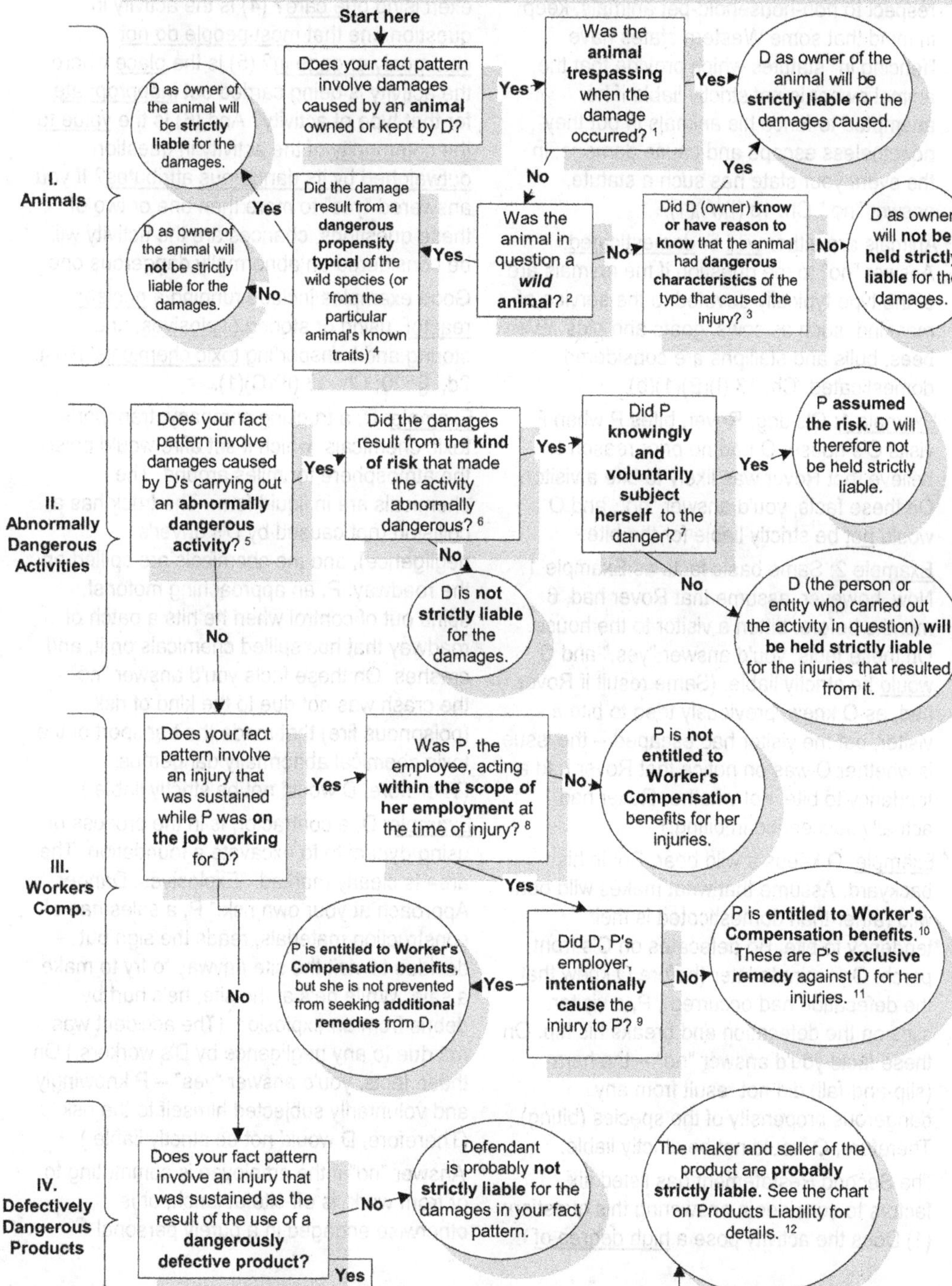

See footnotes on next page

Notes to
Figure 13 (Strict Liability)

[1] If the animal is a "household pet" like a cat or dog, answer "no." (That's because the rule of strict liability for trespassing animals doesn't apply to household pets.) Also, even with respect to non-household-pet animals, keep in mind that some Western states have "fencing in" statutes which provide that the animal owner is *not* strictly liable if he attempted to fence his animals in but they nonetheless escape and cause damage; in the event your state has such a statute, answer "no." Ch. 13 (I)(A)(1).

[2] Animals are either wild or domesticated. Answer "no" to the question if the animals are of the type typically devoted to the service of mankind, such as cows, goats and pigs. Even bees, bulls and stallions are considered domesticated. Ch. 13 (I)(B)(1)(b).

[3] Example 1: O's dog, Rover, bites P when P visits O's house. O had no prior reason to believe that Rover was likely to bite a visitor. On these facts, you'd answer "no", and O would not be strictly liable for the bite.

Example 2: Same basic facts as Example 1. Now, however, assume that Rover had, 6 months before, bitten a visitor to the house. On these facts, you'd answer "yes," and O would be strictly liable. (Same result if Rover had, as O knew, previously tried to bite a visitor, but the visitor had escaped -- the issue is whether O was on notice that Rover had a tendency to bite, not whether Rover had actually succeeded in biting.)

[4] Example: O keeps a wild boar, Bo, in his backyard. Assume that what makes wild boar wild rather than domesticated is their tendency to bite. Bo defecates on O's front porch. One minute later (before O knew that the defecation had occurred), P, a visitor, slips on the defecation and breaks his hip. On these facts you'd answer "no" -- the harm (slip-and-fall) did not result from any dangerous propensity of the species (biting). Therefore, O would not be strictly liable.

[5] The Second Restatement has listed six factors to consider in answering this question: (1) Does the activity pose a high degree of risk that some harm to people or property will result? (2) If the activity results in harm, is the harm likely to be of a serious nature? (3) Is it impossible to eliminate the risk of harm by exercising due care? (4) Is the activity in question one that most people do not commonly engage in? (5) Is the place where the activity is being carried out inappropriate for that type of activity? And (6) Is the value to the community of the activity in question outweighed by its dangerous attributes? If you answered "yes" to more than one or two of these questions, chances are the activity will be considered an abnormally dangerous one. Good examples include running a nuclear reactor, using or storing explosives, and storing and transporting toxic chemicals. Rest. 2d, §520; Ch. 13 (II)(C)(1).

[6] Example: D, a trucking company, transports toxic chemicals, which if set afire would poison the atmosphere for miles around. The chemicals are in liquid form. The truck has a collision (not caused by D's driver's negligence), and the chemicals are spilled on the roadway. P, an approaching motorist, spins out of control when he hits a patch of roadway that has spilled chemicals on it, and crashes. On these facts you'd answer "no" -- the crash was not due to the kind of risk (poisonous fire) that made the transport of the toxic chemical abnormally dangerous. (Therefore, D would not be strictly liable.)

[7] Example: D, a contractor, is in the process of using dynamite to excavate a foundation. The area is clearly marked, "Explosives. Danger. Approach at your own risk." P, a salesman of construction materials, reads the sign but decides to visit the site anyway to try to make a sale. While he's at the site, he's hurt by debris from an explosion. (The accident was not due to any negligence by D's workers.) On these facts, you'd answer "yes" -- P knowingly and voluntarily subjected himself to the risk. (Therefore, D would not be strictly liable.)

[8] Answer "no" if the employee is commuting to or from work, is off-site at lunch, or is otherwise engaged in a purely personal

Notes (p. 2) to Figure 13 (Strict Liability)

activity. In addition, if the employee is drunk or doing something illegal, most states hold that she is not acting "within the scope of employment" -- even if she thinks she is doing her job at the time. Ch. 13 (IV)(B).

9 Example: D (the owner of a company) and P, an employee, get into an argument about how the work is to be done. D gets frustrated at P and throws a wrench at him. P falls trying to get out of the way, and is badly hurt. On these facts, you'd answer "yes." (Therefore, P can get Workers Comp even in the unlikely event that P was found negligent for bringing the encounter about. Furthermore, P could also bring a common-law assault claim against D, though D might get a credit for Workers Comp payments received by P.)

An important question is whether you should answer "yes" where D intentionally ignores a safety regulation that would have shielded P from the kind of accident that then occurs. Most (but not all) courts have answered "no" in this safety-regulation situation. Ch. 13 (IV)(D)(1)(a).

10 Worker's Compensation is a form of "no fault" insurance that the employer is required provide and pay for. In general, benefits will be paid for injuries sustained by the employee on the job, regardless of the employer's or the employee's fault. Note, however, that under Worker's Compensation statutes, plaintiffs are not entitled to recover anything for their pain and suffering. Ch. 13 (IV)(A)(3).

11 Although Workers Comp is P's sole remedy against D (the employer), P is not foreclosed (even he receives Workers Comp) from suing other parties who may be liable, though he'll have to show some independent tort ground, such as intentional tort, negligence or product liability.

Example: P, who works for Emp, loses his hand while operating a machine manufactured by Manu and sold by Manu to Emp years before. The injury occurs because of a dangerous defect in the way the machine guards against chopping of operators' hands. P's sole remedy against Emp will be Workers Comp, even if Emp was negligent in how it chose, installed or maintained the machine, or in how it instructed P on its use. But P is still free to bring a product liability suit (whether based on negligence or strict product liability) against Manu.

7 The product liability flowchart on is Figure 14.

Figure 14

Strict Products Liability

This chart will help you determine whether D (a manufacturer, distributor or retailer of a product) should be held strictly liable for damages caused as a result of a defective product. (This chart does not cover the two other theories on which a manufacturer or seller might be liable for injuries caused by the product: negligence and breach of warranty.) You should re-use the chart for each possible defendant.

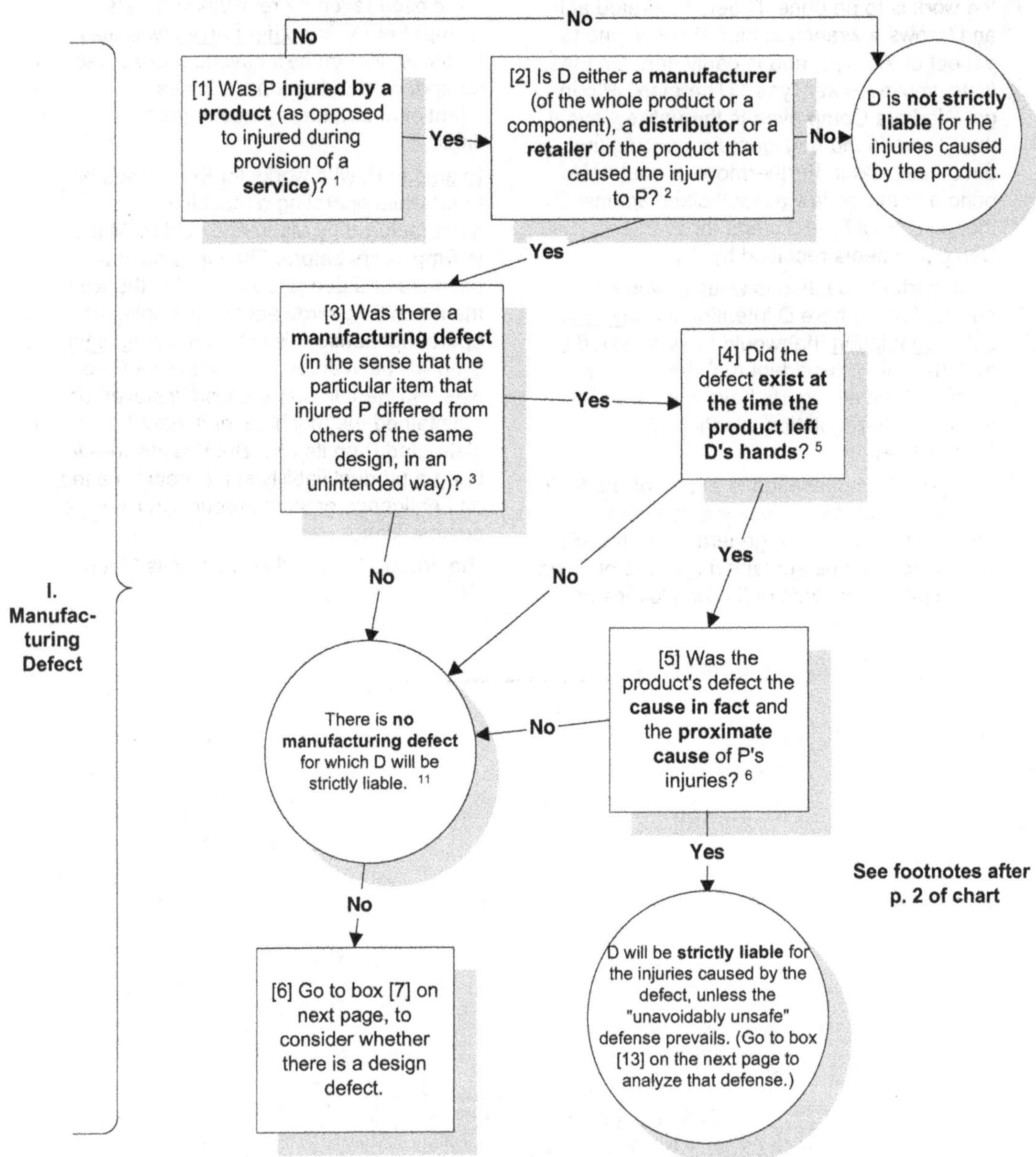

Figure 14 (p. 2)

Strict Products Liability

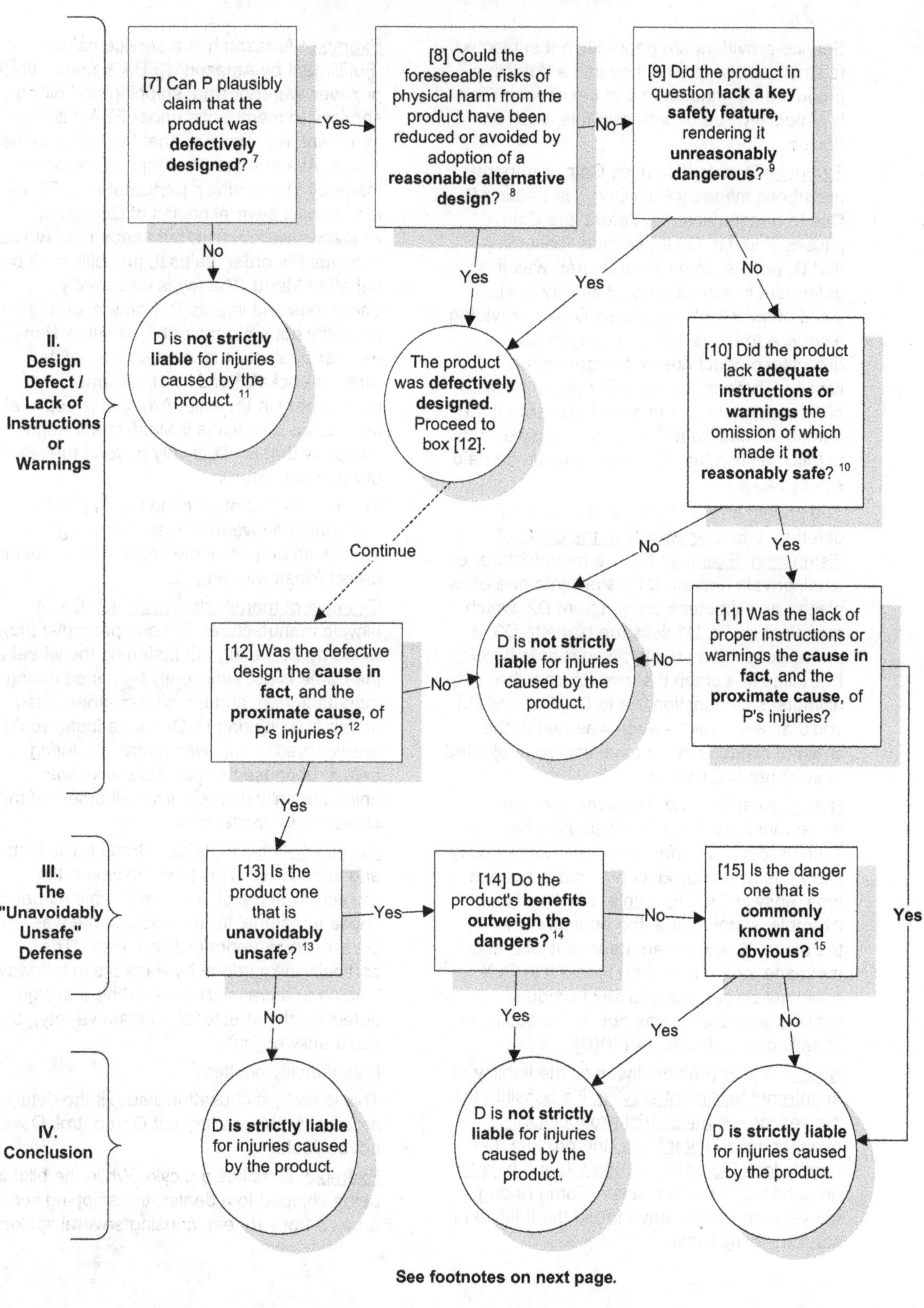

See footnotes on next page.

Notes to Figure 14 (Strict Products Liability)

[1] Service-providers are generally not subjected to strict liability, even if they use a defective product during the course of the service. This is especially true of professionals, such as doctors.

Example: D, a dentist, uses Cain, a general anesthetic made by Pain Corp., in treating P. Due to a manufacturing defect, the Cain causes P to die. On these facts (assuming that D, not the Cain manufacturer, was the defendant in a strict product liability suit), you'd answer "no" -- because D was providing a service to P, his use of a dangerously defective product does not trigger strict liability. That's true even if D was planning to bill P separately for the anesthetic. (But if the defendant was Pain Corp., you'd answer "yes" to this question, and Pain Corp. could be held strictly liable.)

[2] You should answer "yes" to this question if defendant falls anywhere in the chain of distribution. Example: D1 is a manufacturer of small private aircraft. D1 installs into one of its planes an altimeter it bought from D2, which manufactured it. D1 sells the plane to D3, a professional plane dealer, who resells it to P. P is killed in a crash that results from the altimeter's malfunction. As to D1, D2, and D3, you'd answer "yes" -- each was part of the chain of distribution, so each can be subjected to strict product liability.

Note 1: Keep in mind, however, that the defendant must be in the business of selling such products. If defendant does not normally carry this type of product but sold it this one time, answer "no." Example: On the above example, suppose that the original owner of the plane, X, was an amateur pilot who used the plane for 2 years, then resold it to P. X could not be subjected to strict product liability, because he was not "in the business" of selling aircraft. Ch. 14 (III)(B).

Note 2: If your problem involves the liability of an Internet fulfillment service, it's possible that the service will have strict product liability even though it never "sold" the product, but merely took the order, shipped it, and billed it on behalf of the actual seller. Some (though not yet most) cases have found the fulfillment service strictly liable.

Example: Amazon has a service called "Fulfillment by Amazon" ("FBA"), under which it provides warehousing, shipping and billing services to merchants; under FBA it is the merchant, not Amazon, that holds title to the goods. Assume that P orders a Dragon toy made by Manu, which participates in FBA -- Manu ships several copies of Dragon to Amazon's warehouse, but keeps title. Amazon receives P's order, ships it, and bills for it on behalf of Manu. The toy is defectively dangerous and injures P. Some courts (though probably not yet a majority) will allow P to recover against Amazon, because of its "deeper pockets" and its significant involvement in the sale. Amazon is especially likely to be held liable if Manu is a foreign company that is effectively beyond the reach of American courts.

[3] This question is attempting to get you to distinguish between a "manufacturing" defect (dealt with on p. 1 of the chart) and a "design" defect (dealt with on p. 2).

Example of manufacturing defect: D is a bicycle manufacturer. On one particular bicyle made by D, the lug nut fastening the wheel to the frame is not sufficiently tightened during manufacturing, and the bike crashes when ridden fast, injuring P. On these facts, you'd answer "yes" -- this was a manufacturing defect, because this particular bike was unintentionally different from all others of the same model made by D.

Example of design defect: Same basic facts as above example. This time, however, the problem with the bike is that for this model, D chose a material for the spokes that was very likely to crack under ordinary wear. The particular bike ridden by P cracks in this way, leading to a crash. This would be a design defect (of the structurally-unsafe variety), so you'd answer "no".

[4] [Intentionally omitted]

[5] This is really a causation issue: if the defect arose after the product left D's control, D will not be liable.

Example: D makes a bicyle. While the bike is being shipped to a dealer, the shipping service drops it from 15 feet, causing several spokes

Notes (p. 2) to Figure 14 (Strict Products Liability)

to crack invisibly. The bike then crashes. On these facts, you'd answer "no" -- because the defect did not exist until after the bike left D's control, D won't be strictly liable for a manufacturing defect. (There might still be an issue about whether the *design* was defective for not being able to resist the kind of impact that occurred, but this page of the chart is only dealing with *manufacturing* defects.)

[6] Plaintiff bears the burden of proof on this issue (as on all the issues in prior boxes). Therefore, unless P can demonstrate that, more likely than not, the defect was the cause in fact and proximate cause of P's injuries, you must answer "no" (and P loses).

For instance, there is often a serious causation issue in toxic tort cases. Example: D makes a fertilizer, FerBen, that it sells to many farmers, who put it on their fields. The Ps, residents of nearby homes who become sick with a variety of symptoms, sue D on a strict product liability theory. Unless the Ps can show that it's more likely than not that their symptoms are due to a dangerous defect in FerBen, you'd answer "no", and the Ps would lose.

If P (or some third-party user) allegedly "misused" the product, D may defend on the grounds that the misuse prevents the product itself from being the proximate cause of the injury (i.e., that the misuse is a superseding cause). However, unless the misuse is virtually unforeseeable, this defense is unlikely to prevail. For more about this defense, see n. 12 below.

[7] For a discussion of the difference between a design defect and a manufacturing defect, see n. 3 above.

[8] P has the burden of showing that there was a reasonable alternative design (RAD) available that would have reduced or avoided the risks.

Example: P, a police officer, is injured when a bullet pierces a bullet-proof vest made by D. Unless P can show that a vest strong enough to block the bullet would have been feasible (e.g., not hopelessly heavy, and not too wildly expensive) under technology available at the time the vest P wore was made, you would have to answer "no" for this box, and P would lose on strict liability.

[9] Answer "yes" if a safety feature could have been installed on the product at little expense, compared to the cost of the product itself and the magnitude of the danger that exists without the feature. If no other manufacturers have the safety feature, this is relevant to -- but not dispositive of -- the issue. Ch. 14 (IV)(E).

[10] Failure to give adequate instructions or warnings, when doing so would reduce risk, is a separate ground of liability — the failure can turn an otherwise perfectly-safe design into an unreasonably unsafe product.

Example: D designs a lawn mower in a way that makes it reasonably safe, given its need to have a sharp rapidly-spinning blade. Inherent in the mower's design is that grass cuttings are ejected to the left of the mower. D fails to warn users not to stand to the mower's left. P, a child, stands to the left of the mower while his father operates it. P is blinded by a stone thrown from the mower. Even though the design was otherwise reasonably safe, D will be strictly liable if a court believes that a warning would have reduced the chance of this type of accident.

Note 1: There is an aspect of negligence — of the balancing of costs against benefits — in modern courts' treatment of the duty to warn. For instance, if a risk is very remote, and also very hard to avoid even if one knows about it, a court might conclude that there is no duty to warn about it because the costs of the warning (including the risk of distracting the user from other, more significant risks) outweigh the benefits.

Note 2: Even if the product arguably lacked adequate warnings or instructions, D may have a "pre-emption" defense – if D can show that a federal statute or regulation approved the warnings/instructions actually used by D, and that Congress intended not to allow states to impose different or additional warning or instruction obligations, the states will be pre-empted from letting P recover on a failure-to-warn theory.

Note 3: if your case involves the failure to warn of the dangers of a generic drug, consider the possibility that P may be able to recover against the maker of the brand-name version of the drug rather than the maker of the

Notes (p. 3) to Figure 14 (Strict Products Liability)

generic version that harmed P.

Example: D1 invents and gets regulatory approval for an anti-nausea drug, Dramic. (This is the "brand-name" version of the drug.) D2 then properly manufactures a generic version of Dramic called Dramo. As is required by regulators, D2 copies the exact text of the warning label from Dramic. Due to faulty research by D1, the warning label on Dramic (and thus on Dramo) fails to warn that the drug sometimes causes a fatal allergic reaction in people who are allergic to peanuts. P takes a dose of Dramo, and suffers a fatal allergic reaction. Some courts (though probably not most) will permit P's estate to recover against D1 (the brand-name manufacturer), even though the particular pill taken by P was made by D2. The theory is that it was up to D1, the drug's inventor, to devise a proper warning label, so that only D1 (not D2, which was required by federal regulators to simply copy the brand-name label) will have strict product liability for failure-to-warn.

[11] But go to box [10], to see whether there may be a failure to give adequate instructions or warnings — this is a separate possible ground for liability, even if the product's design was not defective.

[12] Only answer "yes" if the defect itself caused the problem. If some other unforeseeable event was a superseding cause, answer "no" to this question.

If P (or someone else) misuses the product, the misuse may prevent the defect from being deemed the proximate cause of the injury. But this is generally true only if the misuse in essentially "unforeseeable." Thus unless P (or some user other than P) used the product is some really bizarre way, or deliberately disregarded a manufacturer's warning, the misuse will probably be considered foreseeable, and therefore will not be a superseding cause. Ch. 14 (V.)(I).

Example: P buys a lawnmower, which has printed on it a bold-faced warning, "Make sure not to put your foot in the path of the mover, or you may cut off your foot." P doesn't read the message, puts his foot in the path of the mower, and cuts it off. A safer design (such as a foot-guard making it harder for the foot to slip under the mower) might have avoided the accident. Since P's "misuse" is somewhat foreseeable, and since P didn't read the message, a court will probably hold that despite the misuse the design defect caused the accident, so you'd answer "yes".

[13] Answer "yes" if the product, though perfectly manufactured, will cause harm in some percentage of users. The classic example is many prescription drugs or vaccines -- at least at present, for many drugs and vaccines there is simply no way of making (or administering) the product that reduces to zero the risk that it will harm the user, perhaps because of an unanticipated allergic reaction.

[14] Some products, such as prescription drugs and vaccines, are of benefit to a great number of people even though a few users will experience dangerous side effects. When that is the case (and assuming that there's no easy way to tell in advance which users will have the problem), the manufacturer or retailer will not be strictly liable for the injuries caused. Ch. 14 (III)(D).

[15] Examples: A knife is obviously dangerous if used carelessly, because it may cut. And a gun is obviously dangerous if used carelessly when loaded, because it may shoot. So you'd answer "yes" to this question if P is claiming that an ordinary knife or gun is defective.

However, before you answer "yes", be sure that the design defect that P is alleging really does stem from the obvious and inevitable nature of the product. If P is instead alleging a non-obvious dangerous defect in a product that also has obvious dangers, answer "no."

Example: P claims that a particular gun made by D is dangerously defective not simply because like all guns it might fire by accident, but rather, because it has an unusually sensitive trigger that's *especially* likely to fire without the user's intent. On these facts, you'd answer "no" -- the extra-sensitive trigger is not an obvious defect.

Figure 15
Defamation

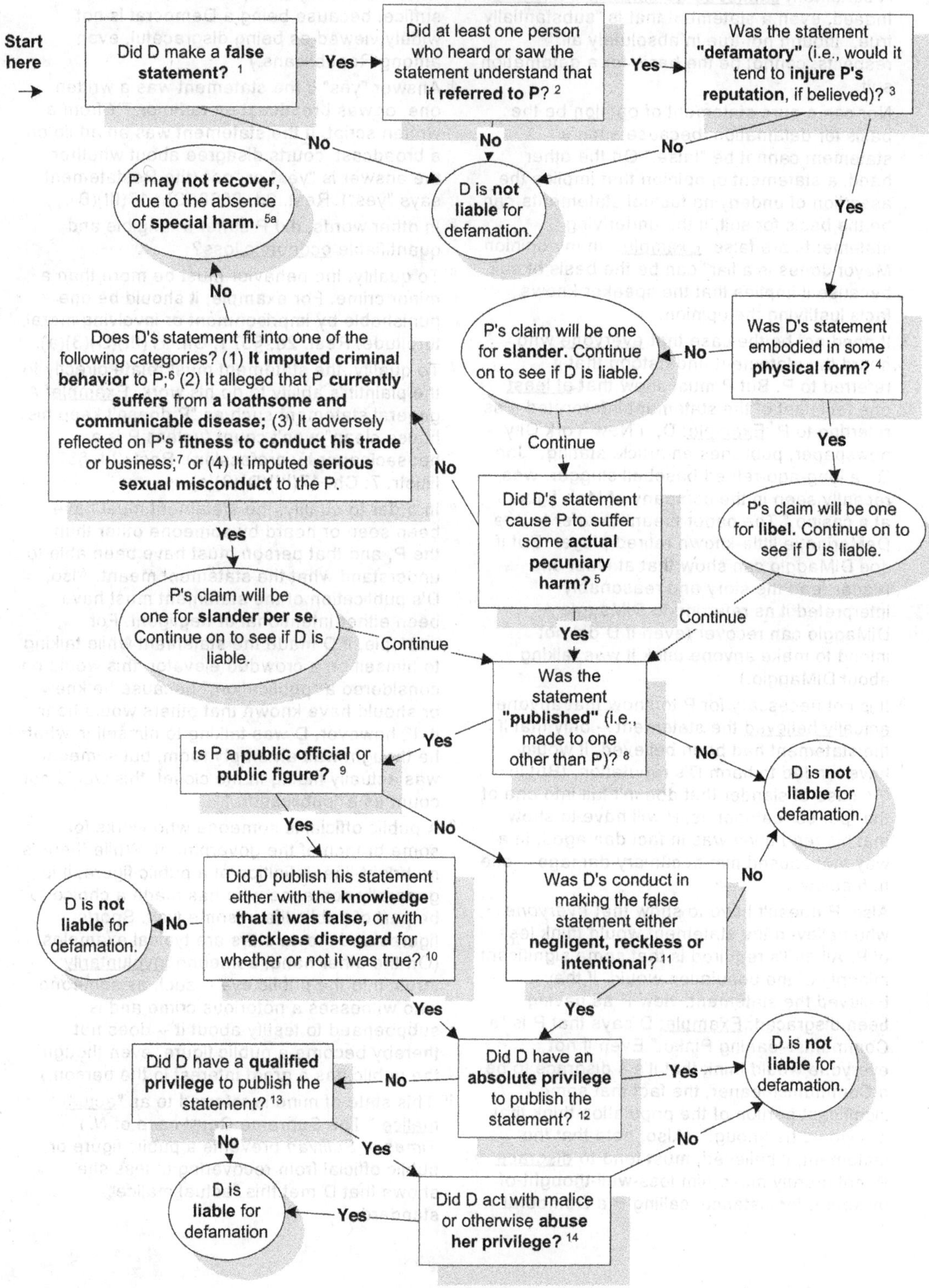

See footnotes on next page

Notes to Figure 15 (Defamation)

[1] A statement cannot be defamatory if it is true. Indeed, even a statement that is "substantially true," though not true in absolutely all respects, cannot be the basis for a defamation suit.

Nor can a pure statement of opinion be the basis for defamation, because such a statement cannot be "false." On the other hand, a statement of opinion that implies the assertion of underlying factual statements can be the basis for suit, if the underlying statements are false. Example: "In my opinion Mayor Jones is a liar" can be the basis of suit, because it implies that the speaker knows facts justifying the opinion.

[2] It need not be the case that everyone who heard the statement understood that it referred to P. But P must show that at least one recipient of the statement interpreted it as referring to P. Example: D, a New York City newspaper, publishes an article stating, "Joe D., a long-ago-retired baseball slugger, was recently seen in the company of Mob figures at a casino." The paper meant to refer to Joe DeMarino, a little-known retired player. But if Joe DiMaggio can show that at least one reader read the story and reasonably interpreted it as referring to DiMaggio, DiMaggio can recover (even if D did not intend to make anyone think it was talking about DiMaggio.)

[3] It is not necessary for P to show that anyone actually believed the statement -- only that if the statement had been believed, it would have tended to harm D's reputation. (But in the case of slander that doesn't fall into one of the "per se" categories, P will have to show that his reputation was in fact damaged, in a way that caused him pecuniary damage -- see n. 5 below.)

Also, P doesn't have to show that *everyone* who believed the statement would think less of P. All that's required is that some significant minority of the population would, if they believed the statement, view P as having been disgraced. Example: D says that P is "a Communist-leaning Pinko." Even if not everyone would think that it's a disgrace to be a Communist-leaner, the fact that some significant portion of the population think that it is would be enough. (Also, note that the statement, if believed, must tend to disgrace P, not merely make him less-well-thought-of by some: for instance, calling P a Democrat when he's really a Republican would not suffice, because being a Democrat is not widely viewed as being disgraceful, even among Republicans.)

[4] Answer "yes" if the statement was a written one, or was broadcast on radio or TV from a written script. If the statement was an ad lib on a broadcast, courts disagree about whether the answer is "yes" or "no" (the Restatement says "yes"). Rest. 2d, §568; Ch. 17(III)(B).

[5] In other words, did P suffer a tangible and quantifiable economic loss?

[6] To qualify, the behavior must be more than a minor crime. For example, it should be one punishable by imprisonment or involving moral turpitude. Rest. 2d, §571; Ch. 17(III)(D)(3)(a).

[7] To qualify, the statement must relate directly to the plaintiff's ability to do his work. Example: A general statement such as "P doesn't keep his house clean" won't count (unless P is a housecleaner by profession). Rest. 2d, §573, Illustr. 7; Ch. 17(III)(D)(3)(c).

[8] In order to qualify, the statement must have been seen or heard by someone other than the P, and that person must have been able to understand what the statement meant. Also, D's publication of the statement must have been either intentional or negligent. For example, if D made the statement while talking to himself on a crowded elevator, this would be considered a "publication," because he knew or should have known that others would hear it. If, however, D was talking to himself in what he thought was an empty room, but someone was actually hiding in the closet, this would not count as a "publication."

[9] A public official is someone who works for some branch of the government. While there is no bright-line definition of a public figure, it is generally someone who has made a choice to be part of public life in some way. Sports figures and movie stars are typical examples. (On the other hand, someone involuntarily thrust into the public eye -- such as someone who witnesses a notorious crime and is subpoenaed to testify about it -- does not thereby become a public figure, even though the public has a great interest in the person.)

[10] This state of mind is referred to as "actual malice." The Supreme Court case of *N.Y. Times v. Sullivan* prevents a public figure or public official from recovering unless she shows that D met this "actual malice" standard.

Notes (p. 2) to Figure 15 (Defamation)

Note that "actual malice" is a term of art -- it does not require that D had any ill will toward P, merely that D made the statement with knowledge of its falsity or reckless disregard of whether it was true.

In order to conclude that D acted with reckless disregard for the truth, there must be evidence that D <u>in fact entertained serious doubts</u> as to the truth of his statement. If D is quite confident that the statement is true, but was really, really sloppy in checking its truth, that's not enough.

[11] States do not, as a matter of non-constitutional state common law, allow even private figures to recover for a non-negligent misstatement, even against a non-media defendant. (It's completely clear, as a constitutional matter, that a media defendant may not be held strictly liable. The Supreme Court has never decided whether the same is true of a non-media defendant, such as a private individual making a statement in a letter to a friend. But all states, as a common-law rather than constitutional-law matter, require the private plaintiff in such a situation to prove that the non-media defendant was at least negligent as to the truth of the statement.) Ch. 17(V)(B)(5).

[12] There is an absolute privilege (i.e., a complete defense to a defamation charge) if the statement was made: (1) pursuant to the course of judicial or legislative proceedings; (2) by a government official in the course of doing her job; (3) by someone to his or her spouse; or (4) with the consent of the plaintiff. Ch.17(VI)(B).

[13] D has a qualified privilege (i.e., a defense to a defamation claim as long as the privilege is not abused) if her statement was made: (1) to protect her own property interests or to protect herself against defamation by the plaintiff; (2) to protect the interests of another (<u>Example</u>: An employer who gives a reference about a former employee is qualifiedly privileged, because she's acting in the interests of the prospective new employer); (3) to protect an interest common to D and the person to whom D spoke; (4) in some states, in exercising the privilege of "neutral reportage." (<u>Example</u>: D, a newspaper, quotes A as saying that B is a thief. B is a private figure. D believes that the charges are probably unfounded, and says so in the article. [B is in fact not a thief.] Some states protect D by means of the privilege for neutral reportage. Without that privilege, D may be liable, since repeating another's false statement, knowing it is probably false, is enough for liability, and inclusion of a statement saying that the accusation may be false is not a defense.) Ch.17(VI)(B).

Also, a federal statute, 47 U.S.C. 230(c)(1), normally gives <u>Internet Service Providers</u> immunity from defamation suits if they publish information supplied by a third person. Ch.17(VI)(D).

[14] Here are some of the ways a qualified privilege will be found to be abused: (1) D's primary purpose in making her statement was something other than protecting the interest for which the privilege is given; (2) the statement was published more widely than necessary; or (3) the statement included more information than was necessary to serve the interest protected by the privilege. Ch.17(VI)(C).

CAPSULE SUMMARY

TABLE OF CONTENTS OF CAPSULE SUMMARY

CAPSULE SUMMARY

CHAPTER 1

INTRODUCTION

I. GENERAL INTRODUCTION

A. Definition of tort: There is no single definition of "tort." The most we can say is that: (1) a tort is a ***civil wrong*** committed by one person against another; and (2) torts can and usually do arise ***outside of any agreement*** between the parties.

B. Categories: There are three broad categories of torts, and there are individual named torts within each category:

1. **Intentional torts:** First, ***intentional*** torts are ones where the defendant desires to bring about a particular result. The main intentional torts are:

   a. ***Battery.***

   b. ***Assault.***

   c. False imprisonment.

   d. ***Infliction of emotional distress.***

2. **Negligence:** The next category is the generic tort of ***"negligence."*** Here, the defendant has not intended to bring about a certain result, but has merely behaved ***carelessly***. There are no individually-named torts in this category, merely the general concept of "negligence."

3. **Strict liability:** Finally, there is the least culpable category, ***"strict liability."*** Here, the defendant is held liable even though he did not intend to bring about the undesirable result, and even though he behaved with utmost carefulness. There are two main individually-named torts that apply strict liability:

   a. Conducting of ***abnormally dangerous activities*** (e.g., blasting); and

   b. The ***selling*** of a ***defective product*** which causes personal injury or property damage.

C. Significance of categories: There are two main consequences that turn on which of the three above categories a particular tort falls into:

1. **Scope of liability:** The three categories differ concerning D's liability for ***far-reaching, unexpected, consequences***. The more culpable D's conduct, the more far-reaching his liability for unexpected consequences — so an intentional tortfeasor is liable for a wider range of unexpected consequences than is a negligent tortfeasor.

2. **Damages:** The ***measure of damages*** is generally broader for the more culpable

categories. In particular, D is more likely to be required to pay punitive damages when he is an intentional tortfeasor than when he is negligent or strictly liable.

D. Exam approach: First, review the fact pattern to spot each individual tort that has, or may have been, committed. Then, for each tort you have identified:

1. **Prima facie case:** Say whether a ***prima facie case*** for that tort has been made.

2. **Defenses:** Analyze what ***defenses*** and justifications, if any, D may be able to raise.

3. **Damages:** Finally, discuss what ***damages*** may be applicable, if the tort has been committed and there are no defenses. Pay special attention to:

   punitive damages;

   damages for ***emotional distress***;

   damages for ***loss of companionship*** of another person;

   damages for ***unlikely and far-reaching consequences***; and

   damages for ***economic loss*** where there has been no personal injury or property damage.

CHAPTER 2

INTENTIONAL TORTS AGAINST THE PERSON

I. "INTENT" DEFINED

A. Meaning of intent: There is no general meaning of "intent" when discussing intentional torts. For each individual intentional tort, you have to memorize a different definition of "intent." All that the intentional torts have in common is that D must have intended to bring about some sort of physical or mental effect upon another person.

1. **No intent to harm:** The intentional torts generally are ***not*** defined in such a way as to require D to have intended to ***harm*** the plaintiff.

   Example: D points a water gun at P, making it seem like a robbery, when in fact it is a practical joke. If D has intended to put P in fear of imminent harmful bodily contact, the "intent" for assault is present, even though D intended no "harm" to P.

2. **Substantial certainty:** If D ***knows with substantial certainty*** that a particular effect will occur as a result of her action, she is deemed to have intended that result.

   Example: D pulls a chair out from under P as she is sitting down. If D knew with "substantial certainty" that P would hit the ground, D meets the intent requirement for battery, even if he did not desire that she do so. [*Garratt v. Dailey*]

a. **High likelihood:** But if it is merely "highly likely," not "substantially certain," that the bad consequences will occur, then the act is not an intentional tort. "Recklessness" by D is not enough.

3. **Act distinguished from consequences:** For "substantially certain" and "intentional," distinguish D's act from the ***consequences*** of that act. The act must be intentional or substantially certain, but the *consequences* need not be.

Example: D intends to tap P lightly on the chin to annoy him. If P has a "glass jaw," which is broken by the light blow, D has still "intended" to cause the contact, and the intentional tort of battery has taken place, even though the consequences — broken jaw — were not intended.

B. Transferred intent: Under the doctrine of ***"transferred intent,"*** if D held the necessary intent with respect to person A, he will be held to have committed an intentional tort against ***any other person*** who happens to be injured.

Example: D shoots at A, and accidentally hits B. D is liable to B for the intentional tort of battery.

II. BATTERY

A. Definition: Battery is the ***intentional infliction of a harmful or offensive bodily contact.***

Example: A intentionally punches B in the nose. A has committed battery.

B. Intent: It is not necessary that D desires to physically ***harm*** P. D has the necessary intent for battery if it is the case ***either*** that: (1) D intended to cause a harmful or offensive bodily contact; or (2) D intended to cause an ***imminent apprehension*** on P's part of a harmful or offensive bodily contact.

Example 1: D shoots at P, intending to hit him with the bullet. D has the necessary intent for battery.

Example 2: D shoots at P, intending to miss P, but also intending to make P think that P would be hit. D has the intent needed for battery (i.e., the "intent to commit an assault" suffices as the intent for battery).

C. Harmful or offensive contact: If the contact is "harmful" — i.e., it causes pain or bodily damage — this qualifies. But battery also covers contacts which are merely ***"offensive,"*** i.e., damaging to a ***"reasonable sense of dignity."***

Example: D spits on P. Even if P is not "harmed" in the sense of being caused physical pain or physical injury, a battery has occurred because a person of average sensitivity in P's position would have her dignity offended.

D. P need not be aware: It is ***not*** necessary that P have ***actual awareness*** of the contact at the time it occurs. (*Example:* D kisses P while she is asleep. D has committed a battery.)

E. Contact beyond level consented to: Battery can occur where P ***consents*** to a certain level of bodily contact, but D ***goes beyond the consented-to level*** of contact. At that point, the consent becomes invalid, and battery results. Look for this "beyond the consented-to level of contact" scenario when the facts involve either a ***sporting event*** or a ***medical/surgical procedure.***

Example: In a pick-up ice hockey game in a park, P and D are skirmishing for the puck near the side wall of the rink. D intentionally delivers a hard body check that throws P into the wall, and the collision between P and the wall badly injures P. D sues P for battery.

If D intentionally delivered a body check (a body contact) that went beyond the level or type of contact D knew or should have known P was impliedly consenting to, then it would constitute battery.

III. ASSAULT

A. Definition: Assault is the intentional causing of an ***apprehension*** of ***harmful or offensive contact.***

Example: D, a bill collector, threatens to punch P in the face if P does not pay a bill immediately. Since D has intended to put P in imminent apprehension of a harmful bodily contact, this is assault, whether D intends to in fact hit P or not.

B. Intent: There are two different intents, either of which will suffice for assault:

1. **Intent to create apprehension:** First, D intends to put P in ***imminent apprehension*** of the harmful or offensive contact, even if D does not intend to follow through (e.g., D threatens to shoot P, but does not intend to actually shoot P); or

2. **Intent to make contact:** Alternatively, D intends to in fact ***cause*** a harmful or offensive bodily contact.

   Example: D shoots a gun at P, trying to hit P. D hopes P won't see him, but P does. P is frightened. The shot misses. This is assault.

3. **Summary:** So D has the requisite intent for assault if D either "intends to commit an assault" or "intends to commit a battery."

C. No hostility: It is not necessary that D bear malice towards P, or intend to ***harm*** her.

Example: D as a practical joke points a toy pistol at P, hoping that P will falsely think that P is about to be shot. D has one of the two alternative intents required for assault — the intent to put P in imminent apprehension of a harmful or offensive contact — so the fact that D does not desire to "harm" P is irrelevant.

D. "Words alone" rule: Ordinarily, ***words alone*** are not sufficient, by themselves, to give rise to an assault. Normally there must be some overt act — a physical act or gesture by D — before P can claim to have been assaulted.

Example: During an argument, D says to P "I'm gonna hit you in the face." This is probably not an assault, if D does not make any gesture like forming a fist or stepping towards P.

1. **Special circumstances:** However, the ***surrounding circumstances***, or D's past acts, may occasionally make it reasonable for P to interpret D's words alone as

creating the required apprehension of imminent contact.

E. Actual contact or apprehension required: Assault requires an ***effect***: P must either actually ***undergo*** a harmful or offensive contact, or be put in ***immediate apprehension*** of such a contact.

1. Unsuccessful prank or bluff: So where D is pulling a ***prank or making a bluff***, if P believes or knows that no imminent harmful or offensive contact will really occur, and none does occur, there is no assault.

Example: D, holding a revolver, walks into P's office and says, "I know you've been having sex with my wife, and I'm gonna blow your head off." The particular gun that D is holding is a toy replica that cannot fire anything, and P knows this because W has told him so on a previous occasion. D has not committed assault — even if D intended to put P in fear of an imminent harmful contact (a bullet), the "result" requirement for assault has not been met because P has not in fact been put in apprehension of such contact.

F. Imminence: It must appear to P that the harm being threatened is ***imminent***, and that D has the ***present ability*** to carry out the threat.

Example: D threatens to shoot P, and leaves the room for the stated purpose of getting his revolver. D has not committed an assault on P.

G. P unaware of danger: P must be ***aware*** of the threatened contact.

H. Threat to third persons: P must have an apprehension that ***she herself*** will be subjected to a bodily contact. She may not recover for her apprehension that ***someone else*** will be so touched.

Example: P sees D raise a pistol at P's husband. D shoots and misses. P cannot recover for assault, because she did not fear a contact with her own body.

I. Conditional threat: Where D threatens the harm only if P does not obey D's demands, the existence of an assault depends on whether D had the ***legal right*** to compel P to perform the act in question.

Example: P, a burglar, breaks into D's house. D says, "If you don't get out, I'll throw you out." There is no assault on P, since D has the legal right to force P to leave.

IV. FALSE IMPRISONMENT

A. Definition: False imprisonment is defined as the intentional infliction of a ***confinement***.

Example: D wants to have sex with P, and locks her in his bedroom for two hours hoping that P will agree. She does not, and D lets her go. This is false imprisonment, because D has intentionally confined P for a substantial time.

B. Intent: P must show that D either ***intended*** to confine him, or at least that D ***knew with substantial certainty*** that P would be confined by D's actions. The tort of false imprisonment cannot be committed merely by negligent or reckless acts.

Example: D, a shopkeeper, negligently locks the store while P, a customer, is in the bathroom. This is not false imprisonment, since D did not intend to confine P.

C. "Confinement": The idea of confinement is that P is held ***within*** certain limits, not that she is prevented from entering certain places.

Example: D refuses to allow P to return to her own home. This is not false imprisonment — P can go anywhere else, so she has not been "confined."

D. Means used: The imprisonment may be carried out by direct physical means, but also by ***threats*** or by the assertion of ***legal authority***.

1. **Threats:** Thus if D threatens to use force if P tries to escape, the requisite confinement exists.
2. **Assertion of legal authority:** Also, confinement may be caused by D's assertion that he has ***legal authority*** to confine P — this is true even if D does not in fact have the legal authority, so long as P reasonably believed that D does, or is in doubt about whether D does.

   Example: Storekeeper suspects P of shoplifting, and says, "I hereby make a citizen's arrest of you." Putting aside whether Storekeeper has a privilege to act this way, Storekeeper has "confined" P, if a reasonable person in P's position would think that Storekeeper had the authority to make such an arrest, even if under local law Storekeeper did not have that authority.

E. P must know of confinement: P must either be ***aware*** of the confinement, or must suffer some actual harm.

Example: P is locked in her hotel room by D, but P is asleep for the entire three-hour period, and learns only later that the door was locked. This is probably not false imprisonment.

V. INTENTIONAL INFLICTION OF EMOTIONAL DISTRESS (IIED)

A. Definition: This tort is the intentional or reckless infliction, by ***extreme and outrageous conduct***, of ***severe emotional or mental distress***, even in the absence of physical harm.

Example: D threatens that if P, a garbage collector, does not pay over part of his garbage collection proceeds to D and his henchmen, D will severely beat P. Since D's conduct is extreme and outrageous, and since he has intended to cause P distress (which he has succeeded in doing), D is liable for infliction of emotional distress. [*State Rubbish Collectors Assoc. v. Siliznoff*]

B. Intent: "Intent" for this tort is a bit broader than for others. There are three possible types of culpability by D: (1) D ***desires*** to cause P emotional distress; (2) D knows with ***substantial certainty*** that P will suffer emotional distress; and (3) D ***recklessly*** disregards the high probability that emotional distress will occur.

Example: D commits suicide by slitting his throat in P's kitchen. D, or his estate, is liable for intentional infliction of emotional distress because although D did not desire to cause distress to P, or even know that distress was substantially certain, he recklessly disregarded the high risk that distress would occur. [*Blakeley v. Shortal's Est.*]

1. **Transferred intent:** The doctrine of ***"transferred intent"*** is applied only in a very ***limited*** fashion for emotional distress torts. So if D attempts to cause emotional distress to X (or to commit some other tort on him), and P suffers emotional distress, P usually will not recover.

   a. **Immediate family present:** The main exception is that the transferred intent doctrine is applied if: (1) D directs his conduct to a member of P's ***immediate family***; (2) P is ***present***; and (3) P's presence is ***known*** to D.

   Example: While P is present, and known to D to be present, D beats up P's father. If P suffers severe emotional distress, a court will probably allow her to recover from D, even though D's conduct was directed at the father, not P.

C. **"Extreme and outrageous":** P must show that D's conduct was ***extreme and outrageous***. D's conduct has to be "beyond all possible bounds of decency."

   Example: D, as a practical joke, tells P that her husband has been badly injured in an accident, and is lying in the hospital with broken legs. This conduct is sufficiently outrageous to qualify. [*Wilkinson v. Downton*]

1. **Bill collectors:** A common fact pattern in which D may be liable for intentional infliction of emotional distress is where D is a ***bill collector***. The collector's conduct can and often will be sufficiently extreme and outrageous to trigger IIED (e.g., repeated abusive phone calls at night; or denouncing P to P's boss or neighbors as a "deadbeat"). And it's no defense to an otherwise proper IIED action that P ***really owed the money*** that D was trying to collect.

D. **Actual severe distress:** P must suffer ***severe*** emotional distress. P must show at least that her distress was severe enough that she ***sought medical aid***. Most cases do not require P to show that the distress resulted in bodily harm.

E. **Constitutional limits on IIED awards:** The ***First Amendment of the U.S. Constitution*** places some important ***limits*** on the right of a state to impose liability for IIED. If the conduct by the defendant that causes the distress is the delivery of a ***message or communication***, a state's act of awarding damages against the defendant for IIED may well violate the defendant's First Amendment freedom of speech.

1. **P is a public figure; rule from defamation cases:** For instance, a plaintiff who is a ***public figure*** (essentially, a famous or newsworthy person) may succeed with a claim for *IIED* based on a communication only if P shows that the defendant either ***knew that his speech was false or recklessly disregarded whether it was true.*** [*Hustler Magazine v. Falwell*]

   Example: *Hustler Magazine* satirizes religious leader Jerry Falwell as a drunken hypocrite who has sex with his mother. *Held*, Falwell cannot recover against *Hustler* for IIED unless he shows that *Hustler* made a false statement about him with knowledge of its falsity or with reckless disregard of its falsity. [*Hustler Magazine v. Falwell*]

2. **Statement on a matter of public concern:** Another way a tort recovery for IIED can violate the defendant's First Amendment rights is if the alleged distress stems from the communicative impact of the defendant's speech, and the speech involves a matter of ***public concern.*** [*Snyder v. Phelps*]

   Example: P is the father of a Marine, Matthew Snyder, recently killed in Iraq. The Ds are members of the Westboro Baptist Church, a church that thinks God punishes the U.S. military for tolerating homosexuality. During the course of Matthew's funeral in Maryland, the Ds, from a public place nearby, carry picket signs with messages like "God hates fags," and "Thank God for Dead Soldiers." (The Ds apparently believe that Matthew was killed because of God's desire to punish the military for not rooting out homosexuality.) P brings a suit against the Ds for intentionally causing him emotional distress. The jury awards P $4 million in damages, based on its conclusion that the Ds' conduct was "outrageous."

   Held (by the U.S. Supreme Court on appeal), for the Ds. Since the Ds' speech was on a matter of "public concern," their First Amendment rights allowed Maryland to regulate that speech only in a "content neutral" manner. Since the jury likely reached its verdict without observing the required "content neutrality," enforcing the resulting damage award against the Ds violated their First Amendment rights. [*Snyder v. Phelps, supra*]

CHAPTER 3

INTENTIONAL INTERFERENCE WITH PROPERTY

I. TRESPASS TO LAND

A. Definition: As generally used, ***"trespass"*** occurs when either: (1) D ***intentionally enters P's land***, without permission; (2) D ***remains*** on P's land without the right to be there, even if she entered rightfully; or (3) D ***puts an object on*** (or refuses to remove an object from) P's land without permission.

B. Intent: The term "trespass" today refers only to ***intentional*** interference with P's interest in property. There is no strict liability.

   Example: D, a pilot, loses control of the aircraft, and the aircraft lands on P's property. This is not trespass to land.

1. **Negligence:** If D ***negligently*** enters P's land, this is generally treated as the tort of negligence, not trespass.

2. **Effect of mistake:** If D has the intent to commit a physical contact with P's land, D will have the requisite intent for trespass even if his decision to make the contact is the result of a ***mistake***. Thus D's mistake about ***legal title*** or ***consent*** won't block liability.

   a. **Reasonableness irrelevant:** This is true even if the mistake is ***reasonable*** (assuming the mistake wasn't induced by anything P did or said).

Example: D, an absentee owner, visits his property, which is a farm. He drives a tractor on what he reasonably thinks is his parcel, but unbeknownst to him (and without negligence on his part), he drives over what is really P's land. This is trespass, despite D's reasonable ignorance of the fact that the land he is entering belongs to someone other than D.

C. Particles and gasses: If D knowingly causes ***objects***, including particles or gases, to enter P's property, most courts consider this trespass.

Example: D's factory spews pollutants onto P's land. This is a trespass. [*Martin v. Reynolds Metals Co.*]

D. Air space: It can be a trespass for a plane to ***fly over*** P's property. However, today most courts find liability only if: (1) the plane enters into the ***immediate reaches*** of the airspace (below federally-prescribed minimum flight altitudes); *and* (2) the flight ***substantially interferes*** with P's use and enjoyment of his land (e.g., by causing undue noise, vibrations, pollution).

II. TRESPASS TO CHATTELS

A. Definition: "Trespass to chattels" is defined as any ***intentional interference*** with a person's ***use or possession*** of a chattel. D only has to pay damages, not the full value of the property (as in conversion, below).

1. Loss of possession: If P ***loses possession*** of the chattel for any time, recovery is allowed even if the chattel is returned unharmed.

Example: D takes P's car for a five-minute "joy ride," and returns it unharmed. D has committed trespass to chattels.

2. Electronic trespass on computer: If D ***interacts with P's computer*** without permission, whether this is trespass to chattels depends on the ***type of harm*** that occurs.

a. No harm to computer or data: Where D's conduct ***does not harm P's computer or the data on it,*** most courts say trespass to chattels does ***not*** occur even though D's interaction with P's computer was uninvited and P is bothered.

Example: D sends lots of emails to P's computer, which P has to take time to delete, but which don't damage the computer or data on it. This is probably not trespass to chattel.

b. Harm done: But if D's conduct *does* harm the computer or data on it, then trespass to chattels does occur.

Example: D puts "spyware" on P's computer that tracks P's keystrokes and slows down the computer's functioning. This is probably trespass to chattels.

Note: The above discussion assumes that the computer data constitutes ***"property"*** for trespass-to-chattels purpose. Most courts today agree that computer files *are* property for this purpose.

III. CONVERSION

A. Definition: Conversion is an ***intentional*** interference with P's possession or ownership of property that is ***so substantial*** that D should be required to pay the property's ***full value***.

> **Example:** D steals P's car, then seriously (though not irreparably) damages it in a collision. D is liable for conversion, and will be required to pay P the full value of the car (though D gets to keep the car).

B. Intent: Conversion is an intentional tort, but all that is required is that D have intended to take possession of the property. Mistake as to ownership will generally not be a defense.

> **Example:** D buys an old painting from an art dealer, and reasonably believes that the art dealer has good title. In fact, the painting was stolen from P years before. D keeps the painting in his house for 10 years. D is liable for conversion, notwithstanding his honest mistake about title.

C. Distinguished from trespass to chattels: Courts consider several factors in determining whether D's interference with P's possessory rights is severe enough to be conversion, or just trespass to chattels. Factors include: (1) duration of D's ***dominion*** over the property; (2) D's ***good or bad faith***; (3) the ***harm*** done to the property; and (4) the ***inconvenience*** caused to P.

D. Different ways to commit: There are different ways in which conversion may be committed:

1. **Acquiring possession:** D takes ***possession*** of the property from P.

   a. **Bona fide purchaser:** Most courts hold that a ***bona fide purchaser*** of ***stolen goods*** is a converter, even if there is no way he could have known that they were stolen.

2. **Transfer to third person:** D can also commit conversion by ***transferring*** a chattel to one who is not entitled to it.

3. **Withholding good:** D may commit conversion by ***refusing to return*** goods to their owner, if the refusal lasts for a substantial time.

4. **Destruction:** Conversion may occur if D ***destroys*** the goods, or fundamentally alters them.

E. Intangibles, including computer files: As with trespass to chattels, if the item is ***"intangible"*** property, check to make sure that in the state in question, the item counts as property for conversion purposes. Most courts today say that ***computer files count.*** Therefore if D permanently deprives P of access to files P owns, D will be liable for conversion in most states.

F. Forced sale: If P is successful with her tort suit, a ***forced sale*** occurs: D is required to pay the ***full value*** of the goods (not just the amount of the use or damage, as in trespass to chattels), but gets to keep the goods.

CHAPTER 4

DEFENSES TO INTENTIONAL TORTS

I. CONSENT

A. Express consent: If P expressly ***consents*** to an intentional interference with his person or property, D will not be liable for that interference.

Example: P says to D, "Go ahead, hit me in the stomach — I'll show you how strong I am." If D does so, P's consent prevents P from suing for battery.

B. Implied consent: Existence of consent may also be ***implied*** from P's conduct, from custom, or from the circumstances.

1. **Objective manifestation:** It is the ***objective manifestations*** by P that count — if it reasonably seemed to one in D's position that P consented, consent exists regardless of P's subjective state of mind.

   Example: D offers to vaccinate all passengers on their ship. P holds up her arm and receives the vaccination. Since it reasonably appeared to D that P consented, there will be consent regardless of P's actual state of mind. [*O'Brien v. Cunard*]

C. Lack of capacity: Consent will be invalidated if P is ***incapable*** of giving that consent, because she is a child, intoxicated, unconscious, etc.

1. **Consent as a matter of law:** But even if P is incapable of truly giving consent, consent will be ***implied*** "as a matter of law" if these factors exist: (1) P is unable to give consent; (2) immediate action is necessary to save P's life or health; (3) there is no indication that P would not consent if able; and (4) a reasonable person would consent in the circumstances.

   Example: P is brought unconscious to the emergency room of D, a hospital. D can perform emergency surgery without P's actual consent — consent will be implied as a matter of law. Therefore, P cannot sue for battery.

D. Exceeding scope: Even if P does consent to an invasion of her interests, D will not be privileged if he goes substantially ***beyond the scope*** of that consent.

Example: P visits D, a doctor, and consents to an operation on her right ear. While P is under anesthetic, D decides that P's left ear needs an operation as well, and does it. P's consent does not block an action for battery for the left-ear operation, since the operation went beyond the scope of P's consent. [*Mohr v. Williams*]

1. **Emergency:** However, in the surgery case, an ***emergency*** may justify extending the surgery beyond that consented to.
2. **Athlete's consent:** Participating in a usually-violent ***sport***, like football or hockey, is generally ***not*** considered to constitute consent to all injuries which may be inflicted by an adversary. Instead, there is an increasing tendency to hold that a player who ***intentionally attacks or injures*** his opponent may be liable in tort.

a. **Scope of implied consent:** So if P impliedly consents to some types of harmful or offensive contact during the sport, fellow-participant D won't be liable for contacts falling within the scope of that implied consent, but ***will*** be liable for contacts going ***beyond*** the ones impliedly consented to.

b. **Significance of sport's rules and customs:** In determining what contacts the player impliedly consented to, most courts attach great weight to the ***rules or customs*** of the sport. Decisions recognize at least three major ***categories*** of contact, and tend to draw different conclusions about whether the plaintiff "impliedly consented" to the contact based on the category the contact falls into:

[1] **Conduct allowed by rules:** The first category consists of contact that is ***expressly allowed*** by the rules and customs of the sport. Where the case falls into this category, in virtually all courts the plaintiff will be held to have ***impliedly consented*** to this type of contact, even if in the particular situation the result is an unexpectedly grave injury.

[2] **Conduct punishable but not "beyond the bounds" of the sport:** The next category consists of conduct that ***violates the rules*** of the sport, but is considered to be essentially ***within the ordinary give-and-take of the sport.*** Conduct would likely fall into this category if it is subject to ***some minor penalty***, but not to a severe punishment like automatic ejection or a multiple-game suspension. Again, most courts would likely hold that such conduct, while against the rules, is of a type that is sufficiently common (and in most instances insufficiently physically dangerous) that the plaintiff should be ***deemed to have impliedly consented to it.***

Example: P and D are playing in an NBA basketball game. D commits a "flagrant foul" on P by grabbing P's arm from behind and throwing him to the ground to prevent him from scoring. (The foul ruling gives P two foul shots, and does not result in D's being ejected or suspended.) P falls, suffering a freak career-ending knee injury when his knee hits the floor. P sues D for battery.

The court would likely hold that judging by the relatively unsevere penalty imposed by the referee, this type of foul is sufficiently ordinary — and sufficiently unlikely to cause severe personal injury — that it should be deemed to be the type of contact to which P implicitly consented by joining the league.

[3] **Reckless or intentionally-harmful conduct beyond the usual bounds:** The final category consists of conduct that not only violates the rules of the sport, but constitutes a ***flagrant violation*** by means of actions that are ***unrelated to the normal method of playing the game***, and that are done ***without any competitive purpose***. Scenarios where D ***intends to physically harm*** his opponent (or ***recklessly disregards*** the danger of such harm), without any *bona fide* belief that D is advancing his own team's competitive interest, are typical of this category. If the case falls into this category, most courts ***allow*** a tort suit (typically one for battery) to be brought by the

injured player against the opponent who committed the violation, and/or the teams that employed that opponent.

Example: P and Clark are NFL players on opposing teams. (Clark plays for the D team.) At the end of a play that goes well for P's team, while P is kneeling and watching the end of the play, Clark comes up behind P and uses his forearm to hit P on the head and neck. Clark strikes this blow (he later testifies) not because he thinks it might help his team, but out of frustration at the play and the fact that his team, D, is losing. The blow fractures P's neck. Therefore, P sues D for the tortious act committed by their employee (Clark). The trial judge, sitting without a jury, rules that P assumed the risk of Clark's conduct, on the theory that "professional football is a species of warfare[.]" P appeals.

Held (on appeal): for P — case remanded for a retrial. The rules and customs of the NFL prohibit the intentional striking of blows. Where one football player intentionally inflicts a serious injury on another, the injured player won't be deemed to have assumed the risk of such a conduct. [*Hackbart v. Cincinnati Bengals, Inc.*]

Note: However, a few cases have ***found for the defendant*** as a matter of law even where the defendant ***intentionally tried to harm*** the plaintiff, or ***recklessly disregarded the high risk*** that the plaintiff would be harmed. These few cases have reasoned that if players and teams have to worry about being held liable in tort for their aggressive on-field acts, their incentive to compete vigorously but lawfully — a desirable thing — will be chilled. [See *Avila v. Citrus Community College District,* holding that P, a varsity college baseball hitter, assumed the risk that the opposing pitcher would intentionally hit him with a pitch as retaliation for the fact that the pitcher's teammate was previously hit by the pitcher for P's team.]

c. **A mere negligent violation of rules:** Where D's conduct in violating the sports rule manifests ***mere negligence*** as to the risk of injury to P (rather than an intention to hurt P or reckless disregard of P's physical safety), ***few if any cases allow recovery***.

E. Consent to criminal acts: Where D's act against P is a ***criminal act***, courts are split. The majority rule is that P's consent is ***ineffective*** if the act consented to is a crime.

Example: P and D agree to fight with each other. In most states, each may recover from the other, on the theory that consent to a crime — such as breach of peace — is ineffective.

II. SELF-DEFENSE

A. Privilege generally: A person is entitled to use ***reasonable force*** to prevent any threatened ***harmful or offensive bodily contact***, and any threatened ***confinement or imprisonment***.

B. Apparent necessity: Self-defense may be used not only where there is a real threat of harm, but also where D ***reasonably believes*** that there is one.

C. Only for protection: The defense of self-defense applies only where D uses the force needed to ***protect himself*** against harm.

1. **Retaliation:** Thus D may not use any degree of force in ***retaliation*** for a tort already committed.

   Example: P hits D with a snowball. Ten minutes later, D hits P with a snowball, in retaliation. D has committed battery on P, because D's act was not done in true self-defense.

2. **Imminence:** D may not use force to avoid harm which is ***not imminent***, unless it reasonably appears that there will not be a later chance to prevent the danger.

   Example: P says to D, "I will beat you up tomorrow." D cannot beat P up today, to prevent tomorrow's attack, unless it appears that there will be no way for D to defend tomorrow.

3. **Verbal provocation:** D may not use self-defense in response to ***verbal provocation***, such as ***taunting or insults***. Self-defense is purely a forward-looking idea: D is entitled to prevent imminent future harm, not redress past harm, especially purely verbal harm.

   Example: P calls D a liar and a cheat in front of D's friends. (Assume that D is not a liar and a cheat, and that P's words constitute slander for which D could recover.) P then says to D, "What're you gonna do about, you coward?" D hits P in the face. P can recover for battery, and D cannot successfully claim self-defense. That's because provocation does not justify self-defense in tort law; only the prevention of imminent bodily harm can justify it.

D. Degree of force: Only the ***degree*** of force necessary to prevent the threatened harm may be used. If D uses more force than necessary, he will be liable for damage caused by the excess.

1. **Deadly force:** Special rules limit the use of ***deadly force***, i.e., force intended or likely to cause death or serious bodily injury.

   a. **Danger must be serious:** D may ***not*** use deadly force unless he himself is in danger of ***death or serious bodily harm***.

      Example: P attacks D with his fists, in a way that does not threaten D with serious bodily harm. Even if there is no other way for D to prevent the attack, D may not use his gun to shoot P, even if the shot is intended only to injure P — D must submit to the attack rather than use deadly force.

E. Retreat: Courts are split on whether and when D has a ***"duty to retreat"*** (i.e., to run away or withdraw) if the threatened harm could be avoided this way.

1. **Restatement view:** The Second Restatement holds that: (1) D may use ***non-deadly force*** rather than retreating; but (2) D may not use ***deadly force*** in lieu of retreating, except if attacked in his ***dwelling*** by one who does not reside in the dwelling.

Example: If P attacks D on the street with a knife, under the Restatement D may use his fists rather than running away, but may not use a gun rather than running away if running away would avoid the danger. If the attack took place in D's home, where P was not also a resident, then D could use the gun.

III. DEFENSE OF OTHERS

A. General rule: A person may use reasonable force to defend ***another person*** against attack. The same rules apply as in self-defense: the defender may only use reasonable force, and may not use deadly force to repel a non-deadly attack.

1. Reasonable mistake: The courts are split on the effect of a ***reasonable mistake***. Older courts hold that the intervener "steps into the shoes" of the person aided, and thus bears the risk of a mistake. But Rest.2d gives a "reasonable mistake" defense to the intervener.

IV. DEFENSE OF PROPERTY

A. General rule: A person may generally use reasonable force to ***defend her property***, both land and chattels.

1. Warning required first: The owner must first make a ***verbal demand*** that the intruder stop, unless it reasonably appears that violence or harm will occur immediately, or that the request to stop will be useless.

B. Mistake: The effect of a ***reasonable mistake*** by D varies:

1. Mistake as to danger: If D's mistake is about whether force is necessary, D is protected by a reasonable mistake.

Example: D uses non-deadly force to stop a burglar whom he reasonably believes to be armed. In fact, the burglar is not armed. D can rely on the defense of property.

2. Privilege: But if the owner's mistake is about whether the intruder has a ***right*** to be there, the owner's use of force will not be privileged.

Example: D reasonably believes that P is a burglar. In fact, P is a friend who has entered D's house to retrieve her purse, without wanting to bother D. Even non-deadly force by D will not be privileged.

C. Deadly force: The owner may use ***deadly force*** only where: (1) non-deadly force will not suffice; and (2) the owner reasonably believes that without deadly force, ***death*** or ***serious bodily harm*** will occur.

Example: D sees P trespassing in P's backyard. D asks P to leave, but P refuses. Even if there is no way to make P leave except by shooting at him, D may not do so, since P's conduct does not threaten D with death or serious bodily harm.

1. Burglary: But a homeowner is generally ***allowed*** to use deadly force against a ***burglar***, provided that she reasonably believes that nothing short of this force will safely keep the burglar out.

D. Mechanical devices: An owner may use a ***mechanical device*** to protect her property only if she would be privileged to use a similar degree of force if she were present and acting herself.

1. **Reasonable mistake:** An owner's right to use a dangerous mechanical device in a particular case will be measured by whether deadly force could have been used against ***that particular intruder***.

    Example: D uses a spring gun to protect his house while he is away. If the gun shoots an actual burglar, and state law would have allowed D to shoot the burglar if D was present, then D will not be liable for using the spring gun. But if a neighbor, postal carrier, or someone else not engaged in a crime happened to enter and was shot, D would not have a "reasonable mistake" defense — since D could not have fired the gun at such a person directly, the spring gun may not be used either.

V. RECAPTURE OF CHATTELS

A. Generally: A property owner has the general right to use reasonable force to ***regain*** possession of ***chattels*** taken from her by someone else.

1. **Fresh pursuit:** The privilege exists only if the property owner is in ***"fresh pursuit"*** to recover his property. That is, the owner must act without unreasonable delay.

    Example: A learns that B has stolen A's stereo and is in possession of it. A may use reasonable force to reclaim the stereo if he acts immediately, but not if he waits, say, a week between learning that B has the property and attempting to regain it.

2. **Reasonable force:** The force used must be reasonable, and ***deadly force*** can never be used.

3. **Wrongful taking:** The privilege exists only if the property was taken ***wrongfully*** from the owner. If the owner parts willingly with possession of the property, and an event then occurs that gives him the right to repossess, he generally will not be able to use force to regain it.

    Example: O rents a TV to A. A refuses to return the set on time. O probably may not use reasonable force to enter A's home to repossess the set, because A's original possession was not wrongful.

B. Merchant: Where a merchant reasonably believes that a person is stealing his property, many courts give the merchant a privilege to ***temporarily detain*** the person for investigation.

1. **Limited time:** The detention must be limited to a short time, generally 10 or 15 minutes or less, just long enough to determine whether the person has really shoplifted or not. Then, the police must be called (the merchant may not purport to arrest the suspect himself).

VI. NECESSITY

A. General rule: Under the defense of ***"necessity,"*** D has a privilege to harm the property interest of P where this is ***necessary*** in order to prevent ***great harm*** to third persons or to the defendant herself.

B. Public necessity: If interference with the land or chattels of another is necessary to prevent a disaster ***to the community*** or to many people, the privilege is that of "***public*** necessity." Here, ***no compensation*** has to be paid by the person doing the damage.

> **Example:** Firefighters demolish D's house, in which a fire has just barely started, because that is the best way to stop the fire from spreading much further. The firefighters, and the town employing them, probably do not have to pay, because they are protected by the privilege of public necessity.

C. Private necessity: If a person prevents injury to himself or his property, or to the person or property of a third person, this is protected by the privilege of "***private*** necessity," if there is no less-damaging way of preventing the harm.

> **Example:** A, while sailing, is caught in very rough seas. To save his life, he may moor at a dock owned by B, and will not be liable for trespass.

1. **Actual damage:** Where the privilege of private necessity exists, it will be a complete defense to a tort claim where P has suffered no actual substantial harm (as in the above example). But if actual damage occurs, P must ***pay for the damage*** she has caused.

   > **Example:** On the facts of the above example, if A's boat slammed into B's dock and damaged it, A would have to pay.

2. **Owner may not resist:** The main purpose of the doctrine of private necessity is to prevent the person whose property might be injured from defeating the exercise of the privilege.

   > **Example:** P moors his ship at D's dock, to avoid being shipwrecked by heavy seas. D, objecting to what he thinks is a trespass, unmoors the ship, causing the ship to be harmed and P to be injured. P may recover from D, because P's mooring was privileged by private necessity and D, therefore, acted wrongfully. [*Ploof v. Putnam*]

VII. ARREST

A. Common law rules:

1. **Arrest with warrant:** Where a police officer executes an arrest with an ***arrest warrant*** that appears to be correctly issued, he will not be liable even if it turns out that there was no probable cause or the procedures used to get the warrant were not proper.

2. **Arrest without warrant:**

   a. **Felony or breach of peace in presence:** A police officer may make a warrantless arrest for a ***felony*** or for a ***breach of the peace,*** if the offense is being committed or seems about to be committed ***in his presence***. A citizen may do the same.

b. Past felony: Once a felony has been committed, an officer may still make a warrantless arrest, provided that he reasonably believes that the felony has been committed, and also reasonably believes that he has the right criminal. A citizen may make an arrest only if a felony has ***in fact*** been committed (though the citizen is protected if she makes a reasonable mistake and arrests the wrong person).

c. Misdemeanor: At common law, no warrantless arrest (either by an officer or by a citizen) may be made for a ***past misdemeanor not involving a breach of the peace***.

3. Reasonable force: One making an arrest may not use more ***force*** than is ***reasonably necessary***.

a. Prevention: Where the arrest is made to ***prevent a felony*** which threatens human life or safety, even deadly force may be used, if there is no other way to prevent the crime. But where the felony does not involve such danger, deadly force may not be used.

b. Apprehension after crime: If a crime has already been committed, the police may use ***deadly force*** only if the suspect poses a significant threat of ***death or serious physical injury*** to others.

Example: Officer spots Burglar escaping after his crime. Officer knows that Burglar is unarmed and unlikely to be violent. Officer may not shoot at Burglar to arrest him, even if there is no other way to make the arrest.

VIII. JUSTIFICATION

A. Generally: Even if D's conduct does not fit within one of the narrower defenses, she may be entitled to the general defense of ***"justification,"*** a catch-all term used where there are good reasons for exculpating D from what would otherwise be an intentional tort.

CHAPTER 5

NEGLIGENCE GENERALLY

I. COMPONENTS OF TORT OF NEGLIGENCE

A. Generally: The tort of "negligence" occurs when D's conduct imposes an ***unreasonable risk*** upon another, which results in injury to that other. The negligent tortfeasor's mental state is irrelevant.

B. Prima facie case: The five components of a prima facie case for negligence action are:

1. Duty: A legal ***duty*** requiring D to conduct himself according to a certain standard, so as to avoid unreasonable risk to others;

2. **Failure to conform:** A failure by D to conform his conduct to this standard. (This element can be thought of as ***"carelessness."***)

3. **Cause in fact:** A showing that D's failure to act with reasonable care was the ***"cause in fact"*** of the injury to plaintiff. Generally, "cause in fact" means a ***"but for"*** cause, i.e., a cause without which the injury wouldn't have occurred.

4. **Proximate cause:** A sufficiently close ***causal connection*** between D's act of negligence and the harm suffered by P that it's fair to hold D liable, as a matter of policy. This is ***"proximate cause."***

5. **Actual damage:** ***Actual damage*** suffered by P. (Compare this to most intentional torts, such as trespass, where P can recover nominal damages even without actual injury.)

   Note: When we say that these five elements make up a "prima facie case" for negligence, what we mean is that if as part of P's case in chief, P fails to prove any of these five elements, D will be entitled to a directed verdict by the judge (and the jury won't even get to deliberate).

II. UNREASONABLE RISK

A. Generally: P must show that D's conduct imposed an ***unreasonable risk of harm*** on P (or on a class of persons of whom P is a member).

1. **Not judged by results:** It is not enough for P to show that D's conduct resulted in a terrible injury. P must show that D's conduct, viewed ***as of the time it occurred***, without benefit of hindsight, imposed an unreasonable risk of harm.

B. Balancing: In determining whether the risk of harm from D's conduct was so great as to be "unreasonable," courts use a ***balancing test***: "Where an act is one which a reasonable [person] would recognize as involving a risk of harm to another, the risk is unreasonable and the act is negligent if the risk is of such magnitude as to ***outweigh*** what the law regards as the ***utility*** of the act or of the particular manner in which it is done."

1. **Small risk of big harm:** Under the balancing test, if a reasonable person would realize that a potential injury, if it came to pass, would be ***extremely grave***, there may be liability even though it was relatively ***unlikely*** that the accident would occur.

   Example: Suppose that D encounters a yellow traffic light while driving his heavy truck into Times Square. He has to decide whether to speed up to make the light, though in any event he intends to keep within the speed limit. D knows that the truck's brakes have been sporadically malfunctioning recently. Assume that D realizes or should realize that if the brakes fail at that moment, numerous people will likely be killed or maimed.

   Even if D reasonably believes that there is only, say, a 2% chance that the brakes will fail at that moment, the potential harm is so great, and the burden of stopping at the yellow light so small, that his conduct in speeding up is probably negligent despite the unlikeliness of a brake failure.

C. Warnings: One of the ways the risks of conduct can be reduced is by giving ***warnings*** of danger. The fact that D gave a warning of dangers to P in particular, or the public in general, is thus a factor that will make it less likely that D will be found negligent when the danger that was warned of results in an accident.

1. **Failure to warn can itself be negligent:** If D ***fails*** to give a warning of a danger that he knows about, and the warning could have been easily given, the mere failure to warn can itself ***constitute negligence.***

2. **Does not immunize D:** However, it's clear that even if D *does* give a warning, this ***does not immunize D*** from negligence liability — if D's activity is unreasonably dangerous (evaluated by balancing its benefits against its risks) despite D's warning to P, D will still be liable.

   Example: Dave, while moving out of his second-floor apartment, throws an old television out the window, aiming for a dumpster on the ground below the window. Just before he throws the TV, he yells out "Look out below." Paula, a pedestrian, does not hear the warning because she is talking on her cellphone. Dave can be found negligent despite having given the warning — it is so dangerous to throw a heavy object out of an upstairs window, and so easy to discard the object by safer means, that the giving of the warning did not make the total benefits of Dave's conduct outweigh its dangers.

III. THE REASONABLE PERSON

A. Objective standard: The reasonableness of D's conduct is viewed under an ***objective standard***: Would a ***"reasonable person*** of ordinary prudence," in D's position, do as D did? D does not escape liability merely because she intended to behave carefully or thought she was behaving carefully.

B. Physical and mental characteristics: The question is whether D behaved reasonably "under the circumstances." "The circumstances" generally include the ***physical characteristics*** of D himself.

1. **Physical disability:** Thus if D has a physical ***disability***, the standard for negligence is what a reasonable person with that physical disability would have done.

   Example: P is blind and is struck while crossing the street using a cane. If the issue is whether P was contributorily negligent, the issue will be whether a blind person would have crossed the street in that manner.

2. **Mental characteristics:** The ordinary reasonable person is *not* deemed to have the particular ***mental*** characteristics of D.

   Example: If D is more stupid, or more careless, than an ordinary person, this will not be a defense.

3. **Intoxication:** Intoxication is no defense — even if D is drunk, she is held to the standard of conduct of a reasonable ***sober*** person.

4. **Children:** A ***child*** is held to the level of conduct of a reasonable person of that ***age*** and ***experience***, not that of an adult.

a. **Adult activity:** But where a child engages in a potentially ***dangerous activity*** normally pursued only by ***adults***, she will be held to the standard of care that a reasonable adult doing that activity would exercise.

Example: Suppose D, a 12-year-old, operates a motorboat. This is an activity that is potentially dangerous and normally pursued by adults. Therefore, D must match the standard of care of a reasonable adult boater.

C. **Custom:** Courts generally allow evidence as to ***custom*** for the purpose of showing presence or absence of reasonable care. However, this evidence is generally ***not conclusive***.

1. **Evidence by D:** Thus where D shows that everyone else in the industry does things the way D did them, the jury is still free to conclude that the industry custom is unreasonably dangerous and thus negligent.

Example: D operates a tugboat without a radio. The fact that most tugboats in the industry do not yet have radios does not prevent the jury from holding that D's lack of a radio was negligent. [*The T.J. Hooper*]

2. **Proof by plaintiff:** Conversely, proof offered by P that others in D's industry followed a certain precaution that D did not, will be suggestive but not conclusive evidence that D was negligent.

D. **Emergencies:** If D is confronted with an ***emergency***, and is forced to act with little time for reflection, D must merely behave as a reasonable person would if confronted with the same emergency, not as a reasonable person would with plenty of time to think.

Example: D is a cab driver. A thief jumps in the cab, points a gun at D's head, and tells him to drive fast. D, in a panic, mistakenly puts the car in reverse and injures P. The issue is whether a cab driver confronted with a gun-pointing thief would or might have behaved as D did, not whether a cab driver in ordinary circumstances would have behaved that way.

E. **Anticipating conduct of others:** A reasonable person possesses at least limited ability to ***anticipate the conduct of others***.

1. **Negligence:** D may be required to anticipate the possibility of ***negligence*** on the part of others.

Example: It may be negligence for D to presume that all drivers near him will behave non-negligently, and that these others will not speed, signal properly, etc.

a. **Parental supervision:** A ***parent*** has a duty to exercise reasonable care to ***supervise the conduct of his or her minor child***, to prevent the child from intentionally harming others or posing an unreasonable risk of harm to others.

i. **Direct liability:** This principle does ***not*** make the parent ***"vicariously liable"*** for the child's torts. Instead, it constitutes ***direct*** negligence by the parent not to use reasonable care in controlling the child, where the parent has the ability to control the child, and knows or should have known of the risk being posed by the child's conduct.

Example: As Mom is aware, Kid, her 10-year-old son, is skateboarding on the sidewalk in front of their house, in a way that poses great danger to pedestrian passersby. Mom knows that she could control Kid to prevent him from skateboarding in this manner, but she unreasonably decides that the risks posed by Kid are small enough to make it not worth Mom's while to intervene. Kid runs into P, a little old lady, who is badly injured.

P can recover against Mom, for failing to use reasonable care to prevent Kid from dangerous skateboarding, given that Mom both (1) knew or should have known that she had the ability to control Kid and (2) knew or should have known that Kid's behavior was risky to pedestrians.

2. **Criminal or intentionally tortious acts:** Normally the reasonable person (and, hence, D) is entitled to presume that third persons will *not* commit ***crimes*** or intentional torts.

   a. **Special knowledge:** But if D has a ***special relationship*** with either P or a third person, or special knowledge of the situation, then it may be negligence for D not to anticipate a crime or intentional tort.

   Example: It may be negligence for D, a psychiatrist, not to warn P that a patient of D's is dangerous to P. [*Tarasoff v. Regents*]

IV. MALPRACTICE

A. Superior ability or knowledge: If D has a ***higher degree*** of ***knowledge***, skill or experience than the "reasonable person," D must ***use*** that higher level.

Example: D, because she is a local resident, knows that a stretch of highway is exceptionally curvy and thus dangerous. D drives at a rate of speed that one who did not know the terrain well would think was reasonable, and crashes, injuring her passenger, P. Even though D's driving would not have represented carelessness if done by a reasonable person with ordinary knowledge of the road, D was responsible for using her special knowledge and is negligent for not doing so.

B. Malpractice generally: Professionals, including doctors, lawyers, accountants, engineers, etc., must act with the level of skill and learning ***commonly possessed by members of the profession in good standing***.

1. **Good results not guaranteed:** The professional will not normally be held to guarantee that a ***successful result*** will occur, only that she will use the requisite minimum skill and competence.

2. **Specialists:** If D holds herself out as a ***specialist*** in a certain niche in her profession, she will be held to the minimum standard of that specialty.

   Example: An M.D. who holds herself out as an ophthalmologist must perform to the level of the minimally competent ophthalmologist, not merely to the minimum level of the internist or general practitioner.

3. **Minimally qualified member:** It is not enough for P to prove that D performed with less skill than the ***average*** member of the profession. D must be shown to have lacked the skill level of the ***minimally qualified member*** in good standing.

   a. **Novice:** One who is just ***beginning*** the practice of his special profession is held to the same level of competence as a member of the profession generally.

      Example: A lawyer who has just passed the bar does not get the benefit of a lower standard — he must perform at the level of minimally competent lawyers generally, not novices.

4. **Community standards:** Traditionally, doctors and other professionals have been bound by the professional standards prevailing in the ***community in which they practice***, not by a national standard.

   a. **Change in rule:** But this rule is on its way out, and many if not most courts would today apply a ***national*** standard. In "modern" courts, P may therefore use expert testimony from an expert who practices outside of D's community.

5. **Informed consent:** In the case of a physician, part of the professional duty is to adequately disclose the ***risks*** of proposed treatment to the patient in advance. The rule requiring adequate disclosure is called the rule of ***"informed consent."*** The doctor must disclose to the patient all risks inherent in the proposed treatment which are sufficiently ***material*** that a reasonable patient ***would take them into account*** in deciding whether to undergo the treatment. Failure to get the patient's adequate consent is deemed a form of malpractice and thus a form of negligence. (In some cases, usually older ones, failure to get informed consent transforms the treatment into battery.)

V. AUTOMOBILE GUEST STATUTES

A. **Generally:** A minority of states still have "automobile guest statutes" on their books. These generally provide that an owner-driver is not liable for any injuries received by his ***non-paying passenger***, unless the driver was grossly negligent or reckless.

VI. VIOLATION OF STATUTE (NEGLIGENCE *PER SE*)

A. **"Negligence *per se*" *doctrine:*** Most courts apply the ***"negligence per se"*** doctrine: when a safety statute has a sufficiently close application to the facts of the case at hand, an unexcused ***violation*** of that statute by D is "negligence *per se*," and thus ***conclusively establishes that D was negligent.***

   Example: D drives at 65 m.p.h. in a 55 m.p.h. zone. While so driving, he strikes and injures P, a pedestrian. Because the 55 m.p.h. limit is a safety measure designed to protect against accidents, the fact that D has violated the statute without excuse conclusively establishes that D was negligent — D will not be permitted to argue that it was in fact safe to drive at 65 m.p.h.

1. **Ordinances and regulations:** In virtually all states, the negligence *per se* doctrine applies to the violation of a ***statute***. Where the violation is of an ***ordinance*** or ***regulation***, courts are split about whether the doctrine should apply.

B. Statute must apply to facts: The negligence *per se* doctrine will apply only where P shows that the statute was intended to guard against the ***kind of injury*** in question.

1. **Protection against particular harm:** This means that the statute must have been intended to protect against the ***particular kind of harm*** that P seeks to recover for.

   Example: A statute requires that when animals are transported, each breed must be kept in a separate pen. D, a ship operator, violates the statute by herding P's sheep together with other animals. Because there are no pens, the sheep are washed overboard during a storm. P cannot use the negligence *per se* doctrine, because the statute was obviously intended to protect only against spread of disease, not washing overboard. [*Gorris v. Scott*]

2. **Class of persons protected:** Also, P must be a member of the ***class of persons*** whom the statute was ***designed to protect***.

   Example: A statute requires all factory elevators to be provided with a certain safety device. The legislative history shows that the purpose was only to protect injuries to employees. P, a business visitor, is injured when the elevator falls due to lack of the device. P cannot use the negligence *per se* doctrine, because he was not a member of the class of persons whom the statute was designed to protect.

3. **Excuse of violation:** The court is always free to find that the statutory violation was ***excused***, as long as the statute itself does not show that no excuses are permitted.

   a. **Typical reasons:** Some typical reasons for finding D's violation to be excused are:

      [a] D was reasonably ***unaware*** of the ***"factual circumstances"*** that made the statute applicable;

      Example: A statute prohibits any contractor from doing excavation within 10 feet of a high-voltage power line. D, a contractor, excavates within 6 feet of such a line. However, D reasonably fails to realize that the line is present because it is obscured by heavy foliage. D knocks down the line, injuring P, a bystander.

      Because D neither knew nor should have known of "the factual circumstances" that made the statute applicable to his particular excavation session, the negligence per se doctrine will not apply to his conduct.

      [b] D made a reasonable and diligent ***attempt*** to comply;

      [c] The violation was due to the ***confusing way*** the requirements of the statute were ***presented to the public***;

      Example: A road sign on Main St. says "No Left Turn." The sign is placed just before two roads turn off of Main St., Maple and Oak. A reasonable driver could be confused about whether the sign means that left turns are prohibited onto Maple, Oak, or both. D, reasonably believing that the sign applies to Maple but not to Oak, turns left onto Oak, and collides with P. D would not be subject to liability under negligence per se, because the confusing nature of the sign would excuse his non-compliance.

[d] Compliance would have involved a ***greater risk of harm.***

4. **Contributory negligence *per se* :** If the jurisdiction recognizes ***contributory negligence***, D may get the benefit of contributory negligence *per se* where P violates a statute.

   Example: Cars driven by P and D collide. If P was violating the speed limit, and the jurisdiction recognizes contributory negligence, D can probably use the negligence *per se* doctrine to establish that P was contributorily negligent.

5. **Compliance not dispositive:** The fact that D has ***fully complied*** with all applicable safety statutes does not by itself establish that he was *not* negligent — the finder of fact is always free to conclude that a reasonable person would take precautions beyond those required by statute.

VII. PROCEDURE IN JURY TRIALS

A. Burden of proof: In a negligence case (as in almost all tort cases) P bears the "burden of proof." This is actually two distinct burdens:

1. **Burden of production:** First, P must ***come forward*** with some evidence that P was negligent, that P suffered an injury, that D's negligence proximately caused the injury, etc. This burden is known as the ***"burden of production."*** This burden shifts from P to D, and perhaps back again during the trial.

2. **Burden of persuasion:** Second, P bears the ***"burden of persuasion."*** This means that as the case goes to the jury, P must convince the jury that it is ***more probable than not*** that his injuries are due to D's negligence.

B. Function of judge and jury

1. **Judge decides law:** The judge decides all questions of ***law***. Most importantly, the judge decides whether reasonable people could differ as to what the facts of the case are; if reasonable people could not differ, the judge will direct a verdict.

   Example: In a car accident case, if the judge decides that D drove so fast that no reasonable person could believe that D acted non-negligently, the judge will take this issue away from the jury. That is, the judge will tell the jury that they *must* find D negligent.

2. **Jury decides facts:** The jury is the finder of the ***facts***. In a negligence case (assuming that the judge does not direct a full or partial verdict), the jury decides: (a) what really happened; and (2) whether D breached his duty to P in a way that proximately caused P's injuries. This means that it is the jury that usually decides whether D's conduct satisfied the "reasonable person" standard.

VIII. *RES IPSA LOQUITUR* — CREATING AN INFERENCE OF NEGLIGENCE

A. Generally: The doctrine of *res ipsa loquitur* ("the thing speaks for itself") allows P to point to the fact of the accident, and to create an ***inference*** that, even without a precise showing of how D behaved, D was probably negligent.

Example: A barrel of flour falls on P's head as he walks below a window on the street. At trial, P shows that the barrel fell out of a window of D's shop, and that barrels do not fall out of windows without some negligence. By use of the *res ipsa loquitur* doctrine, P has presented enough evidence to justify a verdict for him, so unless D comes up with rebuttal evidence that the barrel did not come from his shop or was not dropped by negligence, D will lose. [*Byrne v. Boadle*]

B. Requirements for: Courts generally impose four requirements for the *res ipsa* doctrine:

1. **No direct evidence of D's conduct:** There must be ***no direct evidence*** of ***how D behaved*** in connection with the event.

2. **Seldom occurring without negligence:** P must demonstrate that the harm that occurred ***does not normally occur*** except through the negligence of someone. P only has to prove that ***most of the time***, negligence is the cause of such occurrences.

   Example: If an airplane crashes without explanation, P will generally be able to establish that airplanes usually do not crash without some negligence, thus meeting this requirement.

3. **Negligence most likely by D ("exclusive control"):** P must demonstrate that the negligence was ***probably that of the defendant.*** Sometimes, courts say that the instrumentality that caused the harm must be shown to have been at all times within the "***exclusive control***" of D.

   Example: P, while walking on the sidewalk next to D hotel, is hit by a falling armchair. Without more proof, P has not satisfied the requirement that any negligence was most probably by D (in some courts, the requirement of "exclusive control"), because a guest, rather than the hotel, may well have had control of the chair at the moment it was dropped. [Cf. *Larson v. St. Francis Hotel*]

   a. **Not always required:** But not all courts require P to show that the instrumentality was under D's exclusive control, and the Third Restatement has dropped this requirement.

   b. **Multiple defendants:** If there are ***two or more defendants***, and P can show that at least one of the defendants was in control, some cases allow P to recover. This is especially likely where all of the Ds participate together in an integrated relationship.

   Example: P is injured while on the operating table, and shows that either the surgeon, the attending physician, the hospital, or the anesthesiologist must have been at fault, but is unable to show which one. P gets the benefit of *res ipsa*, and it is up to each individual defendant to exculpate himself. [*Ybarra v. Spangard*]

4. **Not due to plaintiff:** P must establish that the accident was probably not due to his ***own*** conduct.

5. **Evidence more available to D:** Some courts also require that ***evidence*** of what really happened be ***more available to D*** than to P.

   Example: This requirement is satisfied on the facts of *Ybarra*, *supra*, since the Ds obviously knew more than the unconscious patient about who was at fault.

C. **Expert testimony:** As noted, plaintiff has to to show that the type of accident is one that does not normally happen in the absence of negligence by someone, as well as that more likely than not the negligence was probably that of the defendant(s). If the facts are complex or involve ***specialized knowledge*** (e.g., ***technology***), insight into whether the accident would probably have happened without negligence may be ***beyond the expertise of the jury***. In this scenario, most courts today ***allow*** the plaintiff to ***use expert testimony*** to establish these preconditions for *res ipsa*.

1. **Medical malpractice:** Thus expert testimony to show that the requirements for *res ipsa* are satisfied is often allowed in ***medical malpractice*** cases, for instance.

   Example: The three Ds are all members of a surgical team that operates on P's back. P gets a serious infection at the surgical site, and sues on a *res ipsa* theory. *Held*: P may offer expert testimony by other doctors that this sort of surgical-site infection doesn't generally happen without negligence, and that usually the surgical-team members are the ones in control of what infection-control measures are used. [*Sides v. St. Anthony's Medical Ctr*]

D. **Effect of *res ipsa*:** Usually, the effect of *res ipsa* is to permit an inference that D was negligent, even though there is no direct evidence of negligence. *Res ipsa* thus allows a particular kind of circumstantial evidence. When *res ipsa* is used, P has ***met his burden of production***, and is thus entitled to go to the jury.

E. **Rebuttal evidence:**

1. **General evidence of due care:** If D's rebuttal is merely in the form of evidence showing that he was ***in fact careful***, this will almost never be enough to give D a directed verdict — the case will still go to the jury.

2. **Rebuttal of *res ipsa requirements:*** But if D's evidence directly disproves one of the requirements for the doctrine's application, then D will get a directed verdict (assuming there is no prima facie case apart from *res ipsa*).

   Example: If, in a state that requires exclusive control by D, D can show that the instrument that caused the harm was not within his control at all relevant times, the doctrine will not apply, and D may get a directed verdict.

F. **Typical contexts:** Here are a couple of contexts in which the *res ipsa* issue is especially likely to arise:

1. **Airplane accidents:** A commercial ***airplane*** accident in which the plane ***crashes into an obstruction*** like a mountain, often furnishes a good illustration of *res ipsa*.
   a. ***Res ipsa*** **applies:** Today, airplanes don't usually fly into obstructions without someone's negligence, at least in clear weather. Therefore, the estate of a dead passenger will normally be deemed to have established negligence merely by showing that the plane crashed into an obstruction in good weather.
      i. **Rebuttal:** But the airline is always free to try to ***rebut*** the evidence, such as by showing that an unforeseeable explosion caused the airplane to veer off course into the obstruction.
2. **Car accidents:** Plaintiffs often attempt to apply *res ipsa* to ***car accidents***. The analysis varies sharply with whether there are multiple vehicles involved or just one.
   a. **Multiple vehicles:** *Res ipsa* usually does ***not*** apply to car crashes involving ***multiple vehicles.*** In most multi-vehicle crashes, it generally cannot be said that that type of accident does not happen without someone's negligence. Furthermore, even if someone's negligence were probable, usually the negligence of persons other than the defendant (e.g., the plaintiff, driving in a separate car) cannot be sufficiently eliminated by the evidence.
   b. **Single-car accident:** On the other hand, if the accident is a ***single-vehicle one*** (e.g., between a driver and a pedestrian), then *res ipsa* will often ***apply***, since such accidents usually involve driver negligence.

      Example: P, a pedestrian walking along the road, is struck from the rear by D's car. P is probably entitled to use *res ipsa* to create an inference of D's negligence, since such accidents usually involve driver negligence.
      i. **Rebuttal evidence:** But D is always free to come up with evidence ***rebutting*** the *res ipsa* inference of negligence (e.g., that D had an unforeseeable heart attack just before the accident, or, in the above example, that P veered directly in front of D just before the accident).

CHAPTER 6

ACTUAL AND PROXIMATE CAUSE

I. CAUSATION IN FACT

A. Generally: P must show that D's conduct was the ***"cause in fact"*** of P's injury.

B. "But for" test: The vast majority of the time, the way P shows "cause in fact" is to show that D's conduct was a ***"but for"*** cause of P's injuries — ***had D not acted negligently, P's injuries would not have resulted.***

Example: P takes her prescription for a medication to D, her local pharmacy. D mistakenly fills the prescription by giving P pills containing 30 mg of the active ingredient rather than the 20 mg called for by the prescription. After taking the pills, P suffers serious heart arrhythmia, and sues D for this harm. P can recover only if she proves that had D provided the correct, 20 mg, pills, P would not have suffered the arrhythmia. In other words, for P to recover, the trier of fact must be satisfied that the wrong pills were the "but for" cause of P's arrhythmia.

1. **Joint tortfeasors:** There can be ***multiple*** "but for" causes of an event. D1 cannot defend on the grounds that D2 was a "but for" cause of P's injuries — as long as D1 was also a "but for" cause, D1 is viewed as the "cause in fact."

C. Concurrent causes: Sometimes D's conduct can meet the "cause in fact" requirement even though it is *not* a "but for" cause. This happens where two events ***concur*** to cause harm, and either one would have been sufficient to cause substantially the same harm without the other. ***Each*** of these concurring events is deemed a cause in fact of the injury, since it would have been sufficient to bring the injury about.

Example: Sparks from D's locomotive start a forest fire; the fire merges with some other unknown fire, and the combined fires burn P's property. Either fire alone would have been sufficient to burn P's property. Therefore, D's fire is a cause in fact of P's damage, even though it is not a "but for" cause. *Kingston v. Chicago & N.W. Ry.*]

D. Proof of actual cause — generally: The plaintiff bears the burden of proving that the defendant's conduct was the cause in fact of his injury, just as he must bear the burden of proving the other parts of his *prima facie* case. However, he must demonstrate this actual causation merely by a ***preponderance of the evidence.***

1. **Proof of "cause in fact" aspect:** Thus the plaintiff does not have to prove with absolute certainty that had it not been for the defendant's conduct, the injury would not have occurred. All he has to do is to show that it is ***probable*** (***more likely than not***) that the injury would not have occurred without the defendant's act.

E. Actual cause – the "value of a chance" problem: We just saw (in Par. 1 immediately above) that P normally has to show that it's "more likely than not" that D's act was a cause in fact of the injury to P. But now, let's consider the ***converse*** situation, in which P definitely suffered an injury, but there is a ***less than 50/50 chance*** that D caused that injury. In this scenario, application of the traditional "more likely than not" requirement for recovery would mean that P would ***recover $0.*** Do modern courts strictly apply this often-harsh requirement? The answer is generally ***"yes,"*** except for one special case (medical malpractice), which we discuss in Par. 2 below.

1. **The traditional rule:** Thus outside of the special medical-malpractice scenario, if the plaintiff proves that there is a substantial but less than 50/50 chance that the defendant negligently caused the (undisputed) injury, the plaintiff is ***completely out of luck — she recovers $0.***

2. **The medical malpractice scenario:** But there is one ***exception*** to the general rule that where P proves a real but less than 50/50 chance that D caused her harm P recovers nothing. The exception arises in the area of ***medical malpractice***. A patient who proves that the treatment she received from her doctor failed to conform to the reasonable standard of care owed by physicians may recover for medical malpractice, a special type of negligence action. Now, suppose that the nature of the malpractice is that the physician failed to provide a ***timely diagnosis or***

treatment of the patient's disease, and that this delay caused the patient to ***die or suffer a worse medical outcome.*** Suppose further that had the treatment or diagnosis been done promptly and without negligence, there is a real, ***but less than 50/50,*** chance that either the bad outcome would have been delayed, or the patient would have been cured.

a. **Traditional approach denies recovery:** Notice that if the traditional approach is applied, P would be deemed to have failed to prove by the required "preponderance of the evidence" standard (i.e., more likely than not) that D was the cause in fact of her harm, so she would recover nothing. And indeed, a ***substantial minority*** of states still apply this traditional approach.

b. **The "value of a chance" doctrine:** But a ***majority*** of the states that have considered the problem in the last couple of decades have ***declined to follow the traditional rule*** denying all recovery, and instead allow plaintiff P who shows a less than 50/50 chance that prompt-and-appropriate treatment would have avoided the bad outcome to recover for a ***special type of injury,*** namely ***the loss of the opportunity for a better outcome,*** rather than the death or worse outcome. This approach is commonly called the ***"loss of a chance" approach***. Thus in these majority states, P is permitted to recover an amount equal to:

> the ***value the claim would have had*** if the injury was proved more likely than not to have been caused by the malpractice
>
> *times*
>
> the ***percentage chance that a favorable result would have occurred*** had there been no malpractice.

Example: When P begins having some initial symptoms of a stroke, he seeks treatment at D, a physicians' group. D negligently fails to give P timely and adequate stroke-prevention care. P suffers a catastrophic stroke that results in permanent brain damage. Medical evidence demonstrates that in *one-third* of the cases where the patient has initial stroke symptoms like P's, proper and prompt treatment enables the patient to suffer no or reduced stroke complications thereafter. P sues D in Oregon state court to recover for value of this "loss of a chance at recovery." D counters that because P cannot prove that it's "more likely than not" that prompt treatment would have prevented the brain damage, P is not entitled to any recovery at all.

Held (by the Oregon Supreme Court), for P. A "limited loss-of-chance" theory of recovery should be recognized in negligence cases involving medical malpractice in Oregon. Under this theory, "a plaintiff who demonstrates that a physician's negligence reduced his chance of a favorable medical outcome from 33% to 0% [can] recover damages based on the unfavorable medical consequences suffered, but only to the possible extent of ***33% of the damages*** resulting from the adverse medical outcome." [*Smith v. Providence Health & Services*]

F. Multiple fault: If P can show that each of two (or more) defendants was at fault, but only one could have caused the injury, the ***burden shifts*** to each defendant to show that the other caused the harm.

Example: P, D1 and D2 go hunting together. D1 and D2 simultaneously fire negligently, and P is struck by one of the shots. It is not known who fired the fatal shot. The court will put the burden on each of the Ds to show that it was the other shot which hit P — if neither D can make this showing, both will be liable. [*Summers v. Tice*]

1. **The "market share" theory:** In ***product liability*** cases, courts often apply the ***"market share"*** theory. If P cannot prove which of three or more persons caused his injury, but can show that all produced a defective product, the court will require each of the Ds to pay that percentage of P's injuries which that D's sales bore to the total market sales of that type of product at the time of injury. The theory is used most often in cases involving prescription drugs.

   Example: 200 manufacturers make the drug DES. P shows that her mother took the drug during pregnancy, and that the drug caused P to develop cancer. P cannot show which DES manufacturer produced the drug taken by her mother. *Held*, any manufacturer who cannot show that it could not have produced the particular doses taken by P's mother will be liable for the proportion of any judgment represented by that manufacturer's share of the overall DES market. [*Sindell v. Abbott Laboratories*]

   a. **Exculpation:** Courts are split on whether each defendant should be allowed to ***exculpate*** itself by showing that it ***did not make*** the particular items in question — some more modern cases hold that once a given defendant is shown to have produced drugs for the national market, no exculpation will be allowed.

G. Increased risk, not yet followed by actual damage: Where D's conduct has increased the ***risk*** that P will suffer some later damage, but the damage has ***not yet occurred***, most courts ***deny*** P any recovery for that later damage unless he can show that it is more likely than not to occur eventually. But some courts now allow recovery for such damage, discounted by the likelihood that the damage will occur.

II. PROXIMATE CAUSE GENERALLY

A. General: Even after P has shown that D was the "cause in fact" of P's injuries, P must still show that D was the ***"proximate cause"*** of those injuries. The proximate cause requirement is a ***policy determination*** that a defendant, even one who has behaved negligently, should not automatically be liable for ***all*** the consequences, no matter how ***improbable*** or ***far-reaching***, of his act. Today, the proximate cause requirement usually means that D will not be liable for the consequences that are very ***unforeseeable***.

Example: D, driving carelessly, collides with a car driven by X. Unbeknownst to D, the car contains dynamite, which explodes. Ten blocks away, a nurse who is carrying P, an infant, is startled by the explosion, and drops P. P will not be able to recover against D, because the episode is so far-fetched — it was so unforeseeable that the injury would occur from D's negligence — that courts will hold that D's careless driving was not the "proximate cause" of P's injuries.

1. **Multiple proximate causes:** Just as an occurrence can have many "causes in fact," so it may well have more than one proximate cause.

   Example: Each of two drivers drives negligently, and P is injured. Each driver is probably a proximate cause of the accident.

III. PROXIMATE CAUSE — FORESEEABILITY

A. **The foreseeability rule generally:** As the idea is traditionally stated, D is generally liable only for those consequences of his negligence which were ***reasonably foreseeable*** at the time she acted.

   Example: D's ship spills oil into a bay. Some of the oil adheres to P's wharf. The oil is then set afire by some molten metal dropped by P's worker, which ignites a cotton rag floating on the water. P's whole dock then burns. *Held*, D is not liable, because the burning of P's dock was not the foreseeable consequence of D's oil spill, and thus the oil spill was not the proximate cause of the damage. This is true even though the burning may have been the "direct" result of D's negligence. [*Wagon Mound No. 1*]

   1. **Third Restatement:** The Third Restatement applies the same basic concept as the above "foreseeability" principle, but formulates it slightly differently: a defendant is "not liable for harm ***different from the harms whose risk made the [defendant's] conduct tortious.***"

      Example 1: Consider the above example of the oil spill that catches fire. The Third Restatement would presumably agree with the result in the above example: what made D's oil spill tortious was that it was a nuisance (and perhaps a trespass) that risked junking up the wharf with a foreign substance. The risk of a fire from the spill was *not* one of the risks that made the spill tortious, so D isn't liable for it.

      Example 2: D gives a loaded pistol to X, an 8-year-old, to carry across the room and put in a cabinet. While X is carrying the pistol, he drops it. The gun lands on the bare foot of P, X's playmate, and because of its one-pound weight breaks P's toe.

      Under the Third Restatement's "harms that made D's conduct tortious" test, D would not be liable to P, since what made the entrustment of the gun by D to a child negligent was the risk of *shooting* (including a shooting caused by dropping of the gun), not the risk of a foot injury from the weight of the gun if the gun was dropped.

B. **Function of judge and jury:** Is it the ***judge*** or the ***jury*** who decides the issue of proximate cause? The answer is that *both* the judge and the jury participate in deciding this issue, but they participate in different ways.

   1. **Judge formulates the legal rule:** It is up to the ***judge*** to ***formulate the appro-***

priate legal rule in the form of an instruction to the jury.

a. **Judge's "gatekeeper" function:** Although the judge doesn't make the factual determination of whether D proximately caused P's injuries, the judge exercises an important ***"gatekeeper"*** function. That is, the judge can and should ***prevent the case from ever being decided by the jury,*** if the judge decides that ***no reasonable jury could find that the plaintiff has established each element of her prima facie case*** by the required preponderance of the evidence.

Therefore, if the judge decides that on the proof offered by the plaintiff, ***no reasonable jury could decide that it is more likely than not that the defendant proximately caused the plaintiff's injuries***, the ***judge will decide the case*** in favor of the defendant on a motion for summary judgment or for a directed verdict — the jury will ***never get a chance to decide*** whether D proximately caused P's injuries.

2. **Factual determination left to the jury:** But in most negligence cases, the judge will ***not exercise*** her right to ***short-circuit the case*** by taking the decision on proximate cause away from the jury. That is, usually the judge will decide that a reasonable jury could ***go either way*** on this issue; in that case, the judge will instruct the jury on the test for determining proximate cause, and ***will leave it to the jury to apply that test in deciding the factual issue*** of whether the defendant's failure to use due care was so tenuously connected with the harm that proximate cause should be found lacking.

C. **Unforeseeable plaintiff:** The general rule that D is liable only for foreseeable consequences is also usually applied to the ***"unforeseeable plaintiff"*** problem. That is, if D's conduct is negligent as to X (in the sense that it imposes an unreasonable risk of harm upon X), but not negligent as to P (i.e., does not impose an unreasonable risk of harm upon P), P will not be able to recover if through some fluke he is injured.

Example: X, trying to board D's train, is pushed by D's employee. X drops a package, which (unknown to anybody) contains fireworks, which explode when they fall. The shock of the explosion makes some scales at the other end of the platform fall down, hitting P.

Held, P may not recover against D. D's employee may have been negligent towards X (by pushing him), but the employee's conduct did not involve any foreseeable risk of harm to P, who was standing far away. Since D's conduct did not involve an unreasonable risk of harm to P, and the damage to her was not foreseeable, the fact that the conduct was unjustifiably risky to X is irrelevant. D's conduct was not the "proximate cause" of the harm to P. *Palsgraf v. Long Island R.R. Co.*]

D. **Extensive consequences from physical injuries:** A key ***exception*** to the general rule that D is liable only for foreseeable consequences is: once P suffers any foreseeable impact or injury, even if relatively minor, D is liable for ***any additional unforeseen physical consequences***.

1. **Egg-shell skull:** Thus if P, unbeknownst to D, has a very ***thin skull*** (a skull of

"egg-shell thinness"), and D negligently inflicts a minor impact on this skull, D will be liable if, because of the hidden skull defect, P dies. The defendant ***"takes his plaintiff as he finds him."***

E. General class of harm but not same manner: Another exception to the "foreseeable consequences only" rule is that as long as the harm suffered by P is of the ***same general sort*** that made D's conduct negligent, it is irrelevant that the harm occurred in an ***unusual manner***.

Example: D gives a loaded pistol to X, an eight-year-old, to carry to P. In handing the pistol to P, X drops it, injuring the bare foot of Y, his playmate. The fall sets off the gun, wounding P. D is liable to P, since the same general kind of risk that made D's conduct negligent (the risk of accidental discharge) has materialized to injure P; the fact that the discharge occurred in an unforeseeable manner — by the dropping of the gun — is irrelevant. (But D is not liable to Y, since Y's foot injury was not foreseeable, and the risk of it was not one of the risks that made D's conduct initially negligent.)

F. Plaintiff part of foreseeable class: Another exception to the foreseeability rule: the fact that injury to the particular plaintiff was not especially foreseeable is irrelevant, as long as P is a ***member of a class*** as to which there was a general foreseeability of harm.

Example: D negligently moors its ship, and the ship breaks away. It smashes into a draw bridge, causing it to create a dam, which results in a flood. The Ps, various riparian owners whose property is flooded, sue. *Held*, these owners can recover against D, even though it would have been hard to foresee which particular owners might be flooded. All of the Ps were members of the general class of riverbank property owners, as to which class there was a risk of harm from flooding. [*Petition of Kinsman Transit Co.*]

IV. PROXIMATE CAUSE — INTERVENING CAUSES

A. Definition of "intervening cause": Most proximate cause issues arise where P's injury is precipitated by an ***"intervening cause."*** An intervening cause is a force which takes effect ***after*** D's negligence, and which contributes to that negligence in producing P's injury.

1. **Superseding cause:** Some, but not all, intervening causes are sufficient to prevent D's negligence from being held to be the proximate cause of the injury. Intervening causes that are sufficient to prevent D from being negligent are called ***"superseding"*** causes, since they supersede or cancel D's liability.

B. Foreseeability rule: Generally courts use a ***foreseeability*** rule to determine whether a particular intervening cause is superseding.

1. **Test:** If D should have ***foreseen*** the possibility that the intervening cause (or one like it) might occur, *or* if the ***kind of harm*** suffered by P was foreseeable (even if the intervening cause was not itself foreseeable), D's conduct will nonetheless be the proximate cause. But if *neither* the intervening cause nor the kind of harm was foreseeable, the intervening cause will be a superseding one, relieving D of liabil-

ity.

C. Foreseeable intervening causes: Often the risk of a particular kind of intervening cause is the ***very risk*** (or one of the risks) which made D's conduct negligent in the first place. Where this is the case, the intervening cause will almost never relieve D of liability.

Example: D leaves his car keys in the ignition, and the car unlocked, while going into a store to do an errand. X comes along, steals the car, and while driving fast to get out of the neighborhood, runs over P. If the court believes that the risk of theft is one of the things that makes leaving one's keys in the ignition negligent, the court will almost certainly conclude that X's intervening act was not superseding.

1. **Foreseeable negligence:** The ***negligence of third persons*** may similarly be an intervening force that is sufficiently foreseeable that it will not relieve D of liability.

   Example: D is a tavern owner, who serves too much liquor to X, knowing that X arrived alone by car. D also does not object when X gets out his car keys and leaves. If X drunkenly runs over P, a court will probably hold that X's conduct in negligently (drunkenly) driving, although intervening, was sufficiently foreseeable that it should not absolve D of liability.

2. **Criminally or intentionally tortious conduct:** A third person's ***criminal conduct***, or ***intentionally tortious acts***, may also be so foreseeable that they will not be superseding. But in general, the court is more likely to find the act superseding if it is criminal or intentionally tortious than where it is merely negligent.

D. Responses to defendant's actions: Where the third party's intervention is a ***"normal" response*** to the defendant's act, that response will generally ***not*** be considered superseding. This is true even if the response was not all that foreseeable.

1. **Escape:** For instance, if in response to the danger created by D, P or someone else attempts to ***escape*** that danger, the attempted escape will not be a superseding cause so long as it was not completely irrational or bizarre.

   Example: D, driving negligently, sideswipes P's car on the highway. P panics, thrusts the wheel to the right, and slams into a railing. Even though most drivers in P's position might not have reacted in such an extreme or unhelpful manner, P's response is not sufficiently bizarre to constitute a superseding cause.

2. **Rescue:** Similarly, if D's negligence creates a danger which causes some third person to attempt a ***rescue***, this rescue will normally not be an intervening cause, unless it is performed in a ***grossly careless*** manner. D may be liable to the ***person being rescued*** (even if part or all of his injuries are due to the rescuer's ordinary negligence), or ***to the rescuer***.

3. **Aggravation of injury by medical treatment:** If D negligently injures P, who then undergoes ***medical treatment***, D will be liable for anything that happens to P as the result of negligence in the medical treatment, infection, etc.

Examples: P is further injured when the ambulance carrying her gets into a collision, or when, due to the surgeon's negligence, P's condition is worsened rather than improved.

a. **Gross mistreatment:** But some results of attempted medical treatment are so ***gross*** and unusual that they are regarded as superseding.

Example: While P is hospitalized due to injuries negligently inflicted by D, a nurse kills P by giving him an injection of morphine which she knows may be fatal, because she wants to spare him from suffering. D is not liable for P's death because the nurse's conduct is so bizarre as to be superseding.

E. **Unforeseeable intervention, foreseeable result:** If an intervention is neither foreseeable nor normal, but leads to the ***same type of harm*** as that which was threatened by D's negligence, the intervention is usually ***not*** superseding.

Example: D negligently maintains a telephone pole, letting it get infested by termites. X drives into the pole. The pole breaks and falls on P. A properly-maintained telephone pole would not have broken under the blow. Even though the chain of events (termite infestation followed by car crash) was bizarre, X's intervention will not be superseding, because the result that occurred was the same general *type* of harm as that which was threatened by D's negligence — that the pole would somehow fall down. [*Gibson v. Garcia*]

F. **Unforeseeable intervention, unforeseeable results:** If the intervention was not foreseeable or normal, and it produced results which are *not* of the same general nature as those that made D's conduct negligent, the intervention will probably be ***superseding***.

1. **Extraordinary act of nature:** Thus an ***extraordinary act of nature*** is likely to be superseding.

Example: Assume that it is negligent to one's neighbors to build a large wood pile in one's back yard, because this may attract termites which will then spread. D builds a large wood pile. An unprecedentedly-strong hurricane sweeps through, takes one of the logs, and blows it into P's bedroom, killing him. The hurricane will probably be held to be a superseding intervening cause, because it was so strong as to be virtually unforeseeable, and the type of harm it produced was not of the type that made D's conduct negligent in the first place.

G. **Dependent vs. independent intervention:** Courts sometimes distinguish between ***"dependent"*** intervening causes and ***"independent"*** ones. A dependent intervening cause is one which occurs only in ***response*** to D's negligence. An independent intervention is one which would have occurred even had D not been negligent (but which combined with D's negligence to produce the harm). Dependent intervening events are probably somewhat more foreseeable on average, and thus somewhat less likely to be superseding, than independent ones. But a dependent cause can be superseding (e.g., a grossly negligent rescue attempt), and an independent intervention can be non-superseding.

H. Third person's failure to discover: A third person's ***failure*** to ***discover and prevent*** a danger will almost never be superseding. For instance, if a manufacturer negligently produces a dangerous product, it will never be absolved merely because some person further down the distribution chain (e.g., a retailer) negligently fails to discover the danger, and thus fails to warn P about it.

1. **Third person does discover:** But if the third person does ***discover*** the defect, and then willfully and negligently fails to warn P, D may escape liability if D took all reasonable steps to remedy the danger.

    Example: D manufactures a machine, and sells it to X. D then learns that the machine may crush the hands of users. D offers to X to fix the machine for free. X declines. P, a worker for X, gets his hand crushed. X's failure to warn P or allow the machine to be fixed by D probably supersedes, and relieves D of liability because D tried to do everything it could.

CHAPTER 7

JOINT TORTFEASORS

I. JOINT LIABILITY

A. Joint-and-several liability generally: If more than one person is a proximate cause of P's harm, and the harm is ***indivisible***, ***each defendant*** is liable for the ***entire harm***. The liability is said to be ***"joint-and-several."***

Example: D1 negligently scratches P. P goes to the hospital, where she is negligently treated by D2, a doctor, causing her to lose her arm. P can recover her entire damages from D1, or her entire damages from D2, though she cannot collect twice.

1. **Modern trend cuts back on joint-and-several liability:** But there has been a very sharp trend in recent decades to ***cut back***, or even completely ***eliminate***, ***joint-and-several liability.*** This has been mainly due to the rise of comparative negligence as a replacement for contributory negligence. (See *infra*, p. 131).

    a. **Few states keep traditional rule:** As of 2000, only 15 jurisdictions maintained pure joint-and-several liability.

    b. **Hybrids:** About 20 states have replaced joint-and-several liability with one of several ***"hybrid"*** schemes that combine aspects of joint-and-several liability with aspects of pure several liability.

    - ❑ **Hybrid joint-and-several liability with reallocation:** The most common hybrid scheme is this: all defendants are jointly-and-severally liable, but if one defendant turns out to be judgment-proof, the court ***reallocates the damages*** to all other parties (including the plaintiff) in proportion to their comparative fault.

        Example: P sues D1, D2 and D3 for an indivisible harm. P's damages are $100,000. The jury concludes that P is 10% responsible, D1

40%, D2 25% and D3 25%. D1 turns out to be judgment-proof. The court will reallocate based on D1's insolvency, so that D2 and D3 are each jointly-and-severally liable for 50/60ths of $100,000 (i.e., $83,333). The effect is that P and the remaining Ds will ***share the burden*** of D1's insolvency in a ratio to their relative fault.

c. **Pure several liability:** 16 states now have ***pure several liability*** — in these states, a defendant, regardless of the nature of the case, is liable only for her share of total responsibility.

B. Indivisible versus divisible harms: Even where the traditional rule of joint and several liability is in force, it applies only where P's harm is ***"indivisible,"*** i.e., not capable of being ***apportioned*** between or among the defendants. If there is a rational basis for apportionment — that is, for saying that some of the harm is the result of D1's act and the remainder is the result of D2's act — then ***each will be responsible only for that directly-attributable harm.***

1. **Rules on apportionment:** Here is a summary of the rules on when harms will or won't be capable of being apportioned:

a. **Action in concert:** If the two defendants can be said to have acted ***in concert***, each will be liable for injuries directly caused by the other. In other words, apportionment does not take place.

Example: D1 and D2 drag race. D1's car swerves and hits P. D2, even though his car was not part of the collision, is liable for the entire injuries caused by D1's collision, because D1 and D2 acted in concert.

b. **Successive injuries:** Courts often are able to apportion harm if the harms occurred in ***successive incidents***, separated by substantial periods of time.

Example: D1, owner of a factory, pollutes P's property from 1970-1990. D1 sells to D2, who pollutes P's property from 1991-2020. The court will apportion the damage — neither defendant will have to pay for damage done by the other.

i. **Consequence of non-apportionability:** If P is harmed in successive incidents involving multiple Ds, courts will usually place the ***burden of allocating the damages*** on the ***Ds***, not on P. In other words, if no one proves how much of P's damages from the two successive torts are reasonably allocated to D1 and how much to D2, the court will typically make the Ds jointly and severally liable, so that the tortfeasors, not the innocent plaintiff, bear the "burden of unallocability."

Example: D1 and D2 each separately pollutes a stream, poisoning P's livestock, and damaging P by $100,000. Neither D (nor P) offers proof allocating the damages as between D1 and D2. A court will likely hold D1 and D2 jointly and severally liable, on the theory that the uncertainty about how damages should be allocated between the two should hurt them, not P.

ii. **Overlapping:** It may be the case that D1 is jointly and severally liable for the harm caused by both her acts and D2's, but that D2 is liable only for his own. This is especially likely where D2's negligence is in ***response*** to D1's.

Example: D1 negligently breaks P's arm. D2 negligently sets the arm, leading to gangrene and then amputation. D1 is liable for all harm, including the amputation. D2 is only liable for the amount by which his negligence worsened the condition — that is, he's liable for the difference between a broken and amputated arm.

c. **Indivisible harms:** Some harms are ***indivisible*** (making each co-defendant jointly and severally liable for the entire harm, in a jurisdiction following the traditional approach to joint liability).

i. **Death or single injury:** Thus the plaintiff's ***death*** or any ***single personal injury*** (e.g., a broken arm) is ***not divisible***.

ii. **Fires:** Similarly, if P's property is ***burned*** or otherwise destroyed, this will be an indivisible result.

Example: D1 and D2 each negligently contribute to the starting of a fire, which then destroys P's house. There will be no apportionment, so D1 and D2 will each be liable for P's full damages in a state applying traditional joint-and-several liability.

C. **One satisfaction only:** Even if D1 and D2 are jointly and severally liable, P is only entitled to a ***single satisfaction*** of her claim.

Example: P suffers harm of $1 million, for which the court holds D1 and D2 jointly and severally liable. If P recovers the full $1 million from D1, she may not recover anything from D2.

II. CONTRIBUTION

A. **Contribution generally:** If two Ds are jointly and severally liable, and one D pays more than his ***pro rata share***, he may usually obtain partial ***reimbursement*** from the other D. This is called ***"contribution."***

Example: A court holds that D1 and D2 are jointly and severally liable to P for $1 million. P collects the full $1 million from D1. In most instances, D1 may recover $500,000 contribution from D2, so that they will end up having each paid the same amount.

1. **Amount:** As a general rule, each joint-and-severally-liable defendant is required to pay an ***equal share***.

a. **Comparative negligence:** But in ***comparative negligence*** states, the duty of contribution is usually ***proportional to fault***.

Example: A jury finds that P was not at fault at all, that D1 was at fault 2/3 and D2 at fault 1/3. P's damages are $1 million. P can probably recover the full sum from either D. But if P recovers the full sum from D1, D1 may recover $333,000 from D2.

B. Limits on doctrine: Most states ***limit*** contribution as follows:

1. **No intentional torts:** Usually an ***intentional*** tortfeasor may ***not*** get contribution from his co-tortfeasors (even if they, too, behaved intentionally).

2. **Contribution defendant must have liability:** The contribution defendant (that is, the co-tortfeasor who is being sued for contribution) must ***in fact be liable*** to the original plaintiff.

   Example: Husband drives a car in which Wife is a passenger. The car collides with a car driven by D. The jury finds that Husband and D were both negligent. Wife recovers the full jury verdict from D. If intra-family immunity would prevent Wife from recovering directly from Husband, then D may not recover contribution from Husband either, since Husband has no underlying liability to the original plaintiff.

C. Settlements:

1. **Settlement by contribution plaintiff:** If D ***settles***, he may then generally obtain contribution from other potential defendants. (Of course, he has to prove that these other defendants would indeed have been liable to P.)

2. **Settlement by contribution defendant:** Where D1 settles, and D2 — against whom P later gets a judgment — sues D1 for contribution, courts are split among two main approaches:

   a. **Traditional rule:** The traditional rule is that D1, the settling defendant, is ***liable*** for contribution. This is a bad approach, because it sharply reduces a defendant's incentive to settle — she knows that if she settles early, she may be dragged back into extra liability in the form of contribution to the non-settling co-defendants.

   b. **"Reduction of P's claim" rule:** Today, most courts deal with this problem by taking two steps. First, they ***deny contribution*** to non-settlers (or later settlers) from the early settler. But second, they ***reduce the amount of P's claim*** against the non-settlers to reflect the earlier settlement. These courts vary in how they do this:

      i. ***Pro tanto*** **reduction:** Some courts reduce P's claim by the ***dollar amount*** of the settlement (***"pro tanto"*** reduction).

      ii. **Proportional reduction:** On the other hand, some reduce it by the ***proportion*** that the settling defendant's responsibility bears to the overall responsibility of all parties (the ***"comparative share"*** approach.

III. INDEMNITY

A. Definition: Sometimes the court will not merely order two joint-and-severally-liable defendants to split the cost (contribution), but will instead completely ***shift*** the responsibility from one D to the other. This is the doctrine of ***"indemnity"*** — a 100% shifting of liability, as opposed to the sharing involved in contribution.

B. Sample situations: Here are two important contexts in which indemnity is often applied:

1. **Vicarious liability:** If D1 is only ***vicariously liable*** for D2's conduct, D2 will be required to indemnify D1.

   Example: Employee injures P. P recovers against Employer on a theory of *respondeat superior*. Employer will be entitled to indemnity from Employee; that is, Employee will be required to pay to Employer the full amount of any judgment that Employer has paid.

2. **Retailer versus manufacturer:** A ***retailer*** who is held strictly liable for selling a defective injury-causing product will get indemnity from others further up the distribution chain, including the ***manufacturer***.

CHAPTER 8

DUTY

I. DUTY GENERALLY

A. Concept: Generally, a person owes everyone else with whom he comes in contact a general ***"duty of care."*** Normally, you don't have to worry about this duty — it is the same in all instances, the duty to behave with the care that would be shown by a reasonable person. But there are several situations in which courts hold that the defendant owes plaintiff ***less*** than this regular duty. The most important of these situations are:

[1] D generally has no duty to take ***affirmative action*** to help P;

[2] D generally has no duty to avoid causing unintended ***mental suffering*** to P; and

[3] D has no duty to avoid causing ***pure economic loss*** to P in the absence of more tangible types of harm such as physical injury.

II. FAILURE TO ACT

A. No general duty to act: A person generally cannot be liable in tort solely on the grounds that she has ***failed to act***.

1. **Duty to protect or give aid:** This means that if D sees that P is in danger, and fails to render assistance (even though D could do so easily and safely), D is ***not liable for refusing to assist***.

   Example: D, passing by, sees P drowning in a pond. D could easily pull P to safety without risk to D, but instead, D walks on by. D is not liable to P.

B. Exceptions: But there are a number of commonly-recognized ***exceptions*** to the "no duty to act" rule:

1. **Special relationship:** A duty to give assistance may arise out of a ***"special relationship"*** between D and P. Here is a list (from the Third Restatement) of relationships that impose such a duty of care:

   [a] the relationship of "a ***common carrier*** with its ***passengers***";

   [b] "an ***innkeeper*** with its ***guests***";

   [c] "a ***business*** or other possessor of land that ***holds its premises open to the public*** with those who are ***lawfully on the premises***";

   Example: P gets his finger stuck in an escalator operated by D, a store where P is a customer. If D does not give P assistance, D will be liable.

   [d] "an ***employer*** with its ***employees***";

   [e] "a ***school*** with its ***students***";

   [f] "a ***landlord*** with its ***tenants***"; and

   [g] "a ***custodian*** with ***those in its custody***, if the custodian is required by law to take custody or voluntarily takes custody of the other and the custodian has a ***superior ability to protect*** the other." (*Example*: The duty of a jailer to a prisoner.)

   a. **Transient or "ad hoc" relationships:** Plaintiffs have sometimes tried to persuade courts to extend the above list of "special relationships" by adding certain ***"ad hoc"*** relationships, i.e., ***transient relationships*** that were formed shortly before the episode in question. But courts have generally ***rejected*** these attempts.

      i. **No relationship based on "witnessing an emergency":** For example, some plaintiffs have argued that the court ought to recognize a special relationship as existing between a ***person who faces a sudden life-threatening injury*** and another person who ***witnesses that injury at close proximity*** and has the ***opportunity to summon help.*** But this argument has generally been ***rejected*** by the courts, on the theory that recognizing this type of relationship as imposing a duty to summon assistance would swallow up the "no duty to assist" general rule, and would present ***no logical stopping point.***

      Example: P and D used to be a couple, but have broken up. P enters D's trailer without permission, shoots himself, and falls to the floor. D finds P, thinks he has merely pretended to shoot himself, and doesn't call 911, though she could do so easily. P dies, and the facts indicate that he could have been saved if D had called 911 as soon as she found him on the floor. P's estate argues that the court should recognize a special relationship as arising whenever a witness discovers an acute injury to another; such a witness should be found to have the limited duty to use due care in summoning assistance.

      Held, for D; the court will not recognize the "witness to an emergency" relationship urged by the estate. The relationship asserted here does not have either of the elements present in other relationships that have been recognized as creating a duty of assistance: (1) it didn't exist prior to the present occasion; and (2) it did not involve a defendant who had control over either the person in peril or the premises where the peril arose. Imposing a duty to contact emergency assistance on anyone who witnesses another's injury would be a "duty without any practical limit." [*Estate of Cilley v. Lane*]

2. **Defendant involved in injury:** If the danger or injury to P is ***due to D's own conduct***, or to an instrument under D's control, D has the duty of assistance. This is true today even if D acted without fault.

   Example: A car driven by D strikes P, a pedestrian. Even though D has driven completely non-negligently, and the accident is due to P's carelessness in crossing the street, D today has a common-law duty to stop and give reasonable assistance to P.

3. **Defendant and victim as co-venturers:** Where the victim and the defendant are engaged in a ***common pursuit***, so that they may be said to be ***co-venturers***, some courts have imposed on the defendant a duty of warning and assistance. For instance, if two friends went on a jog together, or on a camping trip, their joint pursuit might be enough to give rise to a duty on each to aid the other.

4. **Assumption of duty:** Once D ***voluntarily begins*** to render assistance to P (even if D was under no legal obligation to do so), D must ***proceed with reasonable care***.

   a. **Preventing assistance by others:** D is especially likely to be found liable if he begins to render assistance, and this has the effect of ***dissuading others*** from helping P.

      Example: If D stops by the roadside to help P, an injured pedestrian, and other passers-by decline to help because they think the problem is taken care of, D may not then abandon the attempt to help P.

   b. **Mere promise:** Traditionally, a mere ***promise*** by D to help P (without actual commencement of assistance) was *not* enough to make D liable for not following through. But many modern courts would make D liable even in this situation, if P has a reliance interest.

      Example: D promises P that while P is away on a two-week trip, D will visit P's apartment every day and feed P's dog. D then forgets to do this, and the dog is seriously injured. Today, many courts (and the Third Restatement) would say that D is liable to P, because once he made the promise to render the assistance, he was required to fulfill the promise with reasonable care.

5. **Duty to control others:** If D has a duty to ***control third persons***, D can be negligent for failing to exercise that control.

   a. **Special relationship:** A duty to control a third person may arise either because of a special relationship between D and P, or a special relationship between D and a third person. For instance, some courts now hold that any

business open to the public must protect its patrons from wrongdoing by third parties.

Example: D, a storekeeper, fails to take action when X, an obviously deranged man, comes into the store wielding a knife. P, a patron, is stabbed. Most courts would find D liable for failing to take action.

III. MENTAL SUFFERING

A. Pure mental suffering without physical impact or injury: Suppose the defendant's negligence is the cause in fact of intense ***mental suffering*** to the plaintiff, but this suffering has been produced ***without any physical impact*** upon the plaintiff. Does the absence of any physical impact itself bar plaintiff from recovery? As we'll see, the answer is, "not necessarily."

1. Several categories: We'll look at several distinct types of scenarios:

[1] P suffers a physical impact or direct physical injury, and seeks to ***"tack on"*** to her claim a recovery for emotional distress (though this is not one of the "pure emotional distress" scenarios). (See Par. B below.)

[2] P witnesses an accident; she ***never fears*** for the physical safety of either herself or anyone else during the episode, but suffers emotional distress anyway, for which she seeks to recover. (See Par. C below.)

[3] P witnesses an accident or near-accident, and is ***sufficiently close*** to the dangerous event herself that she is for a time in ***danger of immediate bodily harm***. She escapes the bodily harm, but suffers mental distress from the episode. (See Par. D below.)

[4] P witnesses a ***close relative***, X, suffer a serious bodily injury; P never fears for her own physical safety but nonetheless suffers emotional distress (on account of her concern for X's welfare), for which she seeks to recover. (See Par. E below.)

[5] Same as [4], but the person, X, that P witnesses suffer a serious bodily injury is ***not P's close relative***. Again, P suffers emotional distress for which she attempts to recover. (See Par. F below.)

[6] P suffers emotional distress without ever being herself at risk, and without directly witnessing serious injury to anyone else, but because of the ***special relationship*** between P and D (or between D and a third person, X, who suffers injury), for policy reasons the courts allow P to recover for her own emotional distress. (See Par. G below.)

B. Mental distress damages "tacked on" to case with physical injury: First, let's consider a situation that does not really fall into our "pure mental suffering" category, but that we'll want to compare with the various pure-mental-suffering scenarios we'll be considering. This is the situation in which D causes an ***actual physical injury*** to P's person (or to P's property), and P suffers not just physical injuries but, in addition, mental distress arising out of the episode.

1. P may recover: In this scenario, it's always been clear, in all American courts, that ***D is liable*** not only for the physical consequences of the impact but also for virtually ***all the emotional or mental suffering*** that flows naturally from it. This includes fright at the time of the injury, "pain and suffering" stemming from the injury, anxiety about possibility of a repetition, humiliation from disfigurement, etc. The mental distress claim is said to be ***"tacked on"*** to the claim for physical injury.

2. **"Parasitic" damages:** Such "tacked on" damages from mental suffering are often called ***parasitic*** — they "attach" to the claim for physical injury, analogously to the way a parasite attaches to the host. The usual reason for allowing parasitic damages is that the existence of a physical injury to P provides sufficient assurance that ***the claim of suffering is not being feigned***.

C. **Emotional distress, unaccompanied by fear of impact on anyone:** Next, let's look at the scenario which furnishes probably the ***weakest*** case for allowing P to recover: P ***witnesses*** an accident or near-accident caused by D's negligence, but the danger takes place ***far enough*** from P that she ***never fears an imminent impact*** with her own body, or even with the body of anyone else nearby. Nonetheless, P later suffers mental distress from the episode. In this situation, virtually ***no*** American courts will allow P to recover for her emotional distress, even if that distress has physical manifestations.

Example 1: P is walking in New York City's Times Square. Twenty yards ahead of her, she sees a taxi driven by D speed through a red light, lose control, and crash into a storefront, though miraculously neither D nor anyone else is physically injured. At no time does P believe that she or anyone else is likely to be hit by the cab. Nonetheless, P keeps reliving the near-disaster. She develops nightmares, symptoms of PTSD, and an ulcer.

It is unlikely that *any* American court would allow P to recover. As we'll see, there are several exceptions to the general rule against "stand-alone" recovery for negligent infliction of emotional distress. But here, where P never even briefly feared that either she or anyone else was likely to be hit by the cab, none of these exceptions applies.

1. **"Boundless liability" fear:** Courts' universal rejection of a stand-alone distress claim like the one in the above example stems in part from courts' fear that if such claims were allowed, there would be a ***flood of litigation***, with no way for courts to distinguish genuine claims from ***feigned*** ones. For instance, in the above example letting P recover would raise the possibility that hundreds of similarly-situated people walking or riding in Times Square might bring suit, and there would be no line logically dividing those who should recover from those who shouldn't.

D. **P is within the "zone of danger," and suffers distress:** Our next category is where P witnesses an accident or near-accident, and is ***sufficiently close*** to the dangerous event that she herself is at some point in ***danger of immediate bodily harm***. She escapes the bodily harm, but suffers mental distress from the episode. Courts often describe this situation as one in which the plaintiff was ***"within the zone of danger."***

1. **Most courts allow:** In this "zone of danger" scenario, most courts today ***allow*** the plaintiff to recover for her emotional distress, if plaintiff shows that the distress was ***severe***.

2. **Third Restatement allows:** The Third Restatement similarly allows the plaintiff to recover in this zone-of-danger situation: "An actor whose negligent conduct causes ***serious emotional harm*** to another is subject to liability to the other if the conduct: (a) places the other in ***danger of immediate bodily harm*** and the emotional harm results from the danger[.]"

   Example 2: Same facts as Example 1 above. This time, however, when the taxi driven by D goes out of control, P is standing two feet away. She jumps out of the path of the oncoming cab and barely avoids being hit. If P suffers severe mental distress from constantly re-living the near-accident, most courts (and the Third Restatement) will allow her to recover for that distress, because she was within the "zone of danger."

E. P is a "bystander," and sees a close relative suffer bodily injury: Now, let's turn to the first of two categories in which the plaintiff is a ***"bystander"*** who from a position of safety ***watches another person suffer bodily injury*** due to the defendant's negligence. In the present category, the injured third person is a ***close relative of the plaintiff***, such as the plaintiff's ***parent, sibling,*** or ***child***.

As in the above situation illustrated by Example 2 (where the plaintiff was herself within the "zone of danger"), in the present "bystander watching a close relative be injured" scenario, most courts today ***allow the plaintiff to recover*** for her own distress.

1. **Rationales:** There are two rationales for allowing recovery here: (a) we don't have to worry much about ***fraudulent claims***, since it's highly likely that a person who watches a close relative be injured has indeed suffered great distress; and (b) we don't have to worry about a ***flood of claims***, since the number of people suffering a bodily injury from a given tortious event will be limited, and therefore the number of close relatives watching those injuries occur will also be limited.

2. **Third Restatement allows:** Again, the Third Restatement agrees that the plaintiff should be allowed to recover:

   > An actor who negligently causes ***sudden serious bodily injury to a third person*** is subject to liability for serious emotional harm caused thereby to a ***person who***:
   >
   > (a) ***perceives the event contemporaneously***, and
   >
   > (b) is a ***close family member*** of the person suffering the bodily injury.

   Example 3: P is walking with her 6-year-old son, S, in a cross-walk in Times Square. As P watches, horrified, a taxi negligently driven by D jumps a red light and runs over S, killing him instantly. P suffers severe mental distress from watching the accident and re-living it. Most courts (and the Third Restatement) will allow P to recover against D for her own distress. This recovery is entirely separate, conceptually, from S's estate's right to recover for his bodily injury.

3. **Meaning of "close relative":** Courts vary in ***how close the family relationship must be*** between the bystander/plaintiff and the third person who suffers serious bodily harm.

a. Sibling, parent, child or spouse: A bystander who is the ***sibling, parent, child,*** or ***spouse*** of the person who suffers the bodily harm is likely to be found to be sufficiently closely-related that the bystander can recover for distress.

b. More distant relative: But if the relationship is even a little more ***distant***, courts are likely to ***deny*** recovery. Thus one who witnesses the death or serious injury of a ***fiancé***, a ***cohabiting*** significant other, a ***son-in-law***, or an ***aunt*** or ***uncle*** (even one who has raised the child who suffers the bodily injury) is likely to be ***denied recovery***.

4. Perception must be "contemporaneous": Most courts insist that the bystander must ***perceive*** the accident (the bodily harm to the bystander's close relative) ***"contemporaneously."*** In other words, it's not enough that the bystander learns of the accident very soon ***after*** it occurs. So the following two examples produce opposite legal outcomes:

Example 4: P, sitting on his front porch, watches a car negligently driven by D strike, and badly injure, P's 6-year-old son, S, in the street in front of P's house. Because P has "contemporaneously" perceived the physical injury to S, P will be entitled to recover for P's own mental distress.

Example 5: P is sitting in the kitchen of his house, which looks out only into P's backyard. The doorbell rings, and P's next-door neighbor, X, tells P, "I just saw your son S be hit by a car on the street; the ambulance just took S to the hospital." P rushes to the hospital, where he sees S lying badly injured in the ER. In most courts — and under the Third Restatement — P will not be allowed to recover for his emotional distress, because P did not "contemporaneously" perceive the event that caused the harm to P's close relative.

a. Can "perceive" by another sense: Ordinarily, the contemporaneous "perception" will be by ***sight*** — P observes the accident with his eyes. But ***other senses***, such as ***hearing***, may also suffice, as long as the "perception" is "contemporaneous."

Example 6: Same facts as Example 4 above, except that P, while sitting on his front porch, does not have his distance glasses on, and therefore cannot see what is happening in the street with any detail. But P knows that his son S is playing in the street. P then hears the squeal of D's brakes, and hears S's screams after he is run over. P has sufficiently "perceived" (through his sense of hearing) the event that caused the serious bodily harm to S that he will be permitted to recover for his mental distress.

b. Perception that occurs remotely rather than in person: It's not clear whether the contemporaneous perception has to occur ***"in person,"*** as opposed to via some ***remote, electronic means***. For instance, if P is ***video-Skyping*** with X and sees X hit by a car driven by D, has P met the "contemporaneous perception" requirement? There is little if any case law on the issue so far.

5. Bodily harm witnessed must be serious: The bodily harm that the bystander witnesses must generally be ***serious***. So witnessing a close relative's ***death***, significant permanent ***disfigurement***, or l***oss of a body part or function*** will almost always be sufficient. But ***bruises, cuts, single simple fractures***, and ***other injuries that do not require immediate medical treatment*** will ***rarely be sufficient***.

6. **Bodily injury must be "sudden":** The serious bodily harm suffered by the third person in the plaintiff/bystander's presence must occur in a ***"sudden and dramatic manner,"*** according to most courts.

    Example 7: W works for years at a warehouse owned and operated by D. D negligently stores toxic chemicals there, to which W is unwittingly exposed. Over a period of months, W's health gradually deteriorates, and eventually she is left in a coma. Her husband, H, observes the deterioration with horror, and sues D for distress.

    Even though H has been a "bystander" who has directly witnessed the serious bodily harm suffered by his wife, W, a court will probably *not* allow H to recover for distress, because W's bodily harm was not "sudden."

7. **P need not be in "zone of danger" or fear for own safety:** In the bystander scenario, most courts that allow bystander recovery at all do ***not*** require that the ***bystander himself have ever been in the "zone of danger,"*** i.e., at risk of direct physical harm. In other words, as long as the bystander "contemporaneously perceives" the injury to a close relative, the bystander's own lack of physical danger does not ruin the claim.

    Example: Recall Example 4 on p. 111, where P sits on his porch and watches as his son S is struck down by D's car. The fact that P was never in any physical danger himself during the episode does not nullify P's distress claim.

F. P is a "bystander," and sees a non-close-relative be bodily injured: Now, let's consider the other major category in which a bystander might try to recover: the bystander witnesses serious bodily harm to another person, but this time the bystander and the physically-injured person are ***not close relatives***. In this scenario, ***few if any courts allow*** the bystander to recover for mental distress.

1. **Rationale:** This is one of those situations in which courts fear that allowing recovery will produce a ***flood of claims***, with no easy way to determine which ones are genuine, and no way to avoid subjecting the defendant to potentially boundless liability.

    Example 8: Same basic facts as Example 1 on p. 109. Now, however, P sees the runaway cab strike and kill X, a stranger to P. As in Example 1, P is far enough away (20 yards) from the cab that she never fears that she herself will or may be hit by the cab. Virtually all U.S. courts would deny P the right to recover for her mental distress, even if that distress unquestionably stemmed from seeing the accident and resulted in physical manifestations like ulcers. The same fears of boundless liability and false claims that would result in courts' rejection of P's claim in Example 1 would be cited here.

2. **P not within zone of danger:** The fact that the bystander and the physically-injured person are not close relatives makes the most difference when ***the bystander is never within the zone of danger.*** That's because, in most courts, if the bystander *is* himself within the zone of danger, that fact will ***allow*** the

bystander to recover for emotional distress from the entire episode — the court will typically not try to distinguish between distress from the bystander's own narrow escape and distress from the injury to the nearby non-relative.

G. Special relationship or special activity: Finally, there are a few types of ***"special" situations***, scenarios that involve either a ***special activity*** or a ***special relationship among the parties***, such that courts have decided that the general rule against recovery for negligently-inflicted emotional distress should ***not apply*** even though none of the above exceptions to the general no-liability rule applies. In these special categories, courts have concluded that the ***risk*** of emotional harm to the plaintiff is ***so great***, and the ***number*** of affected plaintiffs likely to be so ***small***, that the court should not worry about either feigned distress or a flood of claimants.

1. **Two main categories:** There are two main scenarios that courts have long recognized as being "special categories" where pure emotional harm should be recoverable:

   a. **Mishandling of bodies:** One is the scenario in which a ***hospital or funeral home*** negligently ***mishandles a corpse***, thereby causing emotional distress to a close relative of the deceased.

   Example: Hospital negligently misidentifies a corpse (that of X), causing the corpse to be cremated instead of sent to a funeral home for burial. X's immediate family learns of the error, and suffers great distress because of it. Most courts would allow the family to recover against Hospital.

   b. **Telegrams announcing death or serious illness:** The other is the scenario in which a ***telegraph company*** negligently and incorrectly announces that *A* is dead or seriously ill, and the telegraph is delivered to *B*, *A*'s intimate family member.

2. **Extension to other situations:** In recent decades, courts have often recognized ***other situations*** as calling for allowing an emotional distress claim that does not fall within either of the above categories, or within any of the physical-impact categories we discussed earlier.

   a. **Factors required:** Here are a few examples, taken from actual cases in which the court declined to rule as a matter of law that P may not recover for distress:

   [1] D, a ***medical clinic*** that has run a blood test on P, negligently (and incorrectly) ***informs P that she is HIV positive***;

   [2] D, an ***obstetrician***, negligently mishandles a ***pregnancy*** of P, a patient, leading to a ***stillbirth*** that causes P great emotional harm;

   [3] D, a ***fast food chain***, negligently serves P a hamburger with human blood on the bun.

H. The "at-risk plaintiff": Claims for negligent infliction of purely emotional distress are sometimes raised by ***"at-risk plaintiffs."*** That is, it is often possible to say that a particular plaintiff, by virtue of his exposure to a certain substance, has suffered an ***increased likelihood of a particular disease*** (e.g., cancer). May such a plaintiff recover for the purely emotional harm of being ***distressed*** by this increased likelihood of illness, assuming that there are no symptoms of the illness itself?

1. **"Cancerphobia":** Liability for emotional distress due to future illness is often referred to by the umbrella (and not-always-accurate) term ***"cancerphobia."*** For simplicity, we'll use this term here.

2. **Hard for P to win:** Plaintiffs have ***rarely succeeded i***n recovering for pure cancerphobia, i.e., cases where the plaintiff cannot show that he has actually suffered bodily harm. Courts put various obstacles in the path of cancerphobia plaintiffs — including obstacles summarized in Pars. 3, 4 and 5 below— and it's the rare plaintiff who can overcome all of these obstacles.

3. **Need actual exposure in toxic cases:** Most of the cases raising the issue of recovery for cancerphobia are ***"toxic tort"*** cases, i.e., cases in which the plaintiff has been or may have been exposed to some toxic substance, whether it is the AIDS virus, hazardous environmental waste, or some other damaging substance. In this situation, most courts have insisted, at a minimum, that plaintiff show ***actual exposure*** to the substance, not merely the ***possibility*** of exposure.

   Example: Suppose that D is a physician who has open lesions on his hands and arms, and who examines many patients, including P, while having those lesions. P later learns that at the time D examined her, D knew that he had AIDS. P has not yet developed AIDS, and there is no evidence that she has had HIV virus particles pass into her body. However, P is very frightened that she will develop AIDS from her exposure to D.

   A court would probably hold that P loses on her "fear of AIDS" theory, because she cannot show that she was "actually exposed" to the HIV virus from D. That is, she will lose unless she can show that more probably than not, some virus particles actually passed from D's body into her own.

4. **Some courts require showing of actual illness:** Some courts have gone even further, and have required that the cancerphobic plaintiff show that more probably than not, he will ***actually contract the illness*** that he is frightened of. In other words, fear of a less-than-probable illness, no matter how devastating the illness would be if it occurred, will ***not suffice***, in these courts.

   Example: In such a court, P in the above example would presumably lose unless she showed not only that she was actually exposed to the HIV virus by D but that she had a greater than 50% chance of contracting AIDS.

5. **Need for danger of "immediate" bodily harm:** Another way that courts often make it hard or impossible to recover for emotional harm from fear of future illness is by insisting that the danger of bodily harm be ***"immediate."***

   a. **Third Restatement:** Thus the ***Third Restatement*** denies recovery for cancerphobia. The Restatement's requirement that the plaintiff can't recover unless she was placed in "immediate" physical danger by the defendant's negligence means that under the Restatement, recovery is ***not allowed*** in cancerphobia cases.

6. **Accompanying physical harm:** But always keep in mind that if there is ***some***

physical harm arising from the episode, the emotional distress will *also* be compensable.

Example: Many workers exposed to *asbestos* have developed a lung abnormality known as "pleural thickening." This thickening is not by itself life-threatening, nor does it even directly impair the patient's life. But courts tend to consider as a form of "bodily harm." And it has been statistically linked to a much higher than normal incidence of certain cancers.

A plaintiff who has suffered pleural thickening is likely to be permitted to recover substantial sums from manufacturer of asbestos to which plaintiff was exposed. Such an award would compensate plaintiff not just for his current physical harm from the pleural thickening itself, but also for his distress at knowing that he has a high risk of future harm.

IV. UNBORN CHILDREN

A. Modern view: Most courts have rejected the traditional view that an infant injured in a pre-natal accident could never recover if born alive. Today, recovery for pre-natal injuries varies:

1. **Child born alive:** If the child is eventually ***born alive***, nearly all courts ***allow*** recovery.

   Example: D makes a drug taken by P's mother while P is a fetus only a few weeks old. P is born with serious birth defects resulting from the drug. Nearly all courts would allow P to recover.

2. **Child not born alive:** Courts are ***split*** about whether suit can be brought on behalf of a child who was *not* born alive. Usually, a court will allow recovery only if it finds that a fetus never born alive is a "person" for purposes of the wrongful death statute.

3. **Pre-conception injuries:** The above discussion assumes that the injury occurred while the child was *in utero*. Suppose, however, that the injury occurred before the child was even ***conceived***, but that some effect from the injury is nonetheless suffered by the later-conceived child. Here, courts are ***split*** as to whether the child may recover.

   Example: P's mother, before getting pregnant with P, takes a drug made by D. The drug damages the mother's reproductive system. When P is conceived, P suffers from some congenital disease or defect (e.g., sterility) as a result. P's mother can clearly recover from D for her own injuries, but courts are split as to whether P can recover against D for these pre-conception events. [*Enright v. Eli Lilly*]

4. **Wrongful life:** If a child is born illegitimate, or with an unpreventable congenital disease, the child may argue that it should be entitled to recover for ***"wrongful life,"*** in the sense that it would have been better off aborted. But almost no courts have allowed the child to make such a wrongful life recovery. Courts do, however, often allow the ***parents*** to recover for their medical expenses, and perhaps their emotional distress from the child's condition.

V. PURE ECONOMIC LOSS

A. The problem generally: Suppose that D behaves negligently towards X, in a way that causes X personal injury or property damage. Suppose further that D's conduct also injures P, but P's only loss is ***economic***, not personal injury or property damage. May P recover in tort from D? As we will see, the traditional general answer is ***"no,"*** but there are some important exceptions.

1. **Tacking on of economic loss to personal or property damage:** Before we begin examining the "three party" situation referred to in the prior paragraph, let's first consider a simpler "two party" situation: D behaves negligently towards P, and causes P both personal injury and economic loss. In this situation, all courts agree (and have always agreed) that P, in addition to recovering for his personal injury, ***may "tack on" his intangible economic harm as an additional element of damages***.

   Example: P owns a retail store, which he personally operates. P is injured by the negligence of D, a careless driver who hits P while P is walking. P can of course recover damages for his physical harm (e.g., his medical bills plus pain and suffering). Once P shows that he has suffered physical harm, he will be permitted to "tack on," as an additional element of damages, his loss of profits from being unable to operate the store. In other words, P's suffering of physical harm qualifies him to recover for the full range of damages which he has suffered, including intangible economic ones.

   a. **Property damage:** Similarly, if P suffers ***property damage*** (even if he does not suffer personal injury), this property damage will qualify him to tack on intangible economic loss as well. Thus suppose, on the facts of the above example, that P's car was struck by D's car, and that as a result: (1) P's car was damaged; (2) P himself was not physically injured; and (3) P lost two days of profits at the store because he could not commute to the store. Once P showed that he suffered direct property damage from P's negligence, all courts would allow him to recover his loss-of-business damages, even though those are purely intangible economic losses.

B. Standard rule disallows pure economic losses: Now, let's return to the three-party situation, in which D's negligence causes physical injury or property damage to *X*, but only economic loss to *P*. Nearly all courts agree that ***P may not recover anything for his economic losses***, since he has not suffered any personal injury or property damage. This is true even though D is clearly a tortfeasor (vis-à-vis X), and even though D's negligence has quite clearly, and foreseeably, brought about the injuries to P. As the idea is often put, a person may not recover for unintentionally-caused ***"pure economic loss."***

1. **Restatement 3d follows this rule:** The Third Restatement of Torts follows this general no-recovery principle: apart from a few exceptional circumstances:

   > a claimant cannot recover for ***economic loss*** caused by (a) ***unintentional personal injury to another party***; or (b) ***unintentional injury to property*** in which ***the claimant has no proprietary interest***.

a. Rationales: There are some strong ***policy reasons*** behind this general rule barring recovery for pure economic loss. Here are two of the leading rationales:

b. Indeterminate and disproportionate liability: Most importantly, if courts allow recovery for economic loss that is not accompanied by personal injury or property damage to the plaintiff, the likely result is ***indeterminate and disproportionate liability.***

c. Other ways for claimants to protect themselves: Second, courts reason that the victims of economic injury can often ***protect themselves effectively by means other than a tort suit.*** For instance, they may be able to ***buy insurance*** against their losses.

2. Contexts in which rule is applied: Here are some of the contexts in which the rule barring recovery for pure economic losses is frequently applied:

a. Blocking of highways/streets and thus access to P's business: Where the defendant negligently causes a street, highway or waterway to be closed, business owners whose property is not directly damaged have often sued, seeking recovery for lost business due to customers' inability to get to the owner's premises. Most cases find against the plaintiff, in a straightforward application of the rule denying recovery for negligently-caused pure economic loss.

b. Toxic torts affecting land or water: In another common scenario, the defendant negligently ***spills toxic substances or pollutants*** onto either a waterway or land, and this "toxic tort" interferes with the economic activities of persons or businesses whose person or property are not directly and physically impacted by the spill. Again, most courts apply the general rule to these non-physically-impacted plaintiffs — unless the plaintiff can show that the defendant negligently created a public nuisance, and that the harm suffered by the plaintiff was different in kind from the harms suffered by other businesses in the area, ***the plaintiff may not recover for its "pure economic loss."***

Example: D ("SoCalGas") supplies millions of people with natural gas from various storage facilities including Aliso, a subterranean former oil reservoir. Because natural gas is odorless, D has added a nausea-causing chemical so that people will notice if a leak happened. A leak from Aliso occurs, releasing 55 tons of natural gas every hour. Residents of the nearby community, Porter Ranch, suffer from unpleasant odors, headaches, dizziness, respiratory problems, nosebleeds and vomiting. While the leak is still flowing, the county health department orders D to establish a relocation program available to any Porter Ranch resident who lives within a certain radius (initially, 5 miles) of the leak site. Altogether, about 15,000 people are eventually relocated, to locations dozens or hundreds of miles away.

The Ps, various businesses in the Porter Ranch area, seek to bring a class action consisting of all persons or entities conducting business within 5 miles of the Aliso facility. They allege that the leak was caused by D's negligence, and that the resulting relocation has deprived many area businesses of customers, causing the class-member businesses to suffer lost earnings. But ***none*** of the class member businesses alleges ***personal injury or property damage*** — every class member seeks recovery for "pure economic loss."

Held (by the California Supreme Court), for D. The court applies the general rule that a defendant has ***no tort duty to guard against negligently causing "purely economic losses."*** So class member businesses that have not suffered non-economic (e.g., physical or property damage) injuries cannot recover anything, because D ***did not owe them any duty*** to avoid negligently causing them economic harm. Pure economic losses are "not self-limiting," so allowing recovery for such losses would "threaten liabilities that are ***indeterminate and out of proportion*** to a defendant's culpability." [*Southern California Gas Leak Cases*]

c. Tort against employee or employer causing economic loss to the other: Similarly, if D ***negligently injures P's employee,*** X, P may not recover for P's economic losses stemming from X's unavailability. And the converse is also true – if D negligently damages X, a business, then P, an employee of X who is deprived of work because of the damage to X, ***may not recover lost wages*** from D.

Example: Goalie is a star soccer player with a long-term contract to play for Metro, a professional soccer team. Driver negligently injures Goalie in a car accident, causing Goalie to miss Metro's season. Assume that by the terms of the Goalie-Metro contract, Metro has to pay Goalie his salary for the season despite his unavailability. Even if Metro can demonstrate with near certainty that Goalie's unavailability has cost Metro $1 million in ticket sales for the season, Metro cannot recover anything at all from Driver.

That's because, although Driver's negligence has caused physical injury *to Goalie* (for which Goalie himself can of course recover against Driver), Metro has suffered only economic loss, unaccompanied by personal injury or damage to Metro's "property."

d. Interruption to power or supplies: Similarly, if D's negligence causes an interruption of the ***flow of goods or services*** that are needed for P's business, but there is no contractual relationship between D and P (and no physical damage to P's property), the general rule prevents P from recovering for its losses.

Example: Contractor, doing excavation work on private property two buildings away from P's factory, negligently severs the power lines that serve the factory, putting P's factory out of business for a day. Assume that the power outage does not cause any damage to P's building or equipment. The rule against recovery for pure economic losses prevents P from recovering from Contractor for these losses.

C. Situations that are exceptions or fall outside of the rule: But there are some important situations that are deemed either to fall outside of the scope of the general no-liability-for-pure-economic-loss rule, or to be exceptions to the rule. Two of the more important such situations are (a) where P has a ***"proprietary interest"*** in property that is physically damaged by D's negligence; and (b) where D has created a

"public nuisance," and P has suffered harm from the nuisance that is "different in kind" from that suffered by other nearby persons.

1. **P has a proprietary interest:** Since the general rule we're discussing bars recovery only for "pure" economic loss, it's not surprising that a plaintiff can recover economic-loss damages if the plaintiff can also show that ***"property" in which she has a "proprietary" interest*** was damaged by the D's negligence, leading to the economic loss.

   a. **P owns and possesses the damaged property:** If P both ***owns and possesses*** the tangible property damaged by D's negligence, it's easy to see how P can recover for economic losses that stem directly from the property damage.

   Example: BargeCo, the owner/operator of a barge, negligently spills chemicals into a harbor. The spilled chemicals flow into the innards of a new custom-designed drill owned by Contractor, a building contractor who is using the drill to finish a construction project owned by Owner at the edge of the harbor. Repair of the drill costs Contractor $10,000, and the process takes a month. Contractor also loses $40,000 because the month's delay causes Contractor to forfeit a "timely completion" bonus in that amount that Contractor would have otherwise received from Owner. (No replacement drill was reasonably available to Contractor sooner because of the drill's custom design.)

   Because Contractor suffered direct damage to its tangible property (the drill), Contractor is entitled to recover from BargeCo not only the repair costs, but the intangible economic loss (the $40,000), since that loss stemmed directly from the same negligent act by BargeCo that caused the property damage.

   b. **P has possession but not ownership; the "proprietary" test:** Where P does ***not own*** the property that's physically damaged, but has the right to ***use or possess*** that property, P can recover for economic loss directly resulting from the episode that damages the property if and only if P's arrangement with the owner included at least one (and in some courts both) of the following attributes:

   [1] ***control*** of the property, and

   [2] the responsibility for ***maintaining and repairing*** the property.

   Example 1 (right to recover economic loss): P rents one floor of a building from O. D, a contractor working for O on the exterior of the building, negligently causes a wall to cave in, blocking P's employees from work for two weeks. Most courts would say that P, as the tenant of a floor of the building, had enough control of its part of the premises to be deemed to have a "proprietary" interest in those premises. In such a court, P would be permitted to recover its economic losses (lost production) for the period when its employees couldn't come to work.

   Example 2 (no right to recover economic loss): P is a railroad that, along with two other railroads, has the right to use a bridge owned and maintained by O. A tugboat owed by D negligently damages the bridge, causing P to have to re-route its shipments for several weeks, at greater cost to P.

A court would probably say that although P had a non-exclusive right to use the bridge, P's lack of complete control (and of the obligation to maintain) the bridge prevented P from having the required proprietary interest in the bridge. If the court so concluded, the court would probably bar P from recovering its economic losses from D, under the general rule preventing recovery of pure economic losses.

2. **Public nuisance with special harm:** Courts generally recognize an exception to the no-recovery-for-pure-economic-losses rule if the defendant's actions create a ***public nuisance,*** but only if the type of economic harm suffered by the plaintiff is ***qualitatively different*** from that suffered by other members of the community.

   a. **Taken from law of nuisance:** This "exception" is really a recognition that the tort of public nuisance has special features that sometimes call for a private right of action for pure economic loss. (See *infra*, p. 000, for a more detailed discussion of private rights of action for public nuisances.)

   b. **"Distinct in kind" requirement:** The requirement for private suits that the plaintiff's losses be ***"distinct in kind*** from those suffered by members of the affected community in general" has quite a lot of bite — where the nuisance has some sort of economic impact on a ***significant number of businesses***, a plaintiff generally ***won't be able to meet*** the "distinct in-kind" requirement merely by showing that her losses are of ***greater magnitude*** than those of most other community members. Rather, the plaintiff typically has to show that something about her situation — usually tied to her particular location — makes her losses of a ***"different kind," not just "different magnitude"*** — from other nearby businesses' losses. The following two examples illustrate the kinds of situations that will or won't meet this "different in kind" requirement.

   Example 1 (not different in kind): A building negligently constructed by D collapses, causing street closings that prevent customers of the Ps' (nearby retail stores) from reaching the Ps' premises. The Ps seek to fit within the public-nuisance exception to the no-recovery-for-pure-economic-loss.

   The Ps have ***not*** shown the requisite "special injury beyond that suffered by the community at large." (Even if the Ps can show that their ***dollar losses were greater*** than those of nearly every other person or business in the area, it's unlikely that the court would find that the "different in kind" requirement was satisfied.)

   Example 2 (different in kind): Restaurant is located on the bank of a river. Many of Restaurant's customers arrive by boat and moor their boat at a dock owned and maintained by Restaurant. Logger floats logs down the river, and negligently allows the logs to become stuck on the river bank near Restaurant's dock, so that Restaurant's customers can no longer arrive by boat. (The log blockage is not located at or immediately adjacent to any part of Restaurant's property.) No other person or business is affected by the blockage.

   A court would likely find that Restaurant has suffered the requisite "distinct in kind" harm. If the court so concluded (and if the court also concluded that the stuck logs constituted a public nuisance), the court would allow Restaurant to recover damages for its lost business from logger.

c. **Commercial fishers as a special case:** Some courts allow ***commercial fishers*** to recover their lost business when the defendant wrongfully pollutes the waterway in which the fishers have been fishing. In such suits, the courts typically conclude that the fishers have met the requirement of showing that their harm is "different in kind" from the losses suffered by the community in general.

D. **Special statutes:** The "rule" barring liability for pure economic losses is a judge-made doctrine, and as such can be overruled by a legislature for all or certain scenarios. And, indeed, there are some important contexts in which state and federal ***statutes overturn*** the common-law no-recovery rule.

1. **Oil spills and the OPA:** For instance, Congress has enacted a special statute that in large part reverses the standard no-recovery-for-pure-economic-losses rule for persons who suffer economic loss as the result of an ***oil spill***. This is the ***Federal Oil Pollution Act of 1990 ("OPA")***, 33 U.S.C. § 2702 et seq.

   Example: Suppose Hotel is located near (but not on) a beach that is fouled by an oil spill, and Hotel loses business because customers cancel their visit when they realize they won't be able to use the beaches. Hotel and its employees can probably both recover under OPA.

E. **Other contexts involving pure economic loss:** Here, we've talked about just one aspect of courts' reluctance to award damage to a plaintiff who has suffered only economic loss — the "three party" scenario in which D tortuously causes personal injury or property damage to *A*, but only economic loss to *B*, who nonetheless sues. But there are a number of ***other scenarios*** that similarly raise the issue of whether a plaintiff who has suffered only economic loss may recover, including scenarios in which the defendant has behaved tortiously only to one person (the one who is now bringing suit). These other scenarios — where the court may or may not award liability for pure economic loss — include misrepresentation, products liability, and interference with contract.

CHAPTER 9

OWNERS AND OCCUPIERS OF LAND

I. OUTSIDE THE PREMISES

A. **Effect outside:** There are special rules lowering a landowner's standard of care. However, these rules do not apply to conduct by the landowner that has effects ***outside*** of his property. Therefore, the general ***"reasonable care"*** standard usually applies to such effects.

1. **Natural hazards:** However, if a hazardous condition exists ***naturally*** on the land, the property owner generally has ***no duty*** to remove it or guard against it, even if it poses an unreasonable danger to persons outside the property. But in an

urban or other thickly-settled area, courts are less likely to apply this traditional rule.

Example: O allows a tree to grow in such a way that it may hit a tall truck passing on the roadway. Traditionally, O may not be held liable to the driver of the truck. But in an urban or suburban context, O might be liable.

2. **Artificial hazards:** Where the hazardous condition is ***artificially*** created, the owner has a general duty to prevent an unreasonable risk of harm to persons outside the premises.

II. TRESPASSERS

A. General rule: As a general rule, the landowner owes ***no duty to a trespasser*** to make her land ***safe***, to ***warn*** of dangers on it, to avoid carrying on dangerous activities on it, or to protect the trespasser in any other way.

Example: P trespasses on D railroad's track. His foot gets caught, and he is run over by a train. Even if the reason that P caught his foot was that D negligently maintained the roadbed, P cannot recover because D owed him no duty before discovering his presence. *Sheehan v. St. Paul Ry. Co.*]

B. Exceptions: There are three main ***exceptions*** to the general rule that there is no duty of care to trespassers:

1. **Constant trespass on a limited area:** If the owner has reason to know that a ***limited portion*** of her land is ***frequently used*** by various trespassers, she must use reasonable care to make the premises safe or at least warn of dangers. This is the ***"constant trespass on a limited area"*** exception.

Example: If trespassers have worn a path across a railroad, the railroad must use reasonable care, such as whistles, when traversing that crossing.

2. **Discovered trespassers:** Once the owner has ***knowledge*** that a particular person is trespassing, the owner is then under a duty to exercise reasonable care for the trespasser's safety.

Example: A railroad's engineer must use reasonable care in stopping the train once he sees P trespassing on the tracks.

3. **Children:** The owner owes a duty of reasonable care to a trespassing ***child*** if all of these requirements are met:

[1] the owner knows that the area is one where children are likely to trespass;

[2] the owner has reason to know that the condition poses an unreasonable risk of serious injury or death to trespassing children;

[3] the injured child either does not discover the condition or does not realize the danger, due to his youth;

[4] the benefit to the owner of maintaining the condition in its dangerous form is slight weighed against the risk to the children; and

[5] the owner fails to use reasonable care to eliminate the danger.

Example: O knows that children often swim in a swimming pool on O's land. One part of the pool is unexpectedly deep. It would not cost very much for O to install fencing. P, a child trespasser, walks on the bottom of the pool, panics after suddenly reaching the deep part, and drowns. O is probably liable to P on these facts.

Note: Traditionally, some or all of these elements are summarized by saying that O is liable for maintaining an ***"attractive nuisance."***

a. **Natural conditions:** The court is less likely to find liability where the condition is a ***natural*** one than where it is artificial.

b. **No duty of inspection:** The child trespass rules do not generally impose any ***duty of inspection*** upon O.

III. LICENSEES

A. **Definition of licensee:** A ***licensee*** is a person who has the owner's ***consent*** to be on the property, but who does ***not have a business purpose*** for being there, or anything else entitling him to be on the land apart from the owner's consent.

B. **Duty to licensees:** The owner does ***not*** owe a licensee any duty to ***inspect for unknown dangers***. On the other hand, if the owner ***knows*** of a dangerous condition, she must ***warn*** the licensee of that danger.

Example: Rear steps leading from O's house to her back yard contain a rotten wood plank. If O knows of the rotten condition, she must warn P, a licensee, if P cannot reasonably be expected to spot the danger himself. But O need not inspect the steps to make sure they are safe, even if a reasonably careful owner would do so.

C. **Social guests:** The main class of persons who qualify as licensees are ***"social guests."***

Example: Even if P is invited to O's house for dinner, P is a "licensee," not an "invitee."

IV. INVITEES

A. **Duty to invitee:** The owner *does* owe an ***invitee*** a duty of ***reasonable inspection to find hidden dangers***. Also, the owner must use reasonable care to take ***affirmative action*** to remedy a dangerous condition.

B. **Definition of "invitee":** The class of invitees today includes: (1) persons who are invited by O onto the land to conduct ***business*** with O; and (2) those who are invited as members of the ***public*** for purposes for which the land is held ***open to the public***.

1. **Meaning of "open to the public":** The ***"open to the public"*** branch of invitees covers those who come onto the property for the purposes for which it is held open, even if these people will not confer any economic benefit on the owner.

Example: P, a door-to-door sales representative, pays an unsolicited sales call on D, a storekeeper. D in fact never buys from such unsolicited callers. However, since P reasonably understood that the premises were held open to salespeople, P is an invitee.

2. **Scope of invitation:** If the visitor's use of the premises goes ***beyond*** the business purpose or beyond the part of the premises held open to the public, that person will change from an invitee to a licensee.

   Example: P visits O's store to buy cigarettes. O then allows P to use a private bathroom in the back of the store not held open to the public. Even though P was an invitee when he first came into the store, he became a licensee when he went into the private bathroom. [*Whelan v. Van Natta*]

C. **Duty of due care:** The owner owes an invitee the duty of ***reasonable care***. In particular:

1. **Duty to inspect:** The owner has a duty to ***inspect*** her premises for hidden dangers. O must use ***reasonable care*** in doing this inspecting. This is true even as to dangers that existed before O moved onto the premises.

2. **Warning:** The giving of a ***warning*** will often, but not always, suffice. If O should realize that a warning will not remove the danger, then the condition must actually be remedied.

3. **Control over third persons:** Reasonable care by O may require that she exercise ***control over third persons*** on her premises.

D. **Firefighters and other public-safety personnel:** Under the common-law ***"firefighter's rule," firefighters, police officers*** and other ***public-safety officials*** who come onto private property in the performance of their duties are treated as ***mere licensees***, so that the owner does not owe them a duty to inspect the premises or to make the premises reasonably safe. The most common application of the common-law doctrine is that a firefighter who is injured while fighting a blaze cannot recover from the owner of the premises, ***even if the owner's negligence caused the fire.***

1. **Status of rule:** A number of states have in recent years expressed dissatisfaction with the firefighter's rule. Some have ***eliminated*** it by statute; others have limited it to the case of firefighters, and have refused to extend it to other rescue workers (e.g., paramedics). Still others limit it to suits against ***landowners***, terming it a rule of "premises liability," not a broad rule against suits by rescue workers.

   a. **Most apply:** But most states ***continue to apply the rule***, at least in the core case: a firefighter injured fighting a fire may not recover against a negligent fire-setter who owns the premises where the injury occurred.

V. REJECTION OF CATEGORIES

A. **Rejection generally:** A number of courts have ***rejected*** the categories of trespasser, licensee and invitee. These courts now apply a general single "reasonable person" standard of liability. California [*Rowland v. Christian*] and New York are included in this group.

1. **Half the states give social guests benefit of duty of due care:** Between the

rejection of categories, and other changes in legal rules, ***social guests*** are in a much better position today than at common law. About half the states have either ***included social guests in the invitee category*** or have completely or partially ***abolished the categories***, so that ***all or most non-trespassing social guests are entitled to reasonable care under the circumstances***.

a. **Not followed as to trespassers:** But most states have been ***unwilling*** to abolish the categories when it comes to ***trespassers***. Most states continue to apply the common-law rule that an owner owes a trespasser no duty of care, and only the duty to refrain from maliciously injuring the intruder.

VI. LIABILITY OF LESSORS AND LESSEES

A. Lessee: A ***tenant*** is treated ***as if she were the owner*** — all the rules of owner liability above apply to her.

B. Lessors: In general, a ***lessor*** is ***not*** liable in tort once he transfers possession to the lessee. However, there are a number of exceptions to this general rule:

1. **Known to lessor, unknown to lessee:** The lessor will be liable to the lessee (and to the lessee's invitees and licensees) for any dangers existing at the start of the lease, which the lessor ***knows or should know about***, and which the lessee has no reason to know about. (This usually does not impose on the lessor a duty to ***inspect*** the premises at the start of the lease.)

2. **Open to public:** If the lessor has reason to believe that the lessee will hold the premises ***open to the public***, the lessor has an affirmative duty to ***inspect*** the premises to find and repair dangers before the lease starts.

3. **Common areas:** The lessor has a general duty to use reasonable care to make ***common areas*** (e.g., the lobby or stairwells of an apartment building) safe.

4. **Lessor contracts to repair:** If the lessor ***contracts***, as part of the lease, to keep the premises in good repair, most courts hold that the landlord's breach of this covenant to repair gives a tort claim to anyone injured. However, P must show that D failed to use reasonable care in performing — it is not enough to show that D breached the contract.

5. **Negligent repairs:** The landlord may incur liability even without a contractual repair obligation if she ***begins*** to make repairs, and either performs them unreasonably, or fails to finish them. This is clearly true where the landlord worsens the danger by performing the repair negligently. Courts are split about what happens where the landlord starts the repair, then abandons it, without worsening the danger.

6. **General negligence standard:** Courts that impose a general negligence standard on occupiers of land often impose a similar general requirement of due care upon lessors.

VII. VENDORS

A. Vendor's liability: Generally, a ***seller*** of land is released from tort liability once he has turned over the property. But there are some exceptions:

1. **Danger to one on the property:** First, suppose the accident happens to one ***on the property*** (e.g., a tenant of the new buyer). Here, you only have to worry about an exception (i.e., post-closing liability of seller to persons on the property) if the seller ***knew or should have known*** of the condition and its dangerousness. If that condition is satisfied, then the duration of the seller's post-closing liability varies depending on whether the seller actively ***concealed*** the danger:

   a. **Seller actively conceals:** If the seller ***actively concealed*** the condition, her liability persists after sale until the buyer ***actually discovers*** the condition and has a reasonable opportunity to correct it (whether the buyer takes the opportunity or not). So here, there's no cut-off if the buyer negligently fails to discover (or fix) the problem.

   b. **Seller doesn't conceal:** If the seller ***didn't actively conceal*** the condition, the seller's liability continues only until the buyer "has had ***reasonable opportunity to discover***" the condition and correct it. In other words here, the seller's liability is ***cut off*** as soon as the buyer ***should have*** discovered and fixed the problem, even if the buyer negligently failed to actually discover it.

2. **Danger to one outside the property:** Essentially the same rules apply to a seller's post-closing liability to one ***outside the property***, except that the seller has longer liability not only for active concealment but for having ***created*** the artificial condition. Thus:

   a. **Seller conceals or created:** If the seller ***actively concealed*** the condition, ***or originally created*** the condition, her liability persists after sale until the buyer actually discovers the condition and has a reasonable opportunity to correct it (whether the buyer takes the opportunity or not). So here, there's no cut-off if the buyer negligently fails to discover (or fix) the problem.

   b. **Seller doesn't conceal or create:** If the seller *neither* actively concealed the condition nor created it, the seller's liability continues only until the buyer "has had ***reasonable opportunity to discover***" the condition and correct it. In other words, here the seller's liability is cut off as soon as the buyer should have discovered and fixed the problem, even if the buyer negligently failed to even discover it.

CHAPTER 10

DAMAGES

I. PERSONAL INJURY DAMAGES GENERALLY

A. Actual injury required: In any action based on negligence, the existence of ***actual injury*** is required. Unlike intentional tort actions, ***nominal*** damages may ***not*** be awarded.

1. **Physical injury required:** Furthermore, P must usually show that he suffered some kind of ***physical*** harm.

   Example: D nearly runs P over. P suffers emotional distress, but no physical manifestation or bodily symptoms from the distress. P may not recover since P had no physical symptoms.

2. **Elements of damages:** But once physical harm has been proven, a variety of damages may be recovered by P. These include:

   a. **Direct loss:** The value of any direct loss of bodily functions. (*Example:* $100,000 for the loss of a leg.)

   b. **Economic loss:** Out-of-pocket ***economic losses*** stemming from the injury. (*Examples:* Medical expenses, lost earnings, household attendant.)

   c. **Pain and suffering:** ***Pain and suffering*** damages.

   d. **Hedonistic damages:** Damages for loss of the ability to ***enjoy*** one's previous life. (*Example:* Compensation for loss of the ability to walk, even if loss of that ability has no economic consequences.)

B. Hedonistic damages: As noted, most courts now allow a jury to award ***hedonistic damages***, i.e., damages for the loss of the ability to ***enjoy life***.

1. **Consciousness required:** Courts are ***split*** about whether P must be ***conscious*** of the loss in order to be able to recover damages. Some states (e.g., New York) do not allow hedonistic damages where P is in a coma.

C. Future damages: P brings only ***one action*** for a particular accident, and recovers in that action not only for past damages, but also for likely ***future*** damages.

1. **Present value:** When P is recovering future values, courts generally instruct the jury to award P only the ***"present value"*** of these losses.

2. **Periodic payments:** Some states now allow D to force P to accept ***periodic payments*** in certain situations. These payments generally terminate upon P's death.

   Example: In New York medical malpractice cases, where the judgment is for more than $250,000, D may pay the judgment by purchasing an annuity for P, which will terminate on P's death.

D. Tax: Any recovery or settlement for personal injuries is ***free*** of ***federal income tax***.

E. The collateral source rule: At common law, P is entitled to recover her out-of-pocket expenses, even if P was ***reimbursed*** for these losses by some ***third party***. This is known as the ***"collateral source rule."***

Example: P has hospital bills of $100,000. A health insurance policy owned by P pays every dime of this. When P sues D, and establishes liability, P may recover the whole $100,000 even though in a sense she has collected twice.

1. **Statutory modifications:** Nearly half the states have ***modified*** the common law collateral source rule in one way or another.

2. **Subrogation:** Where the common law rule remains in effect, P may not get a

windfall after all. An insurance company that makes payments to P will normally be ***subrogated*** to P's tort rights. That is, it is the insurance company, not P, who will actually collect any judgment from D up to the amount of the payments made by the insurer.

F. Mitigation: P has a ***"duty to mitigate."*** That is, P cannot recover for any harm which, by exercise of reasonable care, he could have ***avoided***. In particular, P cannot recover for any harm which would have been avoided had P sought ***adequate medical care***.

1. **Seat belt defense:** In some states, failure to use a ***seat belt*** may deprive P of recovery under the duty to mitigate — if D can show that P would not have been seriously injured had P worn a seat belt, D may escape liability for the avoidable injuries.

II. PUNITIVE DAMAGES

A. Punitive damages generally: Punitive damages can be awarded to penalize a defendant whose conduct is particularly ***outrageous***.

1. **Negligence cases:** In cases of negligence (as opposed to intentional torts), punitive damages are usually awarded only where D's conduct was ***"reckless"*** or ***"willful and wanton."***

   a. **Product liability suits:** Punitive damages are also frequently awarded in ***product liability suits***, if P shows that D knew its product was defective, or recklessly disregarded the risk of a defect.

   b. **Multiple awards:** In a product liability context, a defendant who has made many copies of a defective product may face ***multiple suits***, each awarding punitive damages. The possibility of multiple awards by itself generally does not mean that such awards should not be made. But many courts take into account the possibility of multiple awards in fixing the amount of punitive damages in each case.

2. **Constitutional limits:** The U.S. Constitution places some — but not severe — limits on the award of punitive damages.

   a. **Due process:** A defendant might be able to show that a particular punitive damages award violated its Fourteenth Amendment ***due process*** rights.

      i. **Ratio of actual to punitive:** One of the most important factors in whether an award of punitive damages violates due process is the ***ratio*** of the ***punitive damages*** to the ***compensatory damages.*** The higher this ratio, the more likely it is that a due process violation will be found.

      Example: D, an insurer, refuses in bad faith to settle a claim by X against P, its policy owner. This refusal temporarily places P in fear of having to pay an excess judgment of $136,000. (D eventually pays the judgment all by itself). A state court awards P punitive damages of $145 million, on top of a $1 million compensatory award. *Held*, this award violated D's due process rights. "***Few awards*** [significantly] exceeding a ***single-digit***

ratio between punitive and compensatory damages ... will satisfy due process." [*State Farm Mut. Auto. Insur. Co. v. Campbell*]

III. RECOVERY BY SPOUSE OR CHILDREN

A. General action by spouse: Most states allow the ***spouse*** of an injured person to bring an independent action for his or her own injuries. (*Examples:* A spouse of the injured person may recover for loss of companionship or loss of sex.)

B. Recovery by parent: Similarly, nearly all jurisdictions allow a ***parent*** to recover ***medical expenses*** incurred due to injury to the child. Also, there may be an action for loss of companionship (e.g., the child is in a coma).

C. Child's recovery: Some — but still not most — courts allow a child to recover for loss of companionship or guidance where the parent is injured.

Note: The discussion in paragraphs A, B and C above assumes that the victim is only injured, not killed. Where the victim is killed, the "wrongful death" statutes discussed below apply instead.

D. Defenses: In such third-party actions, generally any ***defense*** which could have been asserted in a suit brought by the injured party may be asserted against the plaintiff.

Example: In a suit by Husband for loss of companionship and sex due to injuries to Wife, D may assert that Wife was comparatively negligent.

1. **Defenses against plaintiff:** Furthermore, defenses may be asserted against the plaintiff even though these could not have been asserted in a suit brought by the victim.

   Example: Husband drives and collides with D; Wife is injured. If Husband sues for loss of companionship, D can raise Husband's comparative negligence as a defense, even though this would not be a defense in a suit brought by Wife.

IV. WRONGFUL DEATH AND SURVIVOR ACTIONS

A. Wrongful death distinguished from survivor: Most states have two types of statutes which take effect when a personal injury victim dies. The "survival" statute governs whether the victim's own right of recovery continues after his death. The "wrongful death" statute governs the right of the victim's survivors (typically, spouse and children) to recover.

B. Survival statutes: The ***survival*** statute in most states provides that when an accident victim dies, his estate may sue for those elements of damages that the victim himself could have sued for had he lived. Thus a survival statute typically allows the estate to sue for pain and suffering, lost earnings prior to death, actual medical expenses, etc. In many states, if death is ***instantaneous***, there is no survival action at all, since all damages are sustained on account of or after the death.

C. Wrongful death: Most states have ***"wrongful death"*** statutes, which allow a defined group to recover for the loss they have sustained by virtue of the decedent's death. Typically, the decedent's ***spouse*** and ***children*** are covered. If the decedent has no spouse or children, usually the ***parents*** are covered.

1. **Elements of damages:** In a wrongful death action, the survivors may recover for: (1) the ***economic support*** they would have received had the accident and death not occurred; and (2) usually, the companionship (including sexual companionship) and moral guidance that would have been given by the decedent. Some — but not most — states also allow the survivors to recover for ***grief***.

   a. **Recovery by parent where child is dead:** Many courts now allow a parent whose child has died to recover for the loss of companionship of that child.

2. **Defenses:** In a wrongful death action, D may assert any defense which he would have been able to use against the decedent if the decedent was still alive and suing in her own name.

   Examples: The decedent's contributory negligence, assumption of risk, consent, etc. will all bar an action for wrongful death by the survivors.

CHAPTER 11

DEFENSES IN NEGLIGENCE ACTIONS

I. CONTRIBUTORY NEGLIGENCE

A. **General rule:** At common law (but rarely under the statutes that exist today) the doctrine of ***contributory negligence*** applies. The doctrine provides that a plaintiff who is negligent, and whose negligence contributes proximately to his injuries, is ***totally barred from recovery***.

   Example: P, while crossing the street, fails to pay attention. D, traveling at a high rate of speed while drunk, hits and kills P. Had P behaved carefully, he would have been able to get out of the way. Even though D's negligence is much greater than P's, in a traditional contributory negligence regime P will be totally barred from recovery because of his contributory negligence.

B. **Standard of care:** The plaintiff is held to the ***same standard of care*** as the defendant (i.e., the care of a ***"reasonable person*** under like circumstances").

C. **Proximate cause:** The contributory negligence defense only applies where P's negligence ***contributed proximately*** to his injuries. The same test for "proximate causation" is used as where D's liability is being evaluated.

   Example: On the facts of the above example, suppose that D was traveling so fast that even had P been careful, D would still have struck P. P will not be barred by contributory negligence, because his negligence was not a "but for" cause, and thus not a proximate cause, of P's injuries.

D. Claims against which defense not usable: Since the contributory negligence defense is based on general negligence principles, it can be used as a bar only to a claim that is itself based on negligence.

1. **Intentional torts:** Thus the defense cannot be used where P's claim is for an ***intentional tort***.

2. **Willful and wanton:** Similarly, if P's conduct is found to have been ***"willful and wanton"*** or ***"reckless,"*** the contributory negligence defense was not allowed. (But if D's negligence is merely "gross," contributory negligence is usually allowed.) The idea is that the defense does not apply where D disregarded a ***conscious*** risk.

II. COMPARATIVE NEGLIGENCE

A. Definition: A ***"comparative negligence"*** system rejects the all-or-nothing approach of contributory negligence. It instead attempts to divide liability between P and D in proportion to their ***relative degrees of fault***. P is not barred from recovery by his contributory negligence, but his recovery is reduced by a ***proportion*** equal to the ratio between his own negligence and the total negligence contributing to the accident.

> **Example:** P suffers damages of $100,000. A jury finds that P was 30% negligent and D was 70% negligent. P will recover, under a comparative negligence system, $70,000 — $100,000 minus 30% of $100,000.

1. **Commonly adopted:** 46 states have adopted some form of comparative negligence. So *contributory* negligence has largely been ***abandoned*** in American law.

B. "Pure" versus "50%" systems: Only 13 states have adopted "pure" comparative negligence. The rest completely bar P if his negligence is (depending on the state) ***"as great"*** as D's, or ***"greater"*** than D's.

C. Multiple parties: Where there are ***multiple defendants***, comparative negligence is harder to apply:

1. **All parties before court:** If all defendants are joined in the same lawsuit, the solution is simple: only the negligence due directly to P is deducted from his recovery.

> **Example:** Taking all negligence by all parties, P is 20% negligent, D1 is 50% negligent, and D2 is 30% negligent. P will recover 80% of his damages.

2. **Not all parties before court:** If not all defendants are before the court, hard questions arise concerning ***joint-and-several liability***. The issue is whether the defendant(s) before the court, who is/are found to be only partly responsible for P's loss, must pay for the whole loss aside from that caused by P's own fault.

> **Example:** P's accident is caused by the negligence of D and X. P sues D, but can't find or sue X. The jury finds that P was 20% responsible; D, 30% responsible; and X, 50% responsible. P's damages total $1 million. It is not clear whether P can collect the full $800,000 from D. Under traditional "joint-and-several liability" rules, P would be able to collect this full $800,000.

a. **Total abolition:** About 1/3 of the states have ***completely abolished*** the doctrine of joint-and-several liability in comparative negligence cases. In these states, all liability is "several." That is, each defendant is ***only required to pay his or her own share*** of the total responsibility. (So in such a state, P in the above example could collect only $240,000 from D, i.e., his 30% share of the overall $1 million in damages.)

b. **Hybrid:** An additional significant number of states have replaced traditional joint-and-several liability with some sort of ***"hybrid"*** approach, which combines aspects of joint-and-several liability and aspects of several liability. (See *supra*, p. 101, for a discussion of these hybrids.)

D. **Last clear chance:** Courts are ***split*** about whether the doctrine of ***last clear chance*** should survive in a comparative negligence jurisdiction.

E. **Extreme misconduct by D:** If D's conduct is not merely negligent, but ***"willful and wanton"*** or ***"reckless,"*** most states nonetheless will reduce P's damages.

1. **Intentional tort:** But if D's tort is ***intentional***, most comparative negligence statutes will *not* apply.

F. **Seat belt defense:** The ***"seat belt defense"*** is increasingly ***accepted*** in comparative negligence jurisdictions. In this defense, D argues that P's injuries from a car accident could have been reduced or entirely avoided had P worn a seat belt; P's damages should therefore be reduced.

1. **Contributory negligence jurisdictions:** In most ***contributory*** negligence jurisdictions, courts ***refuse*** to allow the seat belt defense at all. That is, P's failure to wear a seat belt does not count against his recovery in most courts.

2. **Comparative negligence jurisdictions:** But in states that have comparative negligence, the seat belt defense is more successful. There are various approaches:

[1] D is liable only for those injuries that would have occurred even had P worn a seat belt;

[2] D is liable for all injuries, with a reduction made equal to the percentage of P's fault; and

[3] D is liable for all injuries, but P's fault reduces his recovery for those injuries that would have been avoided.

a. **Effect of statute:** Thirty-two states have ***mandatory*** seat belt use statutes. But the majority of these either prohibit the seat belt defense completely or make the defense almost valueless by allowing only a small reduction of damages.

G. **Imputed comparative negligence:** Occasionally, the fault of one person (call her *A*) may by ***imputed to another*** (*B*), to as to reduce *B*'s recovery.

1. **"Both ways" rule:** But under the so-called ***"both ways" rule,*** this imputation will happen ***only*** if *B* would be vicariously liable (see *infra*, p. C-139) for *A*'s torts. As the Third Restatement puts it, "The negligence of another person is ***imputed*** to a plaintiff ***whenever the negligence of the other person would have been imputed had the plaintiff been a defendant[.]***"

a. **Employer/employee:** This means that if suit is brought by an ***employer*** for damages arising out of an accident involving the employer's ***employee***, any fault by the employee will reduce the plaintiff employer's recovery.

Example: Company hires Worker to drive a delivery truck for Company's business. (Assume that Company is not negligent in selecting or training Worker for this role). Worker has a collision with a car driven by Dave, which damages Company's truck. Company sues Dave for the damage to the truck.

If Worker was negligent in driving the truck, this negligence will be imputed to Company under the "both ways" rule. That's because, if Company were the defendant in a suit by Dave, Company would have been vicariously liable for Worker's negligence under the *respondeat superior* doctrine. Therefore, in a comparative-negligence jurisdiction, Company's recovery will be reduced by the percentage of fault attributable to Worker.

b. **Not attributed from parent to child:** Suppose a ***child is the plaintiff***, the child's parent has contributed to the accident (e.g., by a ***failure to supervise***) and some third party has also been negligent. The both-ways rule normally means that any fault attributable to the child's parents ***won't reduce the child's recovery against the third person***.

Example: Kid is injured in a playground accident, due in part to Guard's failure to supervise rough playing between Kid and Ted, another child. The accident is also due in part to a negligent failure of supervision by Dad, Kid's father, who is also present. Kid has suffered $10,000 in damages, and sues Guard for this sum.

Kid can collect the entire $10,000 from Guard, without reduction for any percentage of fault due to Dad. That's because: (1) Dad would not be vicariously liable for Kid's negligence if Kid were a defendant in an action brought by Ted (since parents are not vicariously liable for their children's torts); (2) consequently, under the "both ways" rule, Dad's fault won't be attributed to Kid, and can't reduce Kid's recovery against either Guard or Dad; and (3) therefore, Dad and Guard are jointly and severally liable, and Guard can be required to pay the whole amount. (Guard could then seek contribution from Dad.)

c. **Driver-passenger scenario (rule not applied):** But there is one major scenario in which courts and/or legislatures usually ***decline to apply*** the both ways rule. Where the ***owner of a vehicle would be vicariously liable for negligence by the driver,*** but the ***owner/plaintiff is a passenger who is injured***, most modern decisions say that the owner's ability to recover from the negligent third-party will ***not be barred or reduced on account of the driver's negligence.***

i. **Restatement approach:** Thus the Third Restatement of Torts, although it generally applies the both ways rule, ***does not apply the rule against the owner-passenger of a vehicle who is injured by a third party*** — the driver's negligence will not be imputed to the plaintiff owner/passenger, even though state law makes the owner liable to third parties for the negligence of a driver who is driving with the owner's permission. See Rest. 3d of Torts (Apport.), § 5, Comment c and Illustration 6.

Example: P is the owner-passenger in a car driven by her husband (H). H drives the car to a restaurant parking lot. While P remains seated, H stops in a travel lane opposite a parking space occupied by a truck driven by D. While H goes into the restaurant to pick up the couple's take-out order, D backs his truck out of his parking space and strikes P's car, injuring her. P sues D for negligence in Maryland court (Maryland being one of the few states still applying contributory negligence). In Maryland, a driver's negligence is imputed to the owner of the vehicle if the driver has the owner's permission to drive it. Therefore, D defends on the grounds that: (1) H was contributorily negligent for leaving the car in the travel lane, and (2) under the both ways rule, H's negligence must be imputed to P, blocking P from any recovery.

Held (by the Maryland Supreme Court), for P. In this special owner-passenger scenario, for public policy reasons the state's general both ways rule ***should not be applied***. The traditional rule imputing the driver's negligence to the owner-passenger was a way of ensuring that if a third party is injured by the driver's negligence, that third party could recover against ***the party most likely to be financially responsible:*** the vehicle's owner (covered by compulsory vehicle owner's insurance). But here the roles are switched: it's the ***third-party driver*** (here, D) whose negligence is a but for cause of injuries to the owner-passenger P, and it's X (the driver operating the car with P's permission) who has also been negligent. Application of the both ways rule here would mean that X's contributory or comparative negligence would bar or reduce P's ability to recover from third-party driver D. This result would be at odds with the imputed negligence doctrine's original purpose, which is to supply a solvent party from whom the injured passenger can recover. [*Seaborne-Worsely v. Mintiens* (Md. 2018)]

III. ASSUMPTION OF RISK

A. Definition: A plaintiff is said to have ***assumed the risk*** of certain harm if she has ***voluntarily consented*** to take her chances that harm will occur. Where such an assumption is shown, the plaintiff is, at common law, completely barred from recovery.

B. Express assumption: If P ***explicitly*** agrees with D, in advance of any harm, that P will not hold D liable for certain harm, P is said to have ***"expressly"*** assumed the risk of that harm.

Example: P wants to go bungee jumping at D's amusement park. P signs a release given to him by D in which P agrees to "assume all risk of injury" that may result from the bungee jumping. If P is injured, he will not be able to sue D, because he has expressly assumed the risk.

1. **Exceptions:** There are three important ***exceptions*** to the general enforceability of

express agreements to assume risk:

[1] first, when the party protected by the clause (typically the defendant) either ***intentionally causes*** the harm, or else brings about the harm by acting in a ***reckless or grossly negligent*** way;

[2] second, when the ***bargaining power*** of the party protected by the clause is ***grossly greater*** than that of the other party, typically a status the court finds to exist only when the good or service being offered is ***"essential"*** (e.g., the services of public carriers or public utilities);

[3] finally, where the court concludes that there is some ***overriding public interest*** which demands that the court refuse to enforce the exculpatory clause.

Example: Even if P signs a contract with D, her doctor, saying, "I agree not to sue you for malpractice if anything goes wrong with my operation," no court will enforce this promise, because of the overriding public interest in not shielding doctors from their own negligence for medical procedures. [*Seigneur v. National Fitness Institute, Inc.*]

C. Implied assumption of risk: Even if P never makes an actual agreement with D whereby P assumes the risk, P may be held to have assumed certain risks ***by her conduct***. Here, the assumption of risk is said to be ***"implied."***

1. **Two requirements:** For D to establish implied assumption, he must show that P's actions demonstrated that she: (1) ***knew of the risk in question***; and (2) ***voluntarily consented*** to bear that risk herself.

   Example: D owns a baseball team. D posts big signs at the gates warning of the danger of foul balls. P has attended many games, and in each game buys a seat right behind home plate, a place where she and all other fans know many foul balls are hit. If P is hit by a foul ball, she will not be able to recover against D even if D negligently failed to screen the home plate area. This is because P knew of the risk in question, and voluntarily consented to bear that risk.

2. **Knowledge of risk:** The requirement that P be shown to have ***known*** about the risk is strictly construed. For instance, the risk must be one which was ***actually*** known to P, not merely one which ***"ought to have been"*** known to her.

3. **Voluntary assumption:** The requirement that P consented ***voluntarily*** is also strictly construed.

   a. **Duress:** For instance, there is no assumption of the risk if D's conduct left P with ***no reasonable choice*** but to encounter a known danger.

   Example: P rents a room in a boarding house from D. She has to use a common bathroom at the end of a hallway. After the lease starts, a hole in the floor leading to the bathroom develops, and D negligently fails to fix it. P knows about the hole, but nonetheless steps in it while going to the bathroom. P will not be barred from recovery by an implied assumption of risk, because D's conduct left P with no reasonable alternative but to walk down the hallway to get to the bathroom.

b. **Choice not created by D:** Where it is ***not D's fault*** that P has no reasonable choice except to expose herself to the risk, the defense ***will*** apply.

Example: P is injured and needs immediate medical help. She asks D — who had nothing to do with the injury — to drive her to the hospital, knowing that D's car has bad brakes. P is deemed to assume the risk of injury due to an accident caused by the bad brakes, because P's dilemma (does she take the ride in D's car with the bad brakes or not?) is not one that D put P into as the result of any wrongdoing by D. (But there would be *no* assumption if D had caused P's original injuries, because D *would* then be the cause of P's dilemma.)

4. **Distinguished from contributory negligence:** Often, P's assumption of risk will also constitute contributory negligence.

Example: P voluntarily, but unreasonably, decides to take her chances as to a certain risk.

a. **Reasonable assumption of risk:** But this is not always true: sometimes conduct that constitutes assumption of risk is *not* contributory negligence.

Example: P, injured, asks for a ride to the hospital in D's car, which P knows had bad brakes. This is assumption of risk, even though P has behaved perfectly reasonably in view of the lack of alternatives.

b. **Defense to reckless conduct:** Distinguishing between assumption of risk and contributory negligence may be important where D's conduct was ***reckless***: contributory negligence is not a defense to reckless conduct, but assumption of the risk generally is.

5. **"Primary" versus "secondary" assumption:** Distinguish between ***"primary"*** implied assumption of risk and ***"secondary"*** implied assumption. In the "primary" case, D is never under any duty to P at all. (*Example:* Foul balls at a baseball game.) In the "secondary" case, D would ordinarily have a duty to P, but P's assumption of risk causes the duty to dissipate. (*Example:* P, injured, asks for a ride to the hospital in D's car, which P knows has bad brakes.)

a. **Effect of comparative negligence statute:** Where there is a ***comparative negligence*** statute, most states eliminate the "secondary" assumption doctrine, but not the "primary" assumption doctrine.

Example 1: In a comparative negligence state, P, knowing of the risk of foul balls, goes to a baseball game and is hit by one. D can still raise assumption of risk as a complete defense, because the assumption here was a primary one — it prevented D from ever having any duty to protect P from foul balls.

Example 2: In a comparative negligence state, Landlord negligently allows Tenant's premises to become highly flammable, and a fire results. Tenant reenters the premises to try to rescue his child, and is injured. This is a "secondary" implied assumption of risk situation. Therefore, most courts would merge assumption of risk into comparative negligence. If Tenant behaved reasonably, his recovery will not be reduced at all. If Tenant behaved unreasonably, his recovery will be reduced only by the percentage of fault.

b. **Sports and recreation:** Within the context of ***sports*** and ***recreation***, ***one participant*** sometimes ***injures the other***. If the risk of this sort of inter-participant injury is found to be "inherent" in the sport or activity, then even in a comparative negligence jurisdiction the plaintiff will not be allowed to recover against the one who injured him, on the theory that the defendant owes no duty to the plaintiff to avoid that sort of risk.

   i. **Ordinary carelessness:** Most courts now hold that in such co-participant sports, ***ordinary carelessness*** is ***inherent*** in the game (and thus covered by "primary" assumption of risk), so that an injured co-participant may recover only if the injury was ***intentional*** or so ***reckless***ly inflicted as to be ***totally outside the range of ordinary activity in the sport.*** For a more extensive discussion, see *supra*, p. 75.

IV. STATUTE OF LIMITATIONS

A. **Discovery of injury:** If P does not ***discover*** his injury until long after D's negligent act occurred, the statute of limitations may start to run at the time of the negligent act, or may instead not start to run until P discovered (or ought to have discovered) the injury.

1. **Medical malpractice:** In ***medical malpractice cases***, statutes and case law today frequently apply the "time of discovery" rule.

   Example: D performs an operation on P in 1970, and leaves a foreign object in P's body. P discovers the problem in 2010, and sues immediately. The statute of limitations is six years on tort actions. Many, probably most, states today would allow P's suit, on the theory that the statute only started to run at the earliest time P knew or should have known that the object was left in his body.

2. **Sexual assaults:** Some states also apply the "discovery" rule to toll the statute of limitations in ***sexual assault*** cases.

   Example: P is sexually abused by D, her father, when P is five years old. P represses the whole episode, but rediscovers it under psychoanalysis at the age of 30. A modern court might allow P to sue at age 31, on the theory that the statute of limitations was tolled until P remembered, or should have remembered, the abuse.

V. IMMUNITIES

A. **Family immunity:** The common law recognizes two ***immunities*** in the family relationship: between ***spouses***, and between ***parent and child.***

1. **Husband and wife:** At common law, inter-spousal immunity prevented suits by one spouse against the other for personal injury.

Examples: If W is injured while a passenger in a car driven negligently by H, W cannot sue H. If H intentionally strikes W, W cannot sue for battery.

a. **Abolition:** But over half the states have now completely ***abolished*** the interspousal immunity, even for personal injury suits. Other states have partially abolished it (e.g., not applicable for intentional torts, or not applicable for automobile accident suits).

2. **Parent and child:** At common law, there is an immunity that bars suit by a ***child against his parents*** or vice versa. Again, many (though not most) states have abolished this immunity, and others have limited it.

B. **Charitable immunity:** ***Charitable organizations***, as well as educational and religious ones, receive immunity at common law.

1. **Abolished:** But more than 30 states have now abolished charitable immunity. Others have cut back on the doctrine (e.g., abolished as to charitable hospitals, or abolished where there is liability insurance).

C. **Governmental immunity:** At common law, there is ***"sovereign immunity,"*** preventing anyone from suing the ***government***.

1. **United States:** Suits against the ***federal government*** are generally allowed today, under the Federal Tort Claims Act (FTCA). But the FTCA does not allow certain types of tort suits.

a. **Discretionary function:** Most important, no liability may be based upon the government's exercise of a ***discretionary or policy-making function***, even if the discretion is abused.

Example: The U.S. government conducts underground testing of biological weapons. The tests are carried out as carefully as can be done, but the government behaves negligently in making the basic decision that such tests can be done safely. Since this high-level decision is "discretionary," P, injured by escaping gas, probably cannot sue under the FTCA.

2. **State governments:** State governments have traditionally had similar sovereign immunity. But most have either completely abolished that immunity, or ***waived*** it selectively.

3. **Local government immunity:** Local government units (cities, school districts, public hospitals, etc.) have traditionally had sovereign immunity as well.

a. **"Proprietary" functions:** But even at common law, where a local government unit performs a ***"proprietary"*** function, there is no immunity. Proprietary functions are ones that have not been historically performed by government, and which are often engaged in by private corporations.

Examples: The running of hospitals, utilities, airports, etc., is generally proprietary, since these are revenue-producing activities; they can therefore be the subject of suit for personal injuries. Police departments, fire departments and school systems are not proprietary, and cannot be sued at common law.

b. **Abolition:** In any event, most states have abolished the general local government immunity, and some that have not done so allow suits where there is liability insurance.

4. **Government officials:** Courts often grant ***public officials*** tort immunity, even where their public employer could be sued.

Examples: Legislators and judges generally receive complete immunity, as long as their act is within the broad general scope of their duties.

CHAPTER 12

VICARIOUS LIABILITY

I. EMPLOYER-EMPLOYEE RELATIONSHIP (*RESPONDEAT SUPERIOR*)

A. ***Respondeat superior*** **doctrine:** If an employee commits a tort during the ***"scope of his employment,"*** his employer will be ***liable*** (jointly with the employee). This is the rule of ***"respondeat superior."***

1. **Applies to all torts:** The doctrine applies to ***all*** torts, including intentional ones and those in which strict liability exists, provided that the tort occurred during the scope of the employee's employment.

B. **Who is an "employee":** *Respondeat superior* is applied to all cases involving ***"employees,"*** but ***not*** to most cases involving ***"independent contractors."*** You must therefore distinguish between these two.

1. **Distinction:** The main idea is that an employee is one who works ***subject to the close control*** of the person who has hired him. An independent contractor, by contrast, although hired to produce a certain result, is not subject to the close control of the person doing the hiring.

a. **Physical details:** The "control" required to make a person an employee rather than an independent contractor is usually held to be control over the ***physical details*** of the work, not just the general manner in which the work is turned out.

Example: A "newspaper boy" is likely to be an independent contractor, not an employee, because the newspaper usually controls only the general terms of employment — such as the time by which the deliveries must take place — not the physical details, such as whether the work should be done by bike or automobile.

C. **Scope of employment:** *Respondeat superior* applies only if the employee was acting ***"within the scope of his employment"*** when the tort occurred. The tort is within the scope of employment if the tortfeasor was acting with an ***intent to further his employer's business purpose***, even if the means he chose were indirect, unwise or even forbidden.

1. **Trips from home:** Most courts hold that where an accident occurs where the

employee is travelling ***from her home*** to work, she is not acting within the scope of her employment. If the employee is ***returning home*** after business, courts are divided.

2. **Frolic and detour:** Even a ***detour*** or side-trip for personal purposes by an employee may be found within the scope of employment if the deviation was "reasonably foreseeable."

   Example: While D, a salesperson, is taking a two-hour trip to visit a business prospect, she makes a five-minute detour to buy a pack of cigarettes. If an accident occurred during the detour, this would probably be held to be "within the scope of employment," so that D's employer would be liable. But a two-hour detour for personal business while on a one-day trip would probably not be within the scope of employment.

3. **Forbidden acts:** Even if the act done was expressly forbidden by the employer, it will be "within the scope of employment" if done in furtherance of the employment.

   Example: D, a storekeeper, expressly orders his clerk never to load a gun while showing it to a customer. The clerk ignores this rule and loads the gun, the gun goes off and the customer is hurt. D will be liable because the loading, though forbidden, was done in furtherance of the employer's business purposes, i.e., sale of guns.

4. **Intentional torts:** The fact that the tort is an ***intentional*** one does not relieve the employer of liability.

   Example: X is a bill collector for D. X commits assault, battery and false imprisonment on P in attempting to collect a debt. D will be liable.

   a. **Personal motives:** But if the employee merely acts from ***personal motives***, the employer will generally not be liable.

      Example: Nurse at D hospital has always hated P because of a prior fight. While P is in the hospital, Nurse kills P. D will not be liable, because Nurse has obviously acted from personal motives, not in an attempt to further D's business.

II. INDEPENDENT CONTRACTORS

A. **No general liability:** As a very general "default" rule, a person who ***hires an independent contractor*** is ***not*** generally liable for the torts of that person. However, there are a number of significant ***exceptions*** to the no-liability general rule.

   1. **Distinguished from employee:** An independent contractor is one who, although hired by the employer to perform a certain job, is not under the employer's immediate control, and may do the work more or less in the manner he himself decides upon. See *supra*, 139.

B. **Exceptions to non-liability:** There are two important exceptions to the rule that an employer is not liable for the torts of his independent contractor.

1. **Employer's own liability:** First, if the employer is ***herself*** negligent in her own dealings with the independent contractor, this can give rise to employer liability.
   a. **Negligent selection:** For instance, suppose the employer ***negligently selects*** an inappropriate contractor, given the requirements of the work — for instance the contractor does not have adequate *experience* in doing the type of project ***safely***. The employer will be directly liable for her negligence in selection, and for the consequences of that negligence.

   Example: Employer selects Contractor to do certain construction renovation work in Employer's store. A reasonable initial investigation by Employer of Contractor's credentials and work experience would have demonstrated that Contractor was not reasonably qualified to do the work safely. Contractor does the work negligently, and the negligent work causes physical injury to P.

   Employer is directly liable for negligently tasking Contractor to do the work, and will therefore be responsible for P's damages.

2. **Vicarious liability for non-delegable duties:** Second, there are some duties of care that are deemed so important that the delegator is liable for negligence by an independent contractor the delegator hires, even if the delegator used all due care in selecting that particular contractor. These are called "***non-delegable duties***," and the delegator/employer is ***vicariously liable*** for the contractor's negligent performance of those non-delegable duties.
   a. **Most important scenarios:** Here are the most important situations in which the duty will be non-delegable and will thus lead to vicarious liability on the employer's part:

      [1] **"Peculiar risk" of harm:** The work is likely to involve a "***peculiar risk"*** of physical injury or property damage to others unless special precautions are taken.

      Example: D owns a private football stadium and the semi-professional team that plays in it. D hires Contractor to install new high-voltage lighting poles in the parking lot. D is not negligent in picking Contractor for this job, since Contractor has adequate experience and safety credentials. Contractor negligently does the work, leaving a pole in such an uninsulated condition that if someone were to touch it, they would be likely to get a high-voltage shock. P, a patron, touches the pole and is shocked.

      Since there is a "peculiar risk" (i.e., a risk of a non-typical type of injury) from high-voltage electrical work that is done without adequate precautions, D will be vicariously liable for Contractor's negligence, in a suit brought by P against D.

      [2] **Abnormally dangerous:** The work is ***abnormally dangerous*** (i.e., ultrahazardous), so that the employer would be strictly liable if he did the work himself (see *infra*, p. 145) rather than via the independent contractor.

[3] **Land possessor:** The employer is a ***possessor or lessor of land,*** and owes a duty of care to the ***public.*** If because of that duty the employer would be liable for negligence in altering or repairing the property himself, the employer will be vicariously liable for comparable negligence committed by the contractor he selects.

Example: O owns a department store. O hires Contractor (properly credentialed) to replace a broken skylight. Contractor does the work negligently. Two months after Contractor turns the repaired area back to O, the skylight falls, injuring P, a patron.

O as the owner of premises open to the public owed a duty of reasonable care to ensure the safety of customers. O will therefore be vicariously liable for the actual negligence of Contractor, since O would have been directly liable for his own negligence if O had done the work himself.

Note about while work is being done: But there's an important clarification to the above rule: it doesn't apply to the contractor's negligence during the period when the contractor is ***actively doing the work,*** and has ***taken over the details of handling of the job*** from the owner.

Example: Same facts as above example. Now, however, assume that Contractor has negligently installed the skylight, but is still in physical possession of, and has responsibility, for the skylight area. (O has let Contractor deal with the details of how the work is to be done safely.) P, a customer, wanders in from an area not under Contractor's control, and is injured when the skylight falls on him. Contractor has also not posted any warning signs.

Since Contractor, not O, was in control of the daily work at the time of the accident, O won't be vicariously liable for Contractor's negligence. (Rationale: We want O to delegate the daily care to the person actually doing the work, and we don't want to encourage micromanagement and meddling by O in that work.)

[4] **Public place:** The work is done in a ***"public place,"*** such as a road, sidewalk, park, etc.

Example: LightingCo hires Contractor to repair a street light (on a public street) that LightingCo. owns and is responsible for illuminating. Contractor negligently does the work, and the streetlight fails soon after. P steps in a pothole which he would have seen had the streetlight been working. Since LightingCo. had the responsibility for maintaining the streetlight in a public place, it is vicariously liable for Contractor's negligence in doing the contracted-for maintenance work.

III. JOINT ENTERPRISE

A. Generally: A ***"joint enterprise,"*** where it exists, may subject each of the participants to vicarious liability for the other's negligence. A joint enterprise is like a partnership, except that it is for a short and specific purpose (e.g., a ***trip***).

1. **Use in auto cases:** The doctrine is used most often in ***auto accident cases***. The negligence of the driver is imputed to the passenger (either to allow the occupant of a second car to recover against the passenger, or to prevent the passenger from recovering against the negligent driver of the other car under the doctrine of imputed contributory negligence).

B. Requirements for joint enterprise: There are four requirements for a joint enterprise: (1) an ***agreement***, express or implied, between the members; (2) a ***common purpose*** to be carried out by the members; (3) a ***common pecuniary interest*** in that purpose; and (4) an equal right to a ***voice*** in the enterprise, i.e., an equal right of control.

IV. AUTO CONSENT STATUTES, THE "FAMILY PURPOSE" DOCTRINE AND BAILMENT

A. Consent statutes: About one quarter of the states have enacted statutes, called "***automobile consent statutes,***" which provide that the owner of an automobile is ***vicariously liable*** for any negligence committed by one using the car with the owner's ***permission***.

B. Automobile insurance omnibus clause: The need for automobile consent statutes is eliminated, in many states, by the fact that the standard ***automobile liability insurance policy*** covers not only the named insured (usually the head of household, who is also generally the owner or co-owner of the automobile), but also any ***member*** of the named insured's household, and any other person who ***uses*** the automobile with the consent of the insured. So the user of the car becomes financially responsible himself, making liability on the part of the owner unnecessary (at least up to the policy limits).

C. Judge-made doctrines: A number of ***judge-made doctrines*** accomplish the same objective of making the car owner vicariously liable for the negligence of one she permitted to use the car.

1. **Joint enterprise:** Often the ***joint enterprise*** doctrine (*supra*, 143), can be used to make one member of the enterprise (e.g., the vehicle owner) vicariously liable for the negligence of another member (e.g., the driver).

2. **Family purpose doctrine:** Another important judge-made doctrine is the ***"family purpose doctrine."*** The doctrine, in force in about 12 states, provides that a car owner who lets ***members of her household*** drive her car for their own personal use has done so in order to further a "family purpose" or family objective, and is therefore vicariously liable. (The doctrine is also sometimes called the ***"family car"*** doctrine.)

D. Bailments: In the absence of a consent statute (and assuming the family purpose doctrine doesn't apply), the mere existence of a ***bailment*** does ***not*** make the bailor vicariously liable for the bailee's negligence.

Example: D lends his shotgun to X. X, while hunting in the woods, negligently fires without noticing P nearby. Even though D is a bailor (he has lent his personal property to X), D does not thereby become vicariously liable for X's negligent use of the bailed property.

1. **Negligence by bailor:** But the bailor may, of course, be negligent herself in entrusting a potentially dangerous instrument to the bailee where she ***should know that the latter may use it unsafely.*** In this situation, the claim is directly against the bailor for ***"negligent entrustment,"*** and there is no vicarious liability.

   Example: In the above example, if D knew that X often hunted while drunk, D's act of entrusting the shotgun to X might itself be negligent, in which case D would be directly (not vicariously) liable to P for the injuries caused by X.

CHAPTER 13

STRICT LIABILITY

I. STRICT LIABILITY GENERALLY

A. Generally: Apart from the special situation of defective products, there are three major contexts in which D can have "***strict liability***" — that is, liability regardless of D's intent and regardless of whether D was negligent. We examine those contexts in this chapter. They are:

[1] strict liability for keeping ***wild or other dangerous animals***;

[2] strict liability for carrying out ***abnormally dangerous*** (or "***ultrahazardous***") ***activities***; and

[3] strict liability on the part of an employer for the ***employee's on-the-job injuries***, a liability that is enforced by ***"workers compensation"*** statutes enacted in all states.

II. ANIMALS

A. Trespassing animals: In most states, the owner of livestock or other animals is liable for property damage caused by them if they ***trespass*** on another's land. This liability is "strict" — even though the owner exercises utmost care to prevent the animals from escaping, he is liable if they do escape and trespass.

B. Non-trespass liability: A person is also strictly liable for non-trespass damage done by any ***"dangerous animal"*** he keeps.

1. **Wild animals:** A person who keeps a ***"wild"*** animal is strictly liable for all damage done by it, as long as the damage results from a ***"dangerous propensity"*** that is typical of the species in question.

Example: D keeps a lion cub, which has never shown any violent tendencies. One day, the cub runs out on the street and attacks P. Even if D used all possible care to prevent the cub from escaping, he is liable for P's injuries, because the cub is a wild animal and the damage resulted from a dangerous propensity typical of lions, that they can attack without warning.

2. **Domestic animals:** But injuries caused by a ***"domestic"*** animal such as a cat, dog, cow, pig, etc., do not give rise to strict liability unless the owner ***knows*** or has ***reason to know*** of the animal's dangerous characteristics.

   Example: Same facts as above example, except that the animal is a dog. If the dog has never attempted to bite anyone before, D is not liable. But if D knew or had reason to know that the dog sometimes attacks people, he would be liable.

III. ABNORMALLY DANGEROUS ACTIVITIES

A. General rule: A person is strictly liable for any damage which occurs while he is conducting an ***"abnormally dangerous"*** activity.

1. **Six factors:** Courts generally consider six factors in determining whether an activity is "abnormally dangerous":

   [1] there is a ***high degree of risk*** of some harm to others;

   [2] the harm that results is likely to be ***serious***;

   [3] the risk ***cannot be eliminated*** by the exercise of reasonable care;

   [4] the activity is ***not common***;

   [5] the activity is not ***appropriate*** for the place where it is carried on; and

   [6] the danger outweighs the activity's ***value*** to the ***community***.

2. **Requirement of unavoidable danger:** Probably the single most important factor is that the activity be one which ***cannot be carried out safely***, even with the exercise of reasonable care.

   Example: D, a construction contractor, carries out blasting operations with dynamite, to excavate a foundation. D uses utmost care. However, a piece of rock is thrown out of the site during an explosion, striking P, a pedestrian on the street. Blasting is an abnormally dangerous activity, in part because it cannot be conducted with guaranteed safety. Therefore, D will be strictly liable for the injury to P.

B. Examples: Here are some types of activities that are generally held to be abnormally dangerous:

1. **Nuclear reactor:** Operation of a ***nuclear reactor***;
2. **Explosives:** The use or storage of ***explosives*** (see above example);
3. **Crop dusting:** The conducting of ***crop dusting*** or spraying;

4. **Airplane accidents:** There usually is *not* strict liability in suits by passengers for ***airplane accidents***. Therefore, in a suit by the estate of a passenger against the airline, the plaintiff must show negligence. (But most courts do impose strict liability for ground damage from airplane accidents.)

5. **Use of firearms:** Similarly, the use of ***firearms*** is usually found ***not*** to be abnormally dangerous, because they can be used very safely if good techniques are employed.

IV. LIMITATIONS ON STRICT LIABILITY

A. **Scope of risk:** There is strict liability only for damage which results from the ***kind of risk*** that made the activity abnormally dangerous.

Example: D operates a truck carrying dynamite, and the truck strikes and kills P. P must show negligence. Transporting dynamite may be ultrahazardous, but P's death has not resulted from the kind of risk that made this activity abnormally dangerous.

1. **Abnormally sensitive activity by plaintiff:** A related rule is that D will not be liable for his abnormally dangerous activities if the harm would not have occurred except for the fact that P conducts an ***"abnormally sensitive"*** activity.

Example: D's blasting operations frighten female mink owned by P; the mink kill their young in reaction to their fright. D is not strictly liable, because P was conducting an abnormally sensitive activity. [*Foster v. Preston Mill Co.*]

B. **Contributory negligence no defense:** Ordinary ***contributory negligence*** by P will usually *not* bar her from strict liability recovery.

1. **Voluntary assumption of risk:** But ***assumption of risk*** is a defense to strict liability. Thus if P ***knowingly and voluntarily*** subjects herself to the danger, this will be a defense, whether P acted reasonably or unreasonably in doing so.

Example: P, an independent contractor, agrees to transport dynamite for D. P understands that dynamite can sometimes explode spontaneously. If such an accident occurs, P cannot recover from D in strict liability, because P has assumed the risk; this is true whether P acted reasonably or unreasonably.

V. WORKERS' COMPENSATION

A. **Generally:** All states have adopted ***workers' compensation*** (WC) statutes, which compensate the employee for ***on-the-job*** injuries without regard either to the employer's fault or the employee's.

1. **No fault:** The employer is liable for on-the-job injuries even though these occur ***completely without fault*** on the part of the employer. Even if the employee is contributorily negligent, the statutory benefits are not reduced at all.

2. **Arising out of employment:** A typical statute covers injuries arising out of and in the ***course of employment***. Thus activities which are purely personal (e.g., injuries suffered while the employee is traveling to or from work) are typically not

covered.

3. **Exclusive remedy:** The WC statute is the employee's ***sole remedy*** against the employer. The employee gives up his right to sue in tort, and does not recover anything for ***pain and suffering***.

   a. **Intentional wrongs:** But if P can show that the employer ***intentionally*** injured him, the employee may pursue a common-law action.

      Example: A few cases have allowed the employee to sue where the employer has willfully disregarded safety regulations. But most have held that the employer's failure to observe safety regulations or to keep equipment in good repair does not amount to an intentional act, and thus does not permit the employee to escape WC as the sole remedy.

   b. **Third parties:** The WC statute does not prevent the worker from suing a ***third party*** who, under common-law principles, would be liable for the worker's injuries.

      Example: At P's job, P uses a machine manufactured by D and sold by D to Employer. If P is injured on the job, he cannot bring a common law action against Employer, but can bring a product liability suit at common law against D.

CHAPTER 14

PRODUCTS LIABILITY

I. INTRODUCTION

A. Three theories: "Product liability" refers to the liability of a seller of a tangible item which, because of a defect, causes injury to its purchaser, user, or sometimes bystanders. Usually the injury is a personal injury. The liability can be based upon any of three theories:

[1] ***Negligence;***

[2] ***Warranty;***

[3] **"*Strict tort liability.*"**

II. NEGLIGENCE

A. Negligence and privity: Ordinary negligence principles apply to a case in which personal injury has been caused by a carelessly manufactured product.

Example: D, a car manufacturer, carelessly fails to inspect brakes on a car that it makes. P buys the car directly from D, and crashes when the brakes don't work. P can recover from D under ordinary negligence principles.

1. **Privity:** Historically, the use of negligence in product liability actions was limited by the requirement of ***privity***, i.e., the requirement that P must show that he contracted ***directly*** with D. But every state has now ***rejected*** the privity require-

ment where a negligently manufactured product has caused personal injuries. It is now the case that ***one who negligently manufactures a product is liable for any personal injuries proximately caused by his negligence***.

Example: D manufactures a car, and negligently fails to make the brakes work properly. D sells the car to a dealer, X, who resells to P. While P is driving, the car crashes due to the defective brakes. P may sue D on a negligence theory, even though P never contracted directly with D.

a. **Bystander:** Even where P is a ***bystander*** (as opposed to a purchaser or other user of the product), P can recover in negligence if he can show that he was a "foreseeable plaintiff."

Example: A negligently manufactured car driven by Owner fails to stop due to defective brakes, and smashes into P, a pedestrian. P can sue the manufacturer on a negligence theory.

B. **Classes of defendants:** Several different classes of people are frequently defendants in negligence-based product liability actions:

1. **Manufacturers:** The manufacturer is the person in the distribution chain most likely to have been negligent. He may be negligent because he:

   [1] carelessly ***designed*** the product;

   [2] carelessly ***manufactured*** it;

   [3] carelessly performed (or failed to perform) reasonable ***inspections*** and tests of finished products;

   [4] failed to package and ship the product in a reasonably safe way; or

   [5] did not take reasonable care to obtain quality ***components*** from a reliable source.

2. **Retailers:** A ***retailer*** who sells a defective product may be, but usually is *not*, liable in negligence. The mere fact that D has sold a negligently manufactured or designed product is ***not by itself*** enough to show that she failed to use due care. The retailer ordinarily has ***no duty to inspect*** the goods. Thus suit against the retailer is now normally brought on a warranty or strict liability theory, not negligence.

3. **Other suppliers:** ***Bailors*** of tangible property (e.g., rental car companies), ***sellers*** and ***lessors*** of real estate, and suppliers of product-related ***services*** (e.g., hospitals performing blood transfusions) may all be sued on a negligence theory.

III. WARRANTY

A. **General:** A buyer of goods which are not as they are contracted to be may bring an action for ***breach of warranty***. The law of warranty is mainly embodied in the ***Uniform Commercial Code*** (UCC), in effect in every state except Louisiana. There are two sorts of warranties, ***"express"*** ones and ***"implied"*** ones.

B. Express warranties: A seller may ***expressly represent*** that her goods have certain qualities. If the goods turn out not to have these qualities, the purchaser may sue for this breach of warranty.

Example: D, a car dealer, promises that a particular car has "shatterproof glass." While P is driving the car, a pebble hits the windshield, shatters the glass, and damages P's eyes. P can sue D for breach of the express warranty that the glass would be shatterproof. [*Baxter v. Ford Motor Co.*]

1. **UCC:** UCC §2-313 gives a number of ways that an express warranty may arise: (1) a statement of ***fact*** or promise about the goods; (2) a ***description*** of the goods (e.g., "shatterproof glass"); and (3) the use of a ***sample or model***.

   a. **Privity:** There is usually ***no*** requirement of ***privity*** for breach of express warranty.

   Example: D manufactures a car, and prepares a brochure stating that the glass is "shatterproof." D sells the car to Dealer, who resells it to P. P never reads the brochure, and is injured when the glass is not shatterproof. P can recover against D for breach of express warranty, because there is no privity requirement, and D's statement was addressed to the public at large.

2. **Strict liability:** D's liability for breach of an express warranty is ***a kind of strict liability*** — as long as P can show that the representation was not in fact true, it does not matter that D reasonably believed it to be true, or even that D could not possibly have known that it was untrue.

C. Implied warranty: The existence of a warranty as to the quality of goods can also be ***implied*** from the fact that the seller has offered the goods for sale.

1. **Warranty of merchantability:** The UCC imposes several implied warranties ***as a matter of law***. Most important is the warranty of ***merchantability***. Section 2-314(1) provides that ***"a warranty that goods shall be merchantable is implied in a contract for their sale if the seller is a merchant with respect to goods of that kind."***

   a. **Meaning of "merchantable":** To be ***merchantable***, the goods must be "fit for the ordinary purposes for which such goods are used."

   Example: A car which, because of manufacturing defects, has a steering wheel that does not work, is not "merchantable," since it is not fit for the ordinary purpose — driving — for which cars are used.

   b. **Seller must be a merchant:** The UCC implied warranty of merchantability arises only if the seller is a ***"merchant with respect to goods of that kind."*** Thus the seller must be ***in business*** and must regularly sell the ***kind of goods*** in question.

   Examples: A consumer who is reselling her car does not make any implied warranty of merchantability; nor does a business person who is selling a piece of equipment used in that person's business rather than held in inventory.

2. **Fitness for particular purposes:** A second UCC implied warranty is that the

goods are ***"fit for a particular purpose."*** Under §2-315, this warranty arises where: (1) the seller knows that the buyer wants the goods for a particular (and not customary) purpose; and (2) the buyer ***relies on the seller's judgment*** to recommend a suitable product.

Example: Consumer tells Shoe Dealer that he wants a pair of shoes for mountain climbing. Dealer recommends Brand X as having good traction. If the shoes don't have good traction, and Consumer falls, he can sue Shoe Dealer for breach of the implied warranty of fitness for a particular purpose.

3. **Privity:** States have nearly all ***rejected*** any ***privity*** requirement for the implied warranties.

   a. **Vertical privity:** Thus ***"vertical"*** privity is not required. In other words, a manufacturer's warranty extends to ***remote purchasers*** further down the line.

   Example: Manufacturer sells a widget to Distributor, who sells to Dealer, who sells to Owner. Owner resells to Buyer. Buyer is injured when the widget does not behave merchantably. In all states, Buyer can sue Manufacturer, despite the lack of any contractual relationship between Buyer and Manufacturer.

   b. **Horizontal privity:** Similarly, ***"horizontal"*** privity is usually not required. In all states, any member of the ***household*** of the purchaser can recover if the member uses the product. In most states, ***any*** user, and even any foreseeable ***bystander***, may recover.

D. Warranty defenses: Here are three ***defenses*** unique to warranty claims:

1. **Disclaimers:** A seller may, under the UCC, ***disclaim*** both implied and express warranties.

   a. **Merchantability:** A seller may make a written disclaimer of the warranty of merchantability, but only if it is ***"conspicuous"*** (e.g., in capital letters or bold print). Also, the word "merchantability" must be specifically mentioned. (Also, the circumstances may give rise to an implied disclaimer, as where used goods are sold ***"as is."***)

2. **Limitation of consequential damages:** Sellers may try to ***limit the remedies*** available for breach (e.g., "Our sole remedy is to repair or replace the defective product"). But in the case of goods designed for personal use ("consumer goods"), limitation-of-damages clauses for ***personal injury*** are automatically ***unconscionable*** and thus unenforceable. UCC §2-719(3).

E. Where warranty useful: Generally, any plaintiff who could bring a warranty suit will fare better with a strict liability suit. But there are a couple of exceptions:

1. **Pure economic harm:** If P has suffered only ***pure economic harm***, he will usually do better suing on a breach of warranty theory than in strict liability. For instance, loss of profits is more readily recoverable on a warranty theory.

2. **Statute of limitations:** The ***statute of limitations*** usually runs sooner on a strict liability claim than on a warranty claim.

IV. STRICT LIABILITY

A. General rule: Nearly all states apply the doctrine of ***"strict product liability."*** The basic rule is that a ***seller*** of a product is ***liable without fault*** for personal injuries (or other physical harm) caused by the product if the product is sold in a ***defective condition.*** Once is defect is shown to have existed, the seller is liable even though he used all possible care, and even though the plaintiff did not buy the product from or have any contractual relationship with the seller.

Example: Manufacturer makes a car with defective brakes. Manufacturer sells that car to Dealer, who resells it to Owner, who resells it to Consumer. Consumer is injured when the car crashes because the brakes don't work. Consumer can recover from Manufacturer in "strict tort liability," by showing that the brakes were in a defective condition at the time the car left the plant. This is true even though Manufacturer used all possible care in designing and building the car, and even though Consumer never contracted with Manufacturer.

1. **Non-manufacturer:** Strict product liability applies not only to the product's manufacturer, but also to its ***retailer***, and any other person in the distributive train (e.g., a wholesaler) who is in the business of selling such products.

   Example: On the above example, Consumer can recover against Dealer, even though Dealer merely resold the product and behaved completely carefully.

2. **Manufacturing, design and failure-to-warn defects:** There are three different types of defects that may exist: (1) a ***manufacturing*** defect; (2) a ***design*** defect; and (3) a ***warning*** defect. It's important to decide which type of defect is or may be at issue, because there are different rules of law governing what constitutes a defect of each type. Here's a brief summary of what each type of defect looks like:

   a. **Manufacturing:** In a ***manufacturing*** defect, a particular instance of the product is different from — and more dangerous than — all the others, because the product ***deviated from the intended design***.

   Example: D makes a bicycle which, because of an air bubble that gets into its front fork during manufacture, has an invisible crack that causes the fork to break while P is riding it. This is a manufacturing defect — this bike is different from the other bikes of the same model, in an unintended way.

   b. **Design:** In a ***design*** defect, all of the similar products manufactured by D are ***the same***, and they all bear a feature whose design is itself defective, and unreasonably dangerous.

   Example: D makes a particular model step-ladder that, when more than 150 lbs. is placed on it, is likely to crack because the wood used is a poor grade. This is a design defect — all the ladders of this model have the same poor wood and the same risk of breakage when used for the intended purpose.)

   Note: Design defects are discussed beginning on p. 155.

c. **Warning:** In a ***failure-to-warn*** case, the maker has neglected to give a warning of a danger in the product (or in a particular use of the product), and this lack of a warning makes an otherwise-safe product unsafe.

Example: D, a prescription drug maker, fails to warn users that the drug causes a serious allergic reaction in 2% of the people who take it.

Note: Failure to warn is discussed beginning on p. 157.

B. What product meets test: A product gives rise to strict liability only if it is ***"defective."***

1. **Meaning of "defective":** In the usual case of a manufacturing (as opposed to design) defect, a product is "defective" if the product "***departs from its intended design*** even though ***all possible care was exercised*** in the preparation and marketing of the product." (Rest. 3d.)

C. Unavoidably unsafe products: A product will not give rise to strict liability if is ***unavoidably unsafe***, and its ***benefits outweigh its dangers***.

1. **Prescription drugs:** For instance, a ***prescription drug*** is not "defective" merely because it causes some side effects and may in an individual case cause more damage than it cures. This is also true of ***vaccines***. In fact, under the new Third Restatement rule, drugs, vaccines, and medical devices will be non-defective (unavoidably unsafe) as long as there is ***even a single group of patients*** for whom the product's benefits outweigh its harms.

   a. **Consequence:** This seems to mean that as long as the drug has a net benefit for one group of patients, the maker doesn't need to make the drug as safe as it could be with reasonable effort! For this reason, many courts have ***rejected*** the Third Restatement drug rule as extreme, and require manufacturers to make reasonable efforts to make the drug as safe as possible.

D. Unknowable dangers: Similarly, if the danger from the product's design was ***"unknowable"*** at the time of manufacture, there will be no liability. See Rest. 3d: a design defect will exist only "when the ***foreseeable*** risks of harm posed by the product could have been reduced or avoided by the adoption of a reasonable alternative design" — so if the risk of harm from the design is unknowable at the time of manufacture, there was no "foreseeable risk" and thus no design-defect liability.

1. **Failure to warn:** Similarly, there can be no ***"failure to warn"*** liability (see *infra*, p. 157) for a danger whose existence was unknowable at the time of manufacture.

E. Food products: Where the product is ***food***, most courts apply a ***"consumer expectations"*** test. Under that test, the food product is defective if and only if it contains an ingredient that ***a reasonable consumer would not expect it to contain***.

Example: D manufactures a chicken enchilada. P, a consumer, chokes on a chicken bone in the enchilada. Under the prevailing view, the bone constitutes a "defect" if and only if a reasonable consumer in P's position would not have expected to find a bone in a chicken enchilada. (But in a minority of courts, P would lose because the bone was "natural" for that type of food product, even though a reasonable consumer might not expect to find the bone there.)

F. Obvious dangers: The fact that a danger is ***"obvious"*** may have an impact on whether the product is deemed defective, and thus on whether D is liable. The treatment of obviousness depends on whether the defect is a manufacturing defect, a design defect, or a failure to warn.

1. **Manufacturing defect:** Where the defect is a ***manufacturing*** defect, the fact that the danger or defect is obvious probably ***won't*** block P from recovering (though under comparative fault — generally applicable in products liability cases, see *infra*, p. 164 — it might reduce P's recovery).

   Example: D makes a can of tuna fish, which contains a sliver of metal in it. P fails to notice the metal and is injured when he swallows it. Even if an ordinary consumer would spot the metal and not eat it, the "obviousness" of the danger won't stop the product from being defective, and P will be able to recover.

2. **Design defect:** If what's alleged is a ***design*** defect, under the modern view the obviousness of the defect is a ***factor*** bearing upon liability, but it ***doesn't automatically*** mean that P can't recover. Instead, the question is whether the design's ***benefits outweigh its dangers***, considering possible alternative designs — if the answer is "no," P can recover even though the dangers were obvious.

   Example: Suppose that D manufactures cigarettes using a particular type of tobacco and a particular curing process, that produces very high tar and nicotine, and thus high risk of cancer. P gets cancer from smoking D's cigarettes. Even if P was perfectly aware of how dangerous D's cigarettes were, this fact won't (in most courts) bar the court from finding that the cigarettes were "defective" and thus from allowing P to recover in products liability.

   So, for instance, if P can show that a cigarette made with a different process would taste as good and have less cancer risk, P could win. (But the test will be a cost-benefit analysis: if P shows merely that a safer cigarette could have been made by reducing the elements that give the cigarette the flavor that most smokers expect, D's process won't be found to be "defective" and P will lose, since the safer cigarette won't have the same "benefits" as D's dangerous one.)

3. **Failure-to-warn:** If the defect or danger is obvious, this will normally ***prevent failure-to-warn liability***. That's because if P is actually aware of the obvious danger the warning won't add anything, and if P isn't aware of the obvious danger he's unlikely to notice or respond to the warning either.

G. Proving the case: P in a strict liability case must prove a number of different elements:

[1] that the item was ***made or sold by the defendant***;

[2] that the product was ***defective***;

[3] that the defect ***caused*** the plaintiff's injuries; and

[4] that the defect ***existed*** when the product ***left the defendant's hands.***

We consider each element in turn.

1. **Manufacture or sale by defendant:** She must show that the item was in fact manufactured, or sold, by the defendant.

2. **Existence of defect:** She must show that the product was ***defective***.

   a. **Subsequent remedial measures:** Most courts ***do not*** allow defectiveness to be proved by evidence that D subsequently ***redesigned*** the product to make it safer.

   b. **Toxic torts:** In the case of a ***"mass toxic tort,"*** plaintiffs often use ***epidemiological*** evidence of defectiveness.

   Example: To prove that DES causes cancer, P offers expert testimony that daughters of women who took DES in pregnancy have a much higher incidence of cancer than those whose mothers did not.

3. **Causation:** P must show that the product, and its defective aspects, were the ***cause in fact***, and the ***proximate cause***, of her injuries.

   a. **Epidemiology:** In ***mass toxic tort*** cases, this element, like existence of a "defect," will often be proved by ***epidemiological*** evidence.

      i. **"General" vs. "specific" causation:** Courts often use the terms ***"general" and "specific" causation*** in toxic tort cases: general causation is a substance's tendency to increase the general incidence of a given disease, and specific causation is the substance's having caused plaintiff's *own* disease.

      ii. **Specific causation required:** Courts normally require ***proof of specific causation*** as part of the plaintiff's prima facie case. However, if plaintiff's only direct proof on the causation issue is proof of general causation, courts will nonetheless permit the jury to ***infer*** specific causation if the proof of general causation is sufficiently strong, so long as there is also some evidence that the plaintiff was ***actually exposed*** to the agent.

      Example: P suffers from a rare cancer. In a suit against D, the maker of a drug called DES, P shows that her mother took DES while pregnant with P. P presents expert testimony showing that daughters of women who took DES in pregnancy are 10 times as likely to get that form of cancer as those whose mothers did not. This proof of "general causation" would probably suffice to allow the jury to infer that DES was the specific cause of P's cancer.

      iii. **The "doubling" rule:** Many courts impose the so-called ***"doubling rule"***: the jury will be permitted to infer specific causation if and only if P shows that the agent ***more than doubles the incidence of the disease*** in the population as a whole. These courts reason that without a doubling, it is not "more likely than not" (the relevant preponderance-of-the-evidence standard) that the agent caused P's particular disease.

4. **Defect existed in hands of defendant:** Finally, P must show that the defect existed ***at the time the product left D's hands***.

a. ***Res ipsa*:** But an inference similar to ***res ipsa loquitur*** is permitted — once P shows that the product did not behave in the usual way, and the manufacturer fails to come forward with evidence that anyone else tampered with it, the requirement of defect in the hands of defendant is satisfied.

H. Bystanders and other non-user plaintiffs: ***Any person who is injured*** due to a dangerously defective product may recover, even if the plaintiff never bought the product. Thus ***family members of buyers, bystanders,*** even ***rescuers,*** may all recover if their injuries are proximately caused by the defect in the product. As the idea is sometimes put, "***privity***" is ***not required*** for strict product liability.

Example: Consumer buys a car from Dealer. The steering wheel fails due to a manufacturing defect, causing the car to swerve and hit Ped, a pedestrian walking on the sidewalk. Ped can recover from Dealer in strict product liability, because his physical injuries were proximately caused by a defective product sold by Dealer. The fact that neither Ped nor any member of his family ever purchased the product in question doesn't matter.

V. DESIGN DEFECTS

A. Definition of "design defect": A ***"design defect"*** must be distinguished from a "manufacturing defect." In a design defect case, all the similar products manufactured by D are the same, and they all bear a feature whose design is itself defective, and unreasonably dangerous.

B. Negligence predominates: Most design defect claims have a heavy ***negligence*** aspect, even though the complaint claims strict liability. As the 3d Restatement puts it, a product has a defective design "when the ***foreseeable risks of harm posed*** by the product ***could have been reduced or avoided by the adoption of a reasonable alternative design*** by the seller or other distributor . . . and the omission of the alternative design ***renders the product not reasonably safe***."

1. **Practical other design:** So P must show that there was a ***"reasonable alternative design" (RAD)***. In deciding whether P's proposed alternative qualifies as an RAD, the court will consider the cost and utility of the alternative, compared with the ***cost and utility*** of D's design.

   Example: D makes a bullet-proof vest, the Model 101, that covers only the wearer's front and back, not sides. P, a police officer, is shot in the side while wearing D's vest. At trial, P says that a design with side protection was an RAD, and that the no-sides design is therefore "defective." Suppose that the side-protection design would have weighed five pounds more and cost twice as much. A court is likely to conclude that the side-protection design is not an RAD, because its cost-benefit ratio is not clearly superior to the Model 101's, since many wearers would prefer the lighter cheaper design over the greater protection.

C. Types of claims: Two types of common design-defect claims are as follows:

1. **Structural defects:** P shows that because of D's choice of materials, the product had a ***structural weakness***, which caused it to break or otherwise become danger-

ous.

2. **Lack of safety features:** P shows that a ***safety feature*** could have been installed on the product with so little expense (compared with both the cost of the product and the magnitude of the danger without the feature) that it is a defective design not to install that feature.

   a. **State of the art:** D will be permitted to rebut this by showing that competitive products similarly lack the safety feature. This is the ***"state of the art"*** defense. But such a showing will not be dispositive — the trier of fact is always free to conclude that all products in the marketplace are defective due to lack of an easily-added feature.

D. Suitability for unintended uses: D may be liable not only for injuries occurring when the product is used as intended, but also for some types of injury stemming from ***unintended uses*** of the product.

1. **Unforeseeable misuse:** If the misuse of the product is ***not reasonably foreseeable***, D has no duty to design the product so as to protect against this misuse.

2. **Foreseeable misuse:** But if the misuse is ***reasonably foreseeable*** by D, D must take at least reasonable design precautions to guard against the danger from that use. (Alternatively, a ***warning*** to the purchaser against the misuse may sometimes suffice.)

   Example: A car is not "intended" to be used in a collision, and most collisions are in a sense "misuse" of the product. Nonetheless, a car manufacturer must design a reasonably *crashworthy* vehicle if it is feasible to do so, because collisions are reasonably foreseeable.

E. Military products sold to and approved by government: If a product is ***sold*** to the ***U.S. government*** for ***military use***, and the government ***approves*** the product's specifications, the manufacturer will generally be immune from product liability even if the design is grossly negligent. [*Boyle v. United Technologies Corp.*]

F. Regulatory compliance defense: Suppose the manufacturer has ***complied with federal or state regulations*** governing the design of the product. At common law, this compliance does ***not*** absolve D of product liability — regulatory compliance is an item of ***evidence*** that the jury may consider, but it is not dispositive.

1. **Labeling:** Thus if government requires that a substance be ***designed*** or ***labeled*** in a particular way, and the manufacturer follows that requirement, under the common-law approach P may still be able to bring a product liability suit on the theory that the design or labeling was inadequate and constituted a defect.

   a. **Preemption:** But if the design or labelling requirement was imposed by ***Congress***, and the court finds that Congress intended to ***preempt*** the states from requiring stricter or different designs or warning labels, then D has a defense. For more about preemption, see p. 166 *infra*.

VI. DUTY TO WARN

A. Significance of the duty to warn: The ***"duty to warn"*** is essentially an ***extra*** obligation placed on a manufacturer.

1. **Manufacturing defect:** Thus if a product is ***defectively manufactured, no warning can save D from strict liability.***

2. **Design defect:** Similarly, if a product is ***defectively designed***, a warning will generally ***not*** shield D from strict product liability.

3. **Properly manufactured and designed product:** If a product is ***properly designed*** and ***properly manufactured***, D must nonetheless give a warning if there is a ***non-obvious*** risk of personal injury from using the product. Similarly, in this situation, D may be liable for not giving ***instructions concerning correct use***, if a reasonable consumer might misuse the product in a foreseeable way.

   Examples: Prescription drugs, even when properly designed and properly manufactured, must contain warnings about side effects. Similarly, a household utility like a lawn mower, if it poses a non-obvious risk of personal injury such as cutting a foot, must contain instructions concerning correct use.

   a. **"Learned intermediary" doctrine for drugs:** In the case of prescription drugs, the warning generally needs to be given only to the ***physician*** — who is a ***"learned intermediary"*** between manufacturer and user — not to the user. See below for more about this.

B. Risk-utility basis: Liability for failure-to-warn is usually based on a negligence-like ***risk-utility analysis.***

1. **Restatement Third approach:** Thus under the Third Restatement, a product will be deemed defective on account of "inadequate instructions or warnings" "when the ***foreseeable risks of harm*** imposed by the product could have been reduced or avoided by the provision of ***reasonable instructions or warnings*** . . . and the omission of the instructions or warnings renders the product ***not reasonably safe***." This sounds very much like the traditional negligence standard, but used in the failure-to-warn context to determine what warnings must be given.

C. Drug cases: The most common category of failure-to-warn cases involves ***prescription drugs***.

1. **Learned intermediary doctrine:** Most courts, and the Third Restatement, recognize a defense that makes the manufacturer's duty to warn in prescription drug cases easier-to-satisfy: the ***"learned intermediary"*** defense. Where the defense is allowed, the manufacturer's duty is generally limited to warning the ***prescribing physician*** rather than the patient. The physician is viewed as a "learned i.e., highly trained intermediary" between the manufacturer and the user; the rationale is that the physician is, in most cases, in the best position to decide whether a drug should be prescribed and when and how its risks should be disclosed.

   a. **Restatement adopts:** The Third Restatement basically ***applies*** the learned intermediary rule as the default rule. The Restatement imposes failure-to-warn liability on a drug or medical device maker only if ***"reasonable instruc-***

tions or warnings regarding foreseeable risks of harm" are ***not provided*** to ***"prescribing and other health-care providers*** who are in a position to reduce the risks of harm in accordance with the instructions or warnings."

i. **Exception:** But the Third Restatement includes an important ***exception*** to this general acceptance of the learned intermediary defense: The language quoted above indicates that if health-care providers will *not* be a position to pass on warnings, the manufacturer has a duty to give the warnings and instructions ***directly to the patient***. So, for instance, if the product is sold over-the-counter to consumers with a mass-media campaign, then warnings must be made to the consumer (e.g., in packaging inserts and/or on TV ads), not just to physicians who might recommend the item to patients.

b. **Exceptions:** Most courts that accept the learned intermediary doctrine recognize several ***exceptions*** to it. The most important one is the one mentioned above in connection with the Restatement: if the health-care provider for that drug will typically not be in a position to pass on the manufacturer's warnings (e.g., because the prescriber will generally not be meeting with the patient about that particular drug), then the doctrine does not apply and the manufacturer must see to it that warnings actually reach the end-user.

2. **Adequacy of warning:** When a warning directly to the end-user is required, the manufacturer must provide, in language comprehensible to a lay person, a warning conveying a fair indication of the ***nature, gravity and likelihood*** of the known or knowable risks of the drug.

3. **Failure-to-warn as main basis for liability:** In the usual situation where a prescription drug is of net benefit to some class of patients, ***defective-design*** liability will not exist. In these situations, therefore, failure-to-warn is the *only* basis for liability. Thus most product liability suits brought against drug companies are premised upon the failure to warn.

4. **Warnings about generic drugs:** ***Generic*** drugs pose a special issue concerning warnings, due to the special way that warnings on generic drugs are regulated by the federal government.

a. **Regulation of warnings:** First, let's look at how the regulation of warning labels by the federal Food and Drug Administration (FDA) ***varies*** as between labeling on the brand-name drug and that on the generic version.

i. **Warnings on brand-name drugs:** When a company makes and proposes to market a ***brand-name*** prescription drug, federal law places on the manufacturer the responsibility for drafting the label for the drug; the label must contain all sorts of federally-dictated information, including such matters as usage instructions (e.g., recommended dosages), contraindications to use, and a listing of the most-common and/or most-serious adverse reactions.

ii. **Warnings on generic drugs:** By contrast, the maker of a ***generic*** drug has far less — essentially zero — responsibility for drafting the warning label for that drug. In brief, the generic maker must place ***"the same"***

label on the drug as the one the FDA has currently approved for the brand-name version. So, for instance, if either the brand-name maker or the generic maker learns of some ***new hazard*** posed by the drug, the generic maker ***may not modify*** the label to warn of the new hazard until the FDA approves the new language (whereas the brand-name maker may, indeed must, ***unilaterally*** change the label, subject to subsequent FDA review).

b. Possible right to sue brand-name maker if P took the generic: What happens when a plaintiff who has taken an arguably-mislabeled ***generic*** drug seeks recovery not from the maker of the generic, but from the ***maker of the branded version,*** perhaps on a misrepresentation theory? After all, it's the branded manufacturer who has written the label and has the responsibility to update the label based on any newly-discovered hazards. But the American law of product liability has always implicitly restricted product liability suits — even suits based on inadequate warning labels — to ones brought against defendants who either ***manufactured*** the particular instance of the defective product that harmed the plaintiff, or who were ***part of the chain that distributed*** that instance. So letting the patient injured by an improperly-labeled generic drug recover from the creator/maker of the branded version would require abandoning this central requirement of product-liability law.

i. Majority rule says that P is out of luck: Indeed, the substantial majority of courts to have considered the issue have held that the plaintiff who took the generic version is ***simply out of luck:*** in these states, there is ***no*** drug-maker from whom the plaintiff can recover. These courts have ***rejected*** the theory that the plaintiff should be able to recover against the ***brand-name manufacturer*** based on fraud or negligent misrepresentation in creating and disseminating the incorrect labeling.

ii. Minority approach allows recovery against branded manufacturer where P took the generic: But a few recent cases have reached the ***opposite result***, by ***allowing*** the plaintiff who consumed an arguably mislabeled generic drug to seek recovery on a ***fraud or misrepresentation theory against the brand-name manufacturer*** who drafted the text of the label used on the generic drug, even though that defendant did not manufacture or distribute the generic drug taken by the plaintiff. [*T.H. v. Novartis Pharmaceuticals Corp.*]

D. Unknown and unknowable dangers: If D can show that it ***neither knew*** nor, in the exercise of reasonable care ***should have known*** of a danger at the time of sale, most courts hold that there was ***no duty to warn*** of the unknown danger.

Example: If D sells a prescription drug without having any ability to know of a particular side effect, failure to warn of that side effect will not give rise to strict product liability.

E. Danger to small number of people: If the manufacturer knows that the product will be dangerous to a ***small number*** of people, the need for a warning will usually turn on the ***magnitude*** of the danger; if the danger is great enough, even a small number of potential bad results will require a warning.

F. Government labelling standards: The scope of D's duty to warn may be affected by the fact that the ***government*** imposes certain ***labeling*** requirements.

1. **Evidence:** If D can show that it has complied with a federal or state labelling requirement, most courts permit this to be shown as ***evidence*** that the warning was adequate. But in most courts, this evidence is not dispositive — the jury is always free to conclude that a reasonable manufacturer would have given a more specific, or different, warning.

2. **Preemption:** But where the labeling requirement is imposed by the ***federal government***, and the court finds that Congress intended to ***preempt*** more-demanding state labeling rules, then compliance with the federal standard *is* a complete defense to P's "failure to warn" claim.

G. Post-sale duty to warn: Courts have disagreed about the extent to which a manufacturer has a duty to make a ***post-sale*** warning about dangers of which the manufacturer was not aware at the time of manufacture.

1. **Duty to warn when manufacturer learns of the risk:** The most common approach is to hold that if the manufacturer eventually ***learns about the risk***, it has an ***obligation to give a post-sale warning,*** assuming the risk is great and the user of the product can be identified. In this situation, a duty to warn probably exists even though the defect was ***not knowable at the time of manufacture***.

2. **Duty to monitor:** Some courts have held that the manufacturer has a duty not only to warn about dangers or defects that it learns about, but also an affirmative duty to ***"keep abreast of the field"*** by ***monitoring the performance and safety*** of its products after sale. Such an affirmative duty of monitoring and testing is most likely to be found in cases involving ***prescription drugs***.

H. Obvious danger: If the danger is ***obvious*** to most people, this will be a factor reducing D's obligation to warn. But where a warning could easily be given, and a substantial minority of people might not otherwise know of the danger, the court may nonetheless find a duty to warn.

I. Hidden causation issue: In any failure-to-warn scenario, be sure to check that the requirement of a ***causal link*** between the failure to warn and the resulting injury is satisfied. If the provision of a warning ***would not have prevented the accident*** from occurring, then the defendant will ***not*** be liable for failing to warn.

1. **Plaintiff who does not read warnings or ignores them:** For example, in a case in which the injured plaintiff is the one who was the user of the product, and the claim is based upon the defendant manufacturer's failure to place a warning label on the product, evidence that the plaintiff ***never read any warning labels*** would prevent failure-to-warn liability. Similarly, if there is evidence that even had plaintiff read the warning, plaintiff would have ***ignored the warning*** and used the product in the same way so that the accident would have happened anyway, failure to warn will not be the basis for liability.

VII. WHO MAY BE A DEFENDANT

A. Goods: In any case involving a ***"good"*** or ***"chattel,"*** both strict and warranty liability will apply to ***any seller*** in the ***business*** of selling goods of that kind.

1. **Retailer:** This means that a ***retail dealer*** who sells the good, but has not manufactured it, will have strict liability as well as warranty liability, even if she could have done nothing to discover the defect. But this is true only if the seller is in the ***business of selling goods of that type*** (so that a private individual selling a good, or a business person selling outside of the usual course of his business, will not have liability).

   a. **Indemnity:** If the retailer is held liable in this way, she will be entitled to ***indemnity*** from the manufacturer or wholesaler, as long as the retailer was not herself negligent.

2. **Used goods:** Courts are split as to whether there is strict or warranty liability for the seller of ***used goods***. Probably most courts would hold that there is no such liability.

   Example: Dealer, a used car dealer, sells a used car to X. The brakes are defective, and X is unable to avoid hitting P, a pedestrian. Most courts would not allow P to recover in strict liability against Dealer.

3. **Fulfillment services:** The rise of ***Internet retailing*** has led to an important issue about who is a seller. We'll focus here on ***Amazon***, the overwhelmingly-dominant Internet merchant (but what we say applies to other internet retailers as well).

   a. **Amazon takes title and re-sells:** Often, Amazon.com acts as a true classic retailer: it buys the product from a supplier, thereby ***taking title*** to the product; it then advertises the product as being sold by Amazon and fulfills the order. Here, it's clear that Amazon is the actual seller of the product and will be strictly liable if the product causes personal injury or property damage, just like a brick and mortar store that sells the product.

   b. **Amazon acts as fulfillment agent:** But the substantial majority of product sales that occur on Amazon.com are made under the company's ***"Fulfillment by Amazon,"*** or ***"FBA,"*** program. Under this program, Amazon ***never takes title:*** the merchant who holds title to the goods (1) ships them in bulk to Amazon for storage in an Amazon warehouse; and (2) relies on Amazon to ***receive the order*** on the Amazon.com website, "pick" the goods for the order and ***ship*** them to the customer. In this FBA scenario, is Amazon is a ***"seller"*** of the product for purposes of strict product liability?

      i. **Cases split:** Cases dealing with this issue are quite ***split***. Here's a summary as of 2022: "By and large, U.S. courts have held that Amazon is ***not strictly liable*** for the goods sold by third parties on Amazon's website. … With that said, the tides may be ***turning***, with several recent decisions ***holding Amazon liable*** for defective products sold by third-party sellers on its website." 107 Cornell L. Rev. 705, 717-718 (2022).

      One of the recent cases finding that Amazon is a seller in these FBA situations is set out in the following example.

Example where Amazon loses: P goes to Amazon.com (D) and buys a dog collar listed by a seller named "The Furry Gang." (Before the sale, The Furry Gang had sent the collar to Amazon's warehouse for storage.) Amazon ships the order without ever taking title to it and remits the sale price to The Furry Gang after subtracting fees. The collar badly injures P, who brings a strict product liability suit. P's suit is solely against Amazon, in part because P can't locate The Furry Gang for service. Amazon defends on the grounds that since it never took title, it cannot be a "seller."

Held, for P. The court will not be guided by who held title. Instead, the court will consider these public-policy factors: [1] whether D was the ***only member of the marketing chain available to the injured plaintiff for redress***; [2] whether the imposition of strict liability on D would serve as an ***"incentive to safety"***; [3] whether D is in a ***better position than the consumer*** to ***prevent the circulation of defective products***; and [4] whether D ***can distribute the cost of compensating for injuries*** resulting from defects (e.g., by charging more or adjusting the sale terms). Here, all four of these factors cut in favor of treating Amazon as a seller for strict product liability purposes, so the court will do so. [*Oberdorf v. Amazon.com Inc.*]

B. Lessor of goods: Courts frequently impose strict liability upon a ***lessor*** of defective goods.

Example: A ***car rental*** company may be strictly liable if it rents a defective car and that car injures a pedestrian due to the defect.

1. **Negligence or warranty liability:** The lessor may also be liable for negligence in failing to discover the defect, or on an implied warranty theory by analogy to the UCC.

C. Sellers of real estate: Sellers of ***real estate*** have also sometimes been subjected to strict and warranty liability when the property turns out to be dangerously defective. But probably only a ***professional builder***, not a consumer who resold the house, would be subject to such liability (unless the consumer actively concealed the facts of which he was aware).

D. Services: One who sells ***services***, rather than goods, does not fall within standard strict liability nor within the UCC implied warranties.

1. **Product incorporated in service:** However, if a product is furnished ***in combination with a service***, then most courts (and the Restatements) ***will*** apply strict liability if the product turns out to be defective.

   Example: P goes to D's beauty parlor to get a permanent. D uses a solution made by a cosmetics company, which badly burns P's scalp. A court will probably hold D strictly liable for the defective solution, even though the product is being furnished in combination with services.

2. **Services by professionals:** But where the services are rendered by a ***health professional,*** she will almost never be liable in either strict tort or warranty, even if she uses a product which is defective.

Example: D is a surgeon, who puts a defective pacemaker into P's heart. D will almost certainly not be held strictly liable for the product defect.

VIII. INTERESTS THAT MAY BE PROTECTED

A. Property damage: All the above analysis assumes that P's injury consists of ***personal*** injury. If P's damages consist only of ***property damage***, special rules may apply:

1. **Strict liability and negligence:** P may generally recover in ***strict liability*** and ***negligence*** even though his damage consists only of property damage rather than personal injury.

   a. **Warranties:** But he might not win on a ***warranty*** theory. If P is suing a ***remote defendant*** (one with whom he did not contract), two of the three alternative versions of UCC §2-318 do *not* allow P to recover for property damage unaccompanied by personal injury.

2. **"Property damage" defined:** Since the rules for recovering for property damage are easier for the plaintiff to satisfy than those for recovering "pure economic" damages, the two must be distinguished.

   a. **Property apart from the defective product:** If P's property apart from the defective product is destroyed (e.g., the product causes a fire that burns down P's house), this obviously ***counts*** as property damage, and is recoverable in strict liability.

   b. **Damage to the product itself:** But where the defect causes the ***product itself*** to be destroyed or visibly harmed (e.g., an automobile catches on fire due to a defective radiator), this is probably ***not*** property damage, and thus ***not recoverable*** in strict liability. Instead, it's intangible economic loss, which as described below usually isn't recoverable in strict liability.

   c. **Loss of bargain:** Similarly, if P's damages stem from the fact that the product simply ***doesn't work*** because of the defect, or is ***worth less*** with the defect than without it, most courts treat this as unrecoverable intangible economic harm (discussed below).

B. Intangible economic harm: Where P's damages are found to be solely ***intangible economic*** ones (as opposed to personal injury or property damage), P will find it much harder to recover.

1. **Direct purchaser:** If P is suing the person who sold the goods to him:

   a. **Warranty:** P can readily recover for breach of ***implied or express warranty***. P can recover the difference between what the product would have been worth had it been as warranted, and what it is in fact worth with its defect. He can also generally recover consequential damages, including lost profits.

   b. **Strict liability and negligence:** P probably won't be able to recover for the intangible economic harm in ***strict liability*** or ***negligence*** — the court will probably hold that the UCC warranty claims were intended as the ***sole remedy*** for intangible economic harm by a purchaser against his immediate seller.

2. **Remote purchaser and non-purchaser:** Where P is suing not his own seller, but a ***remote person*** (e.g., the manufacturer), he will probably ***not*** recover anything if his only harm is an intangible economic one.

   a. **Warranty:** Most courts would deny an implied ***warranty*** claim, on the grounds that P must sue his own immediate seller for such breaches.

   b. **Strict liability:** Almost all courts would deny recovery to the remote buyer for economic harm on a ***strict liability*** theory.

   c. **Negligence:** Most courts deny P recovery in ***negligence*** for pure intangible economic harm.

   d. **Non-purchaser:** The same is true where P is ***not a purchaser at all*** (e.g., P is a ***bystander***) — P probably can't recover on any theory for his intangible economic loss.

   Example: P owns a restaurant, located next door to an office building that is owned by X Corp. and occupied exclusively by X Corp's employees. D manufactures a faulty boiler, which it sells to X Corp. The boiler explodes, damaging X Corp's building extensively. The building damage causes X Corp. to suspend operations for one month while repairs are made. During that month, P's restaurant loses 50% of its revenues, and all its profits, due to the absence of X Corp. employees as customers.

   Even though the defective boiler has caused property damage to X Corp. (for which X will be able to recover on a strict liability theory), *P* will not be permitted to recover in strict liability (or, for that matter, in negligence or warranty) because she has suffered only intangible economic harm.

   e. **Combined:** But remember that if P can show that he has received either physical injury or "property damage," he may then be able to ***"tack on"*** his intangible economic harm as an ***additional*** element of damages. This would certainly be the case in a negligence action, and might possibly be true in a strict liability or warranty action.

IX. DEFENSES BASED ON PLAINTIFF'S CONDUCT

A. **General rule of plaintiff's negligence applies:** Early product liability decisions hesitated to make P's contributory or comparative negligence a defense. But under the modern approach, this has changed: usually, ***whatever*** the jurisdiction's standard method of dealing with plaintiff's negligence is (typically comparative negligence of one sort or another), ***that method applies to product-liability actions***.

   Example: In a typical comparative-negligence jurisdiction, P's comparative negligence in using a defective product will reduce, but not eliminate, D's liability in a strict product liability action.

B. **Different types of negligence by P:** There are a number of different ways in which a plaintiff might behave negligently with respect to a product.

   1. **Failure to discover the risk:** First, P might ***"negligently" fail to discover that there is a defect at all.*** Here, the modern approach essentially agrees with that of

the earlier approach: if P's only fault is to fail to discover the defect, this is probably ***not really "negligence" at all***, since a person is normally entitled to assume that a product is not defective. Therefore, in the ordinary case P's failure to discover the defect will not cause any reduction in her recovery.

2. **Knowing assumption of risk:** Second, P might be fully aware of a product's defectiveness (whether of a manufacturing or design nature), yet voluntarily and unreasonably decide to ***"assume the risk"*** of that defect. In this situation, the modern trend is to ***treat assumption-of-risk as a form of comparative negligence***: to the extent that P's decision to use the product in the face of the known risk was ***unreasonable***, it will cause plaintiff's recovery to be reduced proportionately (and will ***not*** serve as an ***absolute bar*** to recovery).

   Example: P is driving a new car manufactured by D. A warning light suddenly flashes, saying "Overheated engine. Stop immediately." P knows that an overheated engine can often lead to an explosion, with consequent physical danger. P then looks under the hood, and sees that a water hose has ruptured, causing the engine to receive too little water. (Assume that this rupture constitutes a manufacturing defect for which D will be liable under standard strict-liability doctrine.) Nonetheless, P continues to drive for 100 more miles in 90 degree temperatures, even though he is merely taking a pleasure drive. The engine explodes, injuring P.

   Under the Third Restatement and modern approach, P's conduct — though it consists of a voluntary encountering of a known risk — will be treated the same as any other type of plaintiff's negligence. In a pure comparative negligence jurisdiction, therefore, P's recovery will be reduced by an amount representing P's portion of the combined "responsibility" of P and D, but P will still be allowed to make some recovery.

3. **Ignoring of safety precaution:** Suppose P ***consciously fails to use an available safety device***, and is then injured by a product defect that would not have led to injury had the safety device been used. In some situations, the safety device is one provided by the manufacturer of the defective product; in other cases, it is provided by a third party. The analysis is pretty much the same in both types of situations — in most courts the plaintiff's failure to use an available safety device is generally fault that ***reduces*** (but does ***not eliminate***) plaintiff's recovery.

   Example: P, a consumer, purchases a Slicer-Dicer made by D. The Slicer-Dicer is designed to slice, dice, chop, and puree a variety of household products. The Slicer Dicer comes with a hand guard, which when installed prevents the user's hand from getting near the cutting blades. The hand guard is purposely designed to be removable for easy cleaning; the device and its instruction manual both contain a bold-faced warning that the device should not be operated without the hand guard. P removes the hand guard because he finds it easier to use the machine without it; he realizes that there is a greater danger of cutting his hand, but decides to risk it. P's hand slips, and is severely cut by the blades. P sues D on the theory that D's permitting the guard to be removed for separate cleaning constituted a design defect.

In a modern comparative-negligence jurisdiction the court will probably hold that P's use of the product without the guard should reduce, but not eliminate, his recovery.

4. **Use for unintended purpose:** If P totally ***misuses*** the product, D will not be relieved from liability unless the misuse was so ***unforeseeable*** or ***unreasonable*** that either: (1) the misuse ***couldn't reasonably be warned against or designed against***, or (2) the misuse is found to be ***"superseding."***

   Example: D makes a chair with bars across the back. The chair is designed for seating, not climbing. P takes the chair and uses the bars across the back as a step-ladder; he then falls and hurts himself badly. A court would probably hold that the misuse here is so unforeseeable and unreasonable that the risks the design presents (the risk of unsafe climbing) need not be designed against or warned against.

X. DEFENSES BASED ON FEDERAL REGULATION, MAINLY THE DEFENSE OF PREEMPTION

A. **Preemption:** Federal regulation of product safety can have an important impact on consumers' state product-liability rights. In particular, under the doctrine of ***"preemption,"*** federal regulatory action may ***limit the states' freedom to apply their usual rules of tort liability*** to cases involving the regulated product.

1. **The Supremacy Clause:** The concept of preemption is based on the ***Supremacy Clause*** of the U.S. Constitution. That clause says, in essence, that federal law ***takes priority over conflicting state law.***

2. **Preemption, generally:** Here is a brief summary of how preemption works in the context of product-liability law:

   a. **Express preemption:** First — and usually easiest to apply — is ***"express"*** preemption. This occurs when Congress explicitly says that it intends to take away the states' ability to regulate in a particular way. When it is clear that Congress has meant to do this, the Supremacy Clause nullifies any attempt by a state to do what Congress has said the state may not do.

      i. **Express preemption in medical-device cases:** Express preemption is likely to be found, for instance, where the Food and Drug Administration ***pre-approves*** a newly-developed ***medical device*** such as a pacemaker or heart valve. Once this happens, a user of the device will generally not be permitted to recover under state tort law for the device's defectiveness. That's because the court will likely conclude that the federal approval expressly preempts a state from awarding tort damages premised on the device's defectiveness. [*Riegel v. Medtronic Inc.*]

   b. **Implied preemption:** Most real-life controversies involving preemption in tort law, however, involve ***"implied"*** rather than express preemption. That is, Congress (or a federal agency acting under direction from Congress) does not explicitly tell the states that they may not take a particular tort-related action. Instead, Congress or the federal agency enacts a statute or regulation, and a litigant (usually the manufacturer of the product) argues that the federal enactment should be interpreted as displacing a particular state tort-law rule. There are two different ways in which implied preemption can occur in a tort-law context, a ***direct conflict*** and a federal decision to ***occupy*** an ***entire field.***

i. Direct conflict: Sometimes analysis of the federal law and the state law shows that the two are in ***direct conflict***. When this happens, as you'd expect, the state law must yield. The direct conflict can be of two sorts:

(1) Can't comply simultaneously: It is ***impossible*** for the maker of a product to ***comply simultaneously*** with the federal regulation and the state regulation; or

(2) Objectives are inconsistent: The ***objectives*** behind the federal regulation and the state regulation are ***inconsistent***.

Example of (1) (compliance with both is impossible): Suppose that Congress says that every package of cigarettes must contain a label stating, "the Surgeon General has determined that smoking may be hazardous to your health." Suppose then that North Carolina, a tobacco-growing state, passes a statute saying "No health warnings are required in this state on any package of cigarettes." Obviously there is a direct contradiction between the federal and state regulatory schemes — a given cigarette package cannot comply with both. Therefore, the state regulation is invalid.

Example of (2) (conflicting objectives): Suppose that Congress says, "it is the desire of Congress that auto manufacturers be encouraged to install airbags in every automobile produced after the date of this act." To further that objective, Congress gives auto manufacturers a $200 tax credit for every car that is made with an airbag. Texas then passes a statute saying, "in any tort litigation in which the occupant of a vehicle alleges that he or she has been injured by the inappropriate inflation of an airbag, the burden of proving the non-defectiveness of the airbag shall be placed upon the manufacturer." A court might well hold that in view of the strong federal interest in encouraging airbag installation, the Texas statute has a sharply conflicting objective — making airbag installation more burdensome to manufacturers — and that the Texas statute should therefore be deemed impliedly preempted by the federal legislation.

ii. Occupation of entire field: The second form of implied preemption occurs where the federal government is found to have ***intended to occupy an entire field of regulation***. If such an intent is found, then even a state law that does ***not directly conflict*** with the federal law will be preempted.

(1) Need for uniformity: When a court is deciding whether Congress intended to occupy the entire field, the court will give special weight to indications that Congress perceived a need for a ***uniform national rule***, rather than varying state rules. So, for instance, in the medical-device-labeling field, the need for manufacturers to have a ***single nationwide system of labels*** (not state-by-state variations) would be an important factor pointing a court towards the conclusion that Congress intended to occupy the entire field.

c. Implied preemption of state tort remedies: Sometimes a manufacturer succeeds with the argument that federal regulation preempts the states from allowing a plaintiff to recover for a ***common-law tort***. Here, the defendant manufacturer is typically making the argument that merely ***allowing a plaintiff to recover in tort*** would itself constitute an ***implicit*** sort of "regulation" that is inconsistent with the federal regulatory scheme. So these are cases of "implied" (rather than "express") preemption of state law by federal law.

i. Needs direct conflict or impeding of federal enforcement: It is ***not easy*** for a manufacturer to defeat a common-law tort claim by use of an implied preemption defense. As a good rule of thumb, the manufacturer (D) will win with such a defense *only* if it can show that *either:*

[1] the conduct that P argues D was required to take under state common-law rules ***conflicts*** with the federal regulation; or

[2] allowing the tort recovery sought by P ***would impede enforcement*** of the federal regulatory scheme.

Manufacturers will often have a tough time making either of these showings.

ii. Implied preemption in prescription-drug cases: Cases involving ***prescription drugs*** will often be found to involve only "***implied***" preemption. Although Congress has given the FDA authority to regulate prescription drugs just as it allowed the agency to regulate medical devices like the one in *Riegel* (*supra*, p. 166), Congress has ***not expressly dealt with preemption*** in the prescription-drug context. Therefore, prescription-drug cases are harder for the defendant manufacturer to win on a preemption theory than are medical-device cases, because an implied-preemption defense tends to be harder to establish than an express-preemption one. [*Wyeth v. Levine*]

B. Compliance with government standards: Don't confuse the defense of federal preemption of state law with a separate defense, the so-called ***"regulatory compliance"*** defense. The latter defense asserts that because a product complies with a particular government regulation scheme, that compliance automatically means that the product is not defective.

1. Usually rejected: Most jurisdictions do *not* accept the regulatory compliance defense — the plaintiff is free to show that even though the product meets the relevant federal regulatory requirements, the product is nonetheless defective. (However, nearly all states at least allow the fact that the product meets federal regulatory requirements to be admitted as non-dispositive *evidence* of non-defectiveness.) The regulatory compliance defense is discussed *supra*, p. 156.

CHAPTER 15
NUISANCE

I. NUISANCE GENERALLY

A. Type of injury: The term "nuisance" refers not to a type of tort, but to a ***type of injury*** which P has sustained. In the case of "public nuisance," the injury is the loss of any right that P has by virtue of being a "member of the public." In the case of "private nuisance," P's injury is interference with his ***use or enjoyment of his land.***

1. **Three mental states:** A suit for nuisance may be supported by any of the three defendant mental states: (1) intentional interference with P's rights; (2) negligence; or (3) abnormally dangerous activity or other conduct giving rise to strict liability.

II. PUBLIC NUISANCE

A. Definition: A ***"public nuisance"*** is an interference with a ***"right common to the general public."***

1. **Examples:** We talk more below about what is a right "common to the general public." Generally, activities that interfere with ***public waterways, air purity,*** or ***public roads and facilities***, are the most likely to be found to satisfy this standard.

2. **Factors:** Courts look at a number of factors in deciding whether something is a public nuisance, including the ***type of neighborhood***, the frequency/duration, the degree of damage, and the social value of the activity.

   a. **Substantial harm required:** A public nuisance will not be found to exist unless the harm to the public is ***substantial***.

3. **Need not be a crime:** It is no longer the case that for conduct to be actionable as a public nuisance, it must also be a ***crime*** (though the fact the conduct *is* a crime will make it more likely to be held to be a public nuisance).

B. "Right common to general public": The key element of a claim of public nuisance is that the right that is being unreasonably interfered with must be a "right that is ***common to the general public.***"

1. **Has impact:** This requirement of a right common to the general public has considerable ***impact***, in that it prevents many widespread harms from being eligible to be considered public nuisances. As the Second Restatement puts it, to be a right common to all members of the general public the right must be "***collective in nature*** and *not* like the *individual* right that everyone has not to be assaulted or defamed or defrauded or negligently injured."

   a. **What qualifies:** As the idea is sometimes put, the term "public right" is limited to those ***"indivisible resources shared by the public at large***, such as ***air, water, or public rights of way***."

      i. **Interference with just some people:** Even if the interference *is* with a shared resource like air or water, the interference won't qualify if by its nature it affects ***only a few isolated landowners, not the public at large.*** Thus the Restatement says, "the pollution of a stream that merely deprives 50 or 100 lower riparian owners of the use of the water for purposes connected with their land does not for that reason alone become a public nuisance. If, however, the pollution prevents the use of a public bathing beach or kills the fish in a navigable stream and so deprives *all members of the community* of the right to fish, it becomes a public nuisance."

ii. **Interference that occurs within individual private properties:** The "common right" requirement means that typically, a claim that a product has had a particular effect on a piece of ***privately-owned real estate not accessible to the public*** at large will ***fail*** the common-right test.

Examples: Thus claims that manufacturers have infiltrated ***guns*** into neighborhoods, or that manufacturers of ***paints*** have failed to remove lead from them and thus injured children living in buildings painted with these paints, have tended to fail the "common right" standard.

C. Requirement of particular damage: Courts sometime say that a private citizen may recover for his own damages stemming from a public nuisance, but only if he has sustained damage that is different in ***kind***, not just degree, from that suffered by the public generally. However, it's not clear how much impact this so-called requirement has anymore; many newer decisions seem to ignore it.

Example: P is a tenant of a small novelty store on the boardwalk opposite a famous beach; the boardwalk contains hundreds of merchants. D, an oil exploration company, negligently causes an offshore oil spill that fouls the beach for the entire summer, causing P's profits to drop 50% or $20,000, and doing approximately the same to hundreds of the other merchants. It's likely that P can recover from D in public nuisance for his lost profits, notwithstanding that hundreds of other merchants have suffered the same sort of harm to their collective right to an unfouled beach.

D. Within "control" of defendant at time of harm: For public nuisance, courts require that the defendant have had ***control over the instrumentality*** at the ***time of damage*** — it's ***not*** enough that defendant had control at some ***earlier*** point (e.g., at the time of a sale of a product).

Example: In a case by a state against makers of lead-paint that poisoned children in apartment buildings, the Ds (the paint manufacturers) would likely escape liability if the state can't show that when the child plaintiffs were ingesting the lead, the Ds still had the right to abate the nuisance by removing the paint. The fact that the Ds had been in control of the contents of the paint at the time of the much earlier sales to the building owners would be irrelevant — the "control at the time of the harm" requirement is what counts, and is what's not satisfied here.

III. PRIVATE NUISANCE

A. Nature of private nuisance: A ***private nuisance*** is an ***unreasonable interference*** with P's ***use and enjoyment*** of his ***land***.

1. **Must have interest in land:** P can sue based on a private nuisance only if he has an ***interest in land*** that has been affected.

   Example: A fisherman who is injured by an oil spill cannot sue for private nuisance, because no interest in land held by him is affected.

   a. **Tenants and family members:** But a fee simple is not necessary — a ***tenant***, or members of the ***family*** of the owner or tenant, may sue.

2. **Elements:** P must demonstrate ***two*** elements in order to recover: (1) that his ***use and enjoyment of his land*** was interfered with in a ***substantial way***; and (2) that D's conduct was either ***negligent, abnormally dangerous***, or ***intentional***.

B. Interference with use: The interference with P's use and enjoyment must be ***substantial***. If P's damage is merely a small ***inconvenience*** (e.g., somewhat extra noise, mildly unpleasant smells), there will be no recovery.

C. Defendant's conduct: There is ***no general rule of "strict liability" in nuisance***. P must show that D's conduct fell within one of the three classes for tortious defendant conduct: ***negligence, intent***, or ***abnormal dangerousness***.

Example: D, a utility, suddenly spews polluted smoke onto the land of P, a nearby owner. Unless P can show that D was careless in allowing the pollutants, intended to pollute, or was carrying out an abnormally dangerous activity, P cannot recover for private nuisance.

1. **Intentional:** In nuisance cases, D's conduct will be deemed "intentional" even though D did not ***desire*** to interfere with P's use and enjoyment of her land, as long as D ***knew with substantial certainty*** that such interference would occur.

   Example: In the above example, if P put D on notice that pollution was occurring, and D continued with the conduct, the continuing conduct would be deemed intentional, and D could be liable for nuisance.

2. **Unreasonableness:** D's interference with P's interest must be ***"unreasonable."***

   a. **Test for unreasonableness:** The interference will be deemed unreasonable if *either*: (1) the harm to P outweighs the utility of D's conduct; *or* (2) the harm caused to P is greater than P should be required to bear without compensation.

   Example: On the above pollution example, even though operation of a utility is socially beneficial, and even if the social benefits outweigh the damage to P from the pollutants, D probably will have to pay for the polluting because it is not fair that P should have to bear the burden of this pollution without compensation.

3. **Nature of neighborhood:** One important factor in determining whether D's conduct is "unreasonable" is the kind of ***neighborhood*** in which D and P are

located — the more commercial or industrial the neighborhood, the less likely given conduct is to be a nuisance.

D. Remedies: P may be entitled to one or both of the following ***remedies*** for private nuisance:

1. **Damages:** If the harm has already occurred, P can recover ***compensatory damages.***

2. **Injunction:** If P can show that damages would not be a sufficient remedy, she may be entitled to an ***injunction*** against continuation of the nuisance. (But to get the injunction, P probably has to show that the harm to her and to all others similarly situated ***outweighs*** the utility of D's conduct.)

E. Defenses: P's conduct may give rise to the defenses of contributory negligence and/or assumption of risk.

1. **Contributory negligence:** Where the claim is based on D's ***negligent*** maintenance of the nuisance, contributory negligence will normally be a defense.

2. **Assumption of risk:** The defense of ***assumption of risk*** is generally applicable to nuisance cases.

   a. **"Coming to the nuisance":** Most commonly, the defense arises where D claims that P ***"came to the nuisance,"*** i.e., P purchases property with ***advance knowledge*** that the nuisance exists. Today, "coming to the nuisance" is not an absolute defense, but merely ***one factor to be considered*** in determining whether P should win.

   Example: P, a developer, buys a parcel next to D's cattle feed lot, and sells off some of the parcels as homesites. D will be enjoined from operating the feed lot — the manure from which creates flies and odor — even though P came to the nuisance, because the rights of innocent parties, including the homeowners, are at stake. [*Spur Industries, Inc. v. Dell E. Webb Development Co.*]

CHAPTER 16

MISREPRESENTATION

I. INTENTIONAL MISREPRESENTATION ("DECEIT")

A. Definition: The common law action of ***"deceit"*** or "fraud" corresponds to what we today call ***"intentional misrepresentation."***

1. **Elements:** To recover for intentional misrepresentation, P must establish the following elements:

   a. A ***misrepresentation*** by D;

   b. ***Scienter*** (i.e., a culpable state of mind — either knowledge of the statement's falsity or reckless indifference to the truth);

   c. An ***intent to induce the plaintiff's reliance*** on the misrepresentation;

d. ***Justifiable reliance*** by P; and

e. ***Damage*** to P, stemming from the reliance.

B. Misrepresentation: D must make a ***misrepresentation*** to P. Normally, this will be in ***words***.

1. **Actions:** But D's ***actions*** may also constitute a misrepresentation.

   Example: A used car dealer turns back the odometer on a car. This is misrepresentation.

2. **Concealment:** If D intentionally ***conceals*** a fact from P, he will be treated the same way as if he had affirmatively misstated that fact.

3. **Non-disclosure:** If D simply ***fails to disclose*** a material fact (as opposed to taking positive steps to conceal it), it is harder for P to establish the requisite misrepresentation:

   a. **Common law:** At common law, failure to disclose was almost never a misrepresentation.

   b. **Modern view:** In modern courts, the general rule remains that failure to disclose by itself does ***not*** constitute misrepresentation.

      i. **Exceptions:** But modern cases recognize some ***exceptions***, including:

         [1] matters which must be disclosed because of a ***fiduciary relationship*** between the two parties (e.g., lawyer/client);

         [2] matters which must be disclosed in order to prevent a ***partial*** statement of the facts from being misleading;

         [3] ***newly acquired*** information, which, if not disclosed, would make a previous statement misleading; and

         [4] facts ***basic to the transaction***, if the party with knowledge knows of the other's reliance and knows that the other would reasonably expect a disclosure of those facts.

         Example: A homeowner who fails to disclose to the buyer the presence of ***termites*** will today often be found to have made a misrepresentation — this is a fact basic to the transaction that, as the seller should know, a buyer would normally expect to be told about. This represents a change from the common-law rule.

C. Scienter: P must show that D had that culpable state of mind called ***"scienter."*** D acts with scienter if he either:

[1] ***knew or believed*** that he was not telling the truth;

[2] did not have the ***confidence in the accuracy*** of his statement that he stated or implied that he did; or

[3] knew that he ***did not have the grounds*** for a statement that he stated or implied that he did.

1. **Negligence not enough:** Scienter does not exist where D was merely ***negligent*** in making the misrepresentation. (In this instance, a claim for negligent misrepresentation, discussed below, must be brought.)

D. Third-party recovery: Where the fraudulent misrepresentation was not made to P, but to some third person, the rules have changed:

1. **Common law rule:** At common law, D was liable only to those persons whom he ***intended*** to influence by his misrepresentation, and not to others, even though their reliance may have been foreseeable.

    Example: The Ds, directors of a company, prepare an intentionally false prospectus, intending to influence people who buy stock at the initial public offering. P later buys "used" stock from an existing stockholder, and relies on the misrepresentation. At common law, P may not recover against D, because D did not intend to influence P, even though P's reliance was quite foreseeable. [*Peek v. Gurney*]

2. **Modern rule:** But modern cases make it easier for P to recover. Even if D did not intend to influence P, P can recover if she can show that: (1) she is a member of a class which D had ***reason to expect*** would be induced to rely; and (2) the transaction is of the ***same sort*** that D had reason to expect would occur in reliance.

    Example: D falsely claims to have good title in an auto, and sells the car to X, who D knows is wholesaler. X resells to P, repeating the misrepresentation. Under modern law, P could recover against D, because P is a member of a class — ultimate buyers — whom D had reason to expect might rely on the misrepresentation, and the transaction is of the same sort — sale of the car — as D had reason to expect would occur in reliance. [*Varwig v. Anderson-Behel Porsche/Audi*]

E. Justifiable reliance: P must also show that he in fact ***relied*** on the misrepresentation, and that his reliance was ***justifiable***.

1. **Investigation by P:** If, after receiving D's misrepresentation, P makes his ***own investigation***, and ***relies totally*** or almost totally upon this investigation, P will be held not to have met the reliance requirement. (But if the misrepresentation is a ***substantial factor*** in inducing the reliance, P can recover even though his own investigation was also a substantial factor.)

2. **Justifiability:** P must show that his reliance was ***justifiable***.

    a. **No general duty to investigate:** P has no ***duty to investigate*** on his own, even where an investigation could be easily done, and would disclose the falsity of D's statements. (But P may not overlook the ***"obvious"*** — if he does, his reliance is unjustifiable.)

3. **Materiality:** P must show that the fact that he relied on was ***material*** to the underlying transaction.

F. Opinion: It is hard for P to recover for a statement that is fairly characterizable as an ***"opinion."***

1. **Adverse party:** It is especially hard for P to recover where D was an ***"adverse***

party" to P at the time of the misstatements. But even here, P may be justified in relying on D's expression of opinion in one of these special situations. Here are the most important such situations:

a. Special knowledge: D "purports to have ***special knowledge*** of the matter" that the plaintiff does not have and D then actively ***conceals material information.***

Example: The Ps, experienced restaurant operators, negotiate with D, a company that owns a vacant building that the Ps propose to lease for use as a restaurant. During the negotiations, D's representative, Powell, tells the Ps, "The building is in perfect condition. ... [There has] been nothing wrong with the place at all." After the Ps sign the lease and begin remodeling the property, they learn from multiple sources that there was previously a hamburger restaurant there, whose operations were harmed by the building's "very very bad odor." The Ps sue D to recover damages for fraud. D defends on several grounds, one of which is that Powell's statements were statements of opinion.

Held, for the Ps: Powell's statements about the building's suitability for the Ps' planned restaurant give rise to a fraud claim. This is true even if, as D argues, Powell's statements are properly considered "pure expressions of opinion." Powell and D had a ***one-sided knowledge of past facts.*** Where a lessor has ***"superior personal knowledge,"*** a prospective tenant is entitled to rely on the fact that the lessor ***"will not actively conceal material information."*** *Italian Cowboy Partners, Ltd. v. Prudential Ins. Co. of Am.*]

b. Fiduciary relationship: The defendant "stands in a ***fiduciary*** or other similar relation of trust and confidence" to the plaintiff.

c. Confidence: The defendant "has successfully endeavored to secure the ***confidence***" of the plaintiff.

d. Other: There is some other "special reason" to expect that the plaintiff will rely on the defendant's opinion.

i. Defendant knows of plaintiff's gullibility: For instance, if the defendant knows that the plaintiff is particularly ***gullible*** or unintelligent, and therefore has reason to believe that the plaintiff will be misled by a false statement of opinion, this would be a "special reason" to expect the plaintiff to rely.

e. "Puffing" still not actionable: But ***"puffing"*** or ***"trade talk"*** is *not* actionable.

Example: Car Dealer says to Consumer, "This is the best two-door car for the money." In fact, Car Dealer believes that the car is a terrible value. Consumer cannot recover for intentional misrepresentation, because Car Dealer's statement is obviously "puffing."

2. Opinion of apparently disinterested person: If the opinion is expressed not by one of the parties to a business deal, but by someone whom the plaintiff reasonably perceives as being ***"disinterested,"*** it is ***easier*** for P to recover.

3. **Opinion implying fact:** The above rules apply only to statements of "pure" opinion. Where an opinion either ***expresses*** or ***implies facts***, P can recover for misstatement of the underlying facts.

   a. **Lack of knowledge of inconsistent facts:** Thus an opinion often contains the implied statement that its maker knows of no facts ***incompatible*** with that opinion. If P can show that D really knew facts incompatible with his opinion, P can recover.

   Example: Seller tells Buyer, "In my opinion, this house is structurally sound." Seller really knows that the foundation is badly cracked. Buyer can probably recover.

G. Statements about law: Today, statements involving ***legal principles*** are generally treated the same as any other statement. Thus if D's representation of law includes an implied statement about ***factual*** matters, P may rely upon the factual part of the statement.

Example: T is about to become a tenant in a New York City building owned by L. As L knows, T proposes to operate in the building a business that converts restaurant garbage into fertilizer. The lease contains a representation by L that for zoning purposes, the proposed use will be allowed. P signs the lease, moves in, and starts to convert garbage. However, it turns out that the building's zoning prevents T from doing garbage conversion unless T makes expensive modifications. T sues L for fraud. L defends on the grounds that only a misrepresentation of law rather than of fact is involved, and that misrepresentations about whether the law allows a particular use are always statements of pure opinion, for which state law does not allow recovery in fraud.

Held, for T. The false statement about the building's zoning status was not a pure expression of opinion about the law, but rather a mixed statement of fact and law: when L said that it knew the premises were in an unrestricted district, T properly understood this to mean that L knew, as a fact, that the zoning code allowed the proposed use. Therefore, the false statement was a statement of fact about the building's zoning, not an "opinion of law." [*National Conversion Corp. v. Cedar Bldg. Corp.*]

H. Prediction and intention

1. **Prediction:** If the defendant ***predicts*** that something will happen, this will generally be treated as an opinion, which means that in most instances it cannot be relied on.

2. **Intention:** But where D makes a statement as to her own ***intentions***, this is generally treated as a factual representation that can be relied on.

I. Damages: If the misrepresentation was made directly by D to P, most courts give P the ***"benefit of the bargain"*** measure of damages.

II. NEGLIGENT MISREPRESENTATION

A. General: At common law, there was no action for "negligent misrepresentation." Unless P suffered personal injury or direct property damage (thus enabling her to bring a conventional negligence action), P was out of luck. But today, most courts ***do*** allow recovery for negligent misrepresentation, even where only ***intangible economic harm*** is suffered.

1. **Same requirements:** Most requirements for a negligent misrepresentation action are the same as for an intentional misrepresentation action.

B. Business relationship: Courts are quickest to allow recovery for negligent misrepresentation where D's statements are made in the course of his ***business or profession***, and D had a ***pecuniary interest*** in the transaction. (Thus if D is P's friend, and makes a representation that is not in the course of D's business, P cannot recover.)

C. Liability to third persons: The maker of a negligent misrepresentation is liable to a much ***narrower class*** of third persons than is the maker of a fraudulent misstatement.

1. **Persons intended to be reached:** According to the Second Restatement, D is liable for negligent misrepresentation to a ***"limited group of persons"*** whom D either: (1) ***intends to reach*** with the information; or (2) knows the ***recipient intends to reach***.

   Example: D runs a stock ticker service, which negligently reports that X Corp has declared higher earnings, when in fact its earnings are lower. P, an investor, learns of the "higher" earnings from a subscriber to D's service, and buys the stock, losing money. P probably cannot recover from D, since they were not in contractual privity, and since P was not a member of a "limited group of persons" whom D intended to reach or whom D knew that its subscriber intended to reach.

   a. **Persons covered:** Even though the class of third persons covered is narrow, it is still important. Examples where liability might attach include:

      - ❑ A surveyor knows or should know that his survey will be given to a prospective purchaser, and a purchaser relies on the survey in buying the property;
      - ❑ A lawyer drafts a will negligently cutting out a particular intended heir, and the heir sues the lawyer;
      - ❑ An accountant negligently certifies the books of X Corp, knowing that X Corp plans to seek a loan from Bank; Bank makes the loan, X Corp goes bankrupt, and Bank sues the accountant.

III. STRICT LIABILITY

A. Not generally allowed: Generally, a person has no liability for an ***"innocent"*** misrepresentation. In other words, as a general rule there is no strict liability for misrepresentations. But there are some exceptions, discussed below.

B. Sale, rental or exchange: If two parties are involved in a ***sale***, ***rental*** or ***exchange*** transaction, and one makes a material misrepresentation to the other in order to close the deal, he will be liable even if the misrepresentation is innocent.

1. **Warranty:** Usually, the buyer can get as much relief from a claim of ***breach*** of express warranty as from the tort claim of strict liability for misrepresentation. But P may avoid certain contract defenses by relying on the tort theory rather than the warranty theory (e.g., the parol evidence rule).

2. **Service transactions:** A few courts have applied strict liability where D sells P a ***service***, and makes a misrepresentation.

   Example: An agent for Insurance Co. tells P that the policy he is buying will cover him for liability from drunk driving, and through no fault of the agent, the policy does not in fact cover P for this. Some courts might allow P to recover from the agent.

3. **Privity:** The sale, rental or exchange must have been ***directly*** between P and D.

C. Sale of chattel: A seller of goods who makes any misrepresentation on the label, or in public advertising, will be strictly liable for any ***physical injury*** which results, even if the injured person did not buy the product directly from D.

CHAPTER 17

DEFAMATION

I. GENERAL PRINCIPLES

A. Meaning of "defamation": The tort called ***"defamation"*** is actually two sub-torts, "libel" and "slander." These both protect a person's interest in his ***reputation***. A state's freedom to define these torts as it wishes is sharply curtailed by the First Amendment.

B. Prima facie case: To establish a prima facie case for either libel or slander, P must prove:

1. **Defamatory statement:** A ***false*** and ***defamatory*** statement concerning him;

2. **Publication:** A ***communicating*** of that statement to a person other than the plaintiff (a ***"publication"***);

3. **Fault:** ***Fault*** on the part of D, amounting to at least ***negligence***, and in some instances a greater degree of fault;

4. **Special harm:** Either ***"special harm"*** of a pecuniary nature, or the actionability of the statement despite the non-existence of such special harm.

II. DEFAMATORY COMMUNICATION

A. Injury to reputation: To be defamatory, a statement must have a tendency to ***harm the reputation*** of the plaintiff.

1. **Reputation not actually injured:** For the statement to be defamatory, it need

not have ***actually*** harmed P's reputation. It must simply be the case that, ***if the statement had been believed***, it would have injured P's reputation. (But in most cases of slander, and in cases of libel where the defamatory meaning is not apparent from the face of the statement, P has to prove "special damage," i.e., that his reputation was in fact damaged and caused him pecuniary harm — this is not part of the definition of "defamatory," however.)

B. Meaning attached: Many statements can be ***interpreted in more than one way***. Where this is the case, the statement is defamatory if ***any one*** of the interpretations which a reasonable person might make would tend to injure P's reputation, and P shows that at least one of the recipients did ***in fact*** make that interpretation.

C. Reference to plaintiff: P must show that the statement was reasonably interpreted by at least one recipient as ***referring to P***.

1. **Intent irrelevant:** But P does not necessarily have to show that D ***intended*** to refer to him, rather than to someone else. As a common-law matter (putting aside constitutional decisions), even if D behaved non-negligently and intended to refer to someone else entirely, P can still sue.

2. **Groups:** If D's statement concerns a ***group***, and P is a member of that group, P can recover only if the group is a ***relatively small one***.

   Example: The statement, "All lawyers are shysters," would not be defamatory as to any particular lawyer, assuming there was no evidence indicating that the statement was intended to refer to P in particular.

3. **Reference need not be by name:** If a non-explicit reference to P is reasonably understood as in fact referring to P, it does not matter that P is referred to by a ***different name*** or characterization. This is true even if the publication is labelled a "novel."

D. Truth: A statement is ***not defamatory*** if it is ***true***. At common law, it is always the ***defendant*** who has had the burden of proving truth.

1. **Matters of public interest:** Today, as the result of constitutional decisions, the ***plaintiff*** must bear the burden of proving falsity, if: (1) D is a media organization; and (2) the statement involves a matter of ***"public interest"*** (whether P is a public figure or a private figure).

2. **Private figure, no public interest or non-media defendant:** It is probably the case that the states may still require the ***defendant*** to bear the burden of proving truth if: (1) the defendant is not a media organization; *or* (2) the plaintiff is a private figure and the statement is not of public interest.

3. **Substantial truth:** For truth to be a barrier to recovery, it is not necessary that the statement be ***literally*** true in all respects. Instead, the statement must merely be ***"substantially"*** true.

E. Opinion

1. **Pure opinion:** A statement of ***pure opinion*** can never be defamatory.

Example: "I think Smith is a disgusting person," without any factual basis for this statement either expressed or implied, is a statement of pure opinion and therefore cannot be defamatory.

2. **Implied facts:** But if a statement of opinion ***implies undisclosed facts***, and a statement of those facts would be defamatory, then the statement will be itself treated as defamatory.

   Example: "I think P must be an alcoholic" is probably actionable, because it implies that the speaker knows precise facts about P's alcohol consumption which would justify an opinion of alcoholism.

III. LIBEL vs. SLANDER

A. Significance of distinction: Distinguish between "libel" and "slander." It makes a difference only with respect to the requirement of ***special harm***: to establish slander, P must show that he suffered pecuniary harm (unless the statement falls into one of four special categories). To prove libel, by contrast, P does not have to show such special harm (except, in some courts, if the defamatory nature of the statement is not evident on its face).

B. Libel: Libel consists mainly of all ***written or printed matter***.

1. **Embodied in physical form:** Most states hold that it also includes any communication embodied in ***"physical form."***

   Examples: A phonograph record, or a computer tape, would be libel in most courts.

2. **Radio and TV:** Where a program is ***broadcast*** on radio or TV:

   a. **Written script:** If it originated with a ***written script***, all courts treat it as libel.

   b. **No script:** If the program is "ad libbed" rather than coming from a written script, courts are split as to whether it is libel or slander.

C. Slander: All other statements are ***slander***. An ordinary ***oral statement***, for instance, is slander.

D. Special harm: P may generally establish slander only if he can show that he has sustained some ***"special harm."*** This harm generally must be of a ***pecuniary nature***.

Example: P shows only that his friends believed D's defamatory statements, and the friends now socially reject P. If the statement is slander, and does not fall within one of the four "slander per se" categories, P cannot recover.

1. **"Slander per se":** There are four kinds of utterances which, even though they are slander rather than libel, require ***no showing*** of special harm:

   a. **Crime:** Statements imputing morally culpable ***criminal behavior*** to P.

   b. **Loathsome disease:** Statements alleging that P currently suffers from a ***venereal*** or other loathsome and communicable disease.

c. **Business, profession, trade or office:** An allegation that adversely reflects on P's fitness to conduct her ***business***, trade, profession or office.

Example: "P cheats his customers" would be slander per se.

d. **Sexual misconduct:** Statement imputing serious ***sexual misconduct*** to P.

2. **Libel:** In the case of ***libel***, at common law courts do not require proof of actual harm, and can award ***"presumed"*** damages even without a showing of harm. However, recent Supreme Court decisions cut back on the states' ability to do this:

a. **Matters of public concern:** If the statement involves a matter of public concern or a public figure, and recovery is allowed without proof of "actual malice," presumed damages may not constitutionally be awarded.

b. **Matter of private concern:** But if the defamatory statement does *not* involve a matter of "public concern," presumed damages *may* be allowed, even without a showing of "actual malice."

Example: D, a credit reporting agency, sends a subscriber a written report falsely stating that P, an ordinary private corporation, is insolvent. Since the statement is not of "public interest," P may recover $50,000 presumed damages without showing any financial loss, and without showing that D knew of the falsity or recklessly disregarded the truth. [*Dun & Bradstreet v. Greenmoss Builders*]

c. **Actual malice:** If P does show "actual malice" (that D either knew of the falsity or recklessly disregarded the truth), presumed damages may probably be constitutionally awarded, even if P is a public figure and the matter is one of public interest.

IV. PUBLICATION

A. **Requirement of publication generally:** P must show that the defamation was ***"published."*** "Publication" means merely ***"seen or heard by someone other than the plaintiff."***

1. **Must be intentional or negligent:** D's publication must have been either intentional or negligent. Thus there is no "strict liability" as to the publication requirement.

Example: D makes a defamatory statement to P himself, while in P's office. D does not realize (and isn't negligent in not realizing) that X is standing outside the office listening through a keyhole. X hears the statement. D has no liability for defamation, because he did not intentionally or negligently publish the statement (i.e., communicate it to one other than the plaintiff).

B. **Repeater's liability:** One who ***repeats*** a defamatory statement made by another is held to have published it, and is liable as if he were the first person to make the statement. This is true even if he indicates the source, and indicates that he himself does not believe the statement.

Example: D says, "X told me that P is a thief who steals from his customers, though I doubt it." Technically, D has published the defamatory statement, and can be liable.

V. INTENT

A. Common-law strict liability: At common law, libel and slander were essentially ***strict liability*** torts. P had to show that the ***publication*** occurred due to D's intent or negligence, but did not have to show intent or negligence as to any of the other aspects. For instance, it was irrelevant that D had every reason to believe that the statement was ***true***.

B. Constitutional decisions: But Supreme Court decisions on the First Amendment have eliminated courts' right to impose strict liability for defamation. The precise mental state which D must be shown to have met depends on whether P is a public figure:

1. **Public figure:** If P is a ***"public figure,"*** he can recover only if he shows that D made the statement with either: (1) ***knowledge that it was false***; or (2) ***"reckless disregard"*** of whether it was true or false. [*New York Times v. Sullivan*] (These two alternate states of mind are collectively called ***"actual malice,"*** which is a term of art.)

    a. **Meaning of "reckless disregard":** For P to show that D "recklessly disregarded" the truth, is *not* enough to show that a "reasonably prudent person" would not have published, or would have done further investigation. Instead, P must show that D ***in fact entertained serious doubts*** about the truth of the statement.

2. **Private figures:** But if P is ***neither*** a public official nor a public figure, he is ***not constitutionally required*** to prove that D knew his statement was false or recklessly disregarded whether it was true or false. [*Gertz v. Robert Welch, Inc.*]

    a. **No strict liability:** However, the First Amendment prohibits a state from applying ***strict liability***, even in the "private figure" situation, at least if the suit is against a media defendant. In other words, even in suits brought by private figure plaintiffs, if D is a media defendant P must prove that D was at least ***negligent*** in not ascertaining the statement's falsity.

        i. **Suits by one private person against another:** In suits by a private-figure plaintiff against a ***private individual*** or other ***non-media*** defendant, the Supreme Court has never said whether strict liability is constitutionally allowable. However, virtually all states — as a matter of ***common law***, not federal constitutional law — refuse to allow private-figure plaintiffs to recover against even non-media defendants unless the plaintiff ***shows at least negligence.*** In other words, as a common-law matter, all defamation suits require ***at least a showing that the defendant negligently failed to make reasonable efforts to ascertain the statement's truth or falsity.*** (States are always free to require more than negligence regarding truth, such as recklessness or intent.)

Example: D fires P. P seeks a new job from X. X asks D for a reference. D writes back, "We fired P because P sexually harassed a co-worker." If D's belief that P harassed a co-worker was reasonable, under state common-law principles P cannot recover from D for libel, even if P can prove that the accusation was completely false.

VI. PRIVILEGES

A. Absolute privileges: An ***"absolute"*** privilege applies even if D was motivated solely by malice or other bad motives. The following classes of absolute privilege are usually recognized:

1. **Judicial proceedings:** Judges, lawyers, parties and witnesses are all absolutely privileged in what they say during the course of ***judicial proceedings***, regardless of the motives for their statements.

   Example: D, in a pleading in a civil lawsuit between him and P, calls P a crook. P cannot recover from D for defamation, even if P shows that D knew D's statement was a lie.

2. **Legislative proceedings:** ***Legislators*** acting in furtherance of their legislative functions are absolutely privileged.

3. **Government officials:** Many ***government officials*** have absolute immunity for statements issued in the course of their jobs. Thus all federal officials, and all high state officials, have this privilege.

4. **Husband and wife:** Any communication between a ***husband and wife*** is absolutely privileged.

5. **Consent:** Any publication that occurs with the ***consent*** of the plaintiff is absolutely privileged.

B. Qualified privilege: Other privileges are merely ***"qualified"*** or "conditional" ones. A qualified privilege will be lost if D is acting primarily from ***malice***, or from some other purpose not protected by the privilege.

1. **Protection of publisher's interests:** D is conditionally privileged to ***protect his own interests***, if these are sufficiently important, and the defamation is directly enough related to those interests.

   Example: If D reasonably believes that his property has been stolen by P, he may tell the police of his suspicions. If D's belief is reasonable, he is protected against a slander action by P, even if his suspicions are wrong.

2. **Interest of others:** Similarly, D may be qualifiedly privileged to act for the protection of the ***recipient*** of his statement, or some other third person. The issue is whether D's statement is "within the generally accepted standards of ***decent conduct.***"

   a. **Old boss to new boss:** Thus an ex-employer generally has the right to give information about his ***ex-employee*** to a new, prospective, employer if asked by the latter.

3. **Public interest:** D may be conditionally privileged to act in the ***public interest.***

   Example: A private citizen's reasonable but mistaken accusation made to the police that P committed a crime would be covered.

4. **Report of public proceedings:** There is a conditional privilege to report on ***public proceedings***, such as court cases, legislative hearings, etc.

   Example: D, a newspaper, accurately reports that in a lawsuit, X has called P a crook and a liar. Even if X's statement is completely untrue and was made with malice, D has a qualified privilege to make the report of the public proceeding, and therefore may not be sued for libel.

5. **Neutral reportage:** A few cases have recognized a ***"neutral reportage"*** privilege. Under this privilege, one who ***correctly*** and ***neutrally*** reports charges made by one person against another will be protected if the charges are a matter of ***public interest,*** even if the charges are false.

   Example: D, a newspaper, runs a story saying, "Citizen said at a press conference that he saw Mayor Brown take a bribe from a developer." If Citizen really made these charges, D would be protected under the "neutral reportage" privilege even if D had serious doubts about the truth of the charges. This is so even though D's doubts would cause D's conduct to constitute "actual malice" under *New York Times v. Sullivan.*

C. **Abuse of qualified privilege:** Even where a qualified privilege exists, it may be ***abused*** (and therefore forfeited) in a number of ways.

1. **Actual malice:** Most importantly, the privilege will be lost if D ***knew that his statement was false***, or acted in ***reckless disregard*** of whether it was true.

   Example: D, P's ex-employer, is asked for information by X, P's new prospective employer, concerning P's work. D's clerk negligently misreads the file, and asserts that P was fired for dishonesty, when in fact P quit voluntarily. If the clerk is shown to have behaved recklessly, D's qualified privilege — to protect the interest of a third person by commenting on an employee's fitness — will be deemed abused and thus forfeited. But if the clerk was only negligent, the privilege will probably not be lost.

2. **Excessive publication:** The privilege is abused if the statement is made to persons to whom publication is ***not reasonably necessary*** to protect the interest in question, or if more damaging information is stated than is reasonably needed.

D. **Statutory privileges:** Many states, and the federal government, have enacted a number of ***statutory privileges.***

1. **Internet Service Providers:** One of the most important of these is the federal immunity given to ***Internet Service Providers*** (ISPs) under the Communications Decency Act of 1996. Part of the CDA, 47 U.S.C. § 230(c)(1), says that "***no provider or user*** of an interactive ***computer service*** shall be treated as the ***publisher or speaker of any information*** provided by ***another information content provider.***" This provision amounts to a grant of ***immunity*** from state defamation liability for "publishing false or defamatory material so long as the ***information was***

provided by another party. " [*Carafano v. Metrosplash.com, Inc.*]

Example: D, a corporation, owns the matchmaker.com Internet dating service. Some unknown person posts a dating profile of P (a well-known actress) on the matchmaker.com site, without P's consent. The posting is done in the form of answers to a questionnaire that D requires posters to fill out; many of the questions are in multiple-choice format. The posting includes P's picture, her home address, her e-mail address and various sexually-oriented statements. People who send e-mail to the e-mail address are then given P's home phone number. As a result, P receives numerous phone calls, voice mail messages and e-mails, some of which are sexually explicit or threatening. She sues D in state court for defamation and invasion of privacy. D defends on the grounds that the CDA gives it immunity against all such claims by P. P responds that the CDA immunity does not apply where D supplies part of the defamatory content, and that that is what happened here, since most of the content was formulated in response to matchmaker.com's detailed questionnaire.

Held, for D. The immunity given by the CDA was intended by Congress to be ***"quite robust."*** It is true that the immunity does not apply where the defendant functioned as an "information content ***provider***" for the portion of the statement or publication at issue. But here, the fact that some of the content was formulated in response to D's questionnaire does not mean that D was the provider of the content in question. And the fact that D's site structured and standardized the poster's answers (e.g., by supplying multiple-choice answers for dozens of questions) did not turn D into a supplier of the content in the profile. [*Carafano v. Metrosplash.com, Inc., supra*]

VII. REMEDIES

A. Damages: A successful defamation plaintiff may recover various sorts of damages:

1. **Compensatory damages:** First, of course, P may recover ***compensatory*** damages. These can include:

   a. **Pecuniary:** Items of ***pecuniary loss*** (e.g., P's lost earnings from being fired from her job, due to D's statement to P's boss that D was dishonest in the last job).

   b. **Humiliation, lost friendship:** Compensation for ***humiliation***, lost friendship, illness, etc. (even though these items would not count as "special harm" for purposes of slander).

2. **Punitive damages:** Also, under some circumstances ***punitive*** damages may be awarded:

   a. **Public figure or matter of public interest:** If P is a ***public figure***, or the case involves a matter of ***public interest***, punitive damages may be awarded only on a showing that D knew his statements were false or recklessly disregarded the truth. (That is, the "actual malice" requirement of *New York Times v. Sullivan* extends, as far as punitive damages go, not only to public figures but also to private figures suing on matters of public interest.) [*Gertz v. Robert Welch*]

b. **Private figure/private matter:** But if P is a ***private*** figure and D's statement relates to a private matter, then punitive damages may be awarded even if P shows only that D was ***negligent***.

Example: D, a credit reporting agency, falsely reports to a few subscribers that P, a corporation, is insolvent. Because P is a private figure and the report did not involve any matter of public concern, punitive damages can be awarded, as a constitutional matter. [*Dun & Bradstreet v. Greenmoss Builders*]

3. **Nominal damages:** Even a plaintiff who has suffered no direct loss may recover ***nominal*** damages, to "clear his name." Certainly if P shows knowledge of falsehood or reckless disregard of the truth on the part of D, P may recover nominal damages. It is not clear whether or when a plaintiff who shows less than this may recover nominal damages.

B. **Retraction:** Most states have enacted ***"retraction"*** statutes. Some of these statutes hold that if D publishes a retraction within a certain period, this bars P from recovery. Other statutes merely ***require*** news organizations to grant a right of response to P, without providing that this eliminates P's defamation action.

CHAPTER 18

MISCELLANEOUS TORTS

I. INVASION OF PRIVACY

A. **Four torts:** The so-called ***"invasion of privacy"*** cause of action is essentially four distinct mini-torts. They all involve P's "right to be let alone." The four are:

[1] ***misappropriation*** of P's name or picture;

[2] ***intrusion*** on P's solitude;

[3] undue publicity given to P's ***private life***; and

[4] the placing of P in a ***false light***.

B. **Misappropriation of identity:** P can sue if her ***name or picture*** has been ***misappropriated*** by D for his own financial benefit.

Example: D, a cereal maker, runs an ad containing a photo of P eating D's cereal. P does in fact eat D's cereal, but has never agreed to endorse it. P can recover for appropriation of his picture.

C. **Intrusion:** P may sue if his ***solitude*** is ***intruded upon***, and this intrusion would be "highly offensive to a reasonable person."

Example: P and D are roommates at college; they share a suite, but each has his own small bedroom. D hides a web-cam in P's room, and uses it to stream video on the Internet of P having sex with X. P (as well as X) will have a claim against D for the intrusion-on-solitude branch of invasion of privacy: the use of hidden electronic equipment to monitor P's private space is an intrusion that would be "highly offensive to a reasonable person."

1. **Must be private place:** This "intrusion upon solitude" branch is triggered only where a ***private place*** is invaded. Thus if D takes P's picture in a public place, this will normally not be enough.

D. Publicity of private life: P may recover if D has ***publicized*** the details of P's ***private life***. The effect must be "highly offensive to a reasonable person."

Example: D, a sensationalist newspaper, prints the details of the extramarital sex life of P, who is wealthy but not a public figure. P can recover against D for publicity of private life.

1. **Not of legitimate public concern:** As a constitutional matter, it is probably a requirement for the "publicity of private life" action that the material ***not be of legitimate public concern***.

   Example: If P is on trial for murder, it is not an invasion of his privacy for newspapers to give reports on even minor private details of his past life, such as his sexual history.

E. False light: P can sue if he is placed before the public eye in a ***false light***, and this false light would be highly offensive to a reasonable person.

Example: P is a war hero. D makes a movie about P's life, including fictitious materials such as a non-existent romance. D is liable for invasion of privacy, of the "false light" variety.

1. **Actual malice:** But at least where P is a public figure, he can recover for "false light" only if he can show that D knew the portrayal was false, or acted in reckless disregard of whether it was. In other words, *New York Times v. Sullivan* applies to false light actions by public figures. [*Time, Inc. v. Hill*] Probably private figures do not have to meet this "actual malice" standard.

II. MISUSE OF LEGAL PROCEDURE

A. Three torts: Three related tort actions protect P's interest in not being subjected to ***unwarranted judicial proceedings:*** (1) ***malicious prosecution***; (2) ***wrongful institution of civil proceedings***; and (3) ***abuse of process***.

B. Malicious prosecution: To recover for ***malicious prosecution***, P must prove the following: (1) that D instituted ***criminal proceedings*** against him; (2) that these proceedings terminated ***in favor of P*** (the accused); (3) that D had ***no probable cause*** to start the proceedings; and (4) that D was motivated primarily by some purpose other than bringing an offender to justice.

1. **Initiating proceeding:** P must show that D took an ***active part*** in instigating and encouraging the prosecution.

Example: If D merely states what she believes to be the facts to the prosecutor, and lets the prosecutor decide whether to prosecute, this is probably not "institution" of proceedings. But if D attempts to persuade the prosecutor to prosecute, this will be sufficient.

2. **Favorable outcome:** The criminal proceedings must ***terminate in favor of the accused*** (P). An acquittal will of course be enough; so will a prosecutor's decision not to prosecute (but a plea bargain to a lesser offense will not suffice).

3. **Absence of probable cause:** P must show that D ***lacked probable cause*** to institute the criminal proceedings.

   a. **Reasonable mistake:** If D made a ***reasonable mistake***, she does not lack probable cause.

   b. **Effect of outcome:** The fact that P was ***acquitted*** does not itself establish lack of probable cause. D still has the right to show, in the tort case, by a preponderance of evidence, that P was guilty and that D therefore had probable cause.

4. **Improper purpose:** P must show that D acted out of ***malice***, or for some other purpose than bringing an offender to justice.

C. **Wrongful civil proceedings:** In most states, a tort action exists for wrongful institution of ***civil*** proceedings. The requirements are virtually identical to the "malicious prosecution" action, except that the original proceedings are civil rather than criminal.

1. **Elements:** Thus P must prove that:

[1] D initiated civil proceedings against P;

[2] D did not have probable cause to believe that his claim was justified;

[3] the proceedings were started for an improper purpose (e.g., a "nuisance" suit or "strike suit," brought solely for the purpose of extorting a settlement); and

[4] the civil proceedings were terminated in favor of the person against whom they were brought.

D. **Abuse of process:** The tort of ***"abuse of process"*** occurs where a person involved in criminal or civil proceedings uses various ***litigation devices*** for improper purposes.

Example: Even if a civil suit is properly brought by P, if P then uses his power of ***subpoena*** to harass D or make him settle, rather than for the proper purpose of obtaining his testimony, this is an abuse of process.

III. INTERFERENCE WITH ADVANTAGEOUS RELATIONS

A. **Three business torts:** Three related torts protect business interests: (1) injurious falsehood; (2) interference with contract; and (3) interference with prospective advantage.

B. **Injurious falsehood:** The action for ***"injurious falsehood"*** protects P against certain false statements made against his business, product, or property. Most important is so-called ***"trade libel."*** This occurs where a person makes false statements disparaging P's ***goods or business***.

1. **Elements:** P must prove the following elements for trade libel:

   a. **False disparagement:** D made a ***false statement disparaging*** P's goods, business, etc.

      Example: D falsely states that P is out of business.

   b. **Publication:** P must show that the statement was "published," as the word is used in defamation cases.

   c. **Scienter:** P must show ***scienter*** on D's part. That is, P must show that D knew her statement was false, acted in reckless disregard of whether it was false, or (in some courts) acted out of ill-will or spite for P.

   d. **Special damages:** P must prove ***"special damages,"*** i.e., that P suffered ***"pecuniary"*** harm.

2. **Defenses:** D can raise a number of ***defenses***, including:

   a. **Truth:** that the statement was ***true***; and

   b. **Fair competition:** that D was ***pursuing competition by fair means***. In particular, D is privileged to make ***general comparisons*** between her product and P's, stating or implying that her product is the better one. In other words, "puffing" is protected. But if D makes ***specific*** false allegations against P's product, D will not be protected.

C. Interference with existing contract: The tort of ***"interference with contract"*** protects P's interest in having others perform ***existing contracts*** which they have with him. The claim is against one who ***induces*** another to breach a contract with P.

Example: P, a theater owner, has contracted to have X perform in P's theater on a certain date. D, a competing theater owner, induces X to perform for him on that date instead. P can recover against D for interference with contract.

1. **Privileges:** D can defend on the grounds that his interference was ***privileged.***

   a. **Business competition:** D's desire to ***obtain business*** for herself, however, is ***not*** by itself enough to make her privileged to induce a breach of contract. (But in most courts, if P's contract was ***terminable at will***, D is privileged to induce a termination of it for the purpose of obtaining the business for herself.)

D. Interference with prospective advantage: If due to D's interference, P loses the benefits of ***prospective***, ***potential*** contracts (as opposed to existing contracts), P can sue for ***"interference with prospective advantage."***

1. **Same rules:** Essentially the same rules apply here as for "interference with contract." The big difference is that D has a much greater scope of ***privilege*** to interfere.

a. **Competition:** Most importantly, D's desire to ***obtain the business for herself*** will be enough to give her a privilege, which is usually not the case where there is an existing contract.

Example: P and D are competitors. D learns that P has been pursuing a certain prospect for nine months, and is about to sign a long-term supply contract with that customer. D can jump in, and offer a money-losing low price, even if this is for the sole purpose of weakening P.

IV. INTERFERENCE WITH FAMILY AND POLITICAL RELATIONS

A. **Family:** A family member's interest in having the ***continued affections*** of the other member of his family is sometimes protected.

1. **Husband and wife:** In some states, a jilted ***spouse*** may bring either of two tort claims against an outsider who has interfered with the marital relation:

a. **Alienation of affections:** Some states allow P to sue for ***"alienation of affections"*** against anyone who has caused P's spouse to lose his or her affection for P. (This is usually, but not always, a romantic rival — for instance, the action can be brought against a friend or relative who has convinced the spouse to leave P.) But D has a ***privilege*** to interfere to advance what D reasonably believes to be the alienated spouse's welfare.

b. **Criminal conversation:** A person who has ***sexual intercourse*** with one spouse may be liable to the other for ***"criminal conversation."***

2. **Parent's claim:** A ***parent*** will *not* usually have a tort claim against one who alienates his ***child's affections***. But there are a couple of exceptions, where suit is allowed:

a. **Minor leaves home:** The parent has a claim against the person who has caused his minor child to ***leave home***, or not to return home.

Example: A parent might sue the members of a cult, if the cult induces the minor child to leave home.

b. **Sex:** The parent has a tort claim against anyone who has ***sexual intercourse*** with the parent's minor ***daughter*** (but not son).

B. **Interference with political and civil rights:** There may be a common-law tort action for interfering with P's ***political rights*** (e.g., his right to vote), his ***civil rights*** (e.g., his right to make a public protest), or his ***public duties*** (e.g., his duty to serve on a jury).

1. **§1983 suits for state violation of federal rights:** The most important statute allowing recovery for civil rights violations is the famous federal ***"section 1983,"*** 42 U.S.C. §1983. Section 1983 allows a person to bring a tort action against any person who, ***"under color of" state law***, deprives the plaintiff of "any rights, privileges, or immunities" secured by the ***federal Constitution or a federal statute***. So the basic effect of §1983 is to permit a tort suit by anyone who is injured when a

state or local official violates the plaintiff's federal rights, typically her ***constitutionally-guaranteed civil rights***.

a. Constitutional provisions: Most §1983 actions allege that state or local officials have violated one of these three federal constitutional provisions:

[1] the 14th Amendment's guarantee of ***substantive and procedural due process*** of law, and its guarantee of ***equal protection*** of the laws;

[2] the 4th Amendment's prohibition of ***unreasonable searches and seizures***; and

[3] the 8th Amendment's ban on ***cruel and unusual punishment***. *Id.*

Example (Fourth Amendment): Suppose that Officer, an officer in the City police force, arrests P without probable cause, and then brutally beats P in an unsuccessful attempt to extract a confession. P can recover tort damages from both Officer and City under §1983. Officer has acted "under color of" state law — that is, he has used his official position as justification for his acts. And Officer's conduct amounts to an "unreasonable seizure" under the 4th Amendment. City is vicariously liable under the doctrine of *respondeat superior* (*supra*, p. 139).

b. Limitations: Supreme Court decisions over the last few decades have placed two important ***limits*** on the extent to which suits brought under §1983 can supplement state tort law recoveries.

i. Must show actual damage: First, compensatory damages may not be awarded based on the abstract ***value*** or ***importance*** of the constitutional rights that were violated.

ii. Negligence: Second, where the deprivation of a constitutionally-guaranteed right results from a public official's ***negligence*** rather than intent, §1983 ***may not be used at all***.

Example: P, a prisoner, is attacked by X, a fellow prisoner. Prior to the attack, a prison guard working for D (the state) negligently fails to heed P's warning that X plans to attack him. *Held*, for D: §1983 protects only against intentional, rather than negligent, deprivations of Due Process. So P has only his state-law tort remedies (which, apparently, don't exist here because of sovereign immunity). [*Davidson v. Cannon*]

c. Implied right of action from constitutional provision: Section 1983 allows only actions against state and local government officials, not federal ones. However, when a federal official violates a citizen's constitutional rights, the citizen is often permitted to bring a federal tort-like suit against the official. This occurs because the court finds an ***"implied private right of action"*** for violation of the constitutional provision.

i. **4th Amendment violation:** For example, suppose that a federal law-enforcement official violates P's 4th Amendment right to be free from unreasonable searches and seizures. The Supreme Court has held that P has an implied right to bring a federal civil-damages suit against the official for this violation. [*Bivens v. Six Unknown Named Agents of FBI* (civil suit for money damages allowed against FBI agents for search and arrest made without probable cause).]

EXAM TIPS

TABLE OF CONTENTS of EXAM TIPS

EXAM TIPS

Exam Tips on INTENTIONAL TORTS

For three of the torts covered in this chapter — battery, assault and false imprisonment — you shouldn't have much trouble spotting the tort on an essay exam. The fourth tort — intentional infliction of emotional distress — can be easier to miss. Since these are all "intentional" torts, it's not surprising that the most commonly-tested issues relate to intent. Here are the main things to look for:

Battery

☛ **Battery generally:** Look for a ***battery*** issue whenever you have what seems to be a ***"harmful or offensive contact."***

- ☞ **Definition:** If you spot a battery problem, introduce your discussion with the following definition: "Battery is the intentional infliction of a harmful or offensive bodily contact."

- ☞ **Intent:** ***"Intent"*** is probably the most frequently tested sub-issue in battery.

  - ☛ **Desire to cause contact:** One type of intent is "desire to ***cause contact***." That's a pretty obvious and spottable type of intent. (*Example:* D swings at P and hits him.)

  - ☛ **Desire to frighten:** Another type of intent is "desire to ***frighten***." Remember that even if D didn't intend contact to occur (and just wanted to make P think it would) this "intent to cause assault" is enough for battery, if contact ensues. (*Example:* D swings at P, intending to just miss P's nose, but miscalculates and makes contact.)

  - ☛ **Substantial certainty:** Finally, there's the ***"substantially certain"*** variety of intent — if D knows that a harmful or offensive contact is "substantially certain" to occur, the fact that D doesn't "desire" that contact is irrelevant.

    Example: D is repossessing P's car, while P is on the running board — if D knows that P is substantially certain to fall off, that's enough for battery even though D doesn't desire that P fall.

    - ☞ **Subjective test:** Remember that for "substantially certain," the test is

"subjective" — the issue is what D really thought, not what he "should" have thought, so even if an ordinary person would have realized that a harmful or offensive contact with P was nearly certain, D is protected if he didn't realize this.

☞ **"Very likely" not enough:** Also, "substantially certain" doesn't mean "***very*** likely" — it means "almost certain."

☛ **Transferred intent: *"Transferred intent"*** is often tested — if D tries to make contact with (or frighten) X, and contact ensues with P, that's enough for battery.

☛ **Different type of contact than intended:** Contact of a ***"different sort"*** than intended can suffice.

Example: D tries to ram his car into P's car, but P swerves into a fire hydrant — since P has come into contact with the fire hydrant, it doesn't matter that this contact is different from the "ramming" contact intended by D; D is still liable for battery.

☞ **Definition of "contact":** The nature of ***"contact"*** is often tested:

☛ **"Harmful" or "offensive":** The contact can be either ***"harmful"*** or ***"offensive."*** An "offensive" contact means that as long as P's dignity is harmed, ***no injury*** is necessary.

Example: D pushes P while speaking nastily to him — even if there is no physical harm at all to P, there has been an "offensive" contact.

☛ **Indirect means:** The contact can be by ***indirect*** means, i.e., not necessarily D's person touching P's person.

Examples: D throws an object at P, or hits P with his car, or lets loose an animal to attack P.

☞ **Mechanical devices:** The use of ***"mechanical devices"*** to protect property is often tested, and will typically involve battery unless the property owner had a privilege.

Example: If D puts a security system in his car that administers an electric shock to anybody who tries to touch the car, that's a battery.

☞ **Exceeding a privilege:** Whenever a person seems to ***exceed a privilege***, look for a possible battery.

Example 1: D tries to defend himself against an attack from P, but uses excessive force — D is liable for battery.

Example 2: D uses non-deadly force against one who he thinks is an intruder on D's property, but who is really the mail carrier. Again, that's battery.

☞ **Medical malpractice or sports:** In a ***medical malpractice*** or ***sports*** context, consider the possibility that there may be battery.

Example 1: D is a doctor who fails to get the patient's informed consent before performing a certain procedure; D may be found to have battered the patient.

Example 2: P and D play a contact sport (so P impliedly consents to contacts that are within the usual practices or rules of the sport). D hits or tackles P on purpose, and outside of the rules; D probably has committed battery, by going beyond the scope of what P impliedly consented to.

<u>**Assault**</u>

☛ **Assault generally:** Look for an ***assault*** issue whenever you have a person who is put in ***"apprehension of an imminent harmful or offensive contact"*** by another person.

☞ **Definition to use:** If you have an assault issue, work the following definition into the beginning of your discussion of the issue: "Assault is the intentional causing of an apprehension of harmful or offensive contact."

☞ **Combined with battery:** Anytime you have identified a *battery*, also consider whether there was ***first*** an assault — there usually was. As long as P ***saw was about to happen*** there's an assault just before the battery.

Example: If D swings at P's jaw, there's an assault just before the impact, as long as P saw D's swing.

☞ **Intent:** *Intent* issues are sometimes tested in assault:

☛ **Two possible intents:** Remember that there are two distinct intents, either of which can suffice:

❑ D intends to commit a battery, but fails; ***or***

❑ D intends to put P in apprehension, but not to really cause the contact (so that the intent is "attempt to frighten").

☛ **Transferred intent:** ***"Transferred intent"*** operates in assault cases. Thus if D tries to frighten X (or to make a contact with X), and P thinks that he himself will be hit, then D has assaulted P even if D never intended any effect on P or even saw P.

☞ **Words-alone rule:** Remember the ***"words alone"*** rule — words alone can't constitute an assault. But typically, the facts will show at least some small ***overt act***, which will be enough.

Example: While saying words, D raises his fist, or steps menacingly towards P — that's enough of an overt act to prevent the "words alone" rule from applying, so that there is an assault.

☞ **Imminent contact:** The contact must (in P's mind) be ***"imminent."*** (*Example:* P's fear of being beaten tomorrow isn't enough.)

☞ **Apprehension:** The sub-issues relating to whether P has suffered the requisite ***"apprehension"*** are often tested in assault fact-patterns:

- **Awareness of danger:** Remember that P must be ***aware*** of the danger before it happens, and it's not enough that contact eventually does happen. Be on the lookout for fact patterns that tell you that something is happening ***behind P's back***, or happening just before P comes on the scene — these are typically a tip-off that P may not have seen the contact coming in advance, thus negating assault.

  Example: D aims at P from behind, shoots and misses; P then realizes that he was almost hit — there's no assault.

- **Contact with P's loved one not enough:** Here's a point profs especially love to test: P's apprehension must be that there will be a contact with ***herself***, not a contact with a loved one.

  Example: D shoots at X, while X's mother, P, looks on. If P feared only that the bullet would hit X, not that it would hit P herself, P has not been assaulted.

- **Apprehension of natural event:** P must be apprehensive of a "harmful or offensive contact," but ***not*** necessarily apprehensive of a "battery." That is, if P thinks the contact is some ***natural event*** or some ***unintentional human event***, that can still be enough to satisfy the "apprehension" requirement.

  Example: P sees a "tarantula" that he thinks is real, and that he thinks will bite him. It's really a fake put there by D to scare P. Even though P doesn't think a human was involved, and thus doesn't think that this is an attempt at "battery," it's still an assault because P has been put in apprehension of a harmful or offensive contact.

☞ **Privilege:** As with battery, consider the possibility of assault whenever someone exceeds the scope of a ***privilege***.

  Example: D, a homeowner, shoots at P, who D knows is an unarmed burglar. D misses. Since D wasn't permitted to use deadly force here, he had no defense of self-defense or defense of land, so he has committed garden-variety assault.

False imprisonment

☛ **False imprisonment generally:** Look for the tort of ***"false imprisonment" (FI)*** anytime you see one person ***intentionally confine*** another person ***within boundaries***.

- ☞ **Definition to use:** If you spot an FI issue, lead with the following definition: "False imprisonment occurs when the defendant intentionally confines the plaintiff. The plaintiff is 'confined' when his will to leave a place with fixed boundaries is overcome in a way that would overcome the will of an ordinary person in the plaintiff's position."

- ☞ **Some contexts:** Here are a couple of particular contexts that should clue you to the possibility of FI:

  ❑P is detained in a ***store*** on suspicion of shoplifting;

  ❑P is detained on a ***bus*** or ***train*** on suspicion of not having paid the fare;

  ❑P is ***arrested*** (or otherwise detained by a law enforcement official), and placed in a patrol car, or handcuffed to a post or other fixed support.

- ☞ **Keeping P out of a place not enough:** Remember that the essence of the tort is that P is kept ***"in."*** Keeping P ***"out"*** is not enough, even if the place P is being kept out of is a place where he has the right to be, and even if it's P's own ***home***.

  Example: Landlord keeps P out of P's apartment, by changing the lock. Even if Landlord's conduct is wrongful, there is no FI because P is not being kept "in."

- ☞ **Confinement must be against P's will:** The confinement must be ***"enforced,"*** i.e., it must be ***against P's will***.

  Example: If P is told to "stay here," but a reasonable person in P's position would believe that nothing bad would happen to P if P left, there's no enforced confinement and thus no FI.

  ☛ **Force not required; threats may suffice:** However, remember that "enforcement" may happen even ***without force***. Thus ***threats*** of physical harm or prosecution may be enough to constitute "enforcement" of the confinement. Similarly, assertions of ***legal authority*** to detain P, together with a command that P remain, will usually be enough. (*Example:* "I'm a police officer; get in the patrol car and stay there," would be enough.) The test is always whether an ordinary person in the plaintiff's position would feel that he couldn't leave, or would suffer some harm if he tried to leave.

  ☛ **Store detective:** When a store detective says, "Wait here," to a suspected shoplifter, that's probably "enforcement," even though P realizes that the detective has no official status. On these facts, P can reasonably anticipate that the detective will use force to confine him, or will call the police.

- **P given a choice:** If P is given a ***"choice"*** between staying or leaving, but there is some sacrifice to P's interests that will occur if P leaves, that's still FI if a reasonable person in P's position wouldn't leave.

  Example: If P is stopped on suspicion of shoplifting, and forced to leave his wallet as "security" that he'll answer charges, that's probably a sufficiently unpleasant choice that if P stays, he has suffered FI. However, it's not FI if P takes the deal and leaves, even if it was wrongful for D to put P to this choice.

- **Awareness of confinement required:** P is generally required to be ***aware*** of the confinement while it is going on.

  Example: P is locked in a room while he is asleep; the room is unlocked before P wakes up. This is not FI.

  - **Harm suffered during confinement:** There's one exception to this "awareness required" rule that's recognized by modern courts and the Restatement: if P suffers ***harm*** during the confinement, that's FI even if P was not aware of the confinement while it was occurring.

    Example: P suffers an allergic reaction while locked in his hotel room asleep.

  - **No damage required:** Except for this modern exception to the requirement of awareness, FI will occur even if ***no damage*** to P occurs.

    Example: If D is wrongfully and unreasonably suspected of shoplifting and detained in the store for one half hour, that's FI even if P does not suffer emotional distress or any physical injury.

- **Shopkeeper's privilege:** If your FI fact pattern involves detention of P as a suspected shoplifter, remember to check out the ***"shopkeeper's privilege"*** (discussed *infra*) — most courts let a merchant who reasonably suspects P of shoplifting to detain P for the time reasonably needed to conduct an investigation, and there is no FI even if it turns out that P is innocent.

- **Intent to confine required:** Remember that this tort requires ***intent*** to ***confine***. Mere intent to do an act that has the unexpected effect of confining P is not enough, unless D knew with substantial certainty that confinement would result.

  Example: While P is on an elevator, D stops the elevator to make repairs; if D did not realize that P was on the elevator, there's no FI because there was no intent to confine.

Intentional infliction of emotional distress (IIED)

☛ **IIED generally:** Look for the tort of ***intentional infliction of emotional distress*** (IIED) whenever one person does something to another that seems really ***"outrageous,"*** and the latter suffers great ***anguish***.

☞ **Definition to use:** If you spot an IIED issue, introduce your discussion with the following definition: "The tort of intentional infliction of emotional distress occurs whenever the defendant intentionally or recklessly causes, by outrageous conduct, severe emotional or mental distress in another person."

☞ **Some contexts:** Here are some contexts where you should be on the lookout for an IIED issue:

- ❑The facts mention that P is ***"humiliated"*** or "suffers great distress" (especially where the facts tell you that P seeks medical attention for the distress);
- ❑The facts involve a business dispute where one party spies on another, follows the other, or otherwise ***"harasses"*** the other;
- ❑D is a ***debt collector*** who wrongfully harasses P, or wrongfully repossesses P's goods (or does so rightfully but in an outrageous manner);
- ❑D commits a major ***crime*** against P's person or against the person of P's close relative (e.g., D kidnaps P's child); or
- ❑D plays a really nasty practical joke on P (but in this scenario, you should probably conclude that there is insufficient "outrageousness").

☞ **P's mental state:** P's ***mental state*** is often tested:

☛ **Three types suffice:** Three types of mental state will suffice:

[1] D ***intended*** to bring about the distress;

[2] D knew with ***substantial certainty*** that the distress would result, even if D didn't desire it; or

[3] D ***recklessly disregarded*** the possibility that distress would result. Note that "recklessly disregarded" applies for IIED even though it does not for the other intentional torts (assault, battery and false imprisonment).

☛ **Intent to do physical act:** Intent to do a particular ***physical act*** is not sufficient — the intent must relate to P's distress.

Example: Suppose D intends to repossess P's trailer home, and does so, but it turns out that P wasn't really in default. The mere fact that D intended the act of repossession is not enough to meet the "intent" requirement — unless D intended to cause P anguish, knew P's anguish was substantially certain to occur, or recklessly disregarded the possibility that P would be anguished, the requisite mental state is not present.

☞ **Outrageousness: *"Outrageousness"*** is the most frequently tested issue for IIED:

- **Mere insults not enough: *Mere insults*** are generally ***not*** sufficiently outrageous.
- **P's special sensitivity:** P's special ***sensitivity*** is normally irrelevant — outrageousness is measured by whether D's conduct would cause great distress to a person of ordinary sensitivity. (But if D ***knew*** of P's special sensitivity, then outrageousness is judged by reference to whether a person of P's sensitivity would have been seriously anguished.)
- **Publication of true story:** Publication of a ***true story*** about P probably is not sufficiently outrageous (unless the publication would also constitute invasion of privacy, and perhaps not even then).

☞ **Type of harm:** Requirements for the type of ***harm*** suffered by P are also sometimes tested:

- **Medical attention required:** At a minimum, P must seek ***medical attention*** for the distress. Thus if P is merely "outraged," or somewhat "embarrassed," that's not sufficient (even if the act itself is "outrageous").
- **Physical manifestations:** Some courts hold that the distress must be severe enough to cause ***physical manifestations*** (e.g., sleeplessness) in P. Therefore, if there are no physical manifestations, note that this poses an issue (but also say that most modern courts, and the Restatement, do not require physical harm if P has suffered anguish, has sought medical attention, and the act was "outrageous).

☞ **First Amendment issue:** Be on the lookout for a situation in which the way D commits the IIED is by a ***communication*** as to a ***"matter of public concern."*** Here, you should write that the ***First Amendment*** prevents the state from allowing P to recover unless the jury's determination that the conduct was "outrageous" was made in a strictly "content-neutral" way (something that is almost impossible for a jury to do).

Example: D pickets P's son funeral, with signs saying "God killed P because he was gay, and God punishes gays." When the jury in P's IIED action considers whether D's conduct was "outrageous," the jury must make this decision without considering the "message" communicated by D, since the message is on a topic of "public concern." Since it will be almost impossible for a jury to find outrageousness without considering the message's content, any verdict in P's favor will almost certainly violate D's First Amendment rights. [Cite to *Snyder v. Phelps*, on similar facts.]

Exam Tips on *INTENTIONAL INTERFERENCE WITH PROPERTY*

In a complex fact pattern, the presence of any of the three torts covered in this chapter (trespass to land, trespass to chattels and conversion) is usually pretty easy to spot. By and large, your problem is to determine whether the tort has in fact been committed. Here are particular things to look for:

Trespass to land

☛ **When to spot trespass issue:** Look for ***"trespass to land"*** whenever one person intentionally comes onto another person's land.

☞ **Definition to use:** If you spot a trespass issue, lead with the following definition: "Trespass to land is the intentional unauthorized entry onto the land of another."

☞ **Intent:** Trespass is an ***intentional*** tort. The intent is the intent to ***enter land***, not the intent to harm the defendant or the land in any way.

☛ **Knowing with substantial certainty:** If D knows with ***"substantial certainty"*** that he is entering (or causing an object to enter) land, the intent requirement is met.

Example: Suppose D operates a factory that discharges particles of ash onto P's land, and that D knows that this is happening. D meets the intent requirement for trespass, even though D doesn't "desire" that the particles touch P's land.

☛ **Mistake:** The most frequently tested sub-issue in trespass relates to ***mistake***. As long as D knows he's entering land, the intent requirement is satisfied, and D's mistaken belief (even his ***reasonably*** mistaken belief) that his entry is ***authorized*** is ***irrelevant***.

Example 1: D thinks he's coming onto land owned by X, who has in fact invited D, but D is really by mistake coming onto land owned by P. That's trespass.

Example 2: D thinks he has a legal right to enter P's land to repossess P's car, but P is really paid up so D has no right to be there. Again, that's trespass.

- **No strict liability:** Remember that the term "trespass" refers only to ***intentional*** interference. There is no strict liability.

  Example: D, a pilot, loses control of the aircraft, and the craft crash lands on P's property. This is not trespass. But if the pilot has a mechanical problem and intentionally selects a particular parcel to emergency land on, that probably is trespass, though the pilot may have the defense of necessity.

- **Object caused to land:** Trespass occurs not only where D himself comes onto the land, but also where D causes an ***object*** to come onto the land.

  Example: D puts a car onto P's land, or sends pollutant particles onto P's land.

- **Air space:** Remember that a landowner is deemed to have exclusive possessory rights to at least some of the ***air space*** above the land. Whenever you spot one person ***flying over*** another's land, consider the possibility of trespass.

  - **Navigable air space:** If D is flying high enough that he is within FAA-defined "navigable air space," the states cannot deem him to be trespassing.

  - **Lower than navigable air space:** But if D is flying lower than the limits of navigable air space, some states make this automatically trespass. Most states make it trespass ***only*** if P's use and enjoyment of the land is interfered with (the "implicit nuisance" approach).

- **Nominal damages allowed:** Even if there is ***no actual harm*** to P's land, the tort still takes place as soon as D comes on the property (and P can get ***nominal*** damages).

- **Overstaying an invitation:** Even if D's initial entry is ***"authorized"*** by P (e.g., P invites D on as a business visitor) the entry will ***turn into trespass*** if D ***remains*** after being asked to leave.

<u>**Trespass to chattels**</u>

- **When to look for T/C:** Look for ***"trespass to chattels"*** (T/C) whenever one person intentionally interferes with another's possession of a "thing."

  - **Definition to use:** If you spot a T/C issue, lead with the following definition: "Trespass to chattels is the intentional interference with another's possessory interest in a chattel, resulting in damage to that interest."

  - **Intent:** Most T/C issues relate to ***intent***.

    - **Belief about right or title not relevant:** The relevant intent is the intent to take possession or otherwise affect the chattel. D's belief about his ***right*** to do the act, or about who holds ***title***, is ***not*** part of the requisite intent.

- ☛ **Effect of mistake:** Most often tested is the effect of ***mistake***. In general, mistake is ***never*** a defense to T/C. Thus the following types of mistake (even if ***reasonable***) will all be no defense.

  - ❑ D believes that the chattel already belongs to D.

    Example: D takes P's umbrella in a restaurant, thinking it's his own — this is T/C.

  - ❑ D believes that X has title to the object, and buys the object from X when it really belongs to P.

    Example: X steals a radio from P and sells it to D, who does not know the radio is stolen. D is liable to P for T/C.

  - ❑ D is a creditor who wrongly thinks that he has the right to ***repossess*** P's chattel.

- ☛ **Distinction between intent and accident:** Also, the distinction between intent and ***accident*** is often tested. If D doesn't intend to even make contact with P's possession, and this contact happens by accident, there's no T/C. But you should still discuss T/C (even though the tort hasn't been committed) in this scenario.

  Example: D, while driving either carefully or carelessly, hits and damages P's car without intending any contact. That's not T/C.

☞ **Degree of interference:** The ***degree of interference*** is sometimes tested. T/C takes place as long as there's some ***"damage."*** So there are no ***nominal damages*** as in trespass to land. (*Example:* D picks up P's umbrella, realizes the mistake, and immediately puts the umbrella down. That's not T/C.)

- ☛ **Temporary interference with possession:** But "damage" is deemed to take place even if the only damage is a temporary one to P's right of ***"possession,"*** and the item is returned unharmed.

  Example: D picks up P's umbrella, walks around the block with it, and returns it after noticing the mistake. That's T/C.

☞ **Distinguish from conversion:** Always distinguish between T/C and ***conversion***. Conversion only occurs when the injury to P's interests is so severe that it is appropriate to make D pay for the whole value of the item as opposed to damages for just the interference. (See the discussion of conversion, below, where we cover the factors that go into this distinction.)

Conversion

☛ **Conversion generally:** Look for ***"conversion"*** at the same time you look for T/C. Remember that conversion is more "serious" than T/C.

☞ **Definition to use:** When you spot a conversion issue, use the following definition as your lead-in: "Conversion occurs when the defendant so substantially interferes with the plaintiff's possession or ownership of goods that it is fair to require the defendant to pay the property's full value."

☞ **Intent required:** Conversion is an "intentional" tort — the definition of "intent" is the same as for T/C (so D's mistake about the right to possess, or about who has title, doesn't negate his intent).

☞ **Distinguishing from T/C:** The main issue in conversion is to ***distinguish*** it from T/C. Remember the factors that courts consider:

- **Extent and duration of dominion:** The extent and duration of D's ***"dominion"*** (the greater/longer, the more likely it's conversion).

  Example: If D keeps the item for three months, that's probably conversion.

- **Good or bad faith:** D's ***good*** or ***bad faith***.

  Example: D buys property thinking his seller has good title — this suggests T/C rather than conversion, because D has behaved in good faith.

- **Degree of harm:** The degree of ***harm*** to the property.

  Examples: If the item is given back to P in an unchanged condition except for the passage of time, this suggests T/C rather than conversion. But if D takes P's car for a 10-minute joy ride, and returns it to P with the front end smashed, this suggests conversion.

- **Inconvenience and expense:** The ***inconvenience*** and ***expense*** caused to P.

☞ **Intangible property such as e-files:** For both conversion and trespass, if the ***"property"*** in question is an ***intangible***, point out that the item must be "property" of the sort required for these torts under state law. But remember that today, in most courts ***electronic files are*** deemed to be "property" that can be trespassed on or converted.

☞ **Significance of distinction:** Remember why the distinction between conversion and T/C makes a difference: in T/C, D just pays for the damage, but in conversion there's a ***"forced sale"*** — D "buys" the item for the value it had at the time of the conversion (and gets to keep the item).

- **Value of item is the measure:** If it's conversion, the value of the item is the *sole* measure of damages — the fact that D may have gotten benefits from the item while using it, or that D physically damaged the item, is ***not*** added. Since D is "buying" the item, he gets the right to past benefits, or to commit physical damage, at "no additional charge."

☛ **P's right to elect:** P can always ***"elect"*** to sue for T/C (and get the item back plus damages for the harm) even where the facts would support conversion.

Exam Tips on ***DEFENSES TO INTENTIONAL TORTS***

Once you spot what appears to be an intentional tort, always check for defenses. The main ones to check for are:

[1] ***consent***;

[2] ***self-defense***;

[3] defense of ***others***;

[4] defense of ***property***;

[5] recapture of ***chattels***;

[6] ***re-entry*** on land;

[7] ***necessity***;

[8] ***arrest.***

Here's what to look for as to each:

Consent

☛ **Consent generally:** Whenever your fact pattern involves an intentional tort, be alert to the possibility that P ***consented*** (since consent is a defense to all intentional torts).

☞ **Some contexts:** Here are some typical contexts where there is or may be consent:

❑ P and D engage in a ***contact sport,*** and D then makes a harmful contact with P. As long as the contact was within the rules of the sport, P will be found to have impliedly consented to it. (And even if D *did* violate a rule of the sport, if the contact was part of the ***"ordinary give-and-take"*** of the sport, and was done for competitive purposes, P will still probably be found to have impliedly consented to the conduct.)

❑ P is injured by a mechanical security device (e.g., a spring gun or an electric-shock guard device) — if there's a ***warning*** sign, which P actually saw, he may be deemed to have consented.

❑ P is a suspected shoplifter, who is told to "wait here" by the storekeeper's detective — the circumstances may indicate that P waited voluntarily, in which case there was no true confinement.

❑ P's claim is for ***conversion***, but D reasonably believed that P was letting D have the goods.

Example: P has moved out of an apartment shared with D, and D reasonably thinks that P has abandoned his property, so D sells it.

☞ **Objective test:** Remember that the existence of consent is determined by ***"objective,"*** not "subjective," analysis. That is, the question is always what a reasonable person in ***D's position*** would have ***thought*** that P meant, not what P really meant. Thus consent can be ***"implied"*** by P's conduct or by the surrounding circumstances.

Example: P and D have each consented to the other's practical jokes on past occasions, including frightening "assaults." This may mean that P can't sue for assault when D frightens him with a fake tarantula.

☛ **Exceeding the scope of consent:** But in any consent situation, and especially where the consent is "implied" rather than express, be sure that the ***scope*** of consent hasn't been ***exceeded***.

Example: Even if P and D have sparred before, giving rise to implied consent for a "fight" on the present occasion, this is not consent to D's use of brass knuckles that he has never used before.

☞ **Fraud and mistake: *Fraud*** and ***mistake*** are very frequently tested in the consent context.

☛ **Fraud going to the essence vs. to a collateral aspect:** D's ***fraud*** will vitiate P's consent, if the fraud goes to the ***essence*** (usually, the nature of the contact), but ***not*** if the fraud merely goes to some ***"collateral"*** aspect.

Example: If D tells P an electric cattle prod to be used in an experiment won't hurt P when D knows that it will, this fraud goes to the essence of the contact, and thus vitiates P's consent; P can sue for battery. But D's knowingly false statement to P that P will be paid for undergoing the experiment is "collateral," and therefore doesn't vitiate P's consent; therefore, P can't sue for battery.

☛ **Mistaken consent: *P's "mistaken consent,"*** i.e., his mistake about the nature of the event that will take place, usually does ***not*** vitiate consent (as long as D wasn't aware of P's mistake). This is true even if P would never have consented had he known the true facts.

Example: P consents to have surgery performed on him under anesthetic by D. P is not aware that D has been sued several times for malpractice. D does not realize that P would never consent if he knew these facts. P's consent is valid.

☛ **D's mistake:** ***D's mistake*** about whether P has in fact consented depends on the reasonableness of D's belief — D is protected for his reasonable belief (since the test is always the "objective" standard of what one in D's position should reasonably think), but is not protected from his unreasonable mistakes.

Example: While in P's store, D reads a sign that says, "Take one" — if an ordinary person would realize that the sign refers to brochures, not the merchandise underneath the sign, D will be liable for conversion for taking the merchandise even though D honestly believed that P was consenting.

Self-defense

☛ **Self-defense generally:** If your facts suggest that X is threatened with a battery or false imprisonment, and X ***responds*** with ***force***, consider whether X can assert ***"self-defense"*** as a defense against liability for battery or assault.

☞ **Fight:** Look out for the possibility of self-defense whenever ***two parties fight.*** Even if it is not clear who started it, you should consider each fighter's chances of claiming self-defense.

☞ **Identify the first to commit battery or assault:** Do your best to identify the *first* to commit battery or assault. Being the first has two consequences: (1) the other can now use self-defense; and (2) the initial aggressor ***cannot*** respond to the other's self-defense with self-defense of his own.

Example: *A* insults *B*; *B* swings at *A* and misses; *A* hits *B*; *B* hits *A*. Analysis: *A*'s insults aren't enough to trigger *B*'s right to swing; *B*'s swing was therefore tortious; *A* probably then had the right of self-defense; *B* probably didn't have the right of self-defense in return, because his act was in response to *A*'s valid right of self-defense.

☛ **Recovery by initial aggressor:** But remember that even the "initial aggressor" can use self-defense in response to an inappropriate ***escalation*** of the level of force.

Example: A swings at B without cause; B pulls out a gun; now, A can probably use his own gun in self-defense, because B has gone beyond the scope of reasonable self-defense by answering non-deadly force with deadly force.

☛ **Verbal provocations:** ***Verbal provocations*** (e.g., ***insults***) won't by themselves justify self-defense. (See the next-prior example, in which *A* insults

B, and *B* is not thereby justified in swinging at *A*).

☞ **Mistake:** D can use self-defense even if based on a *mistake*, if D's belief in the need for self-defense was ***reasonable***.

Example: P puts his finger in his pocket and points it at D; if D's belief that P has a gun is reasonable, D can use self-defense even though he is wrong.

☞ **Level of force:** After you determine that D had the right to use self-defense, always examine the ***level of force***. This is probably the most commonly-tested area of self-defense. Here's a recap of the general rules:

- **No more force than reasonably necessary:** D can't use non-deadly force that's more than is reasonably needed in the circumstances;
- **Deadly force used to oppose non-deadly force:** D can't use deadly force to oppose non-deadly force;
- **Retreat:** Even against deadly force, some jurisdictions say D must ***retreat*** instead of using deadly force if he knows he can do so safely (but some of these jurisdictions make an exception where the encounter takes place in D's dwelling, in that they allow D to "stand his ground").
- **Test for deadly force:** Many questions require you to determine whether the force used is ***deadly*** or not. The test is: was the force likely to cause ***death*** or ***serious bodily injury***? This can vary with the circumstances.

  Example: A's fists could be deadly force if A was very skilled or strong, or if his adversary was unskilled, weak or temporarily incapacitated.

Defense of others

- **Defense of others, generally:** It's easy to spot a ***"defense of others"*** (D/O) issue — one person will be coming to the aid of the other, to repel some sort of attack.

☞ **Same issues:** Almost all of the issues discussed above in self-defense can be present in D/O, and the substantive rules are the same. Especially likely: an issue about level of force.

☞ **Defense of stranger:** One special D/O issue: Can you come to the defense of a ***complete stranger***? Most courts now say ***"yes."*** If so, the rules are the same as for defending your relatives or yourself.

☞ **D comes onto scene late:** The biggest issue specific to D/O is this: D comes on the scene ***after the fight has already started***, and doesn't realize that X (who D helps out) was really the initial ***aggressor***. Older cases say D ***"steps into the shoes"*** of X, which means that since X as the aggressor wouldn't have had the right to use self-defense, D can't either (even where D's mistake is "***reasonable***"). But modern courts, and the Restatement, usually let D off the hook for a reasonable mistake here.

Defense of realty and defense of chattels

- **The defenses generally:** Whenever X is attempting to ***evict*** someone from his property, consider whether the defense of ***"defense of realty"*** applies. Whenever X is attempting to keep possession of his personal property, think about the defense of ***"defense of chattels."*** The same rules apply (and the same test issues pop up) as to both. Here, we use the phrase "defense of property" (D/P) to cover both.]
  - **Deadly force not allowed:** Remember that D normally cannot use ***deadly force*** to protect his realty or his chattels. (However, some states allow deadly force to be used to prevent the breaking and entering of a dwelling if there is no other way to stop the entry.)
  - **Mechanical devices:** Frequently-tested: D uses a ***trap*** or other ***mechanical device*** to injure or frighten intruders. Sub-issues:
    - **Analyze as if D was present:** Remember that the case is analyzed as if D had been ***present*** and was using the force in person. So if D couldn't use that particular level of force in person against ***that particular intruder***, he can't do it by mechanical device either.

      Example: D puts a spring gun in his unoccupied farm house. When P, seeking to steal whatever's inside, breaks in, the gun shoots him. If under state law D would not have been privileged to use deadly force in person to protect a non-dwelling (which this is, because it's unoccupied), D's use of the spring gun is not allowed either. Cite to *Katko v. Briney* for this type of fact pattern.
    - **Warnings required:** Most courts say that D must post a ***warning*** unless the danger is obvious (e.g., barbed wire).
    - **Unexpectedly severe injury:** Often, the fact pattern will involve ***unexpectedly severe*** injury to P (the intruder). General rule: if D ***reasonably believed*** that the injuries would be non-existent or not severe, D gets the defense.

      Example: D rigs a device to give a mild shock to anyone who touches his car; P gets shocked, then has an unexpected heart attack. D wins, since the "take the victim as you find him" rule doesn't apply in determining whether D stayed within the D/P privilege in the first place.
  - **D doesn't realize P has privilege:** Another special D/P issue that often arises: D is "defending" his land against P's "intrusion," but in reality P is ***privileged***

to be on the land. In this scenario, D has no privilege to evict P, and is liable for battery if he tries.

- **How this arises:** Usually this scenario occurs when P goes onto D's property to ***reclaim a chattel*** that he reasonably believes D has taken from him. (See "reclaiming of chattel" privilege discussed below.) This scenario can also occur when P is on D's land under the privilege of ***necessity*** (e.g., the crash-landing of P's plane or boat).

Recapture of chattels

- **Recapture generally:** The privilege to ***recapture chattels*** (or "recapture property" or "reclaim property") can pop up in several different contexts.
  - **Two likely scenarios:** The two most likely scenarios in which you should be on the lookout for this privilege are:
    - ❑ D's property is wrongfully taken from him in some sort of street crime (e.g., a mugging), and D either tries to get it back immediately from the criminal's person, or later goes onto the land of the criminal (or the land of some third person who's now in possession of the item) to get it back.
    - ❑ D is a merchant who detains a suspected shoplifter.

Mistake

- **Mistake generally:** ***Mistake*** is sometimes tested — if D is mistaken about whether P wrongfully took the property (or about whether P is in possession of the item), D loses the privilege even if his mistake was "reasonable." (But this isn't true for the merchant's privilege to detain a suspected shoplifter — see below.)
- **Fresh pursuit required:** Remember that D must act ***"promptly"*** to recapture the item. Essentially, this means that D must be acting in ***"fresh pursuit,"*** so even a wait of an hour is probably fatal to the privilege.
- **Shopkeeper's privilege to detain:** Most-often tested: the ***merchant's*** privilege to ***detain a shoplifting suspect*** while investigating. (You can refer to this as the ***"shopkeeper's privilege."***) This is analytically distinct, but related, to the privilege to recapture chattels. The most common sub-issues in the merchant case are:
  - ❑Did D (the merchant) have ***reasonable grounds*** for suspecting P? (It's not required that P actually have committed the shoplifting, so here a "reasonable mistake" by D is protected — but D's suspicion must at least be "reasonable.")
  - ❑Did D take ***too long*** to complete the investigation? (10 minutes or so is

usually the maximum allowed.)

❑Did D stop P outside the ***store's property*** (e.g., as P got into his car located on the street)? Courts are split about whether the privilege extends beyond the store's own property line.

❑Was the detention done in a ***reasonable manner?*** If P was roughed up, handcuffed, or coerced to confess, the privilege is lost.

Necessity

☛ **When to look for necessity:** Be alert for the defense of ***"necessity"*** whenever D intentionally does something to ***protect himself*** or others in an ***emergency***, and this affects the rights (usually the land rights) of P, an innocent person.

☞ **Public vs. private:** When you write your answer, always say whether the applicable doctrine is ***"public"*** necessity or ***"private"*** necessity. "Public" necessity applies only where there's a serious danger to many people; "private" applies where the danger is to D and/or a few others. (The distinction is mainly important on the issue of whether D must pay for the damage caused, as discussed below.)

☞ **Two contexts:** The two most common contexts for "necessity" are:

❑D, who can be either a public official or private citizen, tries to stop the spread of a ***fire*** by destroying P's house, moving things out of P's building, putting barriers on P's property, etc. Prevention of fire is generally "public" necessity.

❑D is a ***pilot*** who makes an "intentional" but emergency landing on P's property. This is usually "private" necessity, at least where the plane is a small private one.

☞ **Must D pay:** The most common issue is, Must D ***pay for the harm***? If the necessity is "private," the answer is "yes." (Therefore, private necessity is usually useless unless the landowner physically resists the privilege, or is seeking nominal damages for trespass.) But if the privilege is "public," the answer is "no."

☛ **Nominal damages:** In the private necessity situation, often the question is whether D is liable for ***nominal damages*** where no actual harm has occurred. Answer: D is not liable.

Example: D crash lands on P's open field, but does no significant damage. D pays nothing.

☞ **Landowner resists:** The most common scenario involving necessity: *A* comes onto *B*'s land under the privilege/defense of necessity, but *B* ***resists***, injuring *A*. Here, *A* can recover against ***B***.

Example: *A* is a pilot who makes an emergency landing on *B*'s property, and is injured. *B* evicts *A*, aggravating *A*'s injuries. *B* is liable to *A* for the aggravation of the injuries, in addition to being unable to recover nominal trespass damages from *A*. But *B* could recover for actual damage to his property that occurred before *B* resisted, assuming that *A*'s necessity was "private."

Arrest and crime-prevention

☛ **Found together:** The privileges of ***"arrest"*** and ***"prevention of crime"*** will often be found together.

- ☞ **D breaks up fight:** A common scenario for prevention-of-crime is that D intervenes to ***break up a fight***. Typically, D injures one of the fighters, who turns out to have been a "non-aggressor" who then sues D for battery. Here, D has the privilege, so long as D's belief and level of force were reasonable.
- ☞ **Citizen's arrest:** A common scenario for arrest is that D is a private individual who makes or tries to make a ***"citizen's arrest"*** for a felony he sees committed, or believes has just been committed. Generally, D has the privilege to make this citizen's arrest as long as the force he uses is reasonable, even if D makes a reasonable mistake about who did it. (But D loses the privilege if there was no felony committed at all.)
- ☞ **Deadly force:** Use of ***"deadly force"*** is often tested.
  - ☛ **Fleeing suspect:** The most common sub-issue is, May either a police officer or a citizen use deadly force to stop a ***fleeing suspect***? Answer: neither may use deadly force unless the suspect poses a threat of ***death*** or ***serious physical injury*** to others.

    Example: Neither a homeowner nor the police may shoot a fleeing burglar in the back, unless there is evidence of the burglar's serious dangerousness. Such "serious dangerousness" might be evidenced by the fact that the burglar is armed.

Exam Tips on NEGLIGENCE

In any fact pattern, you must of course be on the lookout for the distinct tort of "negligence." But the tips in this chapter relate mainly to one sub-issue within the tort of negligence, namely, how to determine whether D "was negligent," i.e., failed to behave with reasonable care.

Elements of negligence

☞ **Elements summarized:** On any set of facts, check whether each participant may have behaved "negligently," i.e., carelessly. Once you find this, check for ***all*** of the elements of the tort of negligence:

- ❑a ***duty*** of reasonable care to the plaintiff, i.e., that there was ***foreseeable danger*** if care was not used (covered in the next chapter);
- ❑failure by D to ***exercise*** that ***reasonable care***;
- ❑***harm*** (usually required to be physical harm or at least danger of physical harm) to P; and
- ❑***causation***, i.e., that the failure of care actually and proximately caused the harm.

(This chapter only deals with second of the above requirements, that D failed to exercise reasonable care.)

☞ **Your job:** Your main job is to spot situations where D *may* have behaved negligently, and to articulate both sides of this issue. There's rarely a "right" or "clear" answer to the question, "Was D negligent?" — that's why the existence of due care is almost always a question left for the jury.

☞ **Vehicle accident:** Be especially careful to check for negligence when the facts involve a ***vehicle accident*** — there are few car or truck accidents on exams where there ***isn't*** a negligence issue.

☛ **Don't presume D was negligent:** Don't presume that D's conduct is definitely negligence, even though it seems to be.

Example: Even if the facts tell you that D took his eyes briefly off the road while driving, consider the possibility that there was a good cause for this, or at least that this was within the range of things that a reasonable driver might do on, say, a long trip.

☞ **Failure to warn:** One type of negligence often tested is the ***failure to warn*** another person about a danger. Here the negligence is a form of "omission," so you can miss the issue if you're not looking carefully for it.

Example: D has car trouble, and parks his car at the side of the road without placing warning flares around it.

☞ **Custom:** The issue of ***"custom"*** comes up often. The fact that a particular precaution is or isn't "customary" in the industry is ***evidence*** of what would be reasonable care, but it's ***not dispositive*** either way. (That is, failure to follow a custom that is usually observed for safety reasons, such as the giving of a particular type of warning, doesn't necessarily mean that D's conduct is negligent; conversely, the giving of, say, a customary warning doesn't necessarily mean that D's conduct wasn't negligent.)

☞ **Engaging in activity as negligence:** Sometimes, the negligence is ***"antecedent,"*** not carelessness right before the accident. That is, D's negligence lies in having put himself in a dangerous position by ***engaging in the activity in the first place***, not in carrying out the activity carelessly.

Example: D takes a prescription drug, then drives and gets into an accident while having an allergic reaction; even if D was as "careful" as his condition let him be at the precise moment of the accident, he may have been negligent in getting in the car at all after taking a new drug with a tendency to cause allergic reactions.

☞ **Children's standard of care:** The standard of care for ***children*** is often tested. This happens both where the child is the defendant and where the child is a plaintiff who might be barred by contributory negligence (or have his recovery reduced by comparative negligence). Remember that in most instances, the test is, "What is the level of care of a ***reasonable child*** of the ***age and experience*** of this child?"

☛ **Adult activity:** But remember that a child engaging in an ***adult activity*** (e.g., water skiing) is evaluated by an adult standard.

☛ **Negligence by adult in entrusting task to child:** A related issue often surfaces: It can be negligence for an adult to ***entrust a task*** to a child when a child wouldn't normally have the skills. (*Example:* It may be negligence to leave a 12-year-old to watch a one-year-old.)

☞ **Parental supervision:** Also, remember that a parent has a duty to exercise reasonable care to ***supervise the conduct of her minor child***, to prevent the child from intentionally harming others or posing an unreasonable risk of harm to them. (If the parent doesn't fulfill this duty, she's "directly liable" for her own negligence, not "vicariously liable" — a parent isn't vicariously liable for the torts of her minor child, even ones committed in the parent's presence.)

☞ **D fails to anticipate another's negligence:** One of the most-tested negligence issues: D negligently fails to ***anticipate the negligence*** (or other wrongdoing) of ***another person***.

Some contexts:

❑ D is a car rental agency that fails to verify that X has a license; X then has an accident, hurting P. D is probably negligent.

❑ D somehow helps X drive while drunk. Thus D may be a bartender or social host who serves X after X is already drunk, or a passerby who helps X start X's car when X is obviously drunk. D is probably negligent.

- ❑ D imposes some sort of hazard which isn't dangerous to others who are paying attention, but is dangerous to a person who isn't paying attention. This is probably negligence.

  Example: D parks his car at the shoulder of a highway, posing a danger only to one such as X who is speeding.) Here, D is probably negligent in not anticipating the negligence of others.

Negligence per se

☛ **Negligence per se, generally:** ***"Negligence per se"*** is one of the very most often-tested issues in all of torts. This is because it's easy for professors to construct fact patterns testing the doctrine, it's easy for students to miss the issue completely (e.g., the statute is buried in a complex fact pattern), and once the student spots the issue, there are still many sub-issues.

☞ **How to spot issue:** Whenever you spot a statute in your fact pattern, and the professor gives you the precise language (or even a pretty precise summary) of the statute, that's a tip-off that you should be looking for a negligence per se issue. (In fact, if the statute relates to some safety issue, negligence per se is practically the ***only*** issue to which the statute is likely to be relevant.)

☞ **Definition of doctrine:** Here's a good statement of the negligence per se doctrine, to begin your answer with: "D is negligent if, ***without excuse***, D ***violates a statute that is designed to protect against the type of accident D's conduct causes***, and the accident ***victim*** is ***within the class of persons the statute is designed to protect.***" Rest. 3d, §14.

☞ **Type of harm:** The single most commonly-tested sub-issue is this: Was the ***type of harm*** that occurred the type of harm the statute was ***designed to prevent***? Usually, the answer is ***"no,"*** but you will often have to speculate about what types of harm the legislature might have had in mind.

☛ **Bureaucratic rules:** This issue is especially likely to occur where the statute is essentially ***bureaucratic***, such as a ***licensing*** requirement.

Examples of the "type of harm" problem:

- ❑ A statute says, "No pilot may take on a passenger for pay unless the pilot has a commercial pilot's license." An accident then happens in flight while P is flying as D's paying passenger, and D has only a regular pilot's license. (Probably you should conclude that the licensing requirement was not enacted for the purpose of avoiding in-flight accidents, in which case the violation would not establish negligence.)
- ❑ A statute says, "No one may leave a parked car with the keys in the

ignition." D violates that statute; the car is stolen, and the thief crashes into P. You have to examine why the legislature passed this statute — was it to prevent accidents from thief-driven cars (in which case the per se doctrine applies), or was it to prevent some other harm (e.g., a child's driving the car), in which case the doctrine does not apply.

☞ **Violation must cause accident:** A related issue is that the violation must ***"cause"*** the accident. (This issue really belongs in the next chapter on causation, but we'll consider it here.) The violation of a regulatory statute — especially a licensing statute — usually is not deemed to be the "proximate cause" of the accident, so the violation gets disregarded.

Example: A statute says, "No one may drive a truck without a $500,000 minimum truck liability insurance policy." An accident occurs to D, an uninsured truck driver. Since the accident would still have happened even with insurance, the causal link between statute violation and accident will probably be found missing. (The same rule usually applies where the violation is not having a required license to engage in the activity.)

☞ **P must be member of protected class:** Here's another often-tested issue: Was P a ***member of the class*** that the legislature intended to protect by means of the statute? Don't be too narrow in interpreting the "protected class." In any event, you'll usually not be able to say for sure, and you just want to spot this issue and argue the pros and cons.

Example: The statute says, "No one may leave a vehicle parked and unattended on a part of a street marked 'school zone.'" P is an adult who crashes into D's unattended car parked in such a zone. You can't know what the legislature intended. Therefore, say that if the legislature intended only to protect school children, P will not get the benefit of the negligence per se doctrine. But discuss the possibility that although the statute is tied into a school zone, it may have been intended to protect ***any member*** of the public (e.g., a child's parent, a visitor to the school, etc.) who is using the street in front of the school, in which case the doctrine would apply.

☞ **Ordinance or administrative regulation:** If the provision is an ***ordinance*** or an ***administrative regulation*** instead of a statute, you should note that not all courts apply the negligence per se doctrine here. (But also note that those courts that don't accept the doctrine would probably accept the violation as at least strong evidence of negligence.)

☞ **Excuse:** Fact patterns often raise the issue of ***"excuse"*** of the violation. D is likely to be "excused" from his non-compliance if either: (1) he couldn't avoid the violation even though he was "careful"; or (2) he chose to violate the statute as the lesser of two evils.

Example: A statute says, "All drivers must keep their brakes in working order at all times." D's brakes fail suddenly, and he crashes into the car ahead of him. If D shows that he had no advance notice that his brakes were failing, he'll probably be deemed to be excused, and the negligence per se doctrine won't apply.

☛ **D's compliance as defense:** Sometimes D's ***compliance*** with a statute poses the converse issue: Does the fact that D complied with a fairly precise statutory safety rule automatically mean that D ***wasn't*** negligent? Usually, the answer is "no" — compliance is at most non-dispositive *evidence* of D's non-negligence.

Res ipsa loquitur

☛ **When to look for RIL issue:** Look for a ***"res ipsa loquitur"*** (RIL) issue whenever there's no direct evidence as to whether D was negligent.

☞ **Requirements:** The requirements for the RIL doctrine in most courts are:

[1] there must be ***no direct evidence*** as to D's precise conduct;

[2] the event must be one that ***normally doesn't occur without negligence by somebody***; and

[3] D must be the ***most likely person*** whose negligence would have caused the event (sometimes clumsily expressed by saying that the event or instrumentality must have been "within D's ***exclusive control***").

☛ **Not hard to spot:** Most of the time, the existence of a RIL issue is easy to spot. The tougher part is determining whether all conditions for the doctrine are satisfied.

☞ **Some contexts:** Some contexts where RIL frequently arises on exams (and can be successfully asserted by the plaintiff):

- ❑ The product is grossly defective, and suit is brought in negligence rather than in strict product liability. (*Examples:* Food with a foreign object in it; exploding containers.) In this "product" situation, RIL is most useful where there is no direct evidence that the manufacturer screwed up, i.e., no information about what happened during the manufacture of that particular item.

- ❑ An airplane crashes into the ground or into an obstruction, and there are no clues as to what caused the accident.

- ❑ A driver hits a pedestrian from the rear, while the pedestrian is walking along the side of the road; the pedestrian dies or doesn't know how the accident happened. (But RIL usually ***doesn't*** apply to ***multiple-vehicle*** accidents, since you can't say that such accidents usually don't occur without the negligence of the particular driver who's the defendant.)

- ❑ P gets surgery, and something unexpected results (e.g., a surgical tool is left inside P's body, or the wrong part of P's anatomy is removed).

☞ **Exclusive control:** The requirement that D be the person most likely to have been negligent is often tested. It's up to you to spot this issue and discuss it, because the facts won't usually tip you off.

Example: P undergoes surgery by D, and a later x-ray shows a surgical tool left in his body. It's up to you to say, "But P will probably have to show that only D was the only one who operated on P, or at least that he's more likely than anyone else to have left the tool in P's body."

- **Machine operated by third person:** Because of the "D is the most likely negligent person" requirement, RIL is not usually successfully used against the manufacturer of an airplane or other machine that has to be operated by a third person — since the manufacturer is not in sole control of the machine at the time of the accident, the doctrine doesn't fit unless negligence can be directly traced to the time of manufacture. (RIL works better against the operator than against the manufacturer, in this operated-machine situation.)

☞ **"Usually doesn't occur without negligence":** The requirement that the accident be of a sort that ***usually doesn't occur without negligence*** is also sometimes tested. Again, the issue is usually hidden — it's up to you to notice that you've been given no information about whether an accident of this type "usually doesn't occur without negligence."

Example: P is killed when a plane piloted by D crashes into a mountain. It's up to you to notice and discuss that you don't know whether this accident is of a type that usually doesn't happen without negligence. You might, for instance, speculate that such accidents may often be due to an undetectably-faulty altimeter or some reason other than negligence.

- **Need not show accident never occurs w/o negligence:** But remember that P doesn't have to show that this type of accident ***never*** occurs without negligence, only that it ***usually*** involves negligence. (That's what allows use of the doctrine in airplane-crash-into-ground suits against airlines.)

- **Expert witnesses:** Also, keep in mind that in technical cases (e.g., ***medical malpractice***), P is generally allowed to use ***expert witnesses*** to show that the accident is one that usually doesn't happen without negligence, and/or that the defendants were the ones in control of whether this type of event occurred.

☞ **Where direct evidence available:** The doctrine is only used as ***indirect evidence*** of negligence. Therefore, it's not used when there is ***direct evidence*** of what caused the episode, or of exactly how D behaved during the event.

- **"All possible care used":** Thus if the facts tell you that D "used all possible care" or some such, then RIL is not used.
- **Info about actual cause present:** Similarly, if the facts tell you that the cause of the particular accident was something other than D's negligence, the fact that the accident falls into a "class" in which RIL usually is used is irrelevant.

  Example: If an airplane crashes, but the facts suggest that a defective altimeter was probably the cause, RIL will not be used in a suit against the pilot.
- **Where specifics of D's conduct known:** If the facts describe D's conduct in detail, and the sole issue is, "Was that conduct reasonably careful?" don't use RIL — it's only used when we don't know the specifics of what D did.

☞ **Cases based on non-negligence theories:** Since the purpose of the doctrine is to produce circumstantial evidence of negligence, it's not used in cases based on a non-negligence theory, such as those based on strict product liability.

Example: The suit involves a product with a foreign object in it. If the suit is brought in strict product liability, we don't use RIL because we only need to know, "Was there a 'dangerous defect?'" not "Did the manufacturer use due care?"

Note: On the other hand, we'll see in the Products Liability chapter that in strict liability cases, courts often give P the benefit of a "res-ipsa-like" inference on the issue of whether the product was defective. Thus here, in the product-with-a-foreign-object-in-it suit, P would get the benefit of an inference that a product with a foreign object in it is usually "defective."

☞ **Function of doctrine:** You may want to point out that, in most states, the function of the RIL doctrine where applicable is to treat P as having produced ***enough evidence of negligence to get to the jury.*** That is, if the RIL is not rebutted, D won't succeed with a motion for a directed verdict alleging that P hasn't proved that D was negligent. (But remember that D is generally allowed to come up with rebuttal evidence that he was in fact careful, or that the accident was in fact caused by someone or something else.)

Exam Tips on *ACTUAL AND PROXIMATE CAUSE*

D can't be liable for negligence (or any other tort) unless he in some sense "caused" the harm to P. When you deal with causation on an exam, you must always deal with two distinct issues: (1) was D the ***"cause in fact"*** or "factual cause" of the harm to P?; and (2) was D the ***"legal cause"*** or ***"proximate cause"*** of the harm to P?

Causation generally

☛ **General tip:** Even if there's no true "issue" on either of these types of causation, you should ***discuss each*** at least briefly in your essay answer, since they're part of P's prima facie case.

Sample answer where both types of causation are clear: "Since D hit P while driving carelessly, D is clearly the 'cause in fact' of P's broken leg, because that leg wouldn't have been broken had D not driven his car into P. Also, D is clearly the proximate or legal cause of the injuries, since it was quite foreseeable that D's careless driving in this situation might cause injury to a pedestrian like P, and there were no intervening factors."

Cause in fact

☛ **Cause in fact generally:** Here's what to look for concerning ***"cause in fact"***:

☞ **"But for" standard:** In virtually every situation except one, use the ***"but for"*** standard — D's negligent act is the "cause in fact" of the harm to P ***if the harm would not have happened "but for" D's negligent act.***

Example: "D's speeding was the 'but for'cause of P's broken leg, because but for D's speeding, D could have stopped or swerved in time, or P could have jumped out of the way. . . ."

☛ **Where but-for test not satisfied:** Usually, the fact pattern on an exam is such that the "but for" test is satisfied. But you must look out for the occasional fact pattern where the accident or injury ***"would have happened anyway"*** even without D's negligence, so the "but for" test is not satisfied.

Example: D1 negligently maintains a telephone pole so it rots. D2 negligently drives his car into the pole, knocking the pole down so it hits P. You should say on your answer something like, "If D2 hit the pole so hard that it would have fallen even had it not been rotten, then the court will treat D1's negligence as not being the "but for" cause, or cause in fact, of the impact to P."

☞ **Substantial-factor test:** The one time you shouldn't use the "but for" test is where the facts disclose two ***"concurrent causes," each of which would have been enough by itself*** to cause the harm. Here, you should use the ***"substantial factor"*** test — if one of the causes was a "substantial factor" in bringing the harm about, it's deemed a cause-in-fact even though the other cause could have sufficed alone. (So both causes are likely to be found "causes in fact" on this scenario.)

Example: D1 and D2 are each bar-owners. Each serves X enough alcohol to get X legally drunk. X hits P with his car. The facts suggest that even a just-barely-legally-drunk driver probably would have hit P. D1 and D2 are each a "substantial factor" in P's injury, and thus each is a cause-in-fact, even though neither is truly a "but for" cause since the accident would have happened based solely on the drinks served by one.

☞ **Standard of proof:** Don't forget the ***standard of proof*** for causation (as well as for the other elements of negligence): P has to prove actual causation by a ***"preponderance of the evidence"*** (i.e, that it's ***"more likely than not"*** that P's injury was caused in fact by D's negligence).

☛ **"Value of a chance":** But in a ***medical-malpractice*** scenario, be on the lookout for a ***"value of a chance"*** problem. Even if correct medical diagnosis and treatment would have increased P's chance of a good outcome but only to less than 50%, P can still recover. What he recovers is the value of a good outcome (compared to the bad outcome P actually suffered), but multipled by a fraction representing the percentage-chance that the good outcome would have occurred with adequate and timely treatment.

Example: Doc fails to catch P's early-stage cancer (which adequate diagnosis would have caught). P dies one year later as a result. Assume that if Doc had caught the cancer at the early stage and treated P right away, P would have had a 30% chance of being cured instead of dying in a year. P can recover from Doc an amount equal to:

(the value of a complete cure) *times*
(30%, the chance that prompt treatment would have cured him).

☞ **Serial causes:** You'll often have two ***serial*** causes. If so, distinguish between two situations:

☛ **Two causes cause a single injury:** In one situation, both causes are necessary (and neither is sufficient alone) to cause a ***single injury***. In that instance, ***both*** are "causes in fact."

Example: D1 drives negligently onto the sidewalk, forcing P, a pedestrian, to jump into the street. D2 comes along driving too fast, and hits P because he can't stop in time. D1's and D2's careless acts are each "but for" causes, and thus "causes in fact," because, as to each, we can say that the impact wouldn't have happened "but for" that careless act.

☛ **Two sets of injuries:** In the other situation, you have two causes, but you have ***two sets of injuries*** (an earlier set and a later set). Here, the earlier tortfeasor will be liable for ***both*** sets of injuries, but the later tortfeasor will typically be liable only for the ***later set*** of injuries.

Example: D1 hits P with his car, breaking P's leg. D2, an ambulance driver, taking P to the hospital, crashes, breaking P's arm. D1 is the cause in fact of both the leg and the arm injuries, but D2 is the cause in fact of *only the arm injury*.

☞ **Speculation:** You'll often have to ***speculate*** in your answer about whether D is a cause in fact, based on "what would have happened" if D had behaved differently. Your speculation is especially likely where D's negligence consisted of ***failing to act***. Keep in mind that the "but for" element merely has to be established as "more likely than not."

Example: D abandons his stalled car in the road, without staying to warn other traffic. P, another driver, hits D's car and injures himself. You don't really know what would have happened if D had stayed around, so you'll have to speculate something like this: "If D had stayed around to warn oncoming traffic, he probably (but not certainly) would have been able to successfully warn P of the danger, thereby avoiding the accident. Consequently, D's failure to stay and warn should probably be treated as the 'but for' cause of P's injuries."

Proximate cause

☛ **Proximate cause, generally:** For ***"proximate cause,"*** here's what to look for:

☞ **Forseeability:** Proximate cause generally boils down to whether the harm was ***"foreseeable."*** If it was reasonably foreseeable that D's behavior might (not would, just might) cause an injury somewhat like the one that happened to P, then you should probably conclude that D's behavior was the proximate cause of P's injury.

☞ **Definition to use:** A good definition of proximate cause to use on an exam is: "Conduct will be deemed to be a proximate cause of harm if the harm was a foreseeable result of the conduct, and if the harm was not brought about by an extraordinary or unforeseeable sequence of events."

☛ **"Scope of risk" standard:** D's act (even though negligent) won't be a proximate cause unless it somehow increased the foreseeable risk of an accident ***of a type like the one that happened***. You may want to quote the Third Restatement's test: a defendant is "not liable for harm ***different from the harms whose risk made the [defendant's] conduct tortious.***"

Example: D builds a building using what he knows to be weak steel. Five years later, an earthquake occurs. The building falls on a gasoline truck, causing gas to leak into the roadway. The gas travels two blocks, to where X is standing. X throws a match, and the ensuing explosion hurts P. P probably loses. The harm whose risk made the use of weak steel negligent might include a building collapse. But it probably doesn't include a building's collapse, during an earthquake, onto a gasoline truck, followed by gasoline spillage that causes an explosion two blocks away. So the injury to P was a "harm different from the harms whose risk made the weak-steel-use negligent," preventing that injury from being the proximate result of D's negligent use of steel.

☛ **Different time or different place:** One common exam fact pattern illustrating this "scope of risks" principle: D's negligence causes someone (D, P or a third person) to be in a particular place at a ***different time*** — or at a ***different place*** altogether — than if D hadn't acted. Assuming that being in the place at that different time or being in that different place wasn't inherently and foreseeably more risky, then D's initial act is ***not*** the proximate cause of the harm that ensues.

Example: D is a pilot who misreads his fuel gauge before taking off, and has less gas than he thinks. D is therefore forced to make a landing at an airport that isn't his final destination. While the plane is on the runway, parked properly, P's plane collides with it. D's negligence is not the proximate cause of the crash, because although it put the plane where it wouldn't have otherwise been, this didn't materially increase the risk of a crash — falling out of the sky, not being parked on a particular runway, was the kind of risk that made D's misreading negligent in the first place.

☛ **Negligence per se:** This "scope of risk" analysis is also used in negligence *per se* cases — if the type of accident that occurred wasn't the type of accident the statute was designed to prevent, then D's violation of the statute isn't the proximate cause of the accident.

Example: A motorist who violates a statute requiring a certain amount of insurance has an accident while driving cautiously — the insurance violation is not the proximate cause of the accident.

☛ **Judge-jury allocation of decision-making:** In any proximate-cause scenario, be alert to the allocation of ***decision-making*** as between ***the judge and the jury***. Remember, the judge instructs the jury on what legal test to apply in deciding whether D's tortious conduct proximately caused the harm to P (and the jury then applies that test). However, if the judge believes that ***no reasonable jury could find*** that D's conduct was the proximate cause of the harm, the judge can ***take the case away*** from the jury (by issuing a directed verdict or summary judgment for D).

☞ **Can go either way:** But say that usually, the judge will conclude that the jury could decide the proximate-cause issue ***either way***, in which case the judge will let the jury make the decision.

☞ **Medical complications:** Unforeseen ***medical complications*** suffered by P are often tested. Here, as long as D was the proximate cause of ***some*** harm to P, the fact that the harm was much worse than anticipated is irrelevant. This is the ***"eggshell skull"*** problem. Quote the classic rule here: "D takes P as he finds him."

Example: P has one eye. D's negligence causes P to lose that eye. D is responsible for total blindness.

☞ **Intervening events:** Most proximate cause issues involve ***intervening events***, either by nature or by people. Whenever you see an initial careless act by one person, followed by another act or event by nature or someone else, that's probably a tip-off to ask whether the first person's act was the proximate cause of the eventual injury.

- **Foreseeability:** In this "intervening event" situation, the basic issue is still ***foreseeability*** — if the intervening act/event was reasonably foreseeable, it doesn't block the first event from being a proximate cause. If the intervening act/event was unforeseeable, it's probably ***"superseding,"*** i.e., it prevents the first act from being the proximate cause.

- **Dependent vs. independent intervening acts:** Courts sometimes distinguish between ***"dependent"*** and ***"independent"*** intervening acts. (On this view, a dependent act occurs in response to D's act, such as a rescue of a victim injured by D, whereas an independent act would have happened anyway but without the bad consequences.) However, the distinction is not that significant — you may want to classify the particular event, but then you should probably ignore the distinction.

- **Negligence or intentional wrongdoing of third persons:** Many fact patterns involve D's failure to foresee the ***negligence or intentional wrongdoing of third persons***. Often, the facts will be such that this third-party wrongdoing is foreseeable, and thus not superseding. *Examples:*

  - ❑ D leaves the key in the ignition of his car. The risk that X will steal the car and injure a pedestrian is probably foreseeable (and is probably part of the same general risk that makes leaving a key in the ignition negligence in the first place), so D will be the proximate cause of the injury to the pedestrian.

  - ❑ D leaves explosives around. X, a terrorist, steals them. (This is foreseeable, if one who deals in explosives should know that these are attractive to terrorists or other criminals.)

  - ❑ D leaves his car in an intersection where no parking is allowed. Careful drivers would be able to avoid it, but the car is hit by a careless speeding driver, X. D will still be a proximate cause of the damage.

(As a general rule, the negligence of other drivers on the road is probably ***always*** foreseeable, so a third party's negligence in driving is almost never superseding.)

☛ **Rescuers: *Rescuers*** are often part of the fact pattern. General rule: the rescue is a foreseeable response to an accident or injury. Therefore, the initial tortfeasor will still be on the hook when either the injured person is hurt worse, or the rescuer is hurt. This is true even if the rescuer behaves negligently. Quote Cardozo: "Danger invites rescue."

Example: D hurts P. P is then injured worse when the ambulance is speeding to the hospital and gets into an accident. D is responsible for the worsened injuries to P.

☞ **Firefighters' rule:** But if it's the ***rescuer*** that gets hurt, check to see whether she's a firefighter, police officer, or other person "paid to assume" that type of risk. Most states apply the ***"firefighters' rule,"*** under which such ***professional-risk-takers can't recover*** against the person who negligently caused the need for the rescue.

☛ **Medical malpractice:** Remember that ***medical malpractice*** is usually deemed foreseeable and thus not superseding.

Example: D1 hurts P slightly. D2, a doctor, hurts P worse while treating him. D1 is the proximate cause of the whole set of injuries.

☞ **Gross medical negligence:** But "gross" medical negligence (e.g., the doctor operates on the wrong leg) is probably superseding.

☞ **Responsibility-shifting:** Sometimes ***"responsibility shifting"*** is tested. If X is ***aware*** of the risk caused by D, but ***consciously disregards*** that risk, then X's going forward generally supersedes, and shifts the risk away from D to X. This principle applies in strict products liability, not just negligence cases.

Example: D manufactures a car. Two years later, D discovers that a part was defective, and notifies X (the owner) that D is recalling the car and will fix it for free. X gets the message, but declines to take up the offer. Three years later, X sells the car to P, who is later injured in a crash caused by the defect. X's conscious disregard of the risk will probably be deemed to shift the responsibility away from D to X, so P can't recover from D. (But this probably isn't true where X doesn't get the recall message; here, D's initial fault is still the proximate cause of P's injury.)

Exam Tips on JOINT TORTFEASORS

Whenever you have multiple tortfeasors, consider whether they will be ***"jointly and severally liable."***

Joint tortfeasors, generally

☞ **General rule:** If more than one person is an actual and proximate cause of P's harm, and the harm is indivisible, each D is liable for the ***entire harm***.

☞ **Indivisible harm:** Often-tested issue: "Was the harm to P ***indivisible***?" If not, there is no joint-and-several liability.

Example: D1 and D2 shoot at P. D1 hits P in the leg, D2 hits him in the eye. If we can apportion the harm, including pain and suffering — which we can do here — then there's no joint-and-several liability; each D pays only for the harm he himself caused.

☛ **Burden of proof:** If the harm is theoretically divisible, but P has no allocation evidence (i.e., P can't show which of two or more Ds was responsible for which harm), the court may put the ***burden of proof on the Ds*** to show this.

Example: P shows that D1 and D2, acting separately, poisoned his stream by pollution at different times. If P can't come up with evidence of which harms were due to which D's acts, the court may say that it's up to the Ds to produce such proof, and if they can't they're jointly and severally liable.

☞ **P can collect entire amount of any D:** If joint-and-several liability applies, then P can collect the ***entire amount*** from whichever single defendant he wishes. Alternatively, he may collect some from each. (P is of course limited to one total recovery.)

☞ **Two contexts:** Two common contexts for joint-and-several liability:

- ❑ ***Employer/employee*** — each is jointly and severally liable (the employer on a "vicarious liability" theory).
- ❑ Where a ***dangerous product*** injures the consumer, both the ***manufacturer*** and the ***retailer*** will be jointly and severally liable if P recovers in strict product liability.

☞ **Relation to comparative negligence:** A issue that's very often tested: The interaction between traditional joint-and-several liability and ***comparative*** negligence.

- ☛ **Joint & several liability persists:** If there is no statute dealing specifically with this interaction, then joint-and-several liability ***persists*** as to that portion of the total fault that is not the plaintiff's.

  Example: P has total, indivisible, injuries of $100,000. The jury finds that P was 30% at fault, D1 was 50% at fault and D2 20%. The jurisdiction has a comparative negligence statute, but no statute addressing joint-and-several liability. P can only collect $70,000, which he can collect all from D1, all from D2 or in a mix.

- ☛ **Statutes:** Some states now have special statutes limiting joint-and-several liability in connection with comparative negligence. If your facts are silent about whether such a statute is in force, you might want to give the traditional analysis as in the prior paragraph, and then speculate.

  Example: "But the state may have a statute, as a number of states now do, abolishing joint-and-several liability for any defendant found to be less than 50% at fault for the accident."

Contribution

- ☛ **Contribution generally:** Whenever you have multiple tortfeasors, consider whether one has the right to ***contribution*** from the other(s). Contribution is a ***cost-sharing*** in favor of one who has paid ***more than his proportionate share*** of the total liability.

  - ☞ **Common-law approach:** Under classic common-law contribution, the court makes each defendant pay an ***equal*** net amount.

    Example: D1 and D2 are found jointly and severally liable for P's $100,000 in injuries. P collects $70,000 from D1 and $30,000 from D2. Under the common-law approach, D1 can get contribution of $20,000 from D2, since this is the amount needed to equalize their shares.

  - ☞ **Intentional tortfeasors:** No contribution right is given to an ***intentional*** tortfeasor (even against another intentional tortfeasor).

  - ☞ **Comparative negligence:** The most commonly-tested issue is the interaction between contribution and ***comparative negligence***. Here, most comparative negligence states have statutes requiring contribution ***in proportion to fault***.

    Example: P has a $100,000 loss. The jury says that P was 25% responsible, D1 25% and D2 50%. Assume that P recovers the whole $75,000 from D1 (which he can, provided the state doesn't have a statute changing the traditional joint-and-several liability rule in comparative negligence cases). In most states, D1 can get contribution of $50,000 from D2, since that's the amount that would adjust the shares of D1 and D2 in proportion to the jury's finding of fault.

Indemnity

☛ **Indemnity generally:** Whenever you have multiple tortfeasors, consider whether one has the right to be ***indemnified*** by the other(s). Indemnity refers to a ***complete reimbursement***, not a cost-sharing. It is usually given where one tortfeasor is clearly less culpable than the other.

☞ **D is vicariously liable:** Most commonly, the right of indemnity exists where one D is only ***vicariously*** liable, and the other is directly liable. *Examples:*

- ❑ Employer can get indemnification from Employee (assuming that employer had no direct fault, and his only liability was vicarious).
- ❑ Retailer can get indemnity from Manufacturer in a strict product liability case. (In fact, anyone in a distribution chain held strictly liable can recover against ***anyone higher up*** in the chain — so Retailer can get indemnity from Wholesaler, and Wholesaler can in turn get indemnity from Manufacturer.)
- ❑ Where Owner is liable for accident by Driver from having allowed Driver to drive Owner's vehicle (this is the result of Owner consent statute), Owner will get indemnity from Driver.

Exam Tips on DUTY

Be on the lookout for three special types of situations: (1) D ***fails to act***; (2) P claims ***"mental suffering"*** without physical impact; and (3) D suffers solely ***"intangible economic harm."***

Failure to act

☛ **Failure to act, generally:** Look for situations where D ***fails to act***.

☞ **No duty to assist:** The core rule, of course, is that a person generally has ***no duty to assist another***, even where he could do so easily. Occasionally, this general rule is tested — you can spot it because the facts will typically involve a complete stranger who happens to pass by to observe P's peril.

Example: D jogs by, sees P drowning, doesn't pull P out or call for help. D is not liable.

☞ **Exceptions:** Much more often, however, the ***exceptions*** to the general rule of "no duty to render assistance" are what are tested. The most important exceptions are:

☛ **Owner of business premises:** Any ***owner of business premises*** has a duty to help one who is on the premises, regardless of the source of the danger.

Example: If P is choking in D's store, D must attempt to help P even if the choking has nothing to do with D's conduct.

☞ **Common carriers:** A sub-rule: ***Common carriers*** have a special duty to help passengers, including protecting them from third-party wrongdoers.

☞ **University-student:** Similarly, most courts now recognize a special ***university-student*** relationship (so that the university must give assistance to a student it knows or should know is in danger, whether the danger is from drug use or from, say, a poorly-lit parking lot).

☛ **D created the danger:** D has a duty to help if ***D's conduct created the danger*** (even if D did not behave negligently).

Example: D's car hits P when P darts into the street. Even if D drove completely carefully, D has a duty to get medical assistance for P.

☛ **D undertakes to assist:** D has a duty to render assistance if he ***"undertakes"*** to furnish assistance. "Undertaking" clearly includes the situation where D starts to render assistance, and then doesn't follow through.

Example: D drives P partway to the hospital, then puts P off at the side of the road.

☞ **Mere promise to assist:** Testable issue: Does D's mere ***promise*** to render assistance bind D? Most courts today find that a promise alone can be an undertaking, if it induces detrimental reliance by P or others (e.g., others declined to help P thinking D is already giving help).

☞ **D must leave P worse off:** But there's only liability on an "undertaking" theory when D leaves P ***worse off*** than had there been no undertaking ("detrimental reliance").

Example: D passes by, sees P lying injured, and says, "I'll get help." If no one else comes along, until X comes along and gets help, probably D is not liable because he didn't worsen P's status.

Mental suffering

☛ **Mental suffering generally:** Look for situations where P may have a claim for ***"mental suffering."***

☞ **Must be physical manifestation:** First, remember that the courts usually don't allow recovery for ***"pure"*** mental suffering, without any ***physical manifestations***. Thus if P suffers no physical impact ***and*** doesn't get physical symptoms from her asserted suffering (headaches, nausea, etc.), the court is likely to hold that the mental suffering did not merit compensation.

☞ **Tacking on of suffering:** Also, remember that if P has ***direct physical injuries***, the mental suffering can in all courts be ***"tacked on"*** as an additional element of recovery.

Example: P gets a broken leg from a car accident; P can also recover for suffering the pain from the break.

☞ **Where it's important:** Mental suffering thus is an important issue just in those cases where there is ***no direct physical injury***. There are two major fact patterns that pop up on exams:

- **P in physical danger:** First, P is ***herself in physical danger***, and is frightened solely for her own safety. Here, all courts allow P to recover.

  Example: P is about to be run over and jumps out of the way. P can recover for her emotional distress, both at the moment and reliving the near-accident.

- **P witnesses accident:** Second (and more commonly tested), P ***witnesses an accident*** to another person, and P's mental suffering is mainly her fear ***for the other's*** safety. Here, your analysis should go through several stages:

  - ❑ **P within zone of impact/danger:** If P was within the ***"zone of impact"*** or ***"zone of danger,"*** virtually all courts will allow P to recover for mental suffering, both for her fear for her own safety and her fear for the safety of any ***relative*** who may have been hit or almost hit. So if the facts tell you that P was walking alongside of her husband X (or "standing next to" X), and X is run over or otherwise hurt, then P can recover for mental suffering.

  - ❑ **P not within zone of impact/danger:** If P was ***not*** within the zone of impact/danger, but was "present" and ***viewed*** an accident to another, ***some*** (but probably not yet most) courts have abolished the "zone of impact" requirement, and ***allow*** P to recover for fear for the safety of the injured person. However, these courts almost all require that the injured person be a ***close relative***, and also require that P suffer ***serious*** emotional distress. So on these facts, say that P can recover "if the jurisdiction has abolished the zone-of-impact requirement." (Usually, the facts won't make it clear whether the jurisdiction has abolished the requirement.)

Note: In courts that have abolished the "zone of impact" requirement, P can recover not only where she is, say, outside and within a few feet of the accident site, but also where she is ***inside*** and sees the accident through a ***window***.

❑ **P does not see accident:** If P ***does not see*** the accident at all, but merely hears about it later (even just a few moments later), no court seems to let P recover for emotional distress, even if the injured person (call him "X") is P's close relative. So be on the lookout for a fact pattern reading, "A few moments after the accident, P, X's mother, came on the scene . . . ," or "A neighbor rushed to tell P about the accident to X . . . " — there is ***no recovery*** for P's distress in these scenarios. If X is badly hurt or killed, P can recover for loss of consortium — but in this chapter, we're talking about situations where X is either not badly hurt, or not hurt at all, and P has merely suffered fear, not permanent loss.

Intangible economic harm

☛ **Intangible economic harm, generally:** Look out for situations where D suffers pure ***"intangible economic harm"*** (e.g., ***lost business profits***), as distinguished from physical harm or property damage.

☞ **Added to other harms:** First, look for the situation where D suffers intangible economic harm ***in addition to*** physical injury or direct property damage. Here, all courts agree that P may "tack on" his economic loss to the other elements of harm.

Example: P gets a broken leg, and can't operate his store for six months. P can collect the profits he would have made operating the store.

☞ **Only intangible harm:** More difficult (and more likely to be tested) is the situation where P suffers ***only*** intangible economic harm, with no personal injury or property damage.

☛ **Someone must have personal injury or property damage:** First, check that *someone* has suffered personal injury or direct property damage. If there is no such person, then in all courts it's clear that P can't recover for the economic losses.

☛ **P's right to recover for pure economic loss:** Assuming that the person or tangible property of someone other than P was directly injured, then you have an issue about whether P can recover for his pure economic loss from the same episode.

- **Majority view:** Under the ***majority view***, D can't recover at all, because courts fear open-ended liability. (*Example:* P operates a brokerage business. D negligently drives into an electric transformer on the street, knocking out the power to P's business and all others within a 300 yard radius. P can't operate the business for a day, and loses money. Under the majority view, P can't recover, because he has suffered no personal injury or property damage, and his damages are purely economic.)
- **Small minority sometimes allows recovery:** In a few courts, there is no longer any per se rule against recovery of pure economic losses. However, even these courts require that P be part of a relatively small ***"identifiable class"*** that could be foreseen to suffer losses from an act like D's. (*Example:* Under the above brokerage example, P might be able to recover in a few courts, because any business in the relatively small area served by the transformer could be identified in advance as being one that would be economically damaged by D's conduct.)

☛ **Some contexts:** Contexts where the issue of intangible economic harm is likely to arise:

- **Public health hazard:** D launches some ***"public health hazard"*** (e.g., some disease, or some toxic chemical into the air, or some pollutant into the water). (*Example:* The Gulf Oil Spill scenario, where D negligently causes the spill and claims are brought by P, a hotel operator who suffers no direct physical injury or property damage, but loses profits because customers stay away. Under the majority view, absent a statute P cannot recover for this pure economic loss.)
- **Cutting off of public service:** D cuts off some ***vital public service*** (e.g., a bridge or highway, electric or water service, etc.).
- **Injury to employee:** D negligently injures X, a human, and P, X's ***employer***, loses the benefits of X's services for a time, and thus loses profits. (P can't recover from D for P's pure economic losses, even though *X* can recover his lost wages as well as for pain and suffering, medical bills, etc.)

☛ **Basis for claim:** The "intangible economic loss" problem arises both where the claim is based on negligence, and also where it's based on ***strict product liability*** or ***abnormally dangerous activity***. (But it does not arise where the tort is intentional, since here the liability is wide-sweeping, and probably all courts will give recovery for pure intangible economic loss.)

Exam Tips on OWNERS AND OCCUPIERS OF LAND

Nearly every Torts exam contains at least one question involving the obligation of ***owners of land.***

Persons off the land

☛ **Artificial conditions:** Remember that a landowner has a duty to prevent an unreasonable risk of harm to persons ***off the land*** from ***artificial conditions*** on the land.

> **Example:** D burns trash on his land, causing smoke that distracts a driver on the adjacent road; D is probably liable.

☞ **Natural conditions:** Older cases hold that there is no duty to prevent an unreasonable risk from ***natural*** conditions on the land (e.g., a tree), but modern cases, especially ones from urban states, may disagree.

Duty to trespassers

☛ **Duty to trespassers, generally:** Many exam questions involve the owner's duty to ***trespassers***.

☞ **No duty in general:** The general rule is that the owner owes ***no duty*** to a trespasser to make the land safe, or even to warn the trespasser of known dangers. But there are some exceptions.

☞ **Knowledge of presence:** If O has ***knowledge*** of the trespasser's presence, most courts require O to use reasonable care for the trespasser's safety. Usually a ***warning*** of a specific danger will suffice (but the posting of a general "no trespassers" sign will not).

☞ **Trespassing children:** Most commonly tested is the duty to trespassing ***children***. Here, O will be liable if five requirements are all met:

[1] O knows or should know that children are ***likely to trespass*** on that particular part of his land;

[2] O knows or should know that a condition on that part of the land poses an ***unreasonable risk*** of serious injury to trespassing children;

[3] the child has not ***discovered*** the condition or ***does not realize the danger*** because of his youth;

[4] the utility in maintaining the condition is ***outweighed*** by the danger to children; and

[5] O fails to use ***reasonable care*** to eliminate the danger or to protect the children.

The list probably applies only to ***"artificial"*** conditions on the land, not to "natural" conditions; it's not clear whether it applies to "activities" carried out by O on the land.

☛ **Examples** where O may be liable to trespassing children:

- ❑ O maintains a gravel heap which he knows children sled ride down, with the risk that they'll go onto the adjacent roadway and get run over;
- ❑ O maintains a high-tension wire at the top of a pole. The pole has spikes for climbing, and O knows that children from the nearby school often trespass and climb the pole.

Licensees vs. invitees

☛ **Distinction:** Many questions require you to distinguish between ***"licensees"*** and ***"invitees."***

☞ **"Licensee" and "invitee" defined:**

- ❑ A ***"licensee"*** is typically a ***"social guest."***
- ❑ An ***"invitee"*** is one who is either invited by O to conduct ***business*** on the premises, or is a member of the ***public*** coming onto the land for the purposes for which the land is held open to the public.

☞ **Duty to licensee:** The key difference between licensee and invitee is that O has ***no*** affirmative duty to ***make the premises safe*** for the licensee, including no duty to ***inspect*** for hidden dangers (but does have such a duty as to the invitee).

☛ **Public emergency workers:** Commonly-tested: If P is a police officer, fire fighter or other public ***emergency worker***, under the common-law "firefighter's rule" P is probably a licensee, and can't recover for dangers that O should have known about but didn't.

Example: O doesn't know there's a loose step on the way to his basement, and P, a fire fighter going to the basement to check out a blaze, falls. O is not liable even if it was negligent of him not to have discovered and fixed the step.

☛ **Duty to warn:** But it's key to remember that even to a licensee, O has an obligation to ***warn*** of hidden dangers ***known*** to O.

Example: On above example, if O knows the stair is loose, he's got an obligation to warn P, the fire fighter, assuming there's time.

☞ **Duty to invitee:** By contrast, O ***does*** have an affirmative duty to an ***invitee*** to ***inspect the premises*** for hidden dangers, and to ***make the premises reasonably safe.***

☛ **Protection against third-party wrongdoing:** This obligation often includes a duty to protect against wrongdoing — including crimes — by third parties.

Example: If O runs a hotel, O probably has a duty to supply reasonable security in the hotel and its parking lot, and O is liable to a business visitor who is attacked by a third person if reasonable security would have prevented the attack.

☛ **O is not an insurer:** Keep in mind that even to an invitee, O is ***not an insurer***, merely a person having an obligation to behave "reasonably." For instance, if there have been few or no assaults on O's premises previously, O probably isn't liable for failing to have a security officer when an attack finally occurs.

☛ **P is a browser:** Common issue relating to invitee: When O hold his business open to the public, is a P who comes there just to ***browse*** (without making or intending to make a purchase) an "invitee"? Answer: probably "yes," because O could hope to get economic benefit from P either on that or some later occasion.

☛ **P is an independent contractor:** Similar issue: Is a ***worker*** or other ***independent contractor*** engaged by O to work on the premises (e.g., painter or plumber) an "invitee"? Answer: again, probably "yes," because he gives an economic benefit to O.

☞ **Possible abolition of distinction:** In any discussion where you mention the trespasser/licensee/invitee distinction, you should allude to the possibility that the jurisdiction has (as many jurisdictions now have) ***abolished*** this distinction. Say something like: "If the jurisdiction has abolished the distinctions between trespasser, licensee and invitee, it probably imposes a single standard of 'reasonableness under all the circumstances.' In that event, we must consider the foreseeability of P's presence on the premises and the foreseeability of danger to him. O probably would [or would not] be found liable because. . . . "

Lessors' liability

☛ **Lessor's liability generally:** Questions sometime involve the liability of a ***lessor***. The general rule is that the lessor is off the hook once possession is transferred to the lessee.

☞ **Exceptions:** But there are numerous exceptions, including these three big ones:

[1] the lessor is liable to the lessee and to the lessee's invitees/licensees for failure to ***warn*** about any hidden dangers which the lessor ***knows of*** at the beginning of the lease (but the lessor has no duty to inspect to find hidden dangers);

[2] the lessor remains responsible for ***common areas*** (e.g., an apartment lobby, stairway, elevator, etc.); and

[3] some courts now impose a general duty of reasonable care on landlords as to all who come onto the premises (including the licensees/invitees of tenants).

Exam Tips on DAMAGES

Damages issues can and usually will appear as part of virtually every torts essay exam. Here are some things to look for, especially where the question mainly involves a negligence action:

Collateral source rule

- **The collateral source rule, generally:** Be on the lookout for applications of the ***"collateral source"*** rule.
  - **How the rule works:** Remember that under this rule, D doesn't get a ***discount*** to reflect the fact that P may have been ***reimbursed*** for her out-of-pocket expenses associated with the accident from some third party (e.g., a health insurer who pays P's medical bills).
  - **Where the rule applies:** For a collateral source issue to be present, the fact pattern will have to tell you that P has received insurance or some other reimbursement payment (e.g., public disability payments, or sick pay from P's employer).
  - **Joined to other issue:** Often, a collateral source issue will be ***joined*** with a comparative negligence and/or joint-and-several liability issue. Don't be distracted — unless the facts tell you otherwise, assume that the common law collateral source rule is in effect, and therefore don't take into account any reimbursements in figuring out who can recover what from whom.

    Example: P's total damages are $100,000. He is reimbursed by a health insurance company for $20,000, representing his hospital bills. The jury says that P is 25% responsible, D1 25% and D2 50%. In a comparative negligence jurisdiction, with no other relevant statutes, how much can P collect from each defendant? Answer: up to a total combined limit of $75,000 from each of D1 and D2. This answer is the same as it would be if P had not gotten any reimbursement.

☞ **Statutory changes:** You might want to allude to the possibility that the state has abolished or cut back on the collateral source rule, as some states have done.

Example: "Assuming that the state has not abolished the common law collateral source rule, P's recovery will not be reduced. . . ."

Duty to mitigate

☛ **Duty-to-mitigate generally:** Be on the watch for places to apply the plaintiff's ***"duty to mitigate"*** her damages.

☞ **P fails to seek medical attention:** In the garden-variety situation, P fails to seek ***prompt medical attention***, and his problem (caused initially by D) worsens. Under the duty-to-mitigate rule, P can't recover for any damages that would not have been suffered if P had sought prompt medical aid.

☞ **P fails to take safety precaution:** More likely to be tested: P fails to take some ***advance safety precaution***. Here, some (but not most) courts hold that P has violated the duty to mitigate, and is completely blocked from recovery for those injuries that would have been prevented by the precaution. (Note that this defense is a total one, whereas if P's failure to use the device is treated as comparative negligence P's recovery will be only partly reduced.)

Examples:

- ❑ P doesn't wear a seat belt;
- ❑ P doesn't wear a hard-hat while walking in a construction site;
- ❑ P doesn't wear a mask or gloves while working in a hospital.

Punitive damages

☛ **Punitive damages generally:** Occasionally, you will want to note that ***"punitive"*** damages are or may be appropriate.

☞ **Intentional tort:** If the suit is for an ***intentional*** tort (including defamation or invasion of privacy, as well as the intentional torts against the person), punitive damages will often be appropriate. This is especially true where D's conduct is "outrageous," such as where the tort is intentional infliction of emotional distress.

☞ **Negligence cases:** In ***negligence*** cases, note the possibility of punitive damage only where you conclude that D was ***"reckless"*** or ***"willful"*** in his conduct.

Usually, this means that D disregarded what he knew to be a substantial risk of injury to P or others, rather than merely being "inattentive."

Types of damages

☛ **Types of damages:** You should also have a catalog of various *types* of damages in mind, ready to select from as appropriate in the fact pattern. Here is a partial list:

- ❑ Value of a ***lost body function*** (e.g., loss of an arm).
- ❑ ***Pain and suffering.***
- ❑ ***Lost earnings.***
- ❑ ***Emotional distress.***
- ❑ ***Hedonistic damages.*** (These apply where P loses the ability to engage in a pursuit she enjoyed; courts are split about whether this is allowable where P is in a coma.)
- ❑ Loss of ***consortium***. (These apply where the spouse, parent or child of a person who has a physical injury loses some aspect of companionship — thus where H is injured and his wife, W, can't have sexual relations with him, W gets a recovery for the loss of consortium.)
- ❑ ***Survival*** action. (Even though P is dead, his estate is allowed to recover for his pain and suffering, his medical expenses before death, etc.)
- ❑ ***Wrongful death*** action. (Survivors, such as a spouse, children or — if there is no spouse and child, parents — get recovery for their grief, their loss of money that the decedent would have earned and given to them as support, etc.)

Exam Tips on DEFENSES IN NEGLIGENCE ACTIONS

Whenever you identify a negligence issue, be sure to look for two very common defenses: (1) contributory/comparative negligence; and (2) assumption of risk.

Contributory negligence

☛ **Contributory negligence generally:** Always be on the lookout for application of the doctrine of ***contributory negligence*** (CN).

☞ **Absolute defense:** Remember the core principle of common law CN: it's an ***absolute defense***, and wipes out P's claim even if D's negligence is much greater than P's.

☞ **State assumptions:** Unless the fact pattern tells you that comparative negligence is used, assume that you must identify and discuss situations where CN would apply. Therefore, examine the behavior of everyone you've identified as a potential plaintiff, and ask, "Did he/she behave with reasonable care?"

- ☛ **Where it arises:** Usually, CN will consist of P's failing to notice, or disregarding, danger to ***himself*** (not P's imposition of an unreasonable risk to others). There are two types: (1) P should have noticed the danger, and didn't; and (2) P noticed the danger, and unreasonably decided to encounter it anyway.

- ☛ **May also be assumption of risk:** Type (2) above will also constitute "assumption of risk." (The same conduct can be both CN and assumption of risk, and you should say it's both.) Where P notices the danger and disregards it, remember that this isn't ***necessarily*** CN — perhaps P's need was so great that P was ***reasonable*** in subjecting himself to the risk.

  Example: P needs to get to the hospital, and takes a ride from a somewhat drunk driver — P's conduct may have been dangerous but reasonable, in which case it's not CN.

- ☛ **P couldn't have known of danger:** Look out for situations where P ***couldn't have known*** of the danger — it's not CN to fail to protect oneself against unknown danger, and the fact that P "could have protected herself if she had known of the danger" is irrelevant.

- ☛ **Danger in plain view:** Sometimes the facts will tell you that a certain danger is "in plain view." That's a tip-off for the probable existence of CN.

☞ **Discuss possible statutes:** If the facts don't tell you whether the jurisdiction has CN or comparative negligence, discuss ***each***.

Example: "If the jurisdiction has common law contributory negligence, then P will get no recovery because. . . . If the jurisdiction has comparative negligence, then P's claim will be reduced by the proportion of his fault. . . ."

☞ **Children:** Many fact patterns involve ***children***. Remember that the standard is, "What's the reasonable level of care for a child of that age and experience?" Even a child under 10 can be contributorily negligent if he's less careful than an "ordinary" child of that age.

☞ **Causation issue:** Don't forget that CN is only a defense if P's negligence was a ***cause*** (both cause in fact and proximate cause) of P's injuries.

Example: P doesn't wear his seat belt, and crashes due to D's negligence. If P would have died anyway even with a seat belt on, the failure to wear the belt wasn't a cause in fact of P's injuries, and CN will not apply.

☞ **Negligence per se:** A frequently-tested issue: Can CN be a defense where D's liability is based upon a ***statutory*** violation (negligence per se)? Answer: yes — negligence per se is just a special form of negligence by D, so P's CN will be a defense just as in any other negligence case.

☞ **Last Clear Chance:** In any case where you think CN may apply, consider whether the doctrine of ***"Last Clear Chance"*** (LCC) may undo the effect of CN.

- **How LCC works:** Remember that under LCC, if P has negligently put himself in a position of risk, and D then sees (or should see) P's peril in time to avoid the problem, D is said to have had a "Last Clear Chance" to avoid the peril, and that LCC wipes out P's CN.

Comparative negligence

- **Comparative negligence, generally:** Always be on the lookout for opportunities to discuss ***comparative*** negligence.

☞ **Must talk about:** Since the vast majority of states have replaced contributory negligence with comparative, you should talk about comparative whenever the facts indicate that P may have been negligent. Assuming the facts don't say whether the jurisdiction has contributory or comparative, you should talk about ***both*** scenarios, one after the other.

☞ **Main claim must be based on negligence:** Don't forget that comparative negligence can only apply where the main claim is based on ***negligence***. Thus there is no comparative neg. where P's claim is based on fraud (intentional misrepresentation), strict product liability, breach of warranty, etc.

☞ **Pure vs. modified:** If the facts don't say what type of comparative statute the jurisdiction has, you should probably mention that the statute could be either ***"pure"*** or ***"modified,"*** and say how this would affect the outcome. Remember that this distinction only makes a difference where P's negligence is ***at least half*** the total negligence. Thus if P is found 60% responsible for the accident and D 40%, in a "pure" jurisdiction P collects 40% of her total damages, whereas in a "modified" or "50%" jurisdiction, P gets nothing.

- **How to distinguish:** If the fact pattern gives you the actual statutory language, you should be able to tell whether the statute is a pure or modified one. You should recognize a "pure" statute by the fact that it doesn't say anything about P's negligence being "as great as" or "greater than" D's. A modified or 50% statute will have to deal specifically with this "as great as" or "greater than" case.

☞ **Available safety device:** Wherever P has failed to use some ***available safety device*** (e.g., seat belt or helmet), raise the issue of what effect the existence of a comparative negligence statute might have. Courts vary so much on this issue that it's hard to say what the effect might be — the most likely effect is that P's failure to use the device will be just one type of "fault," and that failure will be thrown into the hopper with everything else in computing P's "percentage of fault," which will then be applied to all the injuries.

☞ **Last Clear Chance:** If you're covering the comparative scenario, you need to look out for possible applications of ***Last Clear Chance***. You should say that courts are split about whether the doctrine applies in a comparative negligence situation. Probably a majority would say that the doctrine no longer applies, so that P's recovery is reduced by her fault even if D had a Last Clear Chance to avoid the accident.

☞ **Multiple defendants:** You also need to worry about the interaction between comparative negligence and ***multiple defendants***. There are two main things to worry about:

- **Joint & several liability:** First, once P's recovery has been reduced by his amount of fault, does P still have the right to recover all the "reduced" award from any ***single*** defendant? That is, does joint-and-several liability persist under comparative negligence?
  - ❑ If all Ds are before the court and are solvent, the answer is clearly "yes."
  - ❑ But if one or more Ds were absent or judgment-proof, courts are split on the effect of comparative negligence.

    Example: Assume P 25% at fault, D1 25% and D2 50%; total damages equal $100,000. Assume D2 is judgment-proof. Some courts would allow P to collect the full $75,000 from D1 — so common law joint-and-several liability persists, and D1 suffers the full brunt of D2's unavailability. Other courts say that P and D1 split the burden of D2's unavailability *pro rata*, so that P would collect $50,000 from D1 (i.e., P and D1 would each "suffer" a $25,000 loss from D2's unavailability). Still other courts make the allocation depend on whether P's losses are economic or non-economic, or on some other factor.

    Probably you should just indicate that not all courts honor joint-and-several liability under comparative negligence, if one or more defendants are absent or judgment-proof.

- **Contribution:** The second issue is each D's right of ***contribution*** against other Ds under comparative neg. Here, it depends on whether the state has passed a special statute. If no special statute has been passed, then the existence of comparative doesn't change each D's common-law right to "equal" contribution from the fellow tortfeasors. But many comparative negligence states have passed statutes applying comparative fault to contribution.

Example: Assume $100,000 in total injuries, no fault by P, D1 is found to be 40% at fault and D2 60% at fault. Assume P collects the entire $100,000 from D1. If the state has by statute applied comparative fault to contribution, D1 will be allowed to collect $60,000 contribution, not $50,000, from D2.

☛ **Imputed comparative negligence:** Be prepared to discuss briefly the doctrine of ***"imputed comparative (or contributory) negligence."*** Remember the ***"both ways rule"***: if (and only if) *B* would would be liable for *A*'s torts, then if *B*'s property or person is injured by *C*, *A*'s contributory or comparative negligence will be imputed to *B*, nullifying or reducing *B*'s ability to recover from *C*.

Example: *B* employs *A* as a truck driver. *C*, driving a car, negligently collides with the truck, while it's driven by *A* on business; but *A* is also negligent. *B* sues *C* for damage to the truck. In a comparative negligence jurisdiction, since *B* is liable for *A*'s negligence under *respondeat superior*, *A*'s negligence will be imputed to *B*. Therefore, *B*'s recovery against *C* will be reduced by *A*'s comparative negligence.

☞ **Exceptions:** But remember that there are two important scenarios where the both ways rule ***won't be applied*** so as to impute a person's comparative/contributory negligence to a plaintiff even though the plaintiff would be vicariously liable for that person's negligence.

Scenario 1: Parent fails to supervise Child; Child gets hurt due to the negligence of D (but the accident wouldn't have happened if Parent had supervised reasonably). Under the older view: Parent's contributory or comparative negligence is "imputed" to Child, barring (or in a comparative negligence state reducing) Child's recovery. But the prevailing view today is that there's ***no*** imputed comparative negligence here — so Child can recover in full from D, and it's up to D to get contribution from Parent.

Scenario 2: P is an owner/passenger in a car driven (with P's permission) by Drive. Trucker negligently drives his truck into the car, but Drive is also comparatively negligent. The both ways rule won't be applied to P's suit against Trucker; therefore, P can recover fully for her injuries from Trucker even if under local law Drive's negligence would have been imputed to P on the theory that P could have prevented Drive's negligence.

Assumption of risk

☛ **Assumption generally:** ***"Assumption of risk" (AOR)*** is one of those important issues that's quite possible to miss on an exam, because it can be easily hidden in the fact pattern. For this reason, it's often tested.

☞ **Definition:** First, keep the basic definition of AOR in mind: "P may be barred from recovery when an injury results from a danger of which P was ***aware*** and that P ***voluntarily*** encountered."

Example: D offers P a ride home. P knows that D is slightly drunk. P has other ways to get home, but this way is a little easier. If D crashes because of being drunk, then at common law P is barred from recovery by AOR.

☞ **Where to look:** So look for situations where P knows about a danger in advance, and nonetheless decides to go forward.

☞ **Express/implied distinction:** Distinguish between ***"express"*** and ***"implied"*** AOR. In express, P and D make an explicit agreement that P is taking the risk (e.g., P signs a ***waiver*** form). In "implied," P's conduct, not his words or documents he signs, establish that he voluntarily and knowingly took the risk.

- For "***express***," the general rule is that P is ***bound*** by his agreement to assume. (But there are exceptions, such as where D's ***bargaining power*** is grossly greater than P's, or where D ***intentionally or recklessly*** caused the danger).

- For "implied," P is bound as long as the circumstances demonstrate that he ***knowingly and voluntarily*** assumed the risk.

☞ **Risk known to P:** Most frequently tested issue: Was the risk truly ***known*** to P?

- **Subjective test:** The test is "subjective" — did P ***actually*** know of the risk. It's irrelevant that P ***should*** have known.

  Example: P is driving on a road. D, who is stopped on the road to fix a flat, has put flares 100 feet before his car. If P sees the flares and understands that they are meant to slow down motorists, then if P drives at regular speed he's bound by AOR because he "knows" of the risk of D's vehicle. But if through inattention or otherwise P doesn't see the flares, he doesn't "know" of the risk, even though a reasonably careful driver would know — AOR does not apply.

- **Specificity of P's knowledge:** Also, P's knowledge of the risk must be fairly ***specific***.

  Example: D offers P a ride, and P agrees. P is aware that D is an "average" driver who might get in an accident. P has not assumed the general risk of an accident, because his knowledge is not specific enough.

☞ **Effect of comparative negligence:** Questions sometimes test the effect of comparative negligence on AOR.

- **Express AOR:** In general, comparative negligence has no effect on the "*express*" case (the rules summarized above still apply).

- **Implied AOR:** But in most courts comparative negligence causes ***implied*** AOR to ***disappear*** as an independent defense, and to instead be merged into comparative fault analysis. (That is, if P is unreasonable in taking the risk, his unreasonableness is taken into account in fixing his percentage of fault, and AOR has no independent significance.)

- **Causal link:** Don't forget that there still has to be a ***causal link*** between P's AOR and the harm to P.

  Example: If P agrees to drive with D knowing D has bad brakes, and an accident happens because D makes a turn and fails to see another car, AOR doesn't apply — the risk assumed by P, failure to be able to stop, wasn't the cause in fact of the accident.

- **Strict products liability:** If the suit is in ***strict products liability***, most courts say that AOR ***applies***. Most common scenario: P knows the product lacks a particular ***safeguard*** that D could have put onto it (e.g., roll bars). Majority rule here: P is stuck with AOR.

<u>**Immunity from tort**</u>

- **Immunity, generally:** Questions concerning ***immunity*** from tort don't arise very often.

  - **Spot the occasions:** The most you will probably have to do is to spot the occasions when common-law immunity might have applied:

    [1] ***intra-family*** immunity (one spouse sues the other, and child sues parent);

    [2] ***charitable*** immunity; and

    [3] immunity of ***governmental bodies*** ("***sovereign*** immunity").

    - **What to say:** If you spot a situation in which one of these three immunities might have applied at common law, you should probably say something like: "At common law, the suit would have been blocked by [intra-family] [charitable] [sovereign] immunity, but nearly all states today have abolished this immunity." (If your fact pattern involves the ***federal*** government as defendant, and the claim relates to the government's failure to handle some discretionary or policy-making activity reasonably, you may wish to say that the Federal Tort Claims Act would block the suit because of the ***"discretionary function"*** exception contained in that statute.)

Exam Tips on *VICARIOUS LIABILITY*

Vicarious liability is tested amazingly frequently, out of all proportion to the number of pages it takes to describe the rules governing it. By "vicarious liability" we mean all of the doctrines which may cause one person to become liable for the acts of another, including:

[1] liability of an ***employer*** for acts of her employees;

[2] the occasional liability for the acts of an ***independent contractor*** whom one has engaged;

[3] liability under the theory of ***"joint enterprise"***;

[4] liability pursuant to an ***automobile consent*** statute; and

[5] the now mostly-outmoded doctrine of "imputed contributory negligence."

Here's how to handle each of these:

Respondeat superior

☛ **Respondeat, generally:** Most of all, look out for places to apply ***"respondeat superior" (RS)***.

- ☞ **Typical contexts:** You should be thinking RS whenever you have an employee doing something during the course of his job. The most-typical context: the employee is driving a car or truck for the employer. But there can be many odd-ball contexts (e.g., Employee, while on the job, incorrectly answers a question asked by a customer).

- ☞ **Two-part test:** Remember the two-part test for when RS will apply:

  [1] D2 must be the ***"employer"*** of D1, which means that D2 must have the right to ***control the details*** of D1's performance; and

  [2] D1 must be acting within the ***scope of the employment*** at the time he commits the act in question.

- ☞ **Intentional torts:** RS applies not only to negligence by the employee, but also to ***intentional torts*** committed by the employee within the scope of employment.

  Example: Employee is a truck driver for Trucking Co. Employee gets into a fist-fight with P when P won't move his car so Employee can make a delivery. RS applies to make Trucking Co. liable.

Of course, the fact that the tort is intentional may make it less likely that the tort is in fact committed within the scope of employment, but if it ***is*** within the scope, it's covered by the RS doctrine.

☞ **Independent contractor:** The most-tested issue: the distinction between an employee (where RS applies) and an ***independent contractor*** (where RS does not apply, though other forms of vicarious liability may, as discussed below). The main test is whether the "employer" had the right to ***control the details*** of how the "employee" did the job. Quick rule of thumb: *A* is an employee of *B* if, in the eyes of the community, *A* would be regarded as part of *B*'s ***"regular working staff."*** The real working relationship, not the contractual label, is what counts. Some examples:

- ❑ Where Finance Co. hires Repoman to repossess cars, and Repoman owns his own tow truck, sets his own hours, and does pick-ups for other companies as well as Finance Co., probably Repoman is an independent contractor.
- ❑ Where Auto Rental Co. sends cars to Repairman to be fixed, and Repairman has his own garage and tools, and buys the repair parts with his own cash (even though Auto Rental reimburses), Repairman is probably an independent contractor — Auto Rental is not controlling the details of Repairman's work.
- ❑ Where Parents hire Babysitter and pay by the hour, giving the details of what to do (e.g., "put Baby to bed at 8:00 p.m."), probably Babysitter is an employee, not an independent contractor, even if Parents don't withhold from her pay, or report it, for tax purposes.

☞ **Scope of employment:** Also much tested: Was the act within the ***scope*** of the employee's employment? (If it's not, the employer is not liable under RS, even though the tortfeasor was clearly an employee.) Main test: Was the employee acting to ***further his employer's business purposes***? If so, the act is within the scope of employment even though the means chosen were unwise or even ***forbidden***. Some examples:

- ❑ Part of Employee's job is to test drapes hanging in apartments for fire-resistance. Employer's instructions say, "Never test the drapes while they are in place. Always take them down." Employee is rushing and tests while drapes are hanging, burning down a building. Employee is within the scope of her employment, because she was furthering Employer's purposes (testing of drapes) even though the way she did it was forbidden by Employer.
- ❑ Employee puts in unpaid overtime at the office on the weekend, working on an invention that Employee thinks will help Employer. Employee burns down the building. Employee is probably working within the scope of

employment.

❑ Employee, while driving to make pick-ups of packages for Employer, makes a one-hour detour to visit her doctor to get pills for her allergies. An accident occurs while Employee is in the doctor's parking lot. This is probably not within the scope of employment, but is rather a ***"deviation"*** that doesn't trigger employer liability (i.e., a ***"frolic"*** or ***"detour."***) (But if the detour is brief, and is of the sort employees frequently and foreseeably do within their working day, then a court might find it to be within the scope of employment even though it did not, strictly speaking, benefit the employer.)

☞ **No release of employee:** Keep in mind that the employ*ee* is not released from liability merely because the employer is covered by RS — both employer and employee are jointly and severally liable.

☞ **Employee-to-employer indemnity:** Also, remember that if RS applies, the employee owes ***indemnity*** (full reimbursement) to the employer.

Torts by independent contractors

☛ **Rules on independent contractors:** If you conclude that the tortfeasor is an ***"independent contractor"*** rather than an "employee," the general rule is that the person who engaged him is ***not*** vicariously liable for the contractor's torts. But there are ***exceptions***, where the person hiring the contractor is deemed to have a ***non-delegable duty***:

☞ **Unusually dangerous work:** Most important: if the work is ***unusually dangerous*** (either "inherently"/"unavoidably" dangerous, or poses ***"peculiar risks"*** where not done with appropriate skill and precautions), then the person engaging the independent contractor ***will*** be vicariously liable.

Example: D1, a homeowner, hires D2 to dig a hole for a swimming pool to be put in D1's back yard. D2 doesn't put up barriers, and P, a neighboring child invited to be there, falls in. Probably D1 is vicariously liable, since the nature of the work being done (excavation of a large hole in a residential neighborhood) is dangerous if not accompanied by barriers.

☞ **Other exceptions:** (1) D is a ***landowner*** who has a duty to ***keep the premises safe*** (the above example would qualify for this exception, too); (2) D is causing the contractor to do work in a ***public place*** (e.g., D is a city that hires a contractor to do work on a public road; D is vicariously liable for the contractor's negligent work).

Joint enterprise liability

☛ **What to look for:** Be on the lookout for ***"joint enterprise"*** liability. When two or more people engage in an activity ***"in concert"*** and for shared aims, each can be held liable for the other's torts.

☞ **Car trips:** Most common application for joint-enterprise: Two people go on a ***car trip*** together, sharing driving and/or expenses. The passenger is vicariously liable for the driver's negligence, because they were "joint venturers" or members of a "joint enterprise."

☞ **Other contexts:** Other contexts are possible for "joint enterprise," especially ***recreational*** activities.

Examples:

❑ Golfers who engage in a "long-driving" contest;

❑ Hot-rodders who race each other on the street;

❑ A water skier and the driver of the boat.

☞ **Manufacturer/retailer:** A ***manufacturer*** of goods, and the ***retailer*** who sells the item to the consumer, are usually ***not*** found to be in a joint enterprise, or otherwise liable for each other's torts. Thus if Manufacturer is negligent in designing a product, Retailer is not vicariously liable. (Retailer may have strict product liability for selling a defective and dangerous product, but that's direct rather than vicarious liability, and is not related to anyone's negligence.)

<u>Automobile consent statutes</u>

☛ **Auto consent, generally:** If a driver of a car gets into an accident, consider the possibility that the vehicle's ***owner*** may be vicariously liable even if the owner was not present.

☞ **Statutes:** Some states have ***"Automobile Consent"*** statutes, whose purpose is precisely to make the owner liable for torts committed in the car by anyone who used the car with the owner's consent.

☞ **Absence of statute:** But in a state without such a statute, the ***mere loan*** of one's car to another person does ***not*** make the owner liable. (Remember that the owner may have ***direct*** liability if the owner should have known that the driver was not competent, as where the driver was drunk or unlicensed.)

Exam Tips on ***STRICT LIABILTY***

It's easy for an issue of "strict liability" to be hidden in the fact pattern — D isn't doing anything careless, and isn't trying to hurt anyone, so you can miss the fact that D is engaging in an activity as to which strict liability might attach. In this chapter, we're only worried about two types of activity calling for strict liability: (1) the keeping of animals; and (2) "abnormally dangerous" activities.

Animals

- ☛ **Animals, generally:** Whenever your fact pattern mentions an ***animal*** that does some harm, consider the possibility of strict liability.
  - ☞ **Wild animals:** If the animal is ***"wild,"*** there's strict liability for any damage that results from a "dangerous propensity" of the ***species***.

    Example: If D keeps a leopard as a pet, and the leopard bites a neighbor, strict liability applies, even if this particular leopard had never attacked anyone before. This is so because the tendency to attack is characteristic of the species of leopard, and the species is wild rather than domesticated.

    - ☛ **Causes humans to be scared:** If the wild animal customarily ***causes humans to be scared***, then an injury caused by P's fright *will* trigger strict liability, since fear-causing would be one of the "dangerous propensities" of the species. (*Example:* D's bear gets loose, and frightens P into having a heart attack. Even if the bear would never have hurt P, fear-causing is one of the species' "dangerous propensities," making D strictly liable.)
  - ☞ **Domestic animals:** If the animal is ***"domestic,"*** then there's only strict liability where the owner ***knows*** or has ***reason to know*** of the ***particular animal's dangerous characteristics***.

    Example: Suppose a dog or a horse bites a neighbor. Since both these species are domesticated, there is no strict liability unless the owner knew that this particular animal had a tendency to bite or otherwise attack, in which case the liability is not truly without regard to fault.

    - ☛ **"1 bite free" is not the rule:** Don't say, "Every dog gets one bite free." If D knew that the dog had ***tried*** to bite or attack someone before and failed, D is now liable when the dog succeeds.

Abnormally dangerous (or ultra-hazardous) activities

- ☛ **Generally:** Most questions relating to this chapter concern ***"abnormally dangerous"*** activities (ADA) (also known as ***"ultra-hazardous"*** activities).
  - ☞ **Definition to use:** The general principle, and a good definition to quote on an exam: "One who carries out an abnormally dangerous activity is strictly liable (that is, liable without regard to fault) for any damage that proximately results from the dangerous nature of the activity."
  - ☞ **Common issue:** A common issue is, Is the activity in fact ***"abnormally dangerous"***?

- **Factors:** Try to remember this list of factors:
  - ❑ Existence of a ***high degree*** of risk of ***some*** harm.
  - ❑ Likelihood that if harm does result, that harm will be ***great***.
  - ❑ The ***inability*** to ***eliminate*** the risk by use of ***reasonable care***.
  - ❑ The ***unusualness*** of the activity.
  - ❑ The ***inappropriateness*** of the activity to the ***place*** where it is carried out.
  - ❑ The extent to which the activity's ***value*** to the community is ***outweighed*** by the activity's dangerous attributes.
- **Examples:** Some activities that are usually considered abnormally dangerous:
  - ❑ Blasting or other use of ***explosives***.
  - ❑ Operation of a ***nuclear power plant***.
  - ❑ The conducting of research into contagious viruses, biochemical weapons, etc.
  - ❑ Possibly, the ***transporting*** of ***flammable*** or very ***toxic*** liquids (e.g., propane).

☞ **"Type of risk" issue:** The most frequently-tested ADA issue is, Did the type of harm that occurred result from the ***type of risk*** that made the activity abnormally dangerous in the first place? If not, then strict liability for ADA does not apply.

Example: D uses explosive to blast through rock. The blasting frightens nearby cattle, who stampede and hurt themselves. Probably the risk of frightening animals isn't one of the special risks that makes the use of explosives abnormally dangerous. If so, D is not strictly liable for the damage to the cattle.

☞ **Assumption of risk as defense:** ***Assumption of risk*** is a defense to strict liability (whether for ADA or keeping of wild animals).

Example: If P sees a sign saying, "Blasting, Keep Out," and P enters anyway and gets hurt, he's probably barred by assumption of risk.

☞ **Contributory negligence not a defense:** But ***contributory negligence*** is ***not*** a defense to strict liability.

Example: On the above example, if P negligently failed to read the sign about blasting, and didn't know blasting was going on, his carelessness would not eliminate his recovery in a contributory-negligence state.

- ☛ **Comparative negligence:** On the other hand, in a ***comparative negligence*** jurisdiction, P's negligence probably *will* reduce his recovery even in a suit based on strict liability. (*Example*: On the above blasting example, P's recovery probably will reduce his recovery in a comparative-negligence state).

Workers' compensation

- ☛ **Workers' camp, generally:** ***Workers' compensation*** statutes are rarely tested. But if P is injured during the course of his employment by D, you should briefly mention that any recovery by P against D will probably be limited by the terms of the WC statute (and that P will not have to prove D's negligence in order to recover this limited amount).
  - ☞ **Exclusive remedy:** Remember that the WC statute usually provides the ***exclusive*** remedy for the employee against the owner — the employee does not have the option of suing, proving that the employer was negligent, and recovering traditional tort damages.
  - ☞ **Exception for intentional wrongdoing:** But also remember that most WC statutes provide an ***exception*** where the employer's wrongdoing is ***intentional***. (However, most courts hold that the employer's failure to observe ***safety precautions*** does ***not*** transform the employer's wrongdoing into an intentional tort, so that WC applies even in this situation.)

Exam Tips on ***PRODUCTS LIABILITY***

You'll almost always know when you've got a products liability issue — in the typical situation, some "product" will be sold, and someone will be injured when the product does not perform the way a consumer would expect it to. The hard things to do are: (1) to articulate the various theories on which P can recover; (2) to structure your answer into a sensible order; and (3) to spot and analyze the various sub-issues (e.g., Can a bystander recover? Was the product unavoidably unsafe? Was there a design defect? Was there a failure to warn?).

Structuring your answer

- ☛ **Structure generally:** As to structure, you may want to organize your answer into the following order:

(1) At the top level, arrange it by plaintiff-defendant pair (all claims by P1 against D1, then those by P1 against D2, P2 against D1, etc.);

(2) Then talk about the theories that could be used in each P-D pair.

Example: "P1's suit against D1 could be based either on strict product liability, negligence or breach of express and implied warranty. Probably P1's best results will come from the strict liability theory, because...";

(3) Then, talk about each special issue presented by the fact pattern, discussing all theories of recovery in the context of that special issue. Thus do a complete discussion of the failure to warn (as to negligence, strict liability and warranty), followed by a complete discussion of, say, design, and so on.

Example: "Was the product properly designed? For the negligence claim, the issue is whether the design was done with 'reasonable care.' For the strict product liability theory, the issue is whether the product was designed 'defectively,' which most courts interpret to mean 'designed in such a way as to satisfy the expectations of a reasonable consumer about how the product would perform....'"

__Three theories of recovery__

☛ **Three main theories:** Whenever you have injuries caused by a "product" (as distinguished from a service or an activity), remember that there are ***three main theories*** on which liability might be founded:

[1] ***Negligence*** (the manufacturer's or retailer's failure to use reasonable care in the design, manufacture, labelling or marketing of the product).

[2] ***Breach of warranty*** (which can come in three types: express warranty, implied warranty of merchantability, and implied warranty of fitness for a particular purpose).

❑ "Misrepresentation" is an offshoot of warranty, applicable mainly to cases of inadequate labelling or false advertising.

[3] ***Strict product liability*** (imposed without regard to fault, for a "defective" and "unreasonably dangerous" product).

Note: You should be sure to list and discuss *each of these theories in each instance*, if there's any chance that it might be applied. (Even if the theory won't be successful, it's probably worthwhile to say why it won't be.)

Example: "Because the facts tell us that Manufacturer could not have found the manufacturing defect even through the exercise of due care, probably a recovery against it based on negligence will not be possible."

Negligence recovery

☛ **Negligence generally:** In considering recovery for ***"negligence,"*** here are the main things to look for:

☞ **Ordinary rules apply:** Remember that the ordinary rules of negligence apply — there's nothing very special about negligence in the product context.

☞ **Don't worry about privity:** ***"Privity"*** doesn't matter — as long as P was a "reasonably foreseeable" plaintiff, the fact that she was a remote purchaser, or even a bystander, doesn't prevent her from a negligence recovery against a negligent manufacturer. This is true even if the product went through several different sellers (wholesaler, retailer, original purchaser, etc.).

☞ **Distribution channel:** Your analysis will differ depending on the particular defendant's place in the ***distribution channel***.

☛ **D is manufacturer:** Where D is the ***manufacturer***, the question is always, "Did D use reasonable care in making the product?" This includes component-selection, design, manufacture, post-manufacture inspection, and labelling. Generally, negligence theories are most useful against the manufacturer (as opposed to people further down in the distribution chain).

☛ **D is retailer:** Where D is the ***retailer***, a negligence claim is much less likely to succeed. In the typical case of a manufactured product shipped in a sealed package, the only ways the retailer is likely to be negligent are:

[1] he saw or should have seen from the outside of the package that something was wrong; or

[2] he knew or should have known that this particular manufacturer was likely to be producing bad goods (e.g., a safety recall is in place, which the retailer ignores or negligently fails to know about).

☞ **No duty to inspect:** Most important: the retailer has ***no duty*** to ***inspect*** the goods he sells, so the fact that an inspection would have disclosed a problem is irrelevant.

☞ **No imputation to retailer:** Also, the manufacturer's negligence is ***not imputed*** to the retailer.

☛ **D is not a seller:** Where D is a lessor, bailor, or user (i.e., a "non-seller"), negligence may be your best theory of recovery (because warranty and strict product liability are not always imposed on non-sellers).

☞ **Contributory/comparative negligence:** ***Contributory (or comparative) negligence*** can be a defense to a negligence product liability claim, as in other types of negligence cases.

Example: If P should have noticed that a food product made or sold by D was rotten from its smell, it's probably contributory/comparative negligence for P to eat it.

Breach of warranty

- **Breach of warranty generally:** Be sure to mention ***breach of warranty*** whenever you analyze a product situation. This is the theory of recovery that students most frequently omit.

  - **Express warranty:** One type of breach of warranty is breach of ***express*** warranty. This occurs where the product fails to live up to explicit statements that D has made about it. In the product context, this comes in two main forms:

    [1] D ***advertises*** the goods as having a certain characteristic (e.g., "doesn't cause drowsiness"); or

    [2] the ***labelling*** contains statements about the product.

    - **Picture or model:** Also, the manufacturer's use of a ***picture*** or ***model*** can be an express warranty.

      Example: If the box containing a helmet shows a person riding a motorcycle with the helmet on, that's probably an express warranty that the helmet is suitable for use as a motorcycle helmet.

    - **Retailer's warranty:** A ***retailer*** is deemed to have "made" any express warranty that is contained on the product (and probably to have made any warranty contained in the manufacturer's advertising).

    - **Endorser's liability:** An ***endorser*** can be liable for breach of express warranty.

      Example: If an Olympic champion says in a commercial, "Contains only natural ingredients," she's probably liable for breach of express warranty if the product has harmful artificial ingredients.

    - **Strict liability:** The warranty is ***"strict"*** — it doesn't matter that D used all reasonable care to make the product conform to the warranty, or reasonably thought the product did conform.

    - **Common-law misrepresentation:** Whenever a label or advertising is incorrect, also mention that P can sue for common-law ***misrepresentation***. Cite to Rest. §402B, establishing liability for one who "makes to the public a misrepresentation about a material fact" concerning the product. This theory is useful if the state's warranty law (controlled by the UCC) is narrower than usual (e.g., it allows a disclaimer that would not block misrepresentation liability, or it applies a narrow version of privity cutting off bystanders).

☞ **Implied warranty of merchantability:** When a product is sold by a ***"merchant"*** (one in the business of selling goods of that kind), the merchant is deemed to make an ***implied warranty*** that the goods are ***"merchantable."***

☛ **Definition of "merchantable" to use:** In your discussion of merchantability, you should define the term: "Goods are 'merchantable' if they are 'fit for the ***ordinary purposes*** for which such goods are used.'" There will often be an issue about whether the goods breached this warranty.

Example: P has a rare allergic reaction to a drug. Probably this does not make the drug "unmerchantable," because the "ordinary person" doesn't have this rare allergy.

☛ **Suit against manufacturer:** Normally, the merchantability suit is against the retailer. But the suit can also be against the manufacturer, as long as the manufacturer was in the business of selling goods of that kind.

☞ **Lessor's liability:** Sometimes tested: Can a merchantability suit be brought against one who ***"leases"*** rather than sells the goods? Answer: most courts allow warranty liability here.

☞ **Fitness for particular purpose:** Occasionally, you should mention the implied warranty of ***fitness for a particular purpose***. Look for this fact pattern: D (almost always the retailer, not the manufacturer) knows that P has ***special requirements***, and makes a ***recommendation*** of a particular make and model, which P follows. (The existence of a warranty of fitness for a particular purpose does not displace the warranty of merchantability — both apply.)

☞ **Privity:** For all three types of warranty (express, merchantability, and fitness for a particular purpose), you generally don't have to worry much about ***privity***.

☛ **Remote purchaser:** All of these warranties are now generally held to extend to a ***remote purchaser*** ("vertical" privity).

☛ **Members of purchaser's household; bystanders:** In virtually every state, every member of the purchaser's ***household*** is also covered. In most states, users who didn't buy, and even ***bystanders***, are covered — but since a few states don't extend the warranties this far, you should mention this as an issue if the injured person is a bystander or other non-purchaser.

☞ **Disclaimer:** Warranties can be ***disclaimed***. Most-often tested: a product is marked ***"AS IS."*** This marking generally serves to disclaim the two implied warranties (merchantability and fitness); it's not clear whether the marking wipes out an express warranty contained elsewhere on the product's labelling, though a handwritten notation probably does disclaim any implied warranties on the pre-printed label.

☞ **Intangible economic harm:** If P's sole damages are ***intangible economic harm*** (e.g., lost profits), warranty theory may be P's best bet. P's claim for economic harm is strongest where P bought the item directly from D under an express warranty; it's weakest where P sues on implied warranty and was not a purchaser (e.g., P is a "bystander" whose business is interrupted when the product explodes and cuts off electrical service in the neighborhood).

Strict product liability

☛ **Strict liability, generally:** The bulk of your analysis will typically concern ***strict*** product liability, since most of the time this furnishes P with the best overall chance of recovery.

☞ **Definition to use:** Start your analysis of strict product liability with a definition: "A seller of a product is liable without fault for personal injuries (or other physical harm) caused by the product if the product is sold in a defective condition."

☞ **Requirements:** Here is a ***checklist*** of requirements for the strict liability doctrine:

❑ D must be a ***"seller"***;

❑ D must have been in the ***business*** of selling products ***of this type***;

❑ The product must have been sold in a ***"defective condition"***;

❑ The product must have been expected to, and did, reach the consumer ***without substantial change*** in its condition; and

❑ The product (and in fact its defectiveness) must have been the ***cause in fact***, and the ***proximate cause*** of the damage to P.

☞ **Things to remember:** Two major things to keep in mind:

☛ **Care irrelevant:** It ***doesn't matter*** that D used ***all possible care*** in designing and manufacturing the product (though the unavailability of safer alternatives may contribute to a finding that the product was "unavoidably unsafe," as discussed below).

☛ **Applies to retailers:** The doctrine applies to non-manufacturers who sell, most notably ***retailers*** (even though they couldn't possibly have known of the defect or danger).

☞ **"Defective":** A commonly-tested issue: Was the product in fact ***"defective"***?

☛ **Manufacturing defects:** For manufacturing defects, quote the Rest. 3d's test: "A product contains a ***manufacturing defect*** when the product

departs from its intended design even though all possible care was exercised in the preparation and marketing of the product."

☛ **Food products:** If the product is ***food***, anything ***"foreign"*** is probably a dangerous defect if it could cause physical injury.

Example: Slivers of metal in canned tuna fish.) Anything ***"natural"*** to the food before processing (e.g., in bones in canned salmon) may or may not be a defect — some courts say that natural items in food can never be a defect, but most now say that anything a consumer ***wouldn't expect to find*** in that type of food is a defect, even if it's "natural."

☛ **Breakage or wearing out:** If the product ***breaks*** or ***wears out*** before a reasonable consumer thinks it would/should, this can be a defect.

☛ **Design defects:** ***"Design defects"*** are the most commonly-tested type of defect. Here are the general principles:

❑ Quote the Rest. 3d's definition: "A product is ***defective in design*** when the ***foreseeable risks of harm posed*** by the product ***could have been reduced or avoided by the adoption of a reasonable alternative design*** by the seller or other distributor... and the ***omission of the alternative design renders the product not reasonably safe."*** Notice that this is essentially a ***negligence-based***, risk-utility standard.

❑ Availability of a ***safer*** design is important evidence that the design actually used was "defective."

❑ The fact that "everyone else in the industry designs it this way" is probative, but not binding, on whether the design was defective.

❑ D's failure to include a cost-effective technologically-available ***safety feature*** will often be a design defect. (*Example:* If the technology exists to make a car not start when the seat belt is not attached, it may well be a design defect not to include this feature.)

❑ The ***"state of the art"*** defense will be accepted in design cases — if at the time of manufacture technology did not yet exist (or wasn't cost-effective) to design the device a certain way, the fact that this design became feasible later (before trial) is irrelevant.

☛ **Preemption defense:** In any design-defect or failure-to-warn case, be on the lookout for a possible ***preemption*** defense: if the particular design or warning-label that P says was faulty was imposed by ***Congress***, and the court finds that Congress intended to ***preempt*** the states from requiring stricter or different designs or warning labels, then D has a defense. Remember that this is always a question of ***congressional intent:*** did Congress intend, by imposing the requirement, to block the states from allowing strict product liability against a D who followed the federal rules?

☞ **Unavoidably unsafe:** ***"Unavoidably unsafe"*** products often turn up on exams. There are two different problems:

- ***Case 1 (individual defective item):*** The defect slips in during the manufacturing process, and no better production process, and no amount of inspection, would prevent this particular unit from being "broken" (different and more dangerous than the "standard" one off the assembly line), or allow D to separate that item from the non-broken ones. Courts are split as to whether the product here is "unavoidably unsafe," but the Rest. 3d's view is that the unavoidability of the defect is ***no defense.***

- ***Case 2 (all items are defective):*** Here, ***each*** copy is unsafe, in the sense that the items are all the same, and each poses the same dangers. Here, "unavoidably unsafe" is clearly a defense, at least if the product's overall benefits outweigh its overall dangers.

  ☞ **Prescription drugs:** In this category, the most common example is ***prescription*** drugs. Even if the drug has rare side effects, or causes allergic reactions in a few people, as long as D gives adequate warnings and the drug produces a net benefit to *some* group of patients, then at least according to the Third Restatement the drug is not defective, and the particular P who is injured cannot recover. (But note that most courts *disagree* — even in prescription drug cases, these courts let P win on a strict liability theory if D did not at least make reasonable efforts to make the drug as free from side-effects or allergic reactions as it could.)

☞ **Defective in D's hands:** Be sure that the product was defective ***when it left D's hands.*** Often-tested: the product is OK when it leaves Manufacturer's plant, but because of bad shipping, bad handling by retailer or bad care by purchaser, its condition changes to a dangerous condition.

Example: A bottle leaves Manufacturer's plant OK, gets broken in transit, and P gets glass in her mouth. Manufacturer is not strictly liable.

☞ **Failure to warn:** Many questions involve ***"failure to warn."*** The duty to warn is basically an ***extra*** obligation.

- **No cure by warning:** Thus if the product is basically dangerous either because of a manufacturing defect or a design defect, D can't cure this defect by warning of the dangers.

- **Duty to warn of non-obvious dangers:** Even if the product is designed in a "non-defective" way, D still has a duty to warn of any ***non-obvious*** dangers. Failure to carry out this duty is evaluated in a way that has aspects of both negligence and strict liability.

- ☞ **Inappropriate uses:** Commonly-tested: D must warn that certain ***uses are not appropriate.***

  Example: If a ladder can't take more than a certain amount of weight, and a reasonable consumer would think that it could take more stress than it really can, it's a violation for the manufacturer not to warn of the real limit.

- ☞ **Labeling problem:** Usually, failure-to-warn arises in connection with the ***label.*** So if the fact pattern tells you something about what the label says, that's a tip-off to look for a failure-to-warn problem.

- ☞ **Prescription-drug cases:** Be especially on the lookout for failure-to-warn in ***prescription drug*** cases — there's almost always some side effect or allergy potential, and courts today say that virtually any risk (however small) must be warned of.

- ☞ **Lost warning booklet:** Here's a common scenario: The warning booklet (or box containing the warning) is part of the package when the product leaves the manufacturer, but it's ***lost*** in shipping or lost by the retailer. The manufacturer is protected here by the "when it left defendant's hands" rule, except for situations where the danger is so great that a reasonable exercise of the duty-to-warn required putting the label right on the product itself instead of on packaging.

  Example: A power mower probably needs a warning on a metal plate attached to the mower, not just on the box.

- ☞ **State-of-the-art defense:** If the danger wasn't ***knowable*** at the time of manufacture, most courts say there's no duty to warn of it. This is the ***"state of the art"*** defense.

  Example: If after all reasonable testing, a prescription drug manufacturer doesn't know that a particular side effect can happen, it's not a violation to fail to list this effect.

  - ☞ **Post-sale duty to notify:** But if the manufacturer ***later learns*** of the danger, most courts will impose on it a ***post-sale duty to notify*** the prior buyer or user of the danger, if that person's identity is known.

☛ **Obvious dangers:** There is no duty to warn of a danger that would be ***obvious*** to an ordinary person.

Example: It is obvious that a kitchen knife can cut someone, or that the user of a ladder might fall off. Manufacturers therefore do not have to warn of these dangers.

- **Prescription drugs:** The most important category of failure-to-warn cases involves ***prescription drugs.***
  - **"Learned intermediary" defense:** Keep in mind the ***"learned intermediary"*** defense for drug makers. Where the defense is allowed (as it is in most states), the manufacturer's duty is generally limited to warning the ***prescribing physician*** rather than the patient. So if the manufacturer warned the physician, but the physician didn't adequately warn the patient, the manufacturer is off the hook in a state that allows the learned intermediary defense.
  - **Generic drug:** Where P took a ***generic drug***, consider the possibility that P may be able to bring a failure-to-warn suit not against the maker of the generic, but instead against the maker of the ***brand-name version.*** Courts sometimes allow suit against the brand-name maker (even though it didn't sell the generic that P took) because it's the brand-name maker, not the generic maker, that has the ***responsibility*** for making sure the ***warning label*** adequately discloses the risks of the drug. (The generic maker's duty is simply to use the same warning label as the brand name.)

- **Causation:** Don't forget ***causation***, especially ***proximate*** cause. Even in strict liability (and warranty), these elements must still be proved. So the "defect" (not just the product) must be the proximate cause of D's injuries.
  - **Misuse by purchaser:** Here's the most common scenario: The purchaser ***misuses*** the product in a way that is virtually ***unforeseeable***. This constitutes a ***superseding cause***. (*Example:* P tries to cut his hair with a lawnmower.) But ***foreseeable*** misuse is ***not*** superseding, and most misuse these days is found to be "foreseeable."
    - **Conscious disregard of warning:** If the manufacturer warns against a particular misuse, and P (or whoever is using the product) ***consciously disregards*** the warning, that's probably superseding. (But P's negligent failure to notice the warning is not superseding.)
    - **Failure-to-warn cases:** Causation is especially important in ***failure-to-warn*** cases. Most important context:
      - If D can show that P ***wouldn't have read*** a warning even if one had been given (or would have ***ignored*** the warning if it had been given and P had seen it), then the failure to warn wasn't the proximate or "but for" cause of the accident, and D won't be liable.
  - **Reaction to danger:** A ***reaction*** to an initial danger is often foreseeable, and thus not superseding.

Example: P1 is injured, and P2 tries to help, or just panics. Either way, if P2 gets injured, that's probably a foreseeable response, and thus not superseding.

☛ **Attempted recall:** If Manufacturer discovers a problem and tries to ***recall*** the product to fix it (at Manufacturer's cost), Owner's refusal to allow this is probably superseding.

Example: Manufacturer recalls cars at its own cost; O1 refuses to cooperate; O1 sells to O2; O2 crashes into P when the car breaks. P loses here, because Manufacturer got off the hook once O1 refused to cooperate with the recall.

☞ **Charge by manufacturer:** But if Manufacturer ***charges*** for the attempt to fix, it's not clear whether O's refusal is superseding. (Certainly that refusal is not superseding if Manufacturer's charges for the fix were unreasonably high.)

☞ **Defenses:** Consider some possible defenses to strict product liability:

☛ Courts vary on whether ***contributory and comparative negligence*** are defenses to strict product liability. The modern/Rest. 3d view is that these defenses ***apply the same way*** as they would in a negligence action.

☛ **Assumption of risk:** ***Assumption of risk is*** a defense, if P acted ***unreasonably*** in encountering the danger.

Example: If Manufacturer warns against using a ladder to hold more than 200 lbs., and P knowingly puts 250 lbs. on, P has assumed the risk.

☞ **Reasonable to ignore warning:** But if P is reasonable in ignoring the warning, and the warning unfairly limits the product compared with what a reasonable consumer would expect, P probably is not bound by AOR.

Example: If the reasonable consumer expects a step-ladder to hold at least the weight of an average 175-lb.-man, a warning not to put more than 100 lbs. on probably won't be effective to trigger AOR if P disregards the warning.

☛ **Compliance with safety regs:** ***Compliance*** with ***governmental safety regulations*** is usually ***not*** a defense.

☞ **Preemption:** Watch out for the possibility that the federal government has ***preempted*** the area. For instance, if the federal government has prescribed warning labels, this may mean that the feds have occupied the entire field of labeling. In that case, states cannot impose failure-to-warn liability if the federal labeling rules have been followed. (This is clearly now true for cigarettes — makers who conform to federal cigarette labeling guidelines can't be sued for failure to warn.)

Persons who may sue

☛ **Persons who may sue, generally:** Regardless of the theory of recovery, examine carefully whether P falls within the class of ***persons who may sue***.

- ☞ **P is a remote purchaser:** Where P is a ***"remote"*** purchaser (he bought, but not directly from D), P can probably recover. At least where physical injury occurs, this lack of "vertical" privity is never a defense today, whether the suit is based on warranty (express or implied), negligence or strict product liability.

- ☞ **P is a non-purchaser user:** Where P is a "user" who is ***not*** a purchaser, P is again clearly covered under strict product liability and negligence. Whether she's covered under warranty depends on the precise version of the UCC in force in the state (with some states limiting warranty recovery to purchasers and to members of the purchaser's family).

- ☞ **P is a bystander:** If P is a ***"bystander"*** (neither a purchaser nor a user), the question is closer. Bystander liability is the most commonly tested aspect of who may sue.

  - ☛ **Negligence case:** Under negligence, the bystander may recover if he was ***"reasonably foreseeable,"*** which he will usually be found to be.

    Example: If a plane crashes into P's house due to a manufacturing defect, P will be allowed to recover, because it is foreseeable that someone on the ground might be hurt by a defective plane.

  - ☛ **Warranty case:** Under warranty, P's right to recover depends on state law (as it does for "users" who didn't purchase, discussed above).

  - ☛ **Strict liability case:** Under strict liability, most courts protect virtually any bystander.

    Example: People injured when a defective car or plane crashes, or when defective scaffolding falls down on them as they walk by, are all permitted to recover.

    - ☞ **Unforeseeable manner of harm:** If the way a bystander gets hurt is really strange, consider the possibility that proximate cause is not present because the manner of harm was too unforeseeable.

      Example: D makes a prescription drug, and doesn't warn users of possible drowsiness. X uses the product, gets drowsy, drives his car and crashes the car into a pole, knocking it down; when the pole falls it hits a propane truck, starting a fire, that injures P, a nearby pedestrian.

Probably this was not a foreseeable risk from the mislabelling, in which case there would be no strict liability for D.

Persons who may be liable

☛ **Whether D can be liable:** Be careful to examine whether *D* is the sort of person ***who can be liable*** under the particular theory.

☞ **D is a retailer:** If D is a ***retailer,*** strict liability and warranty, not negligence, are the best theories.

☞ **D has sold used goods:** If D has sold ***used*** goods (e.g., used cars), courts are split. Most courts say that D is not liable in strict liability or implied warranty. But there can still be negligence liability (e.g., D fails to warn of what he knows to be a defect in the item).

☞ **D is a lessor of goods:** If D is a ***lessor*** of goods, courts differ about whether to apply strict liability and warranty. The trend is probably to cover this situation. Certainly D can be liable in negligence under ordinary principles.

☞ **D is a supplier of services:** If D is a supplier of ***services***, with the product used by D only as a ***tool*** during provision of the service, strict liability and warranty do not normally apply.

Example: D, a tattoo artist, uses special needles in doing the tattooing. D would not be strictly liable or liable under warranty, because he was not selling needles. But the manufacturer of the needle could be liable.

☛ **Title transferred to P:** Where ***title*** to the item is ***transferred*** to P as part of the service, courts are split. But most still don't recognize strict liability or warranty liability here.

Example: D, a surgeon, puts a pacemaker into P. If the pacemaker breaks, D is probably not strictly liable or liable under warranty, since the dominant aspect of his performance was as supplier of services, not as reseller of goods.

☞ **Fulfillment services:** If D is a company that ***supplies fulfillment services*** but ***doesn't take title*** to the goods, remember that some courts now ***allow*** P to sue D even though D wasn't truly a "seller."

Example: Suppose X lists a product on the Amazon.com website and uses Amazon's "Fulfillment by Amazon" service (where Amazon stores, picks, ships and bills the goods, but never takes title) to fulfill the order. Mention that some courts now allow an injured buyer to sue Amazon, especially where the actual seller is a foreign company that can't be found for service.

☞ **D is a user:** If D is a ***"user"*** of goods, rather than a seller, D has no strict liability to a bystander. This is an often-tested aspect.

Example 1: D is a carpenter using power tools. As P passes by, a part of the tool flies off and hits him. D is not strictly liable, because D wasn't making any sale. But the manufacturer of the tool could, of course, be strictly liable.

Example 2: D is a store owner who causes an escalator to be installed. P, a customer, is injured on the device. D is not strictly liable because he didn't sell the item to P.

☞ **D is a gift-giver:** If D is a ***gift-giver***, he is not strictly liable.

Example: D buys a teddy bear, and gives it to P as a gift. P chokes on a button from the teddy bear. D is not strictly liable, because D did not make a sale.

☞ **D is an amateur seller:** If D sells the item, but sells as an ***"amateur"*** (i.e., not one in the business of selling goods of that kind), D is not strictly liable.

Example: D owns a candy store. D sells a slightly-used lawn mower that she has used a few times to cut the grass in front of the store. Since D is not in the business of selling goods of this type, D is not strictly liable to the buyer if the mower is dangerously defective.

Damages

☛ **Damages generally:** Don't overlook ***damages***.

☞ **Negligence and strict liability cases require physical impact:** For negligence and strict liability, there must normally be some ***physical impact or injury***.

☞ **Zone of danger rule:** If there's only ***emotional*** damage, then probably the same ***"zone of danger"*** rule applies to strict liability as to negligence, whatever that rule is.

Example: In a state maintaining the zone-of-danger rule for negligence cases, Wife sees Husband mangled by a power mower 30 yards away. Even in strict liability, Wife probably can't recover against the manufacturer of the mower, because she was not physically at risk.

☞ **Property damage:** P can probably recover for ***property damage*** under all three theories (though a few states don't allow recovery for property damage under a warranty claim, if there's no physical injury).

☞ **Intangible economic harm:** If the only damage suffered by P is ***"intangible economic harm"*** (e.g., lost profits) then the choice of theory makes a difference.

- ☛ **Negligence:** For ***negligence***, not all courts allow recovery for intangible economic harm, and those that do require P to be a member of an "identifiable class."

- ☛ **Implied warranty:** For ***implied warranty***, P can recover if he was a direct purchaser. (In this situation, implied warranty is clearly superior to negligence or strict liability as a theory.) If P was a remote purchaser, courts are split. If P was a bystander, most courts do not allow recovery for pure economic harm.

- ☛ **Strict liability:** For ***strict liability***, most courts don't allow recovery for pure economic harm.

  Example*:* Dentist buys a new drill made by Maker. The drill breaks as it's being used on a patient. If Dentist suffers a loss of reputation leading to lost profits, he can't recover in strict liability against Maker.

Indemnity

☛ **Indemnity:** If P can recover against a retailer under warranty or strict liability, the retailer may obtain complete ***indemnity*** from the manufacturer.

Preemption

☛ **Preemption:** Look for the possibility that federal law has ***preempted*** state common-law tort recovery.

- ☞ **Labeling cases:** This is especially likely in ***labeling*** cases, where, say, if the maker follows FDA drug or device labeling rules, it can't at the same time follow state common-law failure-to-warn rules requiring extra or different warnings. State common-law recovery is preempted in this situation.

Exam Tips on *NUISANCE*

It's easy to miss a "nuisance" issue, because it can seem like a number of other torts (e.g., trespass, abnormally dangerous activity, negligence, etc.). In fact, any fact pattern that can be nuisance might also be one or more of these other torts (though usually, the other torts will involve a direct physical impact and nuisance will usually not).

Nuisance generally

☛ **How to spot:** The name of the tort is a good clue to what type of fact pattern you should be looking for: if in colloquial usage what D is doing would be called a "nuisance" by a lay-person, then the tort of nuisance is worth at least thinking about. Look mostly for fact patterns where D has ***not*** caused a ***physical impact*** with P's person or property.

Public vs. private nuisance

- **Types of acts that may qualify:** You have to distinguish between public and private nuisance, of course (more about the distinction below). But the ***same types*** of activity by D tend to characterize the two types of nuisance. Here is a representative sampling of D's conduct that might be either a public or private nuisance:

  - ❑ D makes persistent ***loud noises.***
  - ❑ D releases ***noxious odors.***
  - ❑ D releases ***harmful chemicals*** into the air.
  - ❑ D cuts off the use of a ***public road.***
  - ❑ D cultivates ***disease-ridden animals.***
  - ❑ D maintains an ***unlawful business*** that lowers the local quality of life (e.g., an unlawful bar, gambling parlor or brothel).
  - ❑ D interferes with ***water*** that flows onto P's property (e.g., D dams a stream, preventing it from flowing onto P's property).

- **Public vs. private:** You need to distinguish between public and private nuisance. It's the nature of ***P's interest*** that distinguishes the two. Public nuisance is an interference with a right "common to the general public." Private nuisance is an interference with P's use and enjoyment of his land. The same act by D can be both a public and private nuisance. Normally you should analyze whether the act is a private nuisance first (since that's the better claim for P), and then go on to public nuisance if you conclude that it's not a private one.

Private nuisance

- **Requirements:** For ***private*** nuisance, check for three main things:

  [1] does P have an ***interest in land*** that has been interfered with?;

  [2] is that interference ***"unreasonable"*** and ***"substantial"***?; and

  [3] was D's conduct ***negligent***, ***abnormally dangerous*** or ***intentional***?

  ☞ **Interest in land:** The most commonly-tested aspect is the requirement that P have an ***"interest in land"*** that has been affected.

  Example: P is a fisherman whose livelihood is ruined because D discharges pollution into the coastal waters. P can't recover in private nuisance because his interest in land hasn't been affected. This is true even if P owns land near the coast, because his *use* of the land he owns hasn't been affected by D's wrongdoing.

- **Tenant:** The interest of a ***tenant*** suffices.

- **Individualized harm not required:** If P does own an interest in land that has been interfered with, there's no requirement of "particular harm," i.e., no requirement that P's interest be different from that of others (as there is for public nuisance).

  Example: If D discharges odors into the air, each local landowner who gets substantial smells on his property has met the "interest in land" requirement, and can sue.

- **"Substantial" interference:** The requirement that the interference with P's use be ***"substantial"*** is also often tested.

  - **Personal injury:** If the interference causes ***personal injury*** to P, or ***direct injury*** to his property, the injury is by definition "substantial."

    Example: Pollutants that cause house paints to become discolored, or that cause plants to die, are by definition a "substantial" interference.

  - **Ultra-sensitive plaintiff:** If the interference doesn't cause physical injury or property damage, it's only "substantial" if a person of ***normal sensitivity*** in the community would be seriously bothered. For instance, ***noises*** or ***smells*** will be measured by this "normally sensitive person" standard. This ***"ultra-sensitive plaintiff"*** issue is often tested.

- **Unreasonable conduct:** D's conduct must be ***"unreasonable."*** Courts consider the magnitude of the interference with P's interests. Some also consider the ***social utility*** of D's conduct.

  Example: D runs a large factory that employs many people, and that cannot stop releasing unpleasant smells and noises without prohibitively costly measures. Some courts are more likely to find a private nuisance here than where D's interests are less "weighty." Other courts ***only*** consider the magnitude of the interference with P's interests, not the size of D's countervailing interests.

- **No strict liability:** D's conduct must be shown to be either ***negligent***, ***abnormally dangerous*** or ***"intentional."*** In other words, there is no general strict liability for nuisance.

  - **Intentional nuisances:** Most nuisance conduct is "intentional," meaning that the interference was ***known*** to D to be ***substantially certain*** to occur (not that D "desired" that interference).

Example: D runs his factory carefully. Unbeknownst to him, the factory one day sends out non-dangerous but annoying pollutants that interfere with P's property. This is not private nuisance, because D has not acted negligently or abnormally dangerously, and did not know with substantial certainty that the interference would occur. But if P complained repeatedly, and D didn't change his practice, then D's knowledge that the interference was occurring would turn the interference into an "intentional" one.

☞ **"Coming to the nuisance" defense:** Lastly, the defense of ***"coming to the nuisance"*** is sometimes raised. Look for this whenever the fact pattern tells you that D was engaging in his activity ***before P moved in***. Usually, the fact that P "came to the nuisance" is ***not an absolute defense***, merely one non-dispositive factor in deciding whether D's conduct was unreasonable.

Public nuisance

☛ **Public nuisance generally:** For ***"public nuisance,"*** there's no real definition, only the vague "interference with a right common to the general public" standard. Anything that an entire community would find dangerous or annoying, but that doesn't result in a direct physical impact, is a candidate.

☞ **Requirements:** Here are the requirements for public nuisance:

[1] there must be an interference with a ***"right common to the public"*** (not just an interference with P's own interests);

[2] the interference with the public's interest must be ***"substantial"***; and

[3] in some courts, P's own harm must be ***different in kind*** from that suffered by the public at large (the requirement of ***"particular harm"***).

☞ **Right common to public:** Overwhelmingly, the most commonly-tested aspect is the ***"right common to the public"*** requirement. Every time you have a possible public nuisance issue, you should discuss whether the harm involved a right common to the general public.

Example: Where Ds (manufacturers of lead-based paint) didn't remove the paint from buildings in which young children later ate the paint, freedom from lead poisoning wasn't a "right common to the public at large," so an individual child who ate lead couldn't recover.

Exam Tips on *MISREPRESENTATION*

Whenever one party in your fact pattern ***makes a statement*** to another, and the statement turns out to be ***untrue***, be on the lookout for a "misrepresentation" claim. A misrepresentation issue is usually not one of the major torts contained in a complex multi-issue fact pattern; it's usually hidden away as one of the more minor issues.

Misrepresentation generally; fraud vs. negligent misrepresentation

☛ **How to spot:** When you talk about "misrepresentation" as an independent tort, you're generally looking for misrepresentations that cause only ***intangible pecuniary loss***. For misrepresentations that cause personal injury or property damage, usually the general tort of negligence (if the falsehood was unintentional) is the better tort to concentrate on.

☛ **Intentional vs. negligent:** Remember, of course, that the tort of misrepresentation can be committed intentionally (the action called "fraud" or "deceit," as well as "intentional misrepresentation" — we'll use "fraud" here for shorthand) or, in some states, negligently. For each misstatement, first analyze and discuss whether fraud has been committed, and go on to discuss negligent misrepresentation only if you conclude that fraud hasn't (or may not have been) committed.

☞ **Same elements, generally:** For the most part, the requirements for fraud and negligent misrep. are the same. We'll talk about most exam issues here under "fraud," and under negligent misrep., we'll just focus on the elements that are different.

Fraud (a/k/a deceit)

☛ **Fraud generally:** Here's what to look for on ***fraud***:

☞ **Requirements:** Memorize this list of requirements (it's easy to forget one):

- ❑ A ***misrepresentation*** by D;
- ❑ ***Scienter*** (culpable state of mind by D, essentially either ***knowledge*** of falsity or ***reckless indifference*** to the truth);
- ❑ An intent to ***induce P's reliance*** (or at least a reason to expect that the class of which P is a member would be likely to rely);
- ❑ ***Justifiable reliance*** by P; and
- ❑ ***Damage*** (usually pecuniary) to P stemming from the reliance.

☞ **Falsity:** Don't forget to check that the representation was ***false***. This won't always be obvious.

Example: Insurer says to Claimant, "You have no legal case against us." Claimant settles. It's not clear that this representation was false, so you should discuss the falsity issue.

☛ **Concealment:** Remember that an affirmative act to ***conceal*** a fact from P is the same as asserting the non-existence of the fact.

Example: Seller repaints a cracked engine block in his car. He then sells to Buyer. That's misrepresentation to Buyer concerning the status of the engine block.

☛ **Silence:** Also, ***silence*** can occasionally (though not usually) be the equivalent of an assertion of fact. The most important situations where silence will be an assertion:

[1] D has a ***fiduciary relationship*** to P (*Example:* Lawyer to Client);

or

[2] D knows that P is mistaken about some ***fact basic to the transaction***

Example: Buyer says to Dealer, "I'm paying you $100,000 because I know that's a Picasso"; Dealer stays silent knowing that the picture is a fake or by a lesser artist. Dealer's silence equals misrepresentation because P's mistake is about a fact basic to the transaction.

☞ **D's superior knowledge not sufficient:** The fact that D has ***more knowledge*** about the situation than P is not by itself enough to turn D's silence into misrepresentation, especially where D is the buyer.

Example: Buyer is a jeweler; Seller is an amateur owner; Seller thinks the going rate for used diamonds is $2 per carat when Buyer knows it's $3 per carat — Buyer's silence is not a misrepresentation.

☛ **Promises, or statements of intent:** Look out for statements of ***intention*** where D ***promises*** to do something; the fact that D doesn't keep the promise doesn't alone make it a misrepresentation. But if D ***never intended*** to keep the promise, this is misrepresentation.

☛ **Statements of opinion:** Also, look out for statements of ***opinion***. A statement of opinion isn't normally a "representation."

☞ **D's special knowledge:** But in some situations, it is a misrepresentation for D to say that something is her opinion when it's not. In an "adverse party" situation (P and D are on opposite sides of a proposed transaction), the main example of misrepresentation of present opinion occurs where D has ***special knowledge*** that P doesn't.

Example: "As an art dealer, it's my opinion that this is a Picasso" — if Dealer doesn't really believe this, it's a misrepresentation because of Dealer's supposed special knowledge.

☞ **Statements of law:** Statements of ***law*** are often held to be non-actionable statements of opinion. But if a statement includes an implied statement concerning the underlying facts, that implied statement can be a misrepresentation.

Example: "This house conforms to the zoning code's set-back requirements" — that's an actionable statement of fact, not opinion, about how the house is positioned on the lot.

☞ **Scienter:** Check that D had ***scienter***. In essence, D must either ***know*** the statement was false, lie about ***how much knowledge*** as to the statement's truth, or ***recklessly disregard*** the fact that he doesn't know the truth.

☞ **Intended reliance:** Check that D meant to ***induce P to rely***. If the statement is made directly to P, usually this isn't a problem.

- **Liability to third persons:** D is also liable to ***third persons*** if they are members of a ***class*** which D had ***"reason to expect"*** would rely, and the transaction is of the ***sort*** that D should foresee would or might occur in reliance.

  Example: If D knowingly mislabels goods, D is liable to anyone, even a non-purchaser, who reads the label and relies.

- **Repetition by third person:** A common test issue is that D makes a statement to X, who ***repeats*** it to P. Here, D is not liable, if he had no reason to expect the statement to be repeated to P or relied on by a class of which P is a part.

- **Overheard remark:** Often, exams test the ***"overheard"*** remark (addressed to X, but overheard by P) — normally, the speaker turns out not to be liable, because she had no reason to expect the overhearing.

  Example: Art Expert falsely says to Friend at Dealer's store, "That's a Picasso." Customer overhears, and offers to buy from Dealer without disclosing that she overheard Expert's statement. Expert isn't liable, because he had no intent to induce Customer to rely, and Customer wasn't a member of a class Expert should have expected to rely.

- **Endorser's liability:** An ***endorser*** can have fraud liability to a member of the buying public.

  Example: Olympic Champion says, "I made money with my Burger-Queen franchise." Any member of the buying public who relies by buying a franchise can probably sue Champion if Champion knew his statement was false.

☞ **Reliance:** Check two aspect's of P's ***reliance***: (1) that there was "actual" reliance; and (2) that the reliance was justifiable.

- **Actual reliance:** P must have ***actually*** relied. Often-tested: P ***spots the***

untruth but does the transaction anyway. Here, P couldn't have relied.

Example: D sells P a car, saying that it was never in an accident. In fact, the engine block was cracked in an accident, and had been painted over. P inspects closely and spots the broken engine block, but says nothing, and buys. P has not "actually relied" on the misrepresentation.

- **Justifiable reliance:** P's reliance must be ***"justifiable."*** So if the falsity would be ***"obvious"*** to an ordinary person in P's position, P can't recover. But P has ***no duty to investigate***, and P's ***contributory negligence*** is ***not*** a defense so long as the falsity is not obvious.

- **Measure of damages:** If you conclude that P can recover for fraud, discuss the ***measure of damages.*** In the usual case where P has bought something based on the misrepresentation, courts differ about the measure:

  [1] some courts give P ***"expectation damages,"*** a/k/a the ***"benefit of the bargain"*** (the difference between what the item was really worth and what it would have been worth if it had been as represented);

  [2] other courts (probably a majority) limit P to ***"reliance"*** damages (difference between the amount paid and the real value, without reference to what it would have been worth if it had been as represented).

  Example: D says, "That's a Picasso worth $200,000, but you can buy it for $150,000." P buys for the $150,000. It's really a fake worth only $1,000. Some courts give P $199,000, in expectation damages, but most give just $149,000, in reliance damages.

  - **Subtraction of actual value:** Whichever measure of damages is to be used, don't forget to subtract the ***actual value*** of what P got. (P doesn't get to tender the item back to D in return for not having this subtraction.)

  - **Consequential damages:** Also, look for ***consequential damages***.

    Example: If a car said to be in working order breaks down while P is going to an important meeting, and P has to rent a replacement car, P can recover the cost of the rental as an additional item of damages on top of expectation or reliance.

  - **No emotional-distress damages:** P can only recover ***pecuniary*** damages, not damages for ***emotional distress*** (e.g., disappointment that the representation turned out not to be true).

Negligent misrepresentation

- **Negligent misrepresentation, generally:** If you conclude that P can't recover for fraud, consider a recovery for ***"negligent misrepresentation"*** (NM).

☞ **Intangible economic harm:** Not all courts allow NM where there's only intangible economic harm, and not personal injury or property damage. Point this out in your answer.

☞ **Differences from fraud:** There are three main differences between an action for fraud and one for NM:

[1] D's mental state must be merely negligent, not "intentional" or "reckless";

[2] D must have made the statement ***during the course of his business*** and with a ***pecuniary interest*** in the transaction; and

[3] P must be a person or member of a ***"limited group"*** that D ***intended to reach, or who D knows a recipient*** of the information intended to reach.

☞ **Re-publisher's liability:** A ***"re-publisher"*** can be liable for NM.

Example: X tells Newspaper, "There's no danger of salmonella from chicken as long as it is cooked for at least five minutes at 300 degrees." If Newspaper prints this as a quotation without checking its accuracy, Newspaper may be liable for NM, at least if we ignore the "who may sue" issue discussed below.

☞ **D's pecuniary interest:** Most commonly-tested issue in NM: D must make the statement in the course of his ***business or profession***, and have a ***pecuniary interest*** in the transaction.

☛ **"Curbstone" opinions:** The "pecuniary interest" requirement knocks out ***"curbstone opinions,"*** i.e., statements by professionals that take place outside the office and outside of a paid professional relationship.

Example: Attorney gives unpaid advice to Fred, his friend, at a cocktail party. Fred can't recover for NM from Attorney because Attorney had no pecuniary interest in his statement.

☛ **Statements outside of the business relationship:** The "pecuniary interest" requirement also knocks out situations where D is speaking to a customer, but on a subject that is outside of the business relationship with the customer.

Example: Storekeeper, owner of a hardware store, gives Customer advice about how to make a will. Since the advice has nothing to do with the sale of any product by Storekeeper, probably Storekeeper will be held to have had no pecuniary interest in the transaction.

☞ **Narrow group:** A person making an NM is liable to a ***narrower group*** than the defrauder: he is not liable to those whom he has "reason to expect" will rely, but merely to a ***"limited group"*** that he either ***intended*** to reach, or that he knew the ***recipient*** intended to reach.

Example: D, a newspaper, negligently reports greater earnings by X Corp. than really occurred. Reader buys the stock, and loses money. Because the readership of a general newspaper is not a "limited class," probably Reader may not recover for NM.

☞ **Contributory negligence:** ***Contributory negligence*** is a ***defense*** to NM. So if a reasonable person would investigate, P loses if he didn't. (Contrast this with the "no duty to investigate" rule for fraud.)

Strict liability

☛ **Strict liability:** Very occasionally, ***strict liability*** for misrep. is tested. Most common situations: P and D are parties to a sales or service transaction. Since these situations must involve privity (P and D dealt face-to-face), strict liability here is based as much in contract as in tort.

☞ **Mislabelling:** Also, a seller who ***mislabels*** a product has, in effect, strict liability for misrepresentation for any ***physical injury*** that results. Cite to Restatement §402B on this labelling issue.

Exam Tips on *DEFAMATION*

Defamation issues are pretty easy to spot — you're looking, of course, for situations where someone is saying something that damages somebody else's ***reputation***. But spotting and analyzing the sub-issues can be difficult, especially because of the Supreme Court's constitutional rulings.

Libel/slander distinction

☛ **When to worry about distinction:** Don't get too hung up on the ***libel/slander*** distinction. It only matters when you're worrying about whether P has to prove "special harm," i.e., pecuniary loss. Use the term "defamation" if you're not sure whether the suit is for libel or slander.

Requirements for defamation

☛ **Requirements:** Memorize this list of requirements for defamation (both libel and slander):

❑ A ***false*** and ***defamatory*** statement by D about P;

❑ A ***"publication,"*** i.e., a communicating of that statement by D to one other than P;

❑ The appropriate level of ***fault,*** which is always at least negligence (except possibly in the case of a private figure suing a non-media defendant), and is "actual malice" if P is a public official or public figure;

- ❑ If the action is for slander that is not "slander *per se*," ***"special harm,"*** i.e., damages of a pecuniary nature.

"Defamatory" statement

☛ **"Defamatory" statement:** Check that the statement was ***"defamatory."*** The term means "having a tendency to harm the ***reputation***" of P.

☞ **Listener doesn't believe:** A commonly-tested issue: the fact that the listener/reader ***doesn't believe*** the statement is ***irrelevant*** on the issue of whether the statement is defamatory. (But this may be relevant to whether "special harm" has been shown, where the suit is for slander.)

☞ **"Significant minority" rule:** Some statements would, if believed, hold P up to disgrace or ridicule in the minds of ***some*** but ***not other*** listeners. Here, so long as a ***"significant and respectable minority"*** would have this negative opinion of P, the statement is defamatory even though other people would not have a negative opinion.

> **Example:** "P is gay" is probably defamatory, because a sizeable minority of law-abiding — though perhaps not politically correct — Americans thinks poorly of gay people.

☞ **Ambiguous statements:** Check the meaning of the statement. Where the statement is ***ambiguous***, it's defamatory if a ***"reasonable person"*** might interpret the statement in a defamatory way, and at least one person in fact took this interpretation.

Reference to P, not to someone else

☛ **Reference to P:** Check that the statement referred (and was understood to refer) to *P*, ***not someone else***.

☞ **Indirect references:** If the statement ***doesn't name*** P, but refers to P in a way that some listeners ***understand*** to be a reference to P, that's enough. Often, the ***context*** will make it clear that P is the one referred to.

> **Example:** "A leading member of this college faculty stole a computer" qualifies, if there are people who previously knew that P was the one under suspicion.

☞ **Group libel:** If the statement refers to an ***entire group***, it's defamatory as to the whole group if the group is a small one (probably less than 20 members). If the statement pertains to only one or a few unnamed members of a larger group, the statement is probably not defamatory if there's no way for listeners to know which members are meant.

Falsity of statement

- **Falsity:** Check that the statement was ***false***. If it's true, the Constitution ***forbids recovery***.

  - **Accusations of criminality:** "Falsity" can occasionally be tricky to determine. Watch out especially for statements that are a charge of ***criminality***, whose truth or falsity depends on technical details about the crime.

    Example: D says, "P stole my tools when he quit working for me." If P took the tools by mistake but then failed to return them, this isn't common-law theft, so the statement would probably be ruled to be "false."

    - **"Substantial" truth bars recovery:** But remember that ***"substantial"*** truth will bar recovery, not just literal truth. (However, if D accuses P of one crime, D can't defend by showing that P really committed a different crime, even a closely-related crime.)

  - **Statements of opinion:** Statements of ***"pure opinion"*** can't be defamatory.

    Example: "Our City Manager can't govern his way out of a paper bag" is an opinion, and thus can't be defamatory even if spoken with hatred and a desire to harm.

    - **Implicit assertion of related facts:** But a statement of opinion that contains an ***implicit*** assertion of related ***facts*** can be defamatory as to those facts.

      Example: "In my opinion, P is an alcoholic" contains the implicit statement that D knows facts that would support this opinion; if P never drinks, D loses.

    - **Hyperbole:** If the statement relates to a subject of controversy and public interest, D gets some leeway for ***hyperbole*** and non-literalness.

      Example: "P's position on this issue shows that he must have been high on something" probably isn't intended to be taken literally, so it's an opinion, not a statement of fact.

Fault

- **Fault generally:** Check that D had the requisite degree of ***fault***. Most-often tested: D's degree of fault relative to the ***truth or falsity*** of the statement.

  - **Public figure must show "actual malice":** If P is a ***"public figure"*** or ***"public official,"*** P must prove that D acted with ***"actual malice."*** Remember that this is a term of art, meaning not malice but either: (1) D had ***knowledge*** of the statement's falsity; or (2) D ***recklessly disregarded*** the truth. (Cite to *New York Times v. Sullivan* on this issue.)

- ☛ **Meaning of "reckless":** Also, remember that D is "reckless" only where D ***"in fact entertained serious doubts"*** about the statement's truth. If D was extremely careless in not checking the story, but had no doubts, that's not "reckless disregard" of the truth for *New York Times v. Sullivan* purposes.

☞ **Private figure must show negligence by media:** If P is a ***private*** figure, and D is a ***media*** defendant, P must prove ***at least negligence*** by D in failing to discover the statement's falsity. In other words, states can't impose strict liability here. (Cite to *Gertz v. Robert Welch* on this point.)

☞ **Private figure against non-media defendant:** If P is a ***private*** figure and D is ***not*** a media defendant, the Supreme Court has never imposed a constitutional requirement of negligence or greater. (The Supreme Court simply hasn't spoken on this issue.) So the states are theoretically free to find D ***strictly liable***. However, as a matter of common law, virtually no states impose strict liability as to fault — they all require at least negligence.

- ☛ This issue is frequently tested despite the fact (or perhaps because of the fact) that it's relatively obscure.

    Example: D, P's former boss, says to X, "P is the most dishonest employee I've ever had." D has a reasonable, non-negligent belief that P stole from D. In fact, however, P never committed any crime. Although there's no constitutional rule preventing a state from imposing strict libility on D, no state would do so — P would always be required as a matter of state common law to prove at least that D was negligent in not ascertaining the statement's truth or falsity.

Libel vs. slander

☛ **Libel vs. slander, generally:** At some point in your answer, you should try to determine whether the defamatory statement was ***libel*** or ***slander***.

☞ **Writing vs. speaking:** Essentially, libel is ***written***, and slander is ***spoken***. Broadcast statements are clearly libel if they're done from written scripts; if the broadcast is ad-libbed, courts are split as to whether it's libel or slander.

☞ **Special harm:** There is only one reason you have to worry about the distinction. For libel, P doesn't have to prove "special harm," i.e., that P's financial interests were harmed. For slander, P ***does*** have to prove ***"special harm,"*** i.e., that his financial interests were harmed — unless the slanderous statement falls into one of four special cases (collectively, "slander per se").

- ☛ **Slander per se:** There are four classes that make up ***slander per se:***

  [1] most important (and most often-tested), a statement accusing P of ***criminal behavior***;

  [2] a statement that P has a ***loathsome disease***;

  [3] a statement adversely reflecting on P's fitness for ***conducting her business*** or profession; or

  [4] an allegation of ***sexual misconduct*** by P.

  Example 1: P works for D. D orally tells his friend X that P has stolen D's property. P in his slander suit need not show that he has suffered "special harm," i.e., financial harm from D's statement — D accused P of criminality, and the case is thus for slander per se.

  Example 2: Same basic facts, but now D tells X that P was a completely incompetent employee. Unless P can show that he suffered some financial loss from this statement, P can't recover even nominal damages.

- ☛ **Other person's disbelief:** Where the hearer/reader ***doesn't believe*** the statement, the requirement of special harm (assuming it applies) will virtually never be met.

Publication

☛ **Publication, generally:** Check that ***"publication"*** occurred.

- ☞ **Communication to one other than P:** The most often-tested issue is that "publication" is defined to require communication to ***one other than P***.

  Example: D says to P, "You're a crook." If no one else overhears this, there's been no publication. This is true even if P then repeats the defamatory statement to another.

- ☞ **No strict liability on publication:** Courts do ***not*** impose ***strict liability*** on the publication issue. Thus if D neither knows nor has reason to know that anyone other than P will hear/read the statement, D is not liable.

  Example: D writes a letter to P, saying, "You're a crook." X, P's wife, opens the letter and reads it. If D didn't know and didn't have reason to believe that anyone other than P would read the letter, D is not liable.

- ☞ **Repeaters:** A ***repeater*** is a "publisher," and thus is liable for defamation, on the same rules as the person who originally made the statement.

  - ☛ **Repeater adds disclaimer:** The most-often tested issue: it doesn't matter that the repeater says, "I'm just repeating what so-and-so says," or even,

"I'm quoting so-and-so." It doesn't even matter that the repeater says, "But I ***don't believe*** the statement that I've just repeated." If the underlying statement is false, the repeater faces liability (subject to the rules on fault, e.g., the repeater must have "actual malice" if P is a public figure).

Privileges

- **Privileges generally:** Look for ***privileges*** that might apply as defenses. Here are the most commonly-tested:
  - **Protection of publisher's interest:** The privilege of "protection of the ***publisher's interest***." Most common illustration: D tries to protect/regain his ***property***.

    Example: D thinks P has stolen his property, and he yells, "Stop thief," or accuses P to the police. Even if D's belief is wrong, he is protected by the privilege, so long as he doesn't spread the defamation wider than needed or otherwise abuse the privilege.

  - **Protection of another's interest:** The privilege of "protection of ***another's interest***." Most common illustration: X asks D for a ***job reference*** concerning D's former employee, P. Even if D's statement about P is wrong, D is protected by the privilege.

  - **Protection of common interest:** The privilege of "protection of ***common interest***," i.e., an interest shared by D and the person to whom D speaks.

    Example: D, an officer of one bank, says to X, an officer of another, "I hear that P's been passing bad checks. Have you heard the same?" Since D and X are both interested in stopping bad-check passing, D is protected even if wrong.

  - **Neutral reportage:** The privilege of ***"neutral reportage."*** This is used especially by media reporting on allegations that the reporter has serious doubts about but thinks need public airing.

    Example: D, a reporter, writes, "Well-informed sources inside the D.A.'s Office say P [a public official] is believed to have taken bribes." Even if the reporter thinks that P probably didn't take the bribes, the reporter is protected if she reasonably thinks the accusation is important for the public to know. (Only a few courts have recognized this privilege so far.)

  - **Abuse of privilege:** But remember that all of the above privileges are just ***"qualified"*** ones, so they're ***lost*** if ***abused***. Generally, a privilege is abused if used out of malice, if used for a different purpose than that furthered by the interest (e.g., idle gossip), or if the statement is spread more widely than needed. The privilege is also lost if D's belief as to the statement's truth is ***reckless***. Courts are ***split*** about whether the privilege is lost if D is merely ***neg-***

ligent in his belief that the statement is true.

Presumed damages

- **Presumed damages generally:** Remember that courts are limited in when they can award ***"presumed"*** damages. Presumed damages are compensatory (as opposed to nominal) damages awarded without actual proof of loss, on the theory that such an amount "would normally" be inflicted by the statement in question. At least where D is a ***media defendant*** and the issue relates to a matter of ***public concern***, even a private-figure plaintiff can't be awarded presumed damages unless he shows that D acted with "actual malice" (not just negligence).

Exam Tips on *MISCELLANEOUS TORTS*

Most of the torts in this chapter will appear on exams only as "minor" torts thrown into fact patterns that also involve the "major" torts from other chapters. For instance, the various "invasion of privacy" torts are most likely to be encountered in the same fact pattern as defamation and intentional infliction of emotional distress.

Invasion of privacy

- **Invasion is most important:** The various ***"invasion of privacy"*** torts are overwhelmingly the torts from this chapter that you're most likely to be tested on.
  - **Must identify right one:** You'll get very little credit for just noting that P may be able to sue for "invasion of privacy." The four types are so different that to get credit for spotting the issue, you've got to identify the right one.
  - **List:** Memorize this simplified list of definitions:
    - ***"Appropriation of identity"*** occurs where P's name or likeness has been appropriated by D for D's financial benefit, without P's consent.
    - ***"Intrusion on solitude"*** occurs where D invades P's private space in a manner which would be highly offensive to a reasonable person in P's position.
    - ***"Publicity of private life"*** or ***"public disclosure"*** occurs where D publicly discloses a non-public detail of P's private life, if the effect would be highly offensive to a reasonable person in P's position.
    - ***"False light"*** occurs where D publishes false statements about P which, although not defamatory, would be highly offensive to a reasonable person in P's position.

☞ **Appropriation of identity:** For ***"appropriation of identity,"*** you're typically looking for an ***advertisement*** that claims that P uses or endorses the product.

- **Can be private citizen:** P doesn't have to be a public figure or celebrity to win.

- **Truth is no defense:** It's no defense that the statement is true.

  Example: P, a famous comedian, says on TV, "I always smoke X-Brand cigars." X Co. takes out ads saying, "P smokes only X." X is liable.

- **Newsworthiness defense:** If the disclosure is ***"newsworthy,"*** that's a defense. However, this defense is usually available only to "news stories," not "advertisements," so anything that looks like an endorsement probably won't qualify for this exception.

  Example: If the *National Enquirer* runs a photo of a famous comedian on the cover as part of a news story about the comedian's problems, the fact that the newspaper is "using" the comedian's likeness to sell newspapers is irrelevant — the "newsworthy" defense applies.

  ☞ **Limited interest:** The "newsworthy" exception applies even if the item is of interest only to a small portion of the viewers/readers.

- **No malice required:** P doesn't have to show that D had "malice" of any sort, even if P is a public figure or public official.

☞ **Intrusion on solitude:** For ***"intrusion on solitude,"*** look for a ***physical entry*** into P's ***private place*** (typically a ***home***, ***office*** or ***vehicle***). (*Example:* D breaks into P's office, rifles through P's desk or safe, and copies down information found there.)

- **Highly-offensive standard:** Make sure the intrusion would be "***highly offensive*** to a reasonable person."

  Example: If D is a reporter who interviews P at her home, then without permission goes into P's bathroom to snoop, this probably doesn't meet the "highly offensive" test.

- **No publicity required:** So long as there has been the requisite physical entry, the information does ***not*** have to be ***publicized*** in order for the tort to occur — the intrusion itself constitutes the tort.

- **Surveillance from public place:** Surveillance of P done from and in a ***public place*** doesn't qualify. (*Example:* "Paparazzi" who dog P and shoot her photo constantly while she is in public aren't committing the tort.) If binoculars or telescopes are used from a public place to peer into P's house through a window, this probably qualifies (since it's certainly "highly offensive to a reasonable person").

☞ **Publicity of private life:** For ***"publicity of private life,"*** look for the disclosure of ***details*** that are highly private (and that a reasonable person would find highly offensive to have disclosed).

Example: The precise details of a minor celebrity's sexual preferences and sexual habits would probably qualify.

☛ **Truth is no defense:** The fact that the details are true (and thus the publication is not defamatory) is irrelevant, and in fact this tort is almost always committed by accurate disclosures.

☛ **Public-record defense:** Most commonly-tested aspect: The detail must not be anywhere in the ***public record***. If it's in the public record (even buried away where no one except a reporter has ever noticed it), this is a defense.

Example: If the county real estate records disclose how much P paid for his house and how much he pays in property taxes, this info can be disclosed, even though a reasonable person would find it offensive and even though no member of the public has ever known the information before.

☛ **Legitimate-public-concern defense:** Also, if the item is of ***"legitimate public concern,"*** that's a defense.

Example: If P is now on trial for theft, or is now running for public office, the fact that many years ago P was accused of theft by a former boss is probably of "legitimate public concern."

☞ **False light:** For ***"false light,"*** look for a fact pattern in which P is not defamed, but some ***untrue statement*** about P is published. Often, this statement will make P "look ***better***" than the truth would have.

Example: P is falsely said to have been a hero, or to have won a prize.

☛ **Need not be defamatory:** The statement need not be defamatory.

☛ **Highly-offended standard:** The main issue is whether the reasonable person would be ***"highly offended."*** "Embarrassed" isn't enough.

Example: A false statement that P has won a door prize or raffle probably isn't sufficient.

☛ **Actual malice if P is public figure:** If P is a ***public figure***, P must show ***"actual malice"*** (that D either knew the statement was false or recklessly disregarded its truth). (Cite to *Time v. Hill* on this point.)

☞ **Private figure:** The Supreme Court has never said whether P has to show "actual malice" where P is a ***private figure***. Point out this uncertainty if your fact pattern involves a private figure.

Misuse of legal procedure

☛ **Misuse of legal procedure torts:** The ***"misuse of legal procedure"*** torts (malicious prosecution, wrongful use of civil proceedings and abuse of process) are rarely tested. Just try to memorize the basic definitions and scenarios for them.

Injurious falsehood, interference with contract & interference with prospective advantage

☛ **Not often tested:** The three "business torts" are also not often tested.

- ☞ **Injurious falsehood:** If D makes false statements disparaging P's goods or services, that's ***"injurious falsehood."***

- ☞ **Interference with contract:** If D ***induces X to breach an existing contract*** which X has with P, that's ***"interference with contract."***

  - ☛ **At-will contract:** If the contract is ***"at will"*** (terminable at any time on little or no notice), courts are split about whether and when D can be liable for interfering with it. If D is acting out of spite, or to drive P out of business, D is probably liable; but if D is just offering a better price or better deal to get the business for himself, he is probably not liable.

- ☞ **Interference with prospective advantage:** If D interferes with P's chance to make a contract (or otherwise do business) with X in the ***future***, that's ***"interference with prospective advantage."*** Basically the same rules apply as for interference with existing contract, except that D has a broader set of privileges to use as defenses.

  Example: If D is ***competing***, that's clearly protected by the privilege, whereas D's desire to compete is not protected by the privilege where an existing non-at-will contract is involved.

SHORT-ANSWER QUESTIONS

Note: Here are 69 short-answer questions adapted from the *Law in a Flash* set on Torts.

1. Juliet is gazing at the stars from her balcony, exclaiming dreamily, "Romeo, Romeo, where art thou, Romeo?" A voice from below responds, "Here I am, you moron, give me a hand up." Juliet looks down and sees Romeo climbing up to the balcony. Before she has a chance to help, Romeo loses his footing, and falls, breaking his arm. Juliet races downstairs and tries to set the arm, even though Romeo tells her that she should wait for a doctor. Juliet makes the break much worse by moving the arm the wrong way. Has Juliet committed a battery even though she was only trying to help?

2. Calvin takes his mean-tempered pet tiger, Hobbes, out for a walk to terrorize the neighborhood. He sees little Susie Derkins playing across the street, and yells to her, as he walks toward her, "Hey, you stupid girl! Why don't you come over and say hello to Hobbes!" Calvin's intent is to frighten Susie, but nothing more. Susie stands, frozen with fear. Hobbes snarls at Susie, straining at his leash. The leash breaks, and Hobbes runs over and attacks Susie. Is Calvin liable to Susie for battery?

3. Speed Racer takes his squeeze, Trixie, on a wild spin through town in his hot racing car, the Mach 5. Paying more attention to Trixie than the road, Speed carelessly runs a stop sign and narrowly avoids hitting Chim-Chim, a pedestrian who is crossing the street at a crosswalk. Chim-Chim is terrified. Has Speed Racer committed an assault?

4. Zorro leaves his valuable cape with the cloakroom attendant at a restaurant. When he returns, the attendant wrongfully refuses to hand over the cape, and threatens to burn it. Zorro stays for two hours before he gets the cape back. Can he successfully claim false imprisonment?

5. Pocahontas runs Indian Trader, a novelty shop. It's closing time, and she takes a quick look around the store to see if there are any patrons left. She doesn't see any. In fact, however, John Smith is crouching down behind a counter, looking at the bottom shelf of a display of plastic tomahawks. Pocahontas leaves and locks up the shop, unwittingly locking Smith in the store. False imprisonment?

6. To play a joke on his friend Ethel Rosenberg, Max disguises himself as an FBI agent, comes to Ethel's door, and tells her that her husband Julius has just been arrested for spying and is about to be executed. In fact, Max knows that Julius has been out fishing all day, and that Ethel has been scared sick worrying about him. She screams and faints, and is extremely anguished for months afterwards. When she recovers, she sues Max for intentional infliction of emotional distress. Max defends on the grounds that Ethel's distress has not led to any physical illness or injury (a factually correct statement). Will Max's defense succeed?

7. Cleopatra and her boyfriend, Marc Antony, have a fight at his house. He storms out.

Despondent, Cleopatra goes to his bathroom, gets in the tub, and slashes her wrists. Antony comes back, and finds her in a pool of blood. Shocked and horrified, he rushes her to the hospital. Cleopatra survives. Antony sues her for intentional infliction of emotional distress. She defends on grounds that she didn't intend to distress him. Who wins?

8. Miles Standish likes to take long walks every day along what he believes is the edge of his property, Turkey Ridge. The course he travels is actually on land belonging to Chief Big Foot. Has Standish committed a trespass to land?

9. Jack T. Ripper jumps into H. G. Wells' time machine, mistakenly believing it's his. He takes it on a whirl through time, realizes his mistake, and returns it. Has Ripper committed a trespass to chattels?

10. Icarus asks Orville Wright if he can borrow Wright's wax wings. Wright hands them over, Icarus straps them on, and soars into the wild blue yonder. Unfortunately, Icarus flies too close to the sun, the wings melt, and Icarus isn't too well off, either. Icarus returns the wings to Wright as one solid mass of wax. Wright claims that Icarus has committed a conversion. Icarus claims that since he rightfully borrowed the wings, he can't be liable for conversion. Who's right?

11. Anne Boleyn enters the hospital to have her sinuses drained. While she is anesthetized, her doctor, Ryno Plasty, removes her eleventh finger (which doesn't function anyway), as well. Has Plasty committed a tort?

12. In an NHL playoff hockey game, Wayne Greatsky gets around the player defending him, Mario Lemeow, and scores. Lemeow, enraged at being scored upon, skates up behind Greatsky and hacks at him with his stick. Greatsky falls, strikes his head on the ice, and suffers a career-ending injury. Greatsky sues Lemeow for battery. Lemeow raises the affirmative defense of implied consent. Will this defense succeed?

13. Axel Cutioner tells Mary, Queen of Scots, that he is a magician, and offers her a solid gold ring if she lets him saw her in half. She consents, not realizing the gold ring is cheap plastic, and, in fact, still has Cracker Jack candy stuck to it. When she discovers the fraud, she sues him for battery. Does her consent constitute a valid defense?

14. Ron is a "responsible" rapist — he never rapes anyone without wearing a condom, and he does not carry a weapon. One night, he attempts to rape Lorena, telling her that he'll be gentle and won't hurt her as long as she doesn't resist. He in fact uses no overt force as he puts on a condom and prepares to assault her. Lorena decides (reasonably under the circumstances) that the least deadly way to prevent intercourse is to use a knife she has hidden in her purse; she does so, and castrates Ron. Ron sues Lorena for battery. She defends on grounds of self-defense. Who wins?

15. Fletcher Christian, deck hand on the ship HMS Bounty, plays a practical joke on Captain Bligh. Bligh whips Christian, in violation of Navy regulations. Humiliated, Christian sets Bligh afloat on a raft. When Bligh gets back to civilization and sues Christian, Christian claims he acted in self-defense. Is his defense valid?

16. Aaron Burr is sitting in an aisle seat in the bleachers at a baseball game, minding his own business. Alexander Hamilton walks up to Burr, his arms laden with beer, nachos, and bratwurst. Hamilton sneers, "Get out of my way, you stupid butthead." People in nearby seats titter. Burr gets up and decks Hamilton, sending him sprawling backwards. Hamilton sues Burr for battery. Burr defends on self-defense grounds. What result?

17. Dorothy is out for a drive with her dog, Toto. A howling storm kicks up, and the visibility decreases to almost nothing. Dorothy is terrified, and says, "Toto, I don't think we're in Kansas anymore." She pulls off the road, into the driveway of the Wicked Witch of the West. She grabs Toto and runs into the garage. Wicked Witch sees Dorothy coming and reasonably believes she's trying to steal Witch's magic brooms, which she keeps in the garage. Witch runs out and beats her up. When Dorothy sues Wicked Witch for battery, will Wicked Witch have a valid "defense of property" privilege?

18. Portentia Lardo, circus fat lady, visits the U-Pik-M Meat Market. She browses for a while in the Beef Department. As she leaves, not having purchased anything, a store detective runs up behind her yelling, in front of other shoppers, "Stop! Thief! She has a side of beef under her coat!" She is, indeed, so large that she looks like she's hiding something. Portentia stops, mortified, and the detective catches up to her, saying, "Come with me." She follows him to the store office, where he asks her to take off her coat. She does so. When it's obvious she's only fat and not a thief, he says, "I'm sorry. You can go." Does Portentia have a valid claim against the store?

19. The Minnow, a tiny ship, sets sail from a tropical port for a three-hour tour. Shortly thereafter a fearsome storm kicks up, the tiny ship is tossed, and the crew seeks refuge at a private dock belonging to Snively. If Snively sues for trespass, will he win?

20. Shakespeare, a playwright, is walking down the street. As he passes a doorway, he sees a woman, Lady Macbeth, standing there. She has a glazed look in her eyes, she's holding a cleaver dripping with blood, and her hands are covered with blood as well. Shakespeare slips surreptitiously into a phone booth, calls the police, and emerges, brandishing a gun. He tells Lady Macbeth that if she moves an inch he'll blow her head off. In fact, Lady Macbeth works at the Titus Andronicus Butcher Shop, and she didn't have a chance to wash her hands before she left work. However, when she tries to tell Shakespeare this, he thinks it's a pile of baloney, and doesn't let her go until the police arrive. She sues Shakespeare for false imprisonment. Can he defend on grounds of legal authority?

21. King's Man catapults a styrofoam ball at Humpty Dumpty's forehead, intending only to embarrass him. In fact, Humpty falls and cracks his skull, where a normal person would have been unhurt. Will King's Man be liable for Humpty's injuries?

22. Arthur Fonzarelli is a bored teenager. He rides all over Mayberry on his Harley Davidson just to kill time. Arthur is very concerned about damage to his spotless Harley, so he is always watchful when he rides. One day, however, he runs over Aunt Bea when he is momentarily blinded by the sun. Aunt Bea sues Arthur for negligence on the grounds that there is no social utility in riding around merely to kill time. Will she win?

23. Batman's son, Batboy, is thirteen. One night, while Batman is playing poker with the Commissioner, Batboy sneaks into the Batcave, stuffs a chaw of chewing tobacco in his cheek, jumps into the Batmobile, and takes off like a bat out of hell. Robin is walking his bike across the street at a crosswalk, and Batboy negligently hits him, ruining the bike and injuring Robin. When Robin sues Batboy for negligence, what standard of care will Batboy be held to?

24. The Hotten Swettee Nightshirt Company manufactures children's nightclothes. The cloth it uses is highly flammable. One youngster, Emma Layshen, wearing a Hotten Swettee nightie, naps a bit too close to her night light and is engulfed in flames. When Hotten Swettee is sued in negligence, Hotten Swettee defends by pointing out (correctly) that the industry custom is to use this same kind of cloth for children's nightclothes. Can Emma win?

25. The Han-dee Shop-R Grocery Store is open 24 hours a day, seven days a week, in violation of a Sunday closing law. Pierre Lucky is shopping at Han-dee one Sunday, and is injured when he slips on a ketchup slick in Aisle 3, which had been there for hours. Pierre sues Han-dee for negligence on the basis of opening for business in derogation of the Sunday closing law. Will he win?

26. The State of Anxiety has a criminal statute requiring that people lock their space saucers when they park them in public places. George Jetson carelessly leaves his keys in the ignition and his space saucer unlocked, when he takes his dog Astro to the park one day. Kibbles Enbitts steals the saucer, and goes for a "joy-fly" in it. Enbitts knocks over Mr. Spacely, who's walking along a sidewalk. Spacely sues Jetson for negligence based on Jetson's violation of the statute. Assuming Spacely can prove the statute was designed to protect pedestrians from being hit by stolen saucers, will Jetson be liable, in most jurisdictions?

27. Things are kind of anxious in Europe, and Gavrilo Princip takes to carrying a gun. He's watching a parade one day, when a man next to him, Dr. Pangloss, carelessly drops a peanut into Princip's gun. When Princip tries to shake the peanut out, the gun goes off, killing Archduke Ferdinand and starting World War I. Rupert, who is badly injured in WWI, sues Pangloss for negligently causing Rupert's injuries. Can Rupert win?

28. Benedict Arnold, diplomat, is out riding, and sees his friend, George Washington, slumped beside a tree. Washington has caught a chill, and Arnold helps him up and takes him back to the Arnold home. There, Arnold applies leeches to Washington, which Arnold believes will suck out Washington's "bad blood" and cure him. Arnold's not a doctor, but he remembers hearing that applying leeches sucks out a sick person's "bad blood." In fact, however (and as most people know), antibiotics are the only proper way to treat a chill, and leeches are dangerous. Arnold's treatment worsens Washington's condition. When Washington sues him, Arnold defends on the grounds that he was under no duty to act at all, so he can't be liable. Who's correct?

29. Paula and Pam, who are friends, are out on a walk with Paula's 12-year-old daughter Sheila. While Sheila is walking 10 yards ahead of the two women, she starts to cross the street at a cross-walk. Dan, speeding, goes through a red light and strikes Sheila, knocking her down and paralyzing her from the waist down. Paula and Pam watch the whole event, horrified. Neither ever feels personally in danger of being hit, but both suffer symptoms of Post-Traumatic Stress Disorder for years afterward, with constant nightmares in which they relive seeing Sheila be terribly injured. Paula and Pam each sue Dan for their emotional distress. Under the majority approach to the relevant issues:

(a) Can Paula recover?

(b) Can Pam recover?

30. DrillCo is an oil company that drills for oil off the shore of Hilton Head, South Carolina. Due to DrillCo's negligence in performing the drilling, a large blow-out occurs, and oil is spread onto the shore. Some direct beachfront owners have oil wash up onto their property with harmful direct results to the land. Peg owns and runs a hotel that is two blocks from the waterfront; no part of the hotel is directly touched by the spill, and no guest or member is physically injured. Because the beach is rendered unsightly for a one-year clean-up period, occupancy at Peg's hotel (like that of most local hotel keepers) diminishes by 60%, leaving her with a loss of $100,000 in profits compared with the profits in a normal year. Assume that the facts constitute an actionable public nuisance. Under prevailing modern law, may Peg recover $100,000 in damages from DrillCo? (Assume there are no statutes on point.)

31. Redd Wightenbleu, soldier, survives six tours of duty in Europe during World War II, and is awarded the Purple Heart for bravery. After the war, he returns, victorious, to the states. During the V-E Day celebrations, he is on a sidewalk in front of the Booby von Trapp Hotel, when an armchair falls on his head from an upper story window. He sues the hotel for negligence. Will res ipsa loquitur be applicable?

32. In January 2022 Paula, a 42-year-old woman, asks Doc, a gastroenterologist, to perform a colonoscopy to check for colon cancer. Doc performs the procedure but fails to notice a polyp that, if biopsied, would show Stage 2 colon cancer. A gastroenterologist who performed a colonoscopy with the minimal competency required of G.I. specialists would have spotted the polyp, biopsied it, and recognized that it was cancerous and needed to be removed. In November 2022, a different physician diagnoses Paula with stage IV colon cancer (an invariably fatal condition), and she dies of that disease in January 2023. Had the polyp been removed and standard chemotherapy administered to Paula soon after January 2022, medical statistics show that Paula would have had a 40% chance of being cured and a 60% chance of dying within one year. Her estate is now suing Doc for medical malpractice. Doc defends by arguing (with factual correctness) that even had he correctly spotted Paula's cancerous polyp during the original examination and ensured that she got state-of-the-art treatment for it, more likely than not Paula would have died within a year anyway. Assume that under standard principles for computing damages, if the estate were able to show a more than 50% chance that prompt treatment would have cured her, the appropriate recovery would be $2 million. You represent the estate.

(a) Identify the legal theory that gives your client the best chance of recovering at least something in the action. ____________

(b) Is the legal theory you identified in Part (a) likely to succeed? ____________

(c) If that legal theory is accepted by the court, what is the appropriate amount of damages that the estate should be awarded? ____________

33. Vronsky is raking the leaves in his front yard, and he carelessly blocks the sidewalk with a huge pile of leaf-filled bags. As a result, Anna Karenina must walk out into the heavily-travelled street to get around the pile, and she is run over by a driver who negligently fails to stop in time. Will Vronsky be liable for Anna's injuries?

34. Spross Goose Plane Repairs negligently fixes Amelia Earheart's plane, such that the next time she flies, she crashes and breaks her leg. The leg is set in a cast. Shortly thereafter, she goes rowing on a local lake. The rowboat tips over, and she drowns, the cast pulling her down and making her unable to swim to safety. Will Sprooss be liable for her death?

35. The Hit & Run Railroad Company has tracks running adjacent to Old MacDonald's Farm. It negligently fails to erect fences on either side of the tracks; as a result, Old MacDonald is worried that if he lets his cows graze in the fields surrounding the tracks, they'll wander onto the tracks. But he lets them graze there anyway (he has nowhere else for them to graze), and one of them wanders onto the tracks and is struck by an oncoming train. Old Mac sues Hit & Run; Hit & Run asserts assumption of the risk as a defense. Who wins?

36. Al Bundy drives his car to the Mr. Walletwrench Service Station to get the oil changed. He drives the car into the garage, fumbles around in the back seat to get a newspaper, and opens the door to get out. He does not realize that the car has been hoisted ten feet into the air to facilitate the oil change; he steps into mid-air, falls to the ground, and is injured. He sues the station for negligence in hoisting the car with him in it. Mr. Walletwrench defends on contributory negligence grounds. (The jurisdiction applies this doctrine.) Who wins?

37. Diamond Jim Potluck visits the N-Palatable Diner. As he walks to the counter, he studies the menu board on the wall, looking for the meatloaf of the day. He does not notice that the cellar door, which opens out of the floor, is open. He falls in, injuring himself. Assuming the Diner was more negligent in leaving the cellar door open than Diamond Jim was in failing to notice it, in a contributory negligence jurisdiction will the Diner be liable for Jim's injuries?

38. Paul Revere and William Dawes are each on a casual midnight horseback ride. They run into each other; each is thrown from his respective horse and each is injured. Each sues the other for negligence. Revere suffers \$20,000 in damages and is found to be 25% at fault for the accident. Dawes, who was riding faster, is found to be 75% at fault and suffers \$30,000 in damages. Who owes what to whom, under a comparative negligence statute holding that a plaintiff who is more negligent than the defendant cannot recover?

39. Herman Hermit owns property secluded deep in the woods. Tris Passer, a trespasser, enters Herman's property and stumbles into a snake pit, which Herman has dug as a home for his pet snakes. It is full of thorny plants and disgusting, writhing snakes. When Tris finally escapes, terrified, she sues Herman for negligence. At common law, will she succeed?

40. A housing inspector arrives at the home of Snow White and the Seven Dwarfs. He's heard that more than four unrelated people live there, which is a violation of the local housing code. He asks to examine the basement, which is accessible via an unlit stairway. Snow White and the Dwarfs have been out picking apples, and unbeknownst to them a few of the apples are strewn about the stairway. The inspector trips on one of the apples, falls, and breaks his leg. Are Snow White and the Dwarfs liable for the inspector's injuries?

41. The Heerr Chick-Chick Fried Chicken Store is on premises rented from the Stately Real Estate Company. Heerr stages a publicity stunt whereby it hires a helicopter to drop chickens over the parking lot, foolishly anticipating that the chickens will drop harmlessly to the ground. The chickens fall, Splat! on the parking lot. One chicken lands on Renee Katzendogs, injuring her. Will Heerr be liable to Renee?

42. Harvey Bangbang owns the Shoot 'M Up Gun Store. He strictly instructs his employees not to load guns before demonstrating them to customers. One employee, Annie Oakleaf, is having a hard time selling a gun to a customer, Long John Silver. She loads a gun and fires at a target on the wall. She accidentally shoots Silver's leg off in the process. Will Harvey be liable for Annie's negligence?

43. The Plen-Tee O'Food Company organizes and runs country fairs. For the Lonornament County Fair, Plen-Tee contracts with Circe du Lune, a highly respected holiday-light-show company, to run a laser-guided light show at night. A light show of this sort is perfectly safe if proper techniques are used; but if safety standards are not followed, there is a considerable risk that onlookers will be blinded. Due to Circe's negligent failure to use standard laser precautions while running the show, Patron, an audience member, is blinded. Circe is jugment proof. Will Plen-Tee be liable for Patron's blindness?

44. Allnever Tell gives his four-year-old son, Willie, a real bow and arrow set for Christmas. Willie takes it outside and fires an arrow at his neighbor, Captain Hook, hitting him in the arm. Will Allnever be liable?

45. Caesar and Antony are fighting over possession of an asp which slithered into a street from the woods. As they wrestle over it, Cleopatra walks by, and they accidentally bump into her with the snake. It bites her and she is seriously injured. She sues Caesar (but not Antony) in negligence, and recovers a $100,000 judgment from him. Is Caesar likely to be entitled to contribution from Antony?

46. Pompeii Canned Goods, Inc., ships cans of Vesuvius Stew to the Volcano Grocery Store. The cans are not properly sealed, and are starting to bulge due to bacteria growth. Volcano doesn't notice and puts them on the shelves anyway. Most of the city comes down with salmonella poisoning as a result of eating the tainted stew. One purchaser who becomes violently ill, Frequentus Regurgitus, sues Volcano on a strict product liability theory, and recovers a $100,000 judgment. Is Volcano likely to be able to recover the entire $100,000 from Pompeii?

47. Bugs and Daffy are neighbors. Bugs keeps a Tasmanian Devil as a pet — a mean, vicious beast with slavering jaws. Bugs keeps the Devil in a heavy steel cage in the basement. One day, the Devil chews his way through the bars, tunnels out of the house, and goes to Daffy's house, biting him on the leg. When Daffy sues Bugs, Bugs claims he's not liable because he didn't realize the Devil's dangerous propensities, since the Devil had never escaped before. Who wins?

48. Guy Fawkes carefully burns a pile of leaves in his backyard; he moves all flammable objects away from the area, keeps a fire extinguisher on hand, and douses the flames occasionally to keep them under control. However, a strong gust of wind blows up, carrying sparks 50' to a neighbor's shed, setting it afire. The neighbor sues Guy, claiming he's strictly liable for the damage here. Is the neighbor correct?

49. Slip 'N' Slide Floor Polish, which is poisonous, looks like Flopsy Cola, a popular soft drink, and comes in a soda-like bottle with an easily removable lid. The bottle has a warning, reading: "This product is poisonous. Keep out of reach of children." Little Bobo, three years old, finds a bottle of polish under the kitchen sink, pops the lid off, and drinks the contents of the bottle, making himself seriously ill in the process. Could Slip 'N' Slide be strictly liable for Bobo's injuries?

50. Count Dracula enters the hospital for an operation to correct internal hemorrhaging. During the operation he receives a transfusion of blood infected with the HIV virus, and as a result he contracts AIDS. Can he successfully sue the hospital in strict product liability?

51. Americus Gothic is justly famous in his neighborhood for his delectable acorn jelly. He's not in the retail business, but occasionally he sells a jar to a lucky neighbor. Although Gothic is careful, one batch of his jelly is contaminated and, when his neighbor, Uneeda Purifyre, buys a jar and eats some, she becomes violently ill. Can Uneeda hold Gothic liable in strict liability?

52. Scrubby Dubdub Inc. manufactures equipment for automatic car washes. Spit 'N' Polish reconditions old car wash equipment, rebuilds it, and resells it. The Hot Wax Car Wash buys reconditioned equipment from Spit 'N' Polish. The equipment fails as Lydia Puttputt is getting her car washed. The brushes go crazy and smash her car. She is seriously injured as a result. She sues Scrubby Dubdub in strict liability. Could Scrubby Dubdub be liable?

53. Gore 'N Guts Byproducts opens a factory in which it processes entrails into pet food. Next door is the home of Charles Nifferoo, a fragrance analyst with a necessarily ultra-sensitive nose. Gore does what it can to control the smell associated with its product, but mildly foul odors occasionally emanate from the plant. While most of the neighbors find it a little unpleasant, it drives Charles' sophisticated nostrils crazy. Can Charles recover for private nuisance?

54. Ghosts have become a serious problem to society, including Phantasm Town. The town is happy when the Ghostbusters open up their ghost collection facility there, primarily because it creates jobs for 500 people, and the town is a victim of high unemployment. One of the unfortunate (and unavoidable) by products of ghost collection is that neighboring property occasionally gets "slimed." When Amelia Nebbish's nearby property is slimed, it causes $100,000 in permanent damage. She sues Ghostbusters for private nuisance, seeking damages and an injunction. What likely result?

55. Ratso is a small-time criminal who likes to hang around with shady types. John Dillinger circulates the lie that Ratso is a "stoolie" who's ratted on various local criminals to the police. Ratso sues John for defamation. Was John's statement "defamatory?"

56. Clara Bow is an up-and-coming Hollywood starlet. Brunhilda, jealous of Clara's success, spreads the lie that Clara has been intimate with an entire college football squad. When Clara sues Brunhilda for defamation, must she prove that she suffered pecuniary harm?

57. Socrates is up for parole. Defamitus testifies to the parole board that the parole should be denied because Socrates is a menace to society — he has been known to solicit sexual favors from young boys. This is not true, although Defamitus has good reason to believe it's true. Can Socrates successfully sue Defamitus for defamation?

58. Pierre Exposee, a reporter for the Paris *Clarion du Jour,* publishes a story that the Emperor Napoleon falsified his war record. Pierre has heard the story from a friend, and actually believes it. Nonetheless, the story is wrong — Napoleon's record is bona fide (as Pierre could have determined with only a little further investigation). However, Pierre has despised Napoleon ever since he stole Pierre's girlfriend, Josephine, and Pierre is glad the story hurt Napoleon's reputation. Napoleon sues Pierre for defamation. Can he recover?

59. Gil Ibble, reporter for the Washington Rag during the Lincoln administration, hears a guy in a bar say: "The only way Abe Lincoln got elected was by stuffing ballot boxes!" Ibble figures this would make a great story, and he writes it, fully believing it's true, and not unearthing any evidence to the contrary. In fact, "Honest Abe" didn't stuff any ballot boxes, and he sues Ibble for defamation. Can Abe recover?

60. Dumbo, a home-loving elephant who teaches piano for a living, likes to keep to himself. While reading the local paper one day, he's horrified to see an item in the gossip column, saying that he had just been in the hospital for ear implants. In fact, had the gossip columnist checked her sources, she would have found that Dumbo was in the hospital for an operation on his deviated septum; he's never had an ear implant, his ears are just *naturally* that large. Dumbo sues the paper for defamation. Can Dumbo recover? (Assume that defamation suits by animals follow the same rules as for humans.)

61. Mrs. Tolstoy is jealous of the beautiful and popular Anna Karenina. In an effort to destroy her reputation, Mrs. Tolstoy circulates the story that Anna is an adulteress — she's having an affair with Vronsky. Will the fact that this is true absolve Mrs. Tolstoy from liability, even though she was trying to wreck Anna's reputation?

62. In Smalltown USA, Martha Washington tells her neighbor, Betsy Ross, "Dolly Madison told me Benedict Arnold is a Communist." Arnold is not a Communist, and he sues Washington for defamation. She asserts truth as a defense, proving that Madison, in fact, told her Arnold is a Communist. Will the defense prevail?

63. To cash in on the allure of the famous spy Mata Hari, the Madame X Lingerie Company introduces a line of Mata Hari jewelled bras without Mata Hari's permission. Has the Company committed an invasion of privacy? If so, of what sort?

64. Mr. Magoo is driving his car when he hits a pedestrian, Elastic Man. Elastic files a personal injury claim against Magoo, claiming he's wheelchair bound. Magoo's insurance investigator doesn't believe Elastic's as injured as he says he is. The investigator gets a tip that Elastic's going to be at the park for a picnic, and sure enough, at the appointed time, Elastic shows up at the park. The investigator sits 50 yards away, taking photographs of Elastic as he runs around and contorts himself into a pretzel. Someone mentions to Elastic that he's being photographed. He sues the investigator for invasion of privacy. Will Elastic recover? If so, for what variety of invasion?

65. Noah and Judas are neighbors, who frequently do each other favors. One night, Judas is visiting Noah, and, as he leaves, Noah says: "I'll come out with you as far as the barn. It looks like rain, and I want to make sure the unicorns are securely shut in the barn." Judas says, "Forget it. I'll check on my way home." Judas has no intention of checking, figuring Noah's just being a worrywart. In fact, the unicorns are not securely penned, and they run away and drown in the subsequent flood. Had they been penned, they would have survived. Noah sues Judas for misrepresentation. Judas claims he didn't misrepresent a past or present fact, so the claim will not lie. Who's correct?

66. Betty Omen is considering buying passage on the first voyage of the Titanic. She is at a cocktail party and sees Captain Smith, who is going to command the voyage. Betty walks over and asks the Captain, "Is the Titanic safe?" He responds, "Madame, the Titanic is capable of surviving any impact whatsoever — missiles, nuclear weapons, icebergs, you name it." In fact, Smith doesn't know if this is true; he hasn't seen the ship itself or any technical specifications. Her worries calmed, Betty buys a ticket. The Titanic sinks, but Betty survives. She sues Smith, who has also survived, for intentional misrepresentation. Will she win?

67. Nysen Shiny, travelling cookware salesman, knocks on the door of the Gingerbread House, where Wicked Witch lives. She invites him in. When he tells her he sells cookware, she says, "Oh, good. Do you have a pot large enough to hold two small children?" He responds, "Oh, yes. Our HG pot is the one for you." He excuses himself to make a phone call, and Witch rifles through his briefcase, finding a spec sheet which shows that the HG pot is clearly not large enough to hold two children, and in fact there aren't any that can. However, when Nysen returns, Witch sweetly orders the HG pot, figuring a pot big enough for one kid at a time will have to suffice. The pot arrives, and Witch sues Nysen for misrepresentation. Assume that Witch suffered financial loss from the fact that she could boil only one kid at a time (lower productivity, translating to loss of revenue from sale of magic potions made from the boiled children). Can Witch recover?

68. E. F. Mutton, the hottest stock broker in New Zealand, is at a cocktail party in the U.S. Yves Dropper, another guest at the party, overhears Mutton telling a third guest, Little Lamb, that, based on his confidential sources, the Embraceable Ewe Sweater Company is about to announce a huge quarterly profit, and it's a great time to invest. In fact, Mutton knows that Embraceable Ewe lost big bucks, and Mutton is just trying to buy time in which to unload his own shares. Relying on his statement, Yves invests, and takes a "bleating" when the market drops. Is Mutton liable to Yves for deceit?

69. Vivien Lee is at a Chinese restaurant, and she gets a fortune cookie for dessert. The fortune inside reads: "A phone call tomorrow will make you a millionaire." Thrilled, Vivien stays home all day for the phone call. In the process, she misses her audition for a Civil War movie. The phone call never comes. Furious, she visits her lawyer, Sid Sharky, and he tells her: "You have a valid criminal fraud case against the fortune cookie company." She presses criminal charges against the Phu Yuc Fortune Cookie Company, which produced the fortune. The case is dismissed, and Phu Yuc sues Vivien for malicious prosecution. Will Yuc prevail?

70. Hansel and Gretel are law students at the Gingerbread Law School. There is a bar review expo at school, where all the competing bar review courses display their wares on tables in an auditorium, in an attempt to sign up students. Hansel and Gretel are standing at the Barcrusher Bar Review table, avidly listening to a sales pitch. They're just about to sign up, pen in hand, when Wicked Witch walks over to them and says, "Don't sign up for this before you talk to me about <u>my</u> course. My materials are better than these; they work like magic. Anyway, I have free chocolate chip cookies and beer at my table." (Assume that these statement are arguably true — they're not clear misstatements of the facts.) Witch leads them away by the elbow, and they wind up signing up for Witch's course instead of Barcrusher's. What's Barcrusher's best claim against Witch, and will it succeed?

ANSWERS TO SHORT-ANSWER QUESTIONS

Note: References of the form "Ch.x..." (e.g., "Ch.2(IV)(A)(1)") are to the full-length *Emanuel Law Outlines: Torts*, Eleventh Edition, 2024.

1. Yes. The distinction here is between intent and motive. Intent is the desire to cause a certain immediate result; motive is why the tortfeasor chose to behave a certain way. A battery is the intentional infliction of a harmful or offensive bodily contact. The required intent is the intent to make a contact (or to create an apprehension of a contact). It is not necessary that the defendant desire to harm the plaintiff, as long as he intends the contact and the contact is in fact harmful or offensive. The harmful touching here was mis-setting the arm; Juliet voluntarily set the arm as she did, so she satisfies the intent element of battery. Her motive was to help, but that by itself won't relieve her of liability. Ch.2(IV).

NOTE: Motive isn't an element of any intentional tort, but it can be relevant. It can aggravate, mitigate, or excuse a tort. For instance, acting with malice can justify "punitive" damages. Acting in self-defense can excuse a tort. But there are other motives that don't have an impact on liability for intentional torts. For instance, say Romeo kissed Juliet without her consent. The fact that his motive was to compliment her wouldn't mitigate his liability to her. Similarly, if Juliet pushed Romeo as a joke, the fact that she intended only a joke doesn't change the nature of the act; it's still a battery. Ch.2(IV)(A)(1).

2. Yes. The "intent" requirement for battery is satisfied if D either (a) intended to cause a harmful or offensive contact; *or* (b) intended to cause in another person an apprehension of a harmful or offensive contact. Where D's conduct falls within (b), D will be liable for battery if the conduct causes (directly or indirectly) a harmful or offensive contact. Here, even though the attack itself was unintended, the harmful contact was the result of Calvin's intentional act (taking the mean tiger out and putting it near Susie to frighten her). Since Calvin "set the force [the tiger] in motion," he'll be liable for battery. Ch.2(IV)(D)(1).

3. No. Assault is an "intentional" tort, and the intent required is that D either desired to cause a harmful-or-offensive contact, or desired to place P or another in apprehension of such a contact. Here, Speed Racer may have intended to drive (and even intended to drive extremely fast), but he didn't intend either to hit anyone or frighten anyone, so there's no assault.

RELATED ISSUE: Say that as Speed Racer approaches the stop sign, he sees Chim-Chim, and speeds up with the idea of scaring the bejesus out of Chim-Chim. Since Speed *intends* to scare Chim-Chim, there *would* be an assault.

RELATED ISSUE: Say that as Speed Racer approaches the stop sign, he sees Chim-Chim and, hoping to scare Chim-Chim, aims his car at him, intending to swerve away at the last moment. The car skids and hits Chim-Chim. Speed would be liable for battery (as well as assault) even though he didn't intend to hit Chim Chim, because he intended to *scare* him and he did in fact *touch* him, and that's enough for a battery.

4. **Yes.** A false imprisonment claim requires intentional confinement to a bounded area. The restraint needn't be physical; it can be accomplished by duress. Wrongfully keeping the plaintiff's valuable property is regarded as one type of duress that qualifies.

RELATED ISSUE: The attendant could also be liable for trespass to chattels, by refusing to surrender the chattel on demand of one with the right to possession when the demand is made. (The conduct is probably insufficiently serious for a conversion claim, however.)

5. **No.** False imprisonment is the intentional confinement of someone to a bounded area. Here, Pocahontas didn't intend to confine Smith; she did so accidentally. Without intent, she can't be liable for false imprisonment. At best, she'd be liable for negligence.

RELATED ISSUE: Say instead that Pocahontas is really paranoid about the threat of shoplifting, and falsely and unreasonably believes that Smith stuck one of the plastic tomahawks in his satchel without paying for it. She locks the doors to the shop (intending to confine Smith), and doesn't realize that another customer, John Rolfe, is in the store. If she's liable to Smith for false imprisonment, she'd be liable to Rolfe, as well — even though she didn't intend to confine him. That's because of "transferred intent." When someone intends (to commit a tort against one person, but injury to another results, the actor's intent is said to be "transferred" from the intended victim to the actual one for purposes of establishing an intentional tort. Here, Pocahontas confined Rolfe as well as her intended victim, Smith, so her intent towards Smith will be "transferred" to Rolfe. (Note, by the way, that Pocahontas didn't have a right to detain Smith to investigate for shoplifting, because her belief that he stole something was unreasonable. Detention for shoplifting investigations is only permissible if the merchant's suspicion is reasonable.)

6. **No.** So long as the defendant's conduct has produced serious emotional distress, the fact that that distress is not manifested by physical symptoms (e.g., sleeplessness, nausea, or ulcers) is not fatal to the claim. (Obviously, the presence of physical symptoms makes the distress easier to prove, but physical harm is not actually required.)

On the other hand, the distress must be severe; mere unhappiness, humiliation, or a couple of sleepless nights won't suffice. In general, the more objectively outrageous the conduct, the less proof of great distress is required. Max's conduct here is so completely outrageous that Ethel probably won't need very detailed proof of her distress.

7. **Marc Antony, probably.** Even where conduct is not intentional, but only reckless — that is, the defendant proceeds with a conscious disregard of a high probability that emotional distress will result — most courts hold that a claim for IIED will lie. See, e.g., *Blakeley v. Shortal's Estate*.

NOTE: A minority of courts hold that recklessness is not sufficient, and require intent (that is, intending emotional distress or knowing that it will result from the outrageous conduct).

8. **Yes.** Trespass to land requires intentional physical invasion of another's land. It is defendant's simple intent to enter land that in fact belongs to the plaintiff— not defendant's intent to do so wrongfully — that is the basis of liability. To put it another way, a mistake of fact — even a reasonable one — about who owns the land is no defense to a trespass-to-land claim. Thus even if Standish had hired the best surveyor in the county and the surveyor had (mistakenly) told Standish that Standish owned the land in question, Standish would still lose. PK §13

at 73.

RELATED ISSUE: Remember that Big Foot doesn't have to prove damages as part of his prima facie case — damages don't have to be proven in order to prevail on a trespass to land claim (and Big Foot can recover nominal damages if he can't prove actual damages).

9. Yes. Trespass to chattels consists of intentionally interfering with personal property in someone else's possession. The issue here is whether mistake of fact is a defense to trespass to chattels. In fact, it's not. It's intent to do the act which creates the interference that's required — not to do so *wrongfully*.

NOTE: H. G. Wells won't have to prove actual damages here, because the type of trespass involved was "dispossession" as opposed to "intermeddling." Loss of possession itself, regardless of the length of time involved, is sufficient to satisfy the damage requirement of a trespass to chattels claim. Had Ripper merely interfered with the time machine — for instance, by putting a bumper sticker on it — Wells would have to prove actual damages as part of his trespass claim.

10. Wright's right. Conversion is an intentional interference with the plaintiff's personal property that is so substantial that it's fair to require the defendant to pay the property's full value. Severe damage, destruction, or misuse all qualify as a misappropriation serious enough to constitute conversion. It doesn't matter that the initial entrustment of possession to D was with P's consent; so long as the interference with P's possessory rights went beyond what was consented-to (here, Wright didn't consent to a melt-down), there can be a conversion.

SIMILAR SITUATION: Say Fairy Godmother turns Farmer Brown's coach into a pumpkin. She will be liable for conversion, since *substantial change* to the chattel is sufficient to justify the claim.

11. Yes, he's committed a battery. The focus here is on the role consent plays in battery. Consent is a valid defense to almost every tort, but only within the scope of the conduct the victim consented to, or conduct closely related to that consent. Here, Anne gave her consent to having her sinuses drained. Removing her extra finger would be well outside the scope of her consent, *and since no emergency situation existed to justify it,* Plasty will be liable for battery. Ch.4(II)(E)(2).

NOTE: Don't interpret this too broadly. Many courts have held that during an operation, the plaintiff's consent extends to anything the surgeon considers necessary during the operation (e.g., in an appendicitis operation, the surgeon can puncture cysts he discovers on the plaintiff's ovaries, since that's considered within the plaintiff's consent to the appendicitis operation). *Kennedy v. Parrott* (NC 1956).

12. Probably not. Where people participate in an organized sport, each will be held to have impliedly consented to those harmful or offensive bodily contacts that are an ***ordinary part of the give-and-take of the game,*** even if the contact violates the rules of the game. But a player will generally *not* be held to have impliedly consented to actions by fellow competitors that are "unrelated to the normal method of playing the game," and that are done without any competitive purpose. Here, if Lemeow had, say, tripped Greatsky in an attempt to stop him from scoring, the court would probably hold that Greatsky impliedly consented to that conduct, even though it constituted a foul, because the contact was part of the ordinary give-and-take of professional hockey, and was done for competitive purposes. But when Lemeow struck Greatsky out of frustration, and not until the play was over, a court would likely hold that Lemeow's action was "unrelated to the normal method of playing the game," was not done with a competitive purpose, and was therefore not covered by the consent that Greatsky will be found to have impliedly given by entering the league. Cf. *Hackbart v. Cincinnati Bengals, Inc.* (where one football player struck another out of anger after the play was over, this was not a contact to which the person struck impliedly consented).

13. Yes. The rule on fraud as it relates to consent is that it only invalidates consent if it relates to an *essential* matter, not a collateral one (i.e., an unimportant one). The fraud here relates to a collateral matter, not an essential one; as such, the consent is valid.

RELATED ISSUE: Had Axel not, in fact, been a magician, the fraud would have related to an essential matter and the consent would have been invalid, and Axel would be liable for battery.

Ch.4(II)(F)(1)(a).

14. Lorena. One may not use deadly force (i.e., force intended or likely to cause death or serious bodily injury) unless one is in danger of death or serious bodily harm. Lorena's use of the knife here certainly qualifies as deadly force (even though she was only trying to injure, not kill, Ron). However, courts hold that the threat of rape alone — even if there is no overt threat of additional bodily injury — constitutes a threat of serious bodily injury. Rest. 2d §65(1)(b). Since Lorena did not use more force than the situation seemed to require, she qualifies for the privilege of self-defense.

15. No. The privilege of self-defense only allows one to use reasonable force to prevent threatened harmful/offensive contact or confinement. When Christian set Bligh adrift there was no longer a threat of danger; it was retaliation, which is *not* a valid ground for self-defense. Ch.4(III)(E)(1).

16. Hamilton wins. Self-defense gives one the privilege to use reasonable force to prevent threatened harmful or offensive contact or confinement. The focus here is on whether insults alone can justify the use of force in self-defense, and the rule is that they can't. But don't interpret this too broadly! Insults (or other types of words) *can* help create a threat of imminent physical harm, especially when they're accompanied by threatening physical gestures. Say, for instance, that Hamilton hadn't had his hands full, but rather had waved a fist at Burr in a menacing way as he spoke to him. In *that* case, self-defense would probably be justified, because there's a threat of physical harm, and not just verbal provocation. Cf. Rest. 2d of Torts §69.

17. No. The focus here is on the how the defendant's *mistake* impacts his assertion of the "defense of property" privilege. The answer depends on what it is the defendant's mistaken about. Mistake *negates* the privilege if the mistake consists of a false (even if reasonable) belief that the intruder is not privileged to enter the land. That's the case here; Dorothy entered Witch's land out of necessity, and that's a privilege. Witch was mistaken about Dorothy's privilege to enter, and that mistake negates Witch's defense of property privilege. That means she'll be liable to Dorothy.

RELATED ISSUE: But a reasonable mistake as to *whether force is necessary* will leave the privilege *intact*. For instance, let's say Dorothy really was trying to steal the brooms, but she didn't have any weapons and force wouldn't have been necessary to subdue her. If Witch mistakenly believed force was necessary and it wasn't, and that mistake was reasonable, she'll be able to rely on "defense of property" as a defense.

18. Yes, because the detention wasn't reasonable; she was needlessly humiliated. Although stores have a right to temporarily detain those reasonably suspected of shoplifting, the privilege is limited. It cannot be lengthy (the few minutes here seem reasonable); it cannot exceed the scope of a brief investigation (e.g., the storekeeper cannot use the detention to attempt to coerce payment for the items); and it cannot involve public humiliation. Here Portentia was publicly humiliated by the detective, and so she may have an intentional infliction of emotional distress claim. She may also have a slander claim (since other shoppers heard the false accusation).

RELATED ISSUE: A common claim in instances like this is for false imprisonment. However, since Portentia was not held anywhere for an appreciable length of time, such a claim wouldn't exist here. But Portentia could sue for slander.

19. No. The crew has a private necessity defense, because it seemed necessary to invade Snively's dock to avoid death or serious harm, and the invasion they committed was substantially less serious than the injury they faced. NOTE: Private necessity is analogous to self-defense, but there the *plaintiff* is the source of the threat.

NOTE: The privilege of necessity means the landowner cannot take even what would otherwise be *lawful* action against the entrant. So if Snively turned the boat out to sea, and it was destroyed, Snively would be liable for conversion.

NOTE: The privilege only lasts until the danger has passed. Any excess = trespass.

RELATED ISSUE: Any loss caused to the landowner must be compensated; the private necessity privilege is *limited.*

20. No, because Lady Macbeth didn't commit the crime. When it comes to felonies, a private citizen has a privilege of legal authority only if a felony was in fact committed (with no room for a reasonable mistake), and he's got reasonable grounds to believe the person in question committed it. The problem here is that no felony was in fact committed. As a result, Shakespeare won't have a defense based on legal authority even though his mistake may have been "reasonable." Ch.4(IX)(B)(2)(b).

RELATED ISSUE: Say that Shakespeare had been a police officer, and not a private citizen. Then he <u>would</u> have a defense based on legal authority. That's because the privilege of legal authority for a police officer encompasses a reasonable mistake as to whether a felony was actually committed.

RELATED ISSUE: Say that a murder *had* actually taken place nearby, and the perpetrator had escaped. But let's say that Lady Macbeth is innocent; she really did get bloody at her butcher shop job. Whether or not Shakespeare was a police officer, he would have a good "legal authority" defense. That's because where a felony has in fact been committed, a private citizen won't lose the "legal authority" privilege by arresting the person he reasonably (but wrongly) believes committed the crime.

21. Yes. The rule is that the defendant is responsible for all personal injury to the plaintiff flowing from his wrongful conduct, even if the injury is surprisingly severe. Here, King's Man committed a battery; he intentionally acted to cause harmful or offensive contact with Humpty, so he is responsible for all personal injuries flowing from his conduct. This is known as the "eggshell skull" theory — particularly apropos when applied to Humpty Dumpty!

NOTE: Note that it doesn't matter that King's Man only wanted to embarrass Humpty; his motive won't relieve him of liability. His action could still constitute a battery if he intended the act that brought about harmful or offensive contact, or even if he only intended to create the *apprehension* of such contact.

NOTE: The "eggshell skull" theory applies to all intentional torts, as well as negligence. It is sometimes summed up by the phrase "The defendant takes his plaintiff as he finds him."

22. No. One of the peculiarities of our negligence system is that it usually focuses on the actor's level of care in *carrying out* an activity, rather than on the social utility of the actor's *decision* to engage in the activity at all. Thus, a defendant who carelessly engages in a socially-useful (and low-risk) activity is likely to be liable for damages; whereas one who carefully engages in a risky activity that is not socially beneficial is not likely to be liable. Even though there was virtually no social utility in Arthur's ride, he rode "carefully," in the sense that he was *attentive*. Therefore, he will not be liable for negligence. Ch.5(III)(F).

23. The obligation to operate the Batmobile in the way a reasonable adult of ordinary intelligence would have operated it, even though Batboy is only thirteen. Although the duty owed by a child is *generally* measured as that of an ordinary child of like age, intelligence, education and experience, when children undertake adult activities, like driving cars, they are held to an adult standard of care.

24. Yes. Although custom is admissible as evidence of a minimum standard of due care, it is not conclusive because, as here, an entire industry is capable of negligence. The industry standard here is likely motivated by cost considerations and clearly not by safety concerns; as such, the custom cannot control as a minimum standard of care. Ch.5(IV)(D)(1).

25. No, because Han-dee's violating the Sunday closing law was not the cause of Pierre's injuries. In order for a violation of a criminal statute to provide the basis of a civil negligence claim, the breach of the statute must have caused the injury in question. Here, it didn't. Thus, it is irrelevant in determining Han-dee's liability for his injuries.

RELATED ISSUE: If Pierre sued Han-dee for its negligence in not cleaning up the ketchup earlier, he would probably succeed, since the "hours" it had been there suggest that the store was on notice that there was a danger to customers, and Han-dee carelessly ignored it.

26. Yes, because most jurisdictions view violation of a safety standard embodied in a criminal statute as being conclusive proof of negligence ("negligence per se"), as long as the statute was formulated for the purpose of preventing the kind of harm in question, and the plaintiff is a member of the class the legislature intended to protect. Since the facts tell you to assume that the statute's purpose is to prevent pedestrian accidents involving stolen saucers, and since Spacely is indeed a pedestrian injured in such an accident, the above requirements are satisfied, and Jetson will be automatically deemed to have been negligent.

There are certain situations in which D's non-compliance with the statute will ordinarily be excused (and negligence per se not applied), but none applies to Jetson here:

1. The violation was reasonable in light of D's childhood, physical disability, or physical incapacitation.
2. D reasonably attempted to comply. (E.g., the doorlock suddenly broke and Jetson couldn't get it to work right away).
3. D neither knew nor should have known of the factual circumstances that rendered the statute applicable. (E.g., after Jetson left the car locked, his friend unlocked it without Jetson's knowing about it).
4. The statute's requirements were presented in a confusing way to the public. (E.g., the statute said that it applied only to "cars," and a reasonable person wouldn't know whether a space saucer was a car.)
5. Compliance with the statute would have been more dangerous than violation.

Rest. 3d (Liab. for Phys. & Emot. Harm) §15.

MINORITY RULES: There are two minority viewpoints. One is that breach of statute, where applicable, merely raises a rebuttable presumption of negligence; the other is that the violation should be treated as merely evidence of negligence. Ch.5(VIII).

27. No. Negligence requires duty, breach, causation, and damages. There is no negligence here because Pangloss didn't have a duty to Rupert, anymore than he had such a duty to all the other millions who were harmed in some way by the War. An individual owes a duty only to prevent the foreseeable risk of injury to one in plaintiff's position. In this case, injury to millions of war-injured people is not a foreseeable result of dropping a peanut in a gun — which is really saying that, as a matter of policy, Pangloss will not be held liable for such widespread damages on the basis of his act. (This result is often expressed in terms of proximate cause rather than duty: one is liable only for those consequences that one's carelessness proximately caused.) Ch.6(III).

NOTE: The level of fault bears on the scope of duty. Thus, intentional wrongdoers are commonly held liable for consequences beyond the foreseeable risk created; and, in turn, negligent tortfeasors are responsible for a broader scope of potential damage than those subject to strict liability.

28. Washington. Initially, Arnold was under no duty to act — when he first saw Washington, he could have left him as he found him, without incurring liability. But once he took an affirmative act in an effort to help (in torts lingo, once he "undertook" to help), he then had the obligation to do so in a reasonable, non-negligent way. Consequently, he is liable for using a treatment method that an ordinary citizen of reasonable care would have known was unsafe. Ch.8(II)(A).

29. (a) Yes. Most modern courts allow a bystander to recover for pure emotional distress, if the bystander watches a close relative be severely injured. See, e.g., Rest. 3d (Liab. Phys. & Emot. Harm), §48, which says that a defendant who "causes ***sudden serious bodily injury to a third person***" will be liable for "serious emotional harm" caused to a plaintiff who "***perceives the event contemporaneously***" and who is a "***close family member***" of the third person who suffers the bodily injury. Since the person that Paula watched suffer the "sudden serious bodily injure" was her daughter, Paula meets the "close family member" requirement, and can recover for her pure emotional distress. And that's true even though Paula was never herself within the "zone of danger," i.e., never close enough to the speeding car that she feared that she herself would be hit.

(b) No. If Pam had herself been at some point within the "zone of danger" from the speeding car, most courts would allow her to recover her emotional distress, both distress at the danger to Pam herself and distress at the actual injury to Sheila. But since Pam was never physically in danger, a different rule applies. Under the rule described in sub-paragraph (a) above, Pam would be able to recover for distress at seeing Sheila be injured only if Pam was a "close family member" of Sheila. Since Pam is not a close family member of Sheila, neither the above rule nor any other rule would furnish an exception to the general rule that one may not recover for emotional distress at witnessing, from a safe position, a severe injury to another.

30. No. As a general rule, tortfeasors are not liable to plaintiffs for negligently-caused ***pure economic loss***, i.e., loss that does not occur in conjunction with any property damage or physical injury to that plaintiff. See, e.g., Rest. 3d of Torts (Liab. for Econ. Loss), §7, stating the general rule that "a claimant cannot recover for economic loss caused by (a) unintentional personal injury to another party; or (b) unintentional injury to property in which the claimant has no proprietary interest." This rule applies here, because the facts tell us that DrillCo has negligently caused oil damage to the property of certain beach-front owners, but that there has been no direct property damage to any property in which Peg has a "proprietary interest." (There's no indication that she has any financial interest in any of the beach-front property that was physically affected by the spill.) Therefore, the Restatement — and most courts — would not allow Peg to recover for her pure economic loss, despite the fact that DrillCo's negligence was the factual and proximate cause of that loss. There are some exceptions to this general principle of "no recovery for pure economic loss," but none of those exceptions applies here.

Note, by the way, that the question tells you to assume that there are ***no statutes*** on point. This is an important assumption, because in fact, there *is* a federal statute on point: the federal Oil Pollution Act, 33 U.S.C. §2702 et seq, gives many people and businesses who suffer economic losses from a negligently-caused oil spill into a navigable waterway the right to recover those losses, even if the claimant did not own property that was physically damaged by the spill. So under the OPA, Peg *would* be able to recover her lost profits.

31. No. *Res ipsa loquitur* requires an event that would not normally have occurred in the absence of negligence; the instrumentality must have been in the exclusive control of the defendant; and the plaintiff must not have voluntarily contributed to his injury. The element missing here is the exclusivity of control. Since guests have at least some control over the furniture in hotel rooms, res ipsa loquitur doesn't apply here.

NOTE: The hotel *could* be liable in negligence for failing to take reasonable steps to adequately protect passersby; it's just that res ipsa loquitur isn't the means by which the negligence claim would be proven.

RELATED ISSUE: The hotel could not be strictly liable for Redd's injuries, even if the actual tortfeasor couldn't be identified.

32. (a) The "value of a chance" theory. Under this theory, if accepted by the court, the estate is entitled to recover for a special type of injury, namely, the injury of being deprived of the opportunity (or "chance") of obtaining a better outcome (a cure) than the early death that occurred.

(b) Yes, probably. Most courts that have considered the matter in the last few decades apply the value of a chance theory. Therefore, the estate can recover even though it is "less likely than not" that Doc's negligence was the actual and proximate cause of Paula's death. In other words, the usual rule that a plaintiff cannot recover unless she can show that the defendant more likely than not caused her injury is modified in the medical-malpractice situation to view the injury not as being "deprived of a cure," but rather, being "deprived of the [less than 50/50] chance of a cure."

(c) $800,000. In value-of-a-chance cases, the court takes the value that the claim would have had if P proved that the injury was more likely than not caused by D's malpractice, and multiplies that number by the percentage chance that a favorable result (e.g., a cure) would have occurred had there been no malpractice. Thus the formula is:

> ***$2 Million*** [value of claim if there was a more-than-50% chance that Paula would have been saved by competent and timely treatment] *times* ***40%*** [the likelihood that such treatment would have cured her].

33. Yes, because one is responsible for those intervening causes that are considered "foreseeable." The negligence of drivers on heavily-travelled streets, as here, would be considered foreseeable. What this tells you is that others' negligence *can* be considered foreseeable. Ch.6(III).

34. No, probably. Negligent defendants are liable for damages from foreseeable intervening causes. Where plaintiff's initial injury leaves him susceptible to subsequent diseases or injury, defendant will be liable for these. However, Amelia's death here was not the result of her weakened condition. Drowning is so abnormal a consequence of a broken leg that it will probably be considered a "superseding" cause, relieving Sprooss of liability for Amelia's death.

RELATED ISSUE: If Amelia had tripped while learning to walk again, and broken her hip, the subsequent injury would be considered "foreseeable" and Sprooss would be liable.

35. Old MacDonald. Assumption of the risk requires that plaintiff voluntarily and knowingly undertake a risk. In this instance, Old Mac did know the danger, and subjected his cows to it; however, the element missing is the voluntariness. Old Mac has a right to a moo-moo here and a moo-moo there, here a moo, there a moo, everywhere a moo-moo on his own farm, and Hit & Run can't deny him this right.

36. Mr. Walletwrench. Contributory negligence bars recovery where plaintiff doesn't behave reasonably to protect himself from injury, and he is injured as a result. Here, reasonable behavior would include "looking before you leap," so to speak. Since Bundy didn't do so, and this was a substantial factor in his injury, Mr. Walletwrench won't be liable.

37. No. Under contributory negligence, any negligence on plaintiff's part bars recovery, regardless of how insignificant it is compared to defendant's negligence.

38. Dawes owes Revere $15,000. Revere is only entitled to the portion of his damages caused by Dawes. Since he was 25% responsible, he is entitled to 75% of his damages: .75 x 20,000 = $15,000. Dawes gets no offset by virtue of his own claim: under this "modified" comparative negligence statute (P can't recover anything if he's more negligent than D), Dawes-as-plaintiff is more negligent than Revere-as-defendant, and so collects nothing on his claim. Therefore, Dawes must write Revere a check for $15,000.

COMPARE: Suppose the state had had a "pure" comparative negligence statute (i.e., one in which P can recover from D even if his fault is much greater than D's). In that event, Dawes would be entitled to 25% of $30,000 (or $7,500), which would be subtracted from Revere's $15,000, leaving Revere a net recovery of $7,500.

39. No. Negligence requires duty, breach, causation, and damages. The key here is duty, and to what extent Herman as a landowner owed Tris a duty. Tris was a trespasser, of which there are two types: discovered and undiscovered. The facts suggest (though they don't conclusively establish) that Tris was an "undiscovered trespasser." If so, under the common-law rule Herman owed Tris *no duty at all.* An undiscovered trespasser represents the very lowest category — in terms of the owner's duty to him — of individuals who enter land. (The rule which imposes a duty on landowners for natural conditions which the owner has *altered* applies only to people *outside* the land, so it doesn't apply here.)

RELATED ISSUE: A *"discovered"* trespasser is owed the duty of reasonable care for the trespasser's safety, which is generally satisfied by a warning (e.g., a sign) of dangers that are known to the landowner and that are unlikely to be discovered by the trespasser.

NOTE: Had the hazard been natural (instead of man-made), no liability would attach even if Tris had been discovered. The most common exception to the "no liability for natural conditions" rule is the case of urban landowners, who must inspect and maintain trees on their property to ensure the trees will not fall on others' property or on a public highway.

40. Yes, probably — it depends on whether the inspector was an invitee. If the inspector was a "licensee" (one who enters the land with owner's consent but without a business purpose), the only duty owed to him was to warn him of known dangerous conditions. So if he's considered a licensee, Snow White & Co. aren't liable for his injuries because they didn't know about the apples. If, however, he was an "invitee" (one who enters by express or implied invitation to conduct business with the owner, or enters for purposes for which the land is held open to the public), he could reasonably expect that the owner had made the premises safe for him. So if he was an invitee, Snow White's duty was to inspect for dangerous conditions *and* warn or make safe (a warning being sufficient under most circumstances). Thus if the inspector is considered an invitee, Snow White & Co. will be liable for his injuries. Most courts treat those who visit during normal hours and under normal circumstances, like this, as *invitees*, making it likely that Snow White & Co. will be liable.

NOTE: If the condition is so obvious that the invitee/licensee should have been aware of it, there is no liability on the landowner (since a warning is superfluous).

41. Yes. Lessees of property are liable to the same extent as landowners. Thus, since Renee is an invitee, Heerr must warn her of known dangers ("Warning: Falling Chickens") and inspect the premises to make them safe for her. Dropping a chicken on her head would constitute a breach of Heerr's duty. Ch.9(VIII)(A).

42. Yes, even though Annie had strict instructions not to load the gun. Since the tort occurred within the scope of the employment relationship, and Annie was serving Harvey's objectives (albeit in a prohibited way), Harvey will be liable. To decide otherwise would undermine vicarious liability in general, since employers would almost always escape liability by giving their employees careful instructions.

NOTE: However, an employee's doing what he is expressly told not to do will often be evidence (but non-dispositive) that he was acting outside the scope of employment.

43. Yes. Although employers are in general not vicariously liable for the torts of their independent contractors, they *are* liable in a number of special situations. One of those situations is where the work being delegated to the independent contractor poses a "peculiar risk" of physical harm if not properly done. That's the case here. So even though this was not an ultra-hazardous activity (and Circe would be liable only if negligent, as it was), the mere fact that the activity posed a particular risk of harm if not conducted properly means that Plen-Tee is vicariously liable for the negligence of its independent contractor, Circe. Notice that this result occurs even though Circe was apparently well-qualified for the job when picked by Plen-Tee (so that Plen-Tee was not directly negligent in its own behavior regarding the contractor).

44. Yes. As a general rule, parents are not vicariously liable for their children's torts. However, parents can be *directly* liable for their children's torts under certain circumstances. One such circumstance exists here: when a parent allows the child to use a dangerous object which the child lacks the maturity and judgment to use safely, the parent will be liable for torts committed with the object. It's clearly unreasonable to give a four-year-old a real bow and arrow. That makes Allnever negligent, and makes him liable for Hook's injuries.

45. Yes. Where joint tortfeasors act in concert and their negligence causes harm, and the plaintiff only sues one of the tortfeasors, that tortfeasor can seek contribution (partial reimbursement) from the other joint tortfeasor(s). If the jurisdiction follows comparative negligence, the court will probably apportion the liability between the two in proportion to their fault. In a non-comparative-negligence jurisdiction (and in some comparative-negligence states), the court will split the liability evenly regardless of which tortfeasor was most at fault. Without the doctrine of contribution (which applies in most but not all states), Caesar could not recover anything from Antony, since this is a case of "joint liability": Caesar and Antony acted in concert, and the damages are indivisible. Ch.7(IV)(B).

NOTE: Since Cleopatra recovered the entire judgment from Caesar, her claim has been "satisfied," and she can't proceed against Antony. Also, note that Cleopatra could have sued Caesar and Antony in the same lawsuit, recovered a judgment against them, and then proceeded to collect from either one or partially from both — her choice — until her claim was satisfied. Finally, note that the rule of "contribution" is not applicable to intentional torts.

RELATED ISSUE: Say Antony and Caesar each had an asp, and each negligently let his asp bite Cleo, injuring her with two separate wounds. The damages would be divisible, and thus joint liability would not apply. Ch.7(I)(C).

46. Yes. Keeping in mind that rules on indemnity vary from state to state, a situation like this is one where indemnity would likely be applied. If the defendant is liable only because he failed to discover another's misconduct, he will normally be entitled to indemnity. A manufacturer who produces defective goods will generally be required to indemnify a retailer who resells the goods and incurs strict liability (as long as the retailer did not *know* of the defect). Volcano can recover the entire $100,000 from Pompeii.

NOTE: Where strict liability is involved, all subsequent suppliers can seek indemnity from those before them in the supply chain, so that the manufacturer — or whoever is responsible for the defect — is ultimately responsible as long as the item was in a defective condition unreasonably dangerous to the user or consumer when it left his control. (Strict liability is liability without fault; that is, liability without regard to how careful the defendant was.")

RELATED ISSUE: If Volcano had discovered the flaw and sold the stew anyway, Pompeii probably would be absolved of indemnity liability (as well as absolved of direct liability to Frequentus), since Volcano's act would be so egregious as to "break the chain" of causation.

RELATED ISSUE: If Frequentus had served the stew to a social *dinner guest*, the guest could not sue Frequentus in strict liability, since under strict product liability, the defendant must be engaged in the business of selling goods. However, since strict liability doesn't require privity (a buyer-seller relationship between the plaintiff and defendant), the guest could sue Volcano directly.

47. Daffy. Owners of *wild* animals are strictly liable for the damage caused by their animals, regardless of the owner's knowledge of the animal's dangerous propensities. Injuries caused by *domestic* animals (dogs, cats, cows, pigs, etc.) do not give rise to strict liability unless the owner *knows or has reason to know* of the particular animal's dangerous propensities. (The concept is very loosely expressed by the not-really-correct saying "every dog is entitled to one free bite.") Here, the Devil is a "wild" animal (not domesticated, i.e., not "used in service to mankind"), so Bugs is strictly liable.

DISTINGUISHING WILD ANIMALS FROM DOMESTIC ONES: Consider customs in the community, and the utility of keeping the animal.

48. No. The use of fire is not considered an abnormally dangerous activity, and thus not a source of strict liability. Therefore, the neighbor would have to prove Guy was negligent. Since the facts here indicate he was careful, the neighbor will not recover.

49. Yes. Strict liability applies to products in a defective condition unreasonably dangerous to consumers. Here, it is foreseeable that children will find the bottle, and Slip 'N' Slide designed theirs to look like soda pop. As such, Slip 'N' Slide will likely be strictly liable. The warning won't exculpate Slip 'N' Slide -- a reasonable warning is an additional requirement, added to the requirement that a product not be sold in a defective/unreasonably dangerous condition.

RELATED ISSUE: Slip 'N' Slide would probably also be liable in negligence, since it is unreasonable to put a poisonous product in a container like Slip 'N' Slide's. (Furthermore, it is easy for Slip 'N' Slide to redesign the bottle with a childproof top and different shape.)

50. No. Strict liability can only be imposed for the sale of defective products, not services. Blood transfusions are generally considered a service, not a product, and as a result strict liability cannot be imposed for infusion with infected blood.

51. No. Strict liability can only be imposed against one who is in the *business* of selling goods of the type in question. A casual transaction between neighbors, like this, cannot be the basis of strict liability. Instead, the seller must be a manufacturer, wholesaler (or other middleman), or person in the business of retailing.

52. No. The equipment was substantially altered after it left Scrubby Dubdub — Spit 'N'

Polish rebuilt it. Strict liability requires that there be no substantial change in the product after it leaves defendant. Thus, Scrubby Dubdub will not be liable.

53. No. A private nuisance requires creation of a condition which poses an unreasonable, substantial interference with plaintiff's use or enjoyment of his property. This is an objective test: the interference would have to be offensive, annoying, or inconvenient to an average member of the community; and it would have to be substantial. Since most people are only mildly bothered by the smell, and Charles is driven crazy only because he's ultrasensitive, Gore will win.

COMPARE: Torts like battery, where defendant takes plaintiff "as he finds him," sensitivities and all.

54. Yes to the damages, no to the injunction.

A private nuisance is an unreasonable interference with the use and enjoyment of land, caused by deliberate, negligent, or hazardous conduct. If damages would not be an adequate remedy, plaintiff may be entitled to an injunction, if the harm to plaintiff outweighs the utility of defendant's conduct. The wrinkle in these facts is the *social value* of Ghostbusters' conduct — you're told in the facts how valuable it is, due to the number of jobs it creates. Because shutting the plant down would do serious harm, a court would probably not enjoin its operation. However, since the harm created is serious and there's no indication that paying the damages will shut it down, the damages are likely to be awarded. Rest. 2d §826(b).

55. No. A defamatory statement is one tending to harm one's reputation so as to lower him in the eyes of a respectable segment of the community. The statement here is not defamatory because it didn't tend to harm Ratso's reputation in a respectable segment of the community. The fact that small-time cons give him the cold shoulder doesn't satisfy the "respectable segment" requirement.

56. No. While in the normal case of slander pecuniary damages (known as "special" damages) must be proven, imputing serious sexual misconduct is one of the four exceptions to the rule, known as "slander per se." Thus, Clara will not have to prove special damages in order for her claim to succeed.

Traditionally, only women plaintiffs could get the benefit of having allegations that they committed serious sexual misconduct treated as slander per se. But the 14th Amendment's Equal Protection clause probably means that a state today must protect plaintiffs of either gender the same way, so an allegation that a man has committed, say, fornication or adultery would probably also constitute slander per se. Ch.17(III)(D)(3).

57. No. The statement is subject to a "qualified privilege" because Defamitus is speaking in the public interest. A qualified privilege means the speaker will not be liable for otherwise defamatory statements unless he (1) exceeds the scope of the privilege, or (2) either lacks reasonable grounds for believing the statement, or acts recklessly in determining its truth or falsity (states are split on the reasonable/reckless issue). Neither applies here.

RELATED ISSUE: Were Defamitus speaking without a qualified privilege, the statement would be slander per se, since it imputes both serious sexual misconduct and a crime of moral turpitude — molesting little boys. Thus, Socrates would not have to prove special (pecuniary) damages in a defamation suit against Defamitus.

RELATED ISSUE: Say Defamitus made the statement not because he cares at all about society, but because he wanted to seduce Mrs. Socrates, and figured his chances would be better with Socrates in the slammer. He'd be liable for defamation, because he wouldn't have a qualified privilege — the privilege only applies when the defamer speaks *in furtherance* of the interest protected, not in an attempt to *injure* the plaintiff.

58. No. For plaintiffs who are "public figures," the fault level required for defamation is "actual malice." Actual malice is knowledge of the defamatory statement's falsity, or a reckless disregard for whether it's true — not spite or ill will, which is what's present in these facts. Since Pierre believed (even if unreasonably) that the story was true, there is no malice and the defamation claim will not lie.

NOTE: Here, Pierre was *negligent* (but not reckless) in not investigating the story. As a public figure whose public stature has been attacked, Napoleon cannot recover. If he were a *private figure* he could, since mere negligence is enough to support a defamation claim against a media defendant.

COMMON LAW RULE: Defamation was a strict liability offense, so no fault had to be proven.

RELATED ISSUE: Had the story libeled Napoleon's private life, on an issue not bearing on his fitness for public life, he could probably have recovered on the same basis as a private individual (i.e., a mere showing of negligence).

59. No. In order to recover damages from a media defendant for defamation involving an issue of public interest or concern, a plaintiff who is a public figure or public official must prove "actual malice." Actual malice is knowledge of a defamatory statement's falsity, or reckless disregard for its truth. Recklessness is measured subjectively here, and requires proof that defendant *actually had serious doubts* about the truth of his story. Here, Ibble believes the story is true, so there's no "malice."

NOTE: At common law, defamation was a strict liability offense, so no fault had to be proven.

RELATED ISSUE: Had Ibble asked Lincoln himself, and Lincoln had denied the charge, Ibble might have been reckless in printing the story anyway. (However, not checking sources in and of itself is generally only negligence, not recklessness.)

60. No. The "*New York Times* privilege" protects the media when it publishes matters of public interest or concern about a *public figure* or public official, as long as the publisher doesn't act with *"actual malice"* (knowledge of falsity or a reckless disregard for the truth). Since Dumbo is a private figure, the paper doesn't get the benefit of the *Times* privilege. However, that doesn't mean that Dumbo won't have to prove *any* fault; he'll still have to prove at least *negligence*.

NOTE: Negligence can be shown by, for instance, a failure to check sources. Recklessness, however, requires a subjective evaluation: whether the reporter entertained serious doubts about the truth of what he was printing.

NOTE: At common law, defamation was a strict liability offense, so no fault needed to be proven.

61. Yes. In defamation, truth is always an absolute defense. (Of course, Mrs. Tolstoy could be guilty of other torts, like invasion of privacy through publication of private facts about Anna.)

NOTE: If the defendant is a media defendant and the defamation involves a matter of public concern, the *plaintiff* has to prove the statement is false; otherwise, plaintiff only has to *allege* that it's false — defendant has the burden of proving truth as an affirmative defense.

62. No. While the entire statement need not be literally true in a truth defense, the defamatory "sting" must be proven true. Here, it doesn't matter who said it, it matters that Arnold was called a Communist. For a truth defense to fly, Washington would have to prove Arnold is a Communist.

NOTE: For media defendants and public matters, the *plaintiff* has to prove the statement is false; otherwise, the plaintiff only has to *allege* falsity, and the defendant has to prove truth as an affirmative defense.

63. Yes, of the "misappropriation of identity" variety. Appropriation is the defendant's unauthorized use (appropriation) of plaintiff's name or likeness for defendant's own commercial or business purposes. That's what Madame X did, so it's liable. Note that with a celebrity like Mata Hari, the damages will focus on the *reasonable value* of Madame X's use, such that Madame X won't profit from the appropriation.

NOTE: Consent is a valid defense to invasion of privacy; so, if Mata Hari had consented to the use of her identity, her claim would be defeated.

RELATED ISSUE: Appropriation can also apply to a celebrity's distinctive *voice*. *Midler v. Ford Motor Co.* (1988).

64. No — Elastic will lose. The only plausible invasion-of-privacy claim is for "intrusion on solitude." Intrusion requires intrusion on plaintiff's affairs in a way that would be objectionable to a reasonable person. The intrusion must be into something private; that is, where plaintiff has a reasonable expectation of privacy. That's not the case here; there's no reasonable expectation of privacy in a public park, so there can't be an intrusion.

RELATED ISSUE: Say that the investigator set up a high-powered camera at the top of a ladder at the edge of Elastic's yard, so he could photograph him in his bedroom at night through Elastic's upstairs window. This *would* be an intrusion, since there's a reasonable expectation of privacy in a room not visible from the street.

Ch.18(I); *Jeffers v. Seattle* (WA 1979).

65. Noah. Statements of intention are treated just like statements of fact for misrepresentation purposes. Thus, they can be the source of justified reliance. Here, Noah is justified in modifying his conduct based on Judas' statement of intent. *Note that Noah would have to prove that Judas didn't intend to follow through with his stated intent when he made the statement.*

RELATED ISSUE: It's *predictions* which typically cannot be misrepresentations, as long as the speaker knows nothing to prevent the prediction from coming true.

NOTE: For intentional torts, an intervening cause (like a flood) is much less likely to break the chain of causation, relieving defendant of liability, than in a negligence claim. If Noah's claim were based on negligence (e.g., Judas negligently forgot to check the unicorns), the flood would probably be considered a superseding cause as an unforeseeable "Act of God" breaking the chain of causation from Judas to the loss of the unicorns, such that it would relieve Judas of liability.

66. Probably. Misrepresentation requires a misrepresentation, knowledge of falsity or reckless disregard for the truth (scienter), intent to induce reliance, actual, justified reliance and damages. Here, Smith didn't know whether the Titanic was sinkable or not (and knew he didn't know), but he assured Betty it wasn't. Thus he satisfies the "scienter" requirement with a reckless disregard for the truth, and, as Captain of the ship, his assurance induces justified reliance.

NOTE: Were the Captain merely negligent — offering an opinion based on unreliable information — he could be liable for negligent misrepresentation.

67. No. Misrepresentation requires proof of the misrepresentation itself, knowledge of falsity or reckless disregard for the truth (scienter), intent to induce reliance, actual, justified reliance and damages. Here, Witch <u>investigated</u> and found the fraud and hence <u>didn't rely</u> on the misrepresentation. That means that the actual reliance (causation) element of intentional misrepresentation is missing. Although she was under no duty to investigate, once she did so she was not justified in relying on Nysen's statement.

68. No. Deceit (a/k/a intentional misrepresentation) requires proof of the misrepresentation itself, knowledge of falsity or reckless disregard for the truth (scienter), intent to induce reliance, causation, justified reliance and damages. Here, Mutton did not intend to induce reliance in Yves, so the "intent" requirement of misrepresentation is not satisfied.

RELATED ISSUE: Say that Mutton *did* intend that Yves rely on his statement. Then he *would* be liable, even though his statement is not a statement of fact and therefore not a source of justified reliance. However, here Mutton would be liable, since he has superior knowledge which Yves does not share; furthermore, he knows facts that indicate his opinion is wrong. These elements mean Yves *could* pursue a misrepresentation claim against him.

69. No, probably. Malicious prosecution requires wrongful institution of criminal proceedings against the plaintiff, lack of probable cause, favorable termination for plaintiff, and damages. Here, the "lack of probable cause" element is missing. Probable cause requires a reasonable ground for belief of the accused's guilt. Vivien initiated the proceedings based on Sharky's legal advice that plaintiff was guilty. This was probably enough to give Vivien probable cause to believe in Phu's guilt. Thus, the prima facie case is defeated.

70. Barcrusher's best claim is for interference with prospective advantage, but it'll probably lose. Interference with prospective advantage requires proof of defendant's act, with knowledge and purpose of interference, adversely affecting plaintiff's prospective advantage (a contract is not required). However, anyone can use fair, commercially-acceptable <u>competitive tactics</u> to lure customers away from competitors *before* they sign a contract. That's all Witch did here. As a result, she's not liable.

MULTISTATE-STYLE QUESTIONS

Here are 30 multiple-choice questions, in a Multistate Bar Exam style. These questions are taken from *"The Finz Multistate Method,"* a compendium of 1100 questions in the Multistate subjects written by the late Professor Steven Finz and published by Aspen Publishing. To learn more about this book and other study aids, go to www.AspenPublishing.com.

1. Prescott, who owned an appliance repair shop, was at a cocktail party when he saw Dresden, one of his competitors. Approaching Dresden, Prescott said, "I'm glad to run into you. I was hoping that we could discuss the possibility of going into partnership instead of competing with each other." Dresden responded, "I wouldn't go into business with you because you're the most incompetent person I've ever known." Audit, a customer of Prescott's, overheard the conversation. As a result, the following day, Audit cancelled a contract which she had with Prescott.

   If Prescott asserts a claim against Dresden for defamation, Prescott will be successful if

   (A) Dresden knew or should have known that the statement was defamatory when he made it.

   (B) Dresden knew or should have known that the statement was false when he made it.

   (C) Dresden knew or should have known that the statement would be overheard when he made it.

   (D) Dresden knew or should have known that harm would result from the statement.

2. Preston purchased a box labeled "Generic Breakfast Cereal" from Riteway Supermarket. While he was eating it, he broke a tooth on a stone which the product contained. The product sold by Riteway and labeled "Generic Breakfast Cereal" is furnished by three different companies: Acme, Birdco, and Cullen. Each sells an approximately equal quantity to Riteway. In addition, all package their product in identical wrappers, so that it is impossible to tell which of them furnished any given box of breakfast cereal. Although the companies compete with each other, at Riteway's request they worked together to design the product wrapper.

   If Preston is successful in an action for damages against Riteway, it will probably be because

   (A) Riteway, Acme, Birdco, and Cullen were involved in a concerted action in the manufacture and marketing of the product.

(B) Riteway, Acme, Birdco, and Cullen established standards on an industry-wide basis, which standards made identification of the product's manufacturer impossible.

(C) the negligence of either Acme, Birdco, or Cullen resulted in harm to Preston under circumstances such that it was impossible to tell which of them caused the harm; and Riteway is vicariously liable for that negligence.

(D) either Acme, Birdco, or Cullen manufactured a defective product, and Riteway sold that product while it was in a defective condition.

Questions 3-4 are based on the following fact situation:

Dan, a thirteen-year-old boy, was a member of Survival Scouts, a national young people's organization. As part of a Survival Scout project, he planned to spend an entire weekend camping alone in the woods. Napper, who knew about the project, phoned Dan's mother Mabe the day after Dan left home. Napper said, "We have your son. We've already beaten him up once, just to hear him scream. Next time, we might kill him." Napper instructed Mabe to deliver a cash ransom to a specified location within one hour. Since there was no way to locate Dan's campsite in the woods, Mabe could not find out whether Napper was telling the truth. Horrified that her son might be beaten and injured or killed, she delivered the ransom as instructed. She remained in a hysterical state until Dan returned from his camping trip, and Mabe realized that the ransom demand had been a hoax. Mabe, who already suffered from a heart ailment, had a heart attack the day after Dan's return.

3. If Mabe asserts a claim against Napper for assault, the court should find for

   (A) Mabe, because Napper was aware that his conduct would frighten her.

   (B) Mabe, because the court will transfer Napper's intent.

   (C) Napper, because Mabe did not perceive injury being inflicted upon Dan.

   (D) Napper, because Mabe had no reason to expect to be touched by Napper.

4. If Mabe asserts a claim against Napper for damages resulting from her heart attack on a theory of intentional infliction of emotional distress, the court should find for

   (A) Napper, because the heart attack occurred the day after Dan's return.

   (B) Napper, if Mabe's pre-existing condition made her especially susceptible to heart attack.

   (C) Mabe, if the heart attack was caused by Napper's outrageous conduct.

   (D) Mabe, because Napper should have foreseen that his conduct would result in harm.

5. Dusty was a "crop duster," an occupation which required her to spray insecticides onto growing crops from an airplane which she flew within fifteen feet of the ground. In locating the fields of her customers, she used a map which the county published for that purpose, and on which every parcel of real estate in the area was identified by a parcel number. Arrow, a farmer, hired Dusty to spray his fields with insecticide.

Arrow knew that his farm was identified on the county map as parcel 612, but by mistake told Dusty that it was parcel 621. As a result, Dusty sprayed the farm which the county map identified as parcel 621. That farm belonged to Plower, who had contracted to grow his crop without chemical insecticides and to sell it to an organic produce distributor. As a result of Dusty's spraying, Plower was unable to fulfill his contract and sustained serious economic losses.

If Plower asserts a claim for damages resulting from trespass to land, the court should find for

(A) Plower, because crop dusting is an abnormally dangerous activity.
(B) Plower, because Dusty intentionally flew through the air space above his land.
(C) Dusty, because she reasonably believed that the farm which she was spraying belonged to Arrow.
(D) Dusty, because there was no damage to Plower's land.

6. Nichol, who was 11 years of age, was playing with Paul, who was ten years of age. While they were playing together, Nichol offered to show Paul his new air rifle. The air rifle was manufactured by the Loly Company. Nichol purchased it from Storr, with money which he earned by mowing the lawns of several of his neighbors. While demonstrating the air rifle to Paul, Nichol accidentally shot him with it, severely injuring Paul's eye. Paul subsequently asserted a negligence claim against Storr.

If Paul is successful in his claim against Storr, it will be because a jury finds that

(A) any negligence by Loly Company in the design of the air rifle should be imputed to Storr.
(B) the air rifle was defectively designed.
(C) the air rifle was defectively manufactured.
(D) it was unreasonable for Storr to sell the air rifle to Nichol.

Questions 7-8 are based on the following fact situation:

Pellum was employed by Denner as chief field mechanic. When he received his salary, Pellum noticed that he had not been paid for the overtime which he had worked the previous month. When he complained to Denner about it, Denner said that all company employees were expected to put in extra time when necessary, and that he had no intention of compensating Pellum for the excess hours. Pellum resigned immediately and advised Denner that he would hold the tools which Denner had issued to him until he received payment.

7. Assume for the purpose of this question only that after Pellum's resignation, Denner wrote him a letter in which he said, "You were never any good as a mechanic, and in addition you were the most dishonest employee this company ever had," and that these statements were false. Pellum's mother, who lived with Pellum and frequently

opened his mail, read the letter as soon as it arrived. In an action by Pellum against Denner for defamation, a court should find for

(A) Pellum, because Denner's statements were published to Pellum's mother.
(B) Pellum, only if Denner had reason to know that someone other than Denner would open and read the letter.
(C) Denner, because the statements contained in the letter were communicated only to Pellum.
(D) Denner, because of the employer's privilege.

8. Assume for the purpose of this question only that Pellum applied for a job with Nuco, and that Nuco wrote to Denner asking for an evaluation of Pellum's honesty and ability. Denner wrote a letter to Nuco which stated, "When Pellum left my company a valuable set of tools left with him. This disappearance has never been properly explained or straightened out." As a result, Nuco did not hire Pellum. If Pellum asserts a claim against Denner for defamation, Pellum should

(A) lose, if Pellum did not return the tools which he took when he left Denner's employ.
(B) lose, because Denner's statement was made in response to a specific request by Pellum's prospective employer.
(C) win, because Denner's statement could not have benefitted Denner's own business interests.
(D) win, if Denner's statement accused Pellum of stealing the tools.

9. Arnold was driving north on Canal Street. As he approached the intersection of First Avenue, he noticed that the traffic light was red against him. Preparing to stop, he stepped on his brake pedal. Because the brakes were not working properly, he could not stop, and continued into the intersection. Burger, who was driving east on First Avenue, saw Arnold go through the red light. Because the light was green in his favor, however, Burger did not stop, but continued into the intersection, believing that he could avoid striking Arnold by steering around him. The two vehicles collided in the intersection. Although damage to Arnold's car was minimal, Burger's car was totally destroyed. The jurisdiction has a statute which prohibits entering an intersection against a red traffic signal light and another statute which adopts the all or nothing rule of contributory negligence.

In an action by Burger against Arnold, the court should find for

(A) Arnold, since Burger had the last clear chance to avoid the accident.
(B) Arnold, if it was unreasonable for Burger to enter the intersection when he did.
(C) Burger, if Arnold's violation of statute was a substantial factor in producing the damage.
(D) Burger, since Arnold's conduct was negligence per se.

10. Fridge was the operator of an appliance store. Once, while testing a refrigerator prior to selling it, she discovered a defect in its wiring. Realizing that the defect would make it dangerous for a person to touch the refrigerator while it was plugged in, she resolved not to sell it. Instead, she placed it on the sidewalk in front of her store to attract the attention of passersby. After two years, the refrigerator became so dirty that she decided to get rid of it. In crayon, Fridge wrote "AS IS - $25" on its door. Pally, who was building a food smoker, needed the body of a refrigerator. When he saw the one in front of Fridge's store, he bought it. As she was loading it onto Pally's pick-up truck, Fridge said, "I hope you know that this refrigerator doesn't work." Pally said that he did. When Pally got the refrigerator home he plugged it in, and received a severe electrical shock while attempting to open its door.

    In an action by Pally against Fridge for damages resulting from his injury, the court will probably find for

    (A) Pally, if it was unreasonable for Fridge to sell the refrigerator without warning him about the wiring defect.
    (B) Pally, since the refrigerator was unfit for ordinary use.
    (C) Fridge, since Pally purchased the refrigerator "AS IS."
    (D) Fridge, if it is found that Pally had the "last clear chance" to avoid being injured.

11. The Chemco insecticide factory was located on the edge of the city of Pinetree. When the wind blew from the east, foul-smelling waste gases from Chemco factory chimneys were blown over Pinetree, causing most of the residents to experience a burning of the eyes and throat. Packer was a resident of Pinetree. On several occasions, she attempted to persuade the City Attorney to seek an injunction against Chemco. The City Attorney refused, however, because the City Council was afraid that doing so would drive Chemco from the area. If Packer seeks an injunction by asserting a claim against Chemco on a theory of public nuisance, which of the following would be Chemco's most effective argument in defense?

    (A) The City Attorney's decision is binding.
    (B) Packer has not sustained harm different from that of the general public.
    (C) A private citizen may not seek an injunction against environmental polluters.
    (D) A private citizen may not sue on a theory of public nuisance.

12. When Darren entered a restaurant for lunch, she hung her coat on the coat rack. When she was leaving, she removed from the rack a coat which looked like hers, but which actually belonged to Perdu. At the time she took it, Darran believed it to be her coat, but when she had driven two miles from the restaurant, she realized that it was not hers. She turned around and was driving back to the restaurant when she was involved in an automobile accident. Perdu's coat was completely destroyed in the accident.

    If Perdu asserts a claim against Darran for trespass to chattel, the court should find for

    (A) Perdu, because the coat was completely destroyed after Darran took it.

(B) Perdu, unless the automobile accident in which the coat was destroyed occurred without fault by Darran.
(C) Darran, because she believed the coat to be her own when she took it.
(D) Darran, if she was making a reasonable effort to return the coat when it was destroyed.

13. Michael, who was eleven years old, received a sled manufactured by Rosebud from his uncle as a Christmas present. Since he already had a better sled, Michael sold the Rosebud to his neighbor Petey. Petey was riding the Rosebud sled down a snow-covered hill when one of the bolts which held it together broke, causing the sled to overturn and injure Petey severely. The bolt broke because of a crack which existed when the sled left the Rosebud factory, but which was too minute to be discovered by reasonable inspection. If Petey brings an action against Rosebud, the court should find for

(A) Petey, if the cracked bolt was a defect.
(B) Petey, but only if Michael did not use the sled before selling it to Petey.
(C) Rosebud, since the sale by Michael was outside the regular course of business.
(D) Rosebud, because the crack was too minute to be discovered upon reasonable inspection.

14. Stabel owned and bred horses, and was an excellent rider. He purchased a horse known as Thunder even though he had heard that Thunder was wild and dangerous, because he hoped that he would be able to "break" or train him. Each time Stabel attempted to approach the horse, however, Thunder reared and kicked at him. Finally, Stabel hired a professional horse trainer named Parte to break Thunder. After explaining that Thunder had repeatedly attacked him, Stabel showed Parte to Thunder's corral. While Stabel stood outside watching, Parte entered the corral holding out his hand and making soft murmuring noises to attract Thunder's attention. When Thunder saw Parte, the horse kicked him, fracturing Parte's leg.

If Parte asserts a claim for damages against Stabel, the court should find for

(A) Parte, because Stabel knew that Thunder had a propensity to attack human beings.
(B) Parte, because Thunder was a wild animal.
(C) Parte, because Stabel acted unreasonably in permitting Parte to enter the corral under the circumstances.
(D) Stabel, because Parte knew that Thunder was dangerous when he entered the corral.

15. Penny was attending a nightclub at which Dr. Hypno was performing. Before the show began, a request was made for a volunteer to assist Dr. Hypno with her act, and Penny volunteered. She was taken backstage to Dr. Hypno's dressing room where she and Dr. Hypno had a conversation. Following their conversation, Penny agreed to participate in Dr. Hypno's show. During the course of the performance, Dr. Hypno attempted to hypnotize Penny on stage. She then touched Penny's skin with an electric

cattle-prod (a device which produces an electric shock and is used for handling stubborn cattle) causing her great pain and discomfort.

Penny subsequently instituted an action against Dr. Hypno. In it, she alleged that Dr. Hypno committed various intentional torts against her by touching her with the cattle prod. If one of the following facts were established at the trial, which would be most helpful to Penny in responding to Dr. Hypno's defense of consent?

(A) During the conversation in Dr. Hypno's dressing room, Dr. Hypno stated that she was going to attempt to hypnotize Penny on stage, stated that she was usually successful in hypnotizing volunteers, and stated further that if she was successful, the cattle prod would cause Penny no discomfort.
(B) During the conversation in Dr. Hypno's dressing room, Dr. Hypno promised to pay Penny $100 for participating in the show; she never did pay her; and, in fact, when she promised that she would pay Penny, she did not intend to do so.
(C) During the conversation in Dr. Hypno's dressing room, Dr. Hypno stated that the electric cattle-prod produced a mild electric shock which would cause no real discomfort, when she knew that this was not true.
(D) When Penny consented to participating in Dr. Hypno's act, she did not know that contact with the electric cattle-prod would result in great pain and discomfort.

16. The state governor was attending a major league baseball game when a member of the home team hit a home run. The governor jumped to his feet and cheered loudly, along with the rest of the crowd. Frank, a freelance photographer, snapped the governor's photograph while he was cheering. When the photograph was developed, Frank had it imprinted on targets. Packaging them with toy plastic darts, Frank marketed them under the name of "The Cheering Governor Dart Board Game," selling several thousand. The governor sued Frank for invasion of privacy.

On which of the following theories is the governor most likely to be successful in his action against Frank?

(A) Appropriation of identity.
(B) Public disclosure.
(C) Intrusion.
(D) False light.

17. Alice was driving her automobile on Country Road in the rain when she rounded a bend and saw a cow standing directly in her path. She immediately jammed on her brakes and pulled the steering wheel to the right in an attempt to avoid striking the cow. As a result, she lost control of her car which skidded off the road and into Basil's yard. Basil, who was in the process of installing an automatic watering system, had dug a trench across the yard for pipes. When the wheels of Alice's car hit the trench, the car stopped abruptly, throwing Alice forward into the windshield, and causing her to be injured. In an action by Alice against Basil for negligence, will a court decide that Basil owed Alice a duty of reasonable care?

(A) Yes, if it was foreseeable that persons driving on Country Road might lose control of their vehicles and skid into Basil's yard.

(B) Yes, if, but only if, the cow was in the road because of some conduct by Basil.

(C) No, because it was not unreasonable for Basil to dig a trench on his own land.

(D) No, because Alice was a trespasser.

Questions 18-19 are based on the following fact situation:

Carp, who was building a house on his own property, had posted a sign which said, "No Trespassing." He was working on the framework of his roof when he found that he had brought the wrong hammer onto the roof with him. Without looking to see if anyone was around, he tossed the hammer to the ground, shouting "Heads up!"

Truck was a truck driver assigned to deliver lumber on the street where Carp was building a house. Carp had not ordered lumber, but when Truck saw Carp working on the roof of an unfinished house, he incorrectly assumed that Carp was the person to whom he was supposed to deliver the lumber. He parked his truck at the curb and was walking across Carp's property toward the unfinished house to talk to Carp about the delivery, when he was struck in the head by the hammer thrown by Carp. Truck cried out in pain, and then fell to the ground, unconscious and bleeding. Carp saw it happen, but merely shrugged and continued working.

A moment later a passerby who had seen what happened called an ambulance. When it arrived, Truck was still unconscious. The driver, Ann, loaded Truck into the ambulance and began driving to the hospital. Because of Ann's negligent driving, the ambulance struck a pole. Truck was killed in the crash.

18. Assume for the purpose of this question only that the representative of Truck's estate instituted an appropriate action against Carp, alleging that Carp's failure to call for medical assistance after he saw the hammer strike Truck was negligence. Which of the following comments is most accurate regarding that allegation?

    (A) Carp owed Truck no duty to call for help if Truck was a trespasser.

    (B) Truck's estate is entitled to punitive (exemplary) damages if Carp was substantially certain that there was a possibility of harm resulting from his failure to act.

    (C) Carp's failure to call for medical aid was not a factual cause of harm to Truck, since someone did call a moment later.

    (D) Truck was an invitee since he was a user of the public street who had entered upon adjacent private land.

19. If the representative of Truck's estate instituted an appropriate action against Ann under the state's "wrongful death" statute, the court would be most likely to find for

    (A) Ann, if Carp's conduct was foreseeable.

    (B) Ann, since a rescuer is not under an obligation to use reasonable care in the face of an emergency.

(C) Truck's estate, since Ann's negligence was a proximate cause of Truck's death.
(D) Truck's estate, unless Carp is found to be liable for Truck's death.

20. Darby was towing a small travel-trailer with his automobile when the hitch which attached the trailer to the car broke, causing the trailer to collide with the vehicle of Venden which was parked at the curb. A statute in the jurisdiction provides that "No person shall operate a motor vehicle or trailer on the roads of this state unless said motor vehicle or trailer is covered by a valid policy of liability insurance." Darby was in violation of that statute in that he knew that his trailer was not covered by a valid policy of liability insurance at the time of the accident. Is his violation of statute relevant to the issue of negligence in an action brought against him by Venden?

(A) Yes, because the statute was designed to protect the victims of automobile and trailer accidents.
(B) Yes, because the reasonable person does not knowingly violate a statute.
(C) No, because the law encourages the purchase of automobile insurance, and therefore absolutely prohibits disclosure to the jury about whether or not a defendant was insured.
(D) No, because compliance with the statute does not prevent automobile or trailer accidents.

21. One night police officers Axel and Barber received a message that a burglary was in progress at the Super Grocery Store. Rushing to the location, they discovered that the back door of the store was open. Entering cautiously, they saw two burglars hiding in the storage room. In the ensuing attempt to effect an arrest in the dark, Axel and Barber knocked over several stacks of merchandise, including cases of bottled soda-pop manufactured by Popco. When the stacked groceries fell over during the chase a bottle broke, and a fragment of flying glass struck Officer Axel, injuring him. If Axel institutes an action against Super, Axel will

(A) win, because the fact that he was attempting to apprehend a criminal who was burglarizing Super's store made him an invitee.
(B) win, if, but only if, Super's conduct was a physical cause of the harm.
(C) lose, because he was a bare licensee at the time the injury occurred.
(D) lose, if it was unforeseeable that persons would be chasing around the storeroom in the dark.

Questions 22-23 are based on the following fact situation:

Collins was a well-known collector of art. Dillon was an art dealer who operated a gallery in which she sold paintings and other works of art. One day, while Collins was visiting Dillon's gallery, Dillon showed him a new painting called "The Petticoats" which she had received that day.

"The artist didn't sign it," Dillon said. "But I'm sure it was painted by Degas. That would make it worth at least $250,000."

Collins answered, "It's by Degas, all right. It's worth every cent you're asking. But I already have several paintings by Degas in my collection, and I don't need another."

Barton, who was browsing in Dillon's gallery, overheard the conversation between Collins and Dillon. Barton knew very little about art, but had just inherited a large sum of money. Because he knew that Collins and Dillon were art experts, he believed what he heard them saying. After Collins left the gallery, Barton asked Dillon if she would accept $200,000 for "The Petticoats." Dillon said that she would not take anything less than $250,000. After negotiation, Barton purchased it for $225,000.

Barton subsequently learned that "The Petticoats" had not been painted by Degas, and was worth only $600.

22. If Barton asserts a tort claim for misrepresentation against Dillon, which of the following would be Dillon's most effective argument in defense?

    (A) A statement of opinion cannot be construed as a misrepresentation, since there is no such thing as a false idea.
    (B) Barton did not sustain damage as a result of his reliance on a statement by Dillon.
    (C) Dillon did not know that Barton would rely on the statements which she made to Collins.
    (D) The value of any work of art is a matter of opinion.

23. If Barton is successful in a tort action for misrepresentation, the court is likely to award him a judgment for

    (A) $250,000 (the value which Dillon stated).
    (B) $250,000 (the value which Dillon stated), on condition that Barton return "The Petticoats" to Dillon.
    (C) $225,000 (the price which Barton paid to Dillon).
    (D) $224,400 (the price which Barton paid to Dillon less the value of "The Petticoats").

24. Dalton was an elderly man who lived in a house with a swimming pool in the back yard. Although Dalton enjoyed swimming in the pool, his age and physical infirmity made him unable to clean or maintain the pool himself. Instead, he agreed to allow his fourteen-year-old neighbor Nellie to swim in the pool anytime she wanted to without notifying Dalton or asking his permission, in exchange for Nellie's services in cleaning and maintaining the pool.

    On Friday morning, Nellie thoroughly cleaned Dalton's pool. Later that day, Dalton drained all the water from the pool and did not refill it. Saturday morning, Nellie woke up early and decided to go swimming in Dalton's pool. She put on her bathing suit and went into Dalton's yard, running onto the diving board of his swimming pool and diving in without looking first. Nellie was severely injured when she fell to the concrete bottom of the empty swimming pool.

If Nellie asserts a negligence claim for her injuries against Dalton in a jurisdiction which has a pure comparative negligence statute, the court should find for

(A) Nellie, because the pool constituted an attractive nuisance.

(B) Dalton, because Nellie was a trespasser.

(C) Nellie, if it was unreasonable for Dalton to drain the pool without warning her.

(D) Dalton, if a reasonable person in Nellie's position would have known the risk of diving into an empty swimming pool.

25. Carolyn was driving to visit her fiance who was staying in Smallville, about fifty miles away. Before she left, her friend Frieda asked her to deliver a small package to someone in Smallville. The package contained a bottle of caustic chemical. Because she was afraid that Carolyn would refuse to carry it if she knew its contents, Frieda wrapped the package in brown paper and did not tell Carolyn what was in it. Carolyn placed the package in the glove compartment of her car and began driving to Smallville. Along the way, Carolyn saw Harold hitchhiking by the side of the road. Since they had gone to high school together, Carolyn offered Harold a ride. While Harold was sitting in the front seat beside Carolyn, the package in the glove compartment began to leak, dripping liquid onto Harold's trousers. Without saying anything to Carolyn, Harold opened the glove compartment and removed the wet package. As soon as the caustic liquid touched Harold's hand, it burned his skin severely.

If Harold commences a negligence action against Carolyn in a jurisdiction which has no automobile guest statute and which applies the all-or-nothing rule of contributory negligence, which of the following would be Carolyn's most effective argument in defense?

(A) Harold was a mere licensee, and was only entitled to a warning of those conditions which Carolyn knew were dangerous.

(B) Carolyn could not have known or anticipated that the contents of the package would cause harm to a passenger in her car.

(C) Harold was contributorily negligent in touching the wet package.

(D) Harold assumed the risk of injury resulting from contact with the wet package.

26. Six months after Dr. Danh performed surgery on her, Peck was x-rayed by another doctor. The x-ray disclosed a surgical instrument inside Peck's chest. Danh was the only person who had ever performed surgery on Peck. Peck subsequently asserted a medical malpractice claim against Danh, alleging that Danh had negligently left the surgical instrument inside her while operating on her.

If an expert testifies that surgeons do not usually leave instruments inside a patient's body unless they are acting unreasonably, may Peck rely on res ipsa loquitur in her claim against Danh?

(A) No, because the doctrine of res ipsa loquitur is not applicable to a claim for professional malpractice.
(B) No, because a jury of laypersons is not competent to infer that a physician was negligent.
(C) Yes, because a surgeon is under an absolute duty not to leave instruments inside a patient's body.
(D) Yes, because Danh was the only person who had ever performed surgery on Peck.

27. When Perl, a law student, told her cousin Joe that she needed a place to study, Joe gave her the key to his mountain cabin and said that she could use it. Because Perl had never been there before, Joe drew a map and wrote instructions on how to find it. Perl followed the map and instructions, but when she arrived she found five identical cabins in a row and did not know which one was Joe's. She tried the key which Joe had given her. When it opened the door of one of the cabins, she went inside, believing the cabin to be Joe's.

    Actually, the cabin which Perl entered did not belong to Joe, but to his neighbor Darrin. Joe knew that his key fit the doors of all five of the cabins, but had forgotten to mention it to Perl. While Perl was inside the cabin, she attempted to turn on the gas stove. Because of a defect in the stove, it exploded, injuring Perl.

    If Perl asserts a claim against Darrin for her injuries, the court should find for

    (A) Perl, because the stove was defective.
    (B) Perl, if Darrin should have anticipated that a person would enter his cabin by mistake.
    (C) Darrin, but only if Perl was a trespasser at the time of the explosion.
    (D) Darrin, unless Darrin knew or should have known that someone would be injured by the stove.

Questions 28-29 are based on the following fact situation:

One evening in Alfred's tavern, Yeong, who was 17 years old, drank alcoholic beverages which Alfred sold her. Yeong then left and went to Barney's tavern where she drank alcoholic beverages which Barney sold her. When Yeong left Barney's tavern, she attempted to ride home on her motorcycle. Because Yeong was intoxicated, she struck and injured Palco, a pedestrian. Palco subsequently asserted claims against Alfred and Barney under a state law which provides as follows: "If a minor under the age of 20 years injures another while intoxicated, any person who sold said minor the alcohol which resulted in said minor's intoxication shall be liable to the injured person."

28. Assume for the purpose of this question only that Alfred did not sell Yeong enough alcohol to make Yeong intoxicated, and that the alcohol which Barney sold Yeong would have made Yeong intoxicated even if Alfred had sold Yeong no alcohol at all. In determining Palco's claim against Barney, the court should find that

(A) Barney's conduct was not the cause of Yeong's intoxication because Alfred's conduct was a substantial factor in making Yeong intoxicated.
(B) Barney is liable under the statute even if Barney's conduct did not cause Yeong to become intoxicated.
(C) Barney's conduct was a cause of Palco's injury because Yeong would not have become intoxicated if Barney did not sell Yeong alcoholic beverages.
(D) Barney's conduct was a cause of Yeong's intoxication, but was not a cause of Palco's injury because Yeong's driving superseded it.

29. Assume for the purpose of this question only that the amount of alcohol which Alfred sold Yeong would have made Yeong intoxicated even if Barney sold Yeong no alcohol at all, and that the amount of alcohol which Barney sold Yeong would have made Yeong intoxicated even if Alfred sold Yeong no alcohol at all. Which of the following statements is/are most correct?

I. Alfred did not cause Palco's injury because Barney subsequently sold Yeong enough alcohol to make her intoxicated.

II. Barney did not cause Palco's injury because Alfred had previously sold Yeong enough alcohol to make her intoxicated.

(A) I only.
(B) II only.
(C) I and II.
(D) Neither I nor II.

30. Drinker was obviously intoxicated when he entered Barr's tavern one night and ordered a drink of Old Wheatstraw alcoholic liquor. A statute in the jurisdiction prohibits serving alcoholic liquor to any intoxicated person. Barr knew that Drinker was intoxicated, but because Drinker was a good customer, Barr opened a new bottle of Old Wheatstraw and poured him some of it. After drinking the liquor, Drinker left the tavern and began driving home.

The liquor which Barr served Drinker had been manufactured by Wheatstraw. Before the liquor left Wheatstraw's factory, Fuller, an angry employee, added a poison to it which could not have been discovered by reasonable inspection. While Drinker was driving in a reasonable manner, the poison caused him to die. As a result, Drinker's car struck Prill, injuring her. If Prill asserts a claim against Barr based on Barr's violation of the above statute, which of the following would be Barr's most effective argument in defense against that claim?

(A) Barr did not serve Drinker enough liquor to make him intoxicated.
(B) The statute was not meant to prevent people from drinking liquor which had been poisoned.
(C) Serving liquor to Drinker was not a cause of Prill's injuries.
(D) Fuller's conduct was a superseding cause of Prill's injuries.

ANSWERS TO MULTISTATE-STYLE QUESTIONS

1. **C** Although liability ordinarily results from the publication of false defamatory statements about the plaintiff, the courts have always required that publication be either intentional or the result of negligence. Dresden's statement to Prescott was not a publication, since Prescott is the plaintiff. The fact that it was overheard by Audit does not satisfy the requirement of publication unless either Dresden intended that Audit hear it or Audit heard it as a result of Dresden's unreasonable conduct in the face of the foreseeable risk that Audit would hear it. If Dresden knew that Audit would hear it, he intended the publication. If he should have known that Audit would hear it, he acted unreasonably in saying it.

   The courts have never required proof that the defendant knew the statement to be defamatory, so **A** is incorrect. The United States Supreme Court has held that in some defamation cases the plaintiff must prove that the defendant knew or should have known that the statement was false when he made it. **B** is incorrect, however, because the requirement has not been applied to a defamation action brought by a private person against a non-media defendant. **D** is incorrect because knowledge that harm will result is not an essential element of any defamation case.

2. **D** Strict liability is imposed on the seller of a product which is in a defective condition when sold. Thus, if Riteway sold the product while it was defective, Riteway would be strictly liable no matter who manufactured it.

   Parties who work together to accomplish a particular result are involved in a concert of action which may make any one of them vicariously liable for torts committed by the others. **A** is incorrect, however, because the facts indicate that the manufacturers and retailer did not work together on manufacturing or marketing the product. It has been held that where there are a small number of manufacturers in a particular industry, where all belong to an industry-wide association which establishes industry standards, where those standards result in their products' being defective, and where all members of the industry and the association are named as defendants, liability may be imposed on an industry-wide basis. **B** is incorrect, however, because there is no indications that the number of cereal manufacturers is small or that they belong to an industry-wide association which sets standards or that their standards made the product defective or that all members of the industry and their association have been named as defendants. Under the alternative liability theory, where two or more defendants commit identical acts of negligence under circumstances which make it impossible to tell which one injured the plaintiff, it will be presumed that all of them factually caused the plaintiff's injury. **C** is incorrect, however, because there is no indication that all of the parties named committed identical acts of negligence or that any of them was negligent at all.

3. **D** Assault occurs when, with the intent to induce such apprehension, the defendant induces in the plaintiff a reasonable apprehension that a harmful or offensive contact with the plaintiff will occur. Since Mabe did not fear contact with herself, she was not assaulted.

   A and **B** are incorrect because Napper's conduct did not induce Mabe to apprehend contact with herself. If Napper's conduct did give Mabe reason to apprehend contact with herself, it would not matter whether she had perceived contact with Dan. **C** is, therefore, incorrect.

4. **C** A defendant is liable for intentional infliction of emotional distress if, with the intent to cause emotional distress, he engages in outrageous conduct which causes serious mental suffering. The defendant intends the plaintiff's emotional distress if he desires or knows that it will result from his conduct. Because of the affection normally associated with the parent-child relationship, Napper probably knew (i.e., intended) that his threats to injure or kill Dan would cause his mother to experience emotional distress. If his conduct was outrageous and caused her to experience emotional distress, Napper is liable to her for the distress and any physical manifestations of it.

   A is incorrect because the passage of time is not sufficient to prevent liability for an injury which was caused by the defendant's tortious conduct. If the reasonable person would not have experienced any suffering as a result of Napper's conduct, then a plaintiff who did experience suffering might not be permitted to recover for it because the law does not seek to benefit a supersensitive plaintiff. If the reasonable person would have experienced some suffering, however, the plaintiff will be permitted to recover for her suffering even if a pre-existing condition makes it unusually severe. (This rule sometimes leads courts to exclaim, "The defendant takes the plaintiff as he finds her.") **B** is, therefore, incorrect. **D** is incorrect because liability for intentional infliction of emotional distress requires intent, not merely a foreseeable risk.

5. **B** Trespass to land is an intentional entry on realty possessed by the plaintiff. For this purpose the air immediately above the ground is regarded as part of the realty.

   Without intent, there is no trespass liability. **A** is incorrect because participation in an abnormally dangerous activity does not satisfy the requirement of intent. **C** is incorrect because intent means a desire to enter the land or air space above it (without regard to knowledge of the plaintiff's right). **D** is incorrect because damage to the realty is not an essential element of trespass to land.

6. **D** The facts specify that Paul's claim is for negligence. Negligence is unreasonable conduct. It may be unreasonable to sell a device as dangerous as an air rifle to an eleven-year-old, because the risk that he will use it to shoot another child is foreseeable. In any event, D is the only finding listed which could result in a judgment for Paul.

   A is incorrect because negligence of a manufacturer is not imputed to a retailer. **B** and **C** are incorrect because there is no indication that the harm resulted from any defect in the air rifle or that such a defect resulted from negligence.

7. **B** There can be no liability for defamation unless the defendant intentionally or negligently communicated the defamatory statement to a person other than the plaintiff. Communication of the accusation to Pellum's mother would satisfy this requirement only if Denner knew or should have known that she would see the contents of the letter which contained them.

   A is, therefore, incorrect. **C** is incorrect because the statements actually were communicated to Pellum's mother, who read the letter. Courts have sometimes held that an employer who defames a former employee in a communication with a prospective employer of that former employee is privileged if he believes reasonably and in good faith that his statements are true. This reasoning does not apply to the facts given, however, because Denner's statements were not being made to a prospective employer of Pellum. **D** is, therefore, incorrect.

8. **D** A statement is defamatory if it would tend to hold the plaintiff up to shame, disgrace, or ridicule in the minds of a substantial group of respectable people. Since most respectable people believe that theft is disgraceful, an accusation that the plaintiff is a thief is probably defamatory. In a defamation action, a statement means what the reasonable person reading it would think it means. The reasonable person reading Denner's statement might believe that it accuses Pellum of stealing tools. Whether this is so is a question for the jury, but it is clear that *if* Denner's statement accused Pellum of stealing tools it was defamatory and might lead to liability.

   If Pellum did not return the tools, Denner's statement is literally true. Since a statement means what the reasonable person hearing it would think it means, and since the reasonable person might think that Denner's statement accused Pellum of theft, the literal truth of the statement would not prevent Denner from being liable. **A** is, therefore, incorrect. A defendant may be privileged to make defamatory statements in a reasonable and good faith attempt to protect a legitimate interest. In deciding whether a former employer was acting in good faith when making a defamatory statement to a plaintiff's prospective employer, courts frequently look to whether the former employer made the statement gratuitously (making it less likely that he was acting in good faith) or in response to a request for information (making it more likely that he was acting in good faith). **B** is incorrect, however, because this fact alone is not sufficient to privilege a defendant's publication. **C** is incorrect because if the defendant was acting reasonably and in good faith, the interest which a former employer has in common with a prospective employer might be sufficiently legitimate to make the privilege apply.

9. **B** Under the all-or-nothing rule of contributory negligence, a plaintiff is completely barred from recovering damages if his own unreasonable conduct contributed to their occurrence. Since Burger saw Arnold in the intersection, he was probably guilty of contributory negligence.

   The doctrine of last clear chance does no more than negate the effect of a plaintiff's contributory negligence. If a defendant had "the last clear chance" to avoid injuring the plaintiff, the defendant might be liable in spite of the plaintiff's negligence. The plaintiff never loses a case, however, simply because that plaintiff had the "last clear chance" to avoid being injured. **A** is, therefore, incorrect. **C** and **D** are incorrect for two reasons: first, the presumption which results from a defendant's violation of a statute (sometimes called negligence per se) may ordinarily be rebutted by proof that the violation resulted from circumstances beyond the defendant's control; and, second, even if Arnold could not rebut the presumption that he was negligent, Burger's contributory negligence is still available to him as a defense.

10. **A** Although the phrase AS IS disclaims implied warranties of merchantability or fitness for a particular purpose, it does not free a seller from the duty of acting reasonably. Since it probably was foreseeable that the purchaser of a refrigerator would plug it in even after being advised that it did not work, Fridge had a duty to take reasonable precautions against the harm which might result therefrom. If her failure to warn Pally was unreasonable, it was negligence which was a proximate cause of harm and would result in liability.

    B is incorrect because the phrase AS IS is an effective disclaimer of the implied warranty of merchantability (i.e., fitness for ordinary use). **C** is incorrect because Fridge is still liable under a negligence theory. **D** is based on a misinterpretation of the doctrine of "last clear chance" which accomplishes nothing more than undoing the effect of a plaintiff's contributory negligence. (If a defendant had "the last clear chance" to avoid injuring the plaintiff, the defendant might be liable in spite of the plaintiff's negligence. The plaintiff never loses a case, however, simply because that plaintiff had "the last clear chance" to avoid being injured.)

11. **B** A private individual can successfully assert a claim for public nuisance only if the harm which she sustained was different from that sustained by the general public (i.e., "particular" harm). Since no fact indicates this to be so of Packer, she may not assert the public nuisance claim.

A is incorrect because if Packer had sustained "particular" harm, the decision of the City Attorney would not prevent her from suing for damages. Although it is generally held that a private individual may not seek an injunction on a public nuisance theory, **C** is incorrect because there are other theories on which a private individual may receive an injunction against environmental polluters. **D** is incorrect because a private individual who sustains particular harm as a result of a public nuisance may sue for damages.

12. **A** Trespass to chattel is intentional interference with the plaintiff's chattel resulting in damage. For this purpose, intent consists of a desire or knowledge that the chattel will be involved, without regard to whether the defendant knows that the chattel is the plaintiff's or that the plaintiff's rights are being violated. Interference can consist of any act regarding the chattel which only its rightful possessor is entitled to perform. Since Darren desired to take that particular coat, she had the necessary intent, regardless of her belief that the coat was her own. Since only Perdu was entitled to take the coat, Darren interfered with it. Since the coat was destroyed while Darren possessed it, her interference resulted in damage to Perdu. Darren is, therefore, liable to Perdu for trespass to chattel.

    B is incorrect because the tort was committed when Darren took the coat and the tort led to the coat's destruction. In trespass to chattel, intent does not require knowledge that the chattel belongs to another or that the defendant's act will affect the rights of another. **C** is, therefore, incorrect. Trespass to chattel was committed when Darren took the coat. If she had succeeded in returning the coat, damages might have been mitigated (i.e., reduced), but the tort would not have been undone. **D** is incorrect because her unsuccessful attempt to return the coat could not even mitigate damages.

13. **A** Strict liability is imposed on the seller of a product which is in a defective condition when sold. Since the bolt was cracked when the sled left the Rosebud factory, Rosebud would be liable if the crack constituted a defect.

    B and **C** are incorrect because the use and/or sale by Michael would not prevent the imposition of strict liability if the sled was defective when it left Rosebud's factory so long as such use or sale did not substantially change its condition. **D** is incorrect because strict liability in tort does not depend on unreasonable conduct by the defendant.

14. **D** One who voluntarily encounters a known risk assumes that risk, and is not entitled to damages resulting from it.

    A, B, and **C** are all incorrect since assumption of risk is available as a defense in claims based on negligence or strict liability. In addition, **B** is incorrect because horses are not regarded as wild animals, and **C** is incorrect because the fact that Parte, a professional horse trainer, had been warned of the animal's propensity indicates that Stabel's conduct was reasonable.

15. **C** Consent means willingness, and the affirmative defense of consent is effective because of the rule that a plaintiff who is willing for a particular thing to happen to her has no right to complain when it does. For this reason, a defendant does not commit a tort when she does something to which the plaintiff has consented. If the defendant induces plaintiff's consent by fraud, however, the consent does not have this effect, and does not privilege the defendant's conduct. A defendant induces consent by fraud when she knowingly misrepresents the nature of the act to which the plaintiff is consenting. Thus, if Dr. Hypno told Penny that the cattle prod would produce no real discomfort when she knew that this was false, she fraudulently induced Penny's consent to contact with it, and was not privileged by her consent.

In **A**, Penny consented to the contact even though she was aware that Dr. Hypno was not always successful in hypnotizing volunteers and that if she was not successful in hypnotizing her, the cattle prod might cause discomfort. Since she knew the nature of the act to which she was consenting, her consent would furnish Dr. Hypno with a privilege. **A** is, therefore, incorrect. In **B**, although Dr. Hypno defrauded Penny by promising money which she did not intend to pay, the fraud did not relate to the nature of the act to which Penny was consenting. Dr. Hypno would, therefore, be privileged by her consent, and **B** is, therefore, incorrect. A mistake leading to a consent does not destroy the effect of that consent unless the defendant is aware of the mistake. Since there is no indication in **D** that Dr. Hypno was aware of Penny's mistake regarding the effect of a cattle prod, her consent privileged Dr. Hypno, and **D** is, therefore, incorrect.

16. **A** Appropriation of identity is committed when the defendant, without the plaintiff's permission, uses the plaintiff's identity for a commercial purpose. Since Frank sold games which were imprinted with the governor's likeness, a court could conclude that he has liable for appropriation.

Public disclosure is committed when the defendant publicly discloses a private fact about the plaintiff the disclosure of which would offend the reasonable person in the plaintiff's position. Since a photo of the governor's face as it appeared in a public place is obviously not a private fact, **B** is incorrect. Intrusion is committed by intentionally invading the plaintiff's private space in a manner which would offend the reasonable person in the plaintiff's position. Since Frank snapped the photo in a public place, he did not invade the governor's private space, and **C** is incorrect. False light is committed by publishing false statements about the plaintiff which, although not defamatory, are in some way embarrassing or damaging. Since Frank did not publish any statements about the governor, **D** is incorrect.

17. **A** Holders of land owe a duty of reasonable care to travelers who foreseeably deviate onto the land for reasons related to their use of the adjacent public way.

B is, therefore, incorrect. **C** is incorrect because although the reason given explains why Basil's conduct was not negligent, it fails to explain why he had no duty. Although a landholder generally owes no duty of reasonable care to a trespasser, **D** is incorrect because a strayed traveler as described above is entitled to reasonable care as an exception to the general rule.

18. **C** Conduct is a factual cause of harm if the harm would not have occurred without it. Since medical assistance was summoned just a moment later, and since the facts do not indicate that Truck was worse off for the momentary delay, Carp's failure to summon aid was not a cause of harm.

Most jurisdictions agree that a landholder owes no duty of reasonable care to a trespasser. When the landholder knows of the trespasser's presence, however, and knows that the trespasser has been imperiled by some affirmative act of the landholder, the landholder does have a duty to act reasonably to protect the trespasser from that act. Since Carp knew that his act of throwing the hammer created the need for aid, he probably did owe Truck a duty to act reasonably in summoning it. **A** is, therefore, incorrect. Punitive damages may be available against a defendant who intended harm by his act. Intent requires a substantial certainty that the harm will probably occur, however. Knowledge that harm is *possible* is not intent, and is not sufficient to result in liability for punitive damages. **B** is, therefore, incorrect. A user of the public way who enters upon private land foreseeably and in connection with his use of the public way is entitled to some measure of reasonable care. **D** is incorrect, however, because he does not thereby become an invitee, and, further, because Truck's entry onto Carp's realty was not connected with Truck's use of the public way.

19. **C** Since the death would not have occurred without Ann's negligence, her negligence factually caused it. Since it is obviously foreseeable that an automobile accident will result in the death of a passenger, Ann's negligence was also a legal cause of the harm.

A is incorrect because Carp's conduct preceded Ann's, and is, therefore, not an intervening cause of Truck's death. Although "reasonable care" may require less in an emergency than it does under ordinary circumstances, one faced with an emergency is still required to act as a reasonable person would under similar circumstances. **B** is, therefore, incorrect. Even if Carp is liable for Truck's death, Ann would be liable also if her negligence proximately caused it. **D** is, therefore, incorrect.

20. **D** Violation of statute is relevant to the question of negligence only if the statute violated was designed to protect a class of persons to which the plaintiff belongs against risks like the one which resulted in harm to the plaintiff. Since insurance would not have prevented the trailer hitch from failing, the statute was not designed to protect against the risk that it would. Its violation is, therefore, not relevant.

A is, therefore, incorrect. **B** is incorrect because the violation is not relevant unless the statute was designed to protect against the risk involved. Public policy generally prohibits disclosing to a jury that a defendant was or was not insured. Such disclosure is not *absolutely* prohibited, however, since there are circumstances under which such disclosure could be made to a jury (e.g., to establish ownership of a vehicle). **C** is, thus, based on an overinclusive statement of the law, and is, therefore, incorrect.

21. **D** Negligence is the breach of a duty of reasonable care. A defendant owes a plaintiff a duty of reasonable care when the defendant's conduct creates a foreseeable risk to the plaintiff. If it was unforeseeable that persons would be running about the storeroom in the dark, the stacked groceries did not pose a foreseeable risk to the plaintiff. There would, therefore, be no duty to protect him against them and no negligence.

A is incorrect because an invitee is only entitled to reasonable care, and unless Super's conduct was unreasonable, the duty to Axel was not breached. **B** is incorrect for the same reason, since unless the conduct was negligent there is no liability. The fact, alone, that Axel was a licensee would not be sufficient to defeat his case, since even a licensee is entitled to reasonable warnings about known hidden dangers on the premises. **C** is therefore incorrect.

22. **C** An essential element of tort liability for misrepresentation is the defendant's intent to induce the plaintiff's reliance on the defendant's statement. If Dillon did not know that Barton would rely on the statements which she made to Collins, she could not have intended to induce Barton's reliance on those statements. Since there is no indication that Dillon was aware that Barton had overhead her conversation with Collins, C is correct.

A is overinclusive, and, therefore, incorrect: statements of opinion, especially when made by experts, may be regarded as assertions of fact (i.e., the fact that the speaker actually held that particular opinion). Since Barton paid $250,000 for something worth only $600, based on his belief in what he had overheard Dillon saying, he did sustain damage as a result of his reliance on Dillon's statement. **B** is, therefore, incorrect. **D** is incorrect for two reasons. First, as indicated above, an expert may incur misrepresentation liability by stating that she holds an opinion which she doesn't actually hold. Second, Dillon's statement was not only an evaluation of the painting's value, but included a statement about who had painted it.

23. **D** Since Barton received something for his money, the measure of his damage must consider the value which he has received. In some jurisdictions, damage for misrepresentations is measured by the difference between what the plaintiff received and what the defendant told him he would be receiving (benefit of the bargain theory). In this case, that would be $250,000 less $600, or $249,400. In other jurisdictions, the damage is measured by the difference between what the

plaintiff paid and what he actually received (out of pocket theory). In this case, that would be $225,000 less $600 or $224,400. **D** is, therefore, correct. **A** and **C** are incorrect because they ignore the value of what Barton actually received. **B** is incorrect because it describes a rescission remedy, which may be available in a claim for breach of contract, but is not available in this tort claim for damages.

24. **C** Under pure comparative negligence statutes, a plaintiff's recovery in a negligence action is diminished in proportion to the plaintiff's fault, but is not barred by the plaintiff's own negligence. Thus, Nellie would be entitled to recover part of any damages which she sustained as a result of Dalton's conduct if Dalton's conduct was unreasonable.

In most jurisdictions, a landholder owes a duty of reasonable care to an invitee, but owes no duty of reasonable care to a trespasser. For this purpose, an invitee is one whose presence confers an economic benefit on the landholder, and a trespasser is one who enters without permission. Since Nellie's use of Dalton's pool was consideration for valuable services which she rendered, she was an invitee. Under the "attractive nuisance" doctrine, a trespassing child may be entitled to reasonable care, but it is inapplicable here because Nellie was an invitee rather than a trespasser. **A** and **B** are, therefore, incorrect. If Nellie's conduct was unreasonable, the amount of her damages would be diminished accordingly. **D** is incorrect, however, because in a pure comparative negligence system, the plaintiff's negligence does not completely bar her recovery.

25. **B** Negligence is a failure to act reasonably in the face of a foreseeable risk. If it was not foreseeable that the contents of the package would cause harm to a passenger in her car, Carolyn's conduct with respect to the package could not have been negligent. Although it is not certain that a court would come to this conclusion, the argument in B is the only one listed which is supported by the facts.

A is incorrect because the rule limiting the duty owed to a licensee applies only to conditions of realty occupied by a defendant. Contributory negligence is unreasonable conduct by plaintiff which contributes to the happening of the accident. Since Harold could not have known that the contents of the package were caustic, there is no reason to conclude that his conduct was unreasonable. **C** is, therefore, incorrect. A plaintiff is said to have assumed the risk when he voluntarily encounters a known risk. **D** is incorrect because Harold did not know that the contents of the package were caustic, and touching it did not, therefore, constitute an encounter with a known risk.

26. **D** Under the doctrine of *res ipsa loquitur*, an inference that the defendant acted unreasonably can be drawn from the facts that the injury involved was one which does not usually occur without unreasonable conduct and that the defendant was the only person whose conduct could have caused the injury (i.e., the defendant was in exclusive control of the circumstances). If an expert witness testifies that surgeons do not usually leave instruments inside a patient unless

they are acting unreasonably, Peck can rely on the inference established by *res ipsa loquitur* if she can show that Dr. Danh was the only person who could have left the instrument inside her. Since Danh was the only person who had ever performed surgery on Peck, Danh is the only person who could have left the instrument inside her.

A is incorrect because it is based on an inaccurate statement of law; there are many medical malpractice cases in which the plaintiff is permitted to rely on *res ipsa loquitur*. (Indeed, these cases frequently involve what we have here: foreign objects left in the plaintiff's body during surgery). Ordinarily, in drawing an inference of negligence under the doctrine of *res ipsa loquitur*, a jury relies on what it knows about human experience to determine whether a particular accident is of a kind which does not usually occur without negligence. Because of its lack of specialized knowledge, a jury is not competent to decide whether the particular result of a professional's conduct is one which would not usually occur without negligence. Once a jury has heard testimony to that effect from an expert witness (something that nearly all courts allow), however, the jury may base an inference of negligence on its decision about whether or not it believes that expert. This is a credibility decision which a jury is uniquely competent to make. For this reason, **B** is incorrect. **C** is incorrect because *res ipsa loquitur* is not dependent on the existence of any "absolute duty," but rather on circumstantial evidence which justifies the inference that a particular defendant acted unreasonably.

27. **D** In general, there are only three potential bases for tort liability: intent, negligence, and liability without fault. Liability without fault is ordinarily imposed upon a person who knowingly engages in abnormally dangerous activities or who is a professional supplier of products. Since Darrin was neither, liability without fault cannot bc imposed. Intentional tort liability is imposed upon a defendant who knew to a substantial degree of certainty that his act would harm the plaintiff. Unless Darrin *knew* that the stove would hurt someone, he cannot be liable for committing an intentional tort. Negligence is unreasonable conduct in the face of a risk about which the defendant should have known (i.e., a foreseeable risk). Unless Darrin *should have known* that his stove would injure someone, he cannot be liable for negligence.

Although liability without fault (i.e., strict liability) may be imposed upon a professional supplier who sells a defective product, **A** is incorrect because Darrin was neither a professional supplier of stoves nor did he sell the defective stove. If Darrin should have anticipated that a person would enter his cabin by mistake, he might have owed Perl a duty to act reasonably. **B** is incorrect, however, because there is no fact indicating that he breached that duty by acting unreasonably. It is often held that a landholder owes a trespasser no duty of reasonable care. Thus, if Perl was a trespasser at the time of the explosion, Darrin would probably not be liable to her for negligence. Even if she was not a trespasser, however, Darrin would not be liable unless he knew or should have known that the stove would injure someone. Perl's trespass is, therefore, not the *only* thing that would result in a judgment for Darrin. **C** is, therefore, incorrect.

28. **C** Under the "but for" rule of causation, defendant's conduct is a cause in fact of plaintiff's injury if the plaintiff's injury would not have occurred without it. Since Palco would not have been injured without Yeong's intoxication, and since Yeong would not have become intoxicated without Barney's conduct, Barney's conduct was a cause in fact of Palco's injury.

A is incorrect for two reasons: first, under the given facts it is uncertain whether Alfred's conduct was a substantial factor in making Yeong intoxicated; and, second, even if Alfred's conduct was a cause of the harm (i.e., a substantial factor in producing it), Barney's conduct was also a cause of that harm. **B** is incorrect because the language of the statute ("... any person who sold said minor the alcohol which resulted in said minor's intoxication ... ") indicates that liability depends on a causal relationship between the defendant's conduct and the minor's intoxication. Since Palco's injury would not have occurred without Yeong's intoxication, any cause of Yeong's intoxication must also have been a cause of Palco's injury (see above explanation of "but for" rule). **D** is, therefore, incorrect.

29. **D** Under the "substantial factor" rule of causation, defendant's conduct is a cause of a particular consequence if it was a substantial factor in bringing that consequence about. Conduct which would have produced a particular consequence all by itself was a substantial factor in producing that consequence even if other factors happened to combine with that conduct to bring the consequence about. Since either Alfred's conduct alone or Barney's conduct alone would have made Yeong intoxicated, each was a substantial factor in making Yeong intoxicated. Each was, therefore, a cause of Yeong's intoxication. Under the "but for" rule of causation, a condition is a cause of harm if the harm would not have occurred without that condition. Since Palco's injury would not have occurred had Yeong not been intoxicated, Yeong's intoxication was a cause of Palco's injury. Since the conduct of Alfred and Barney were causes of Yeong's intoxication, and since Yeong's intoxication was a cause of Palco's injury, the conduct of Alfred and Barney were causes of Palco's injury. For this reason, neither I nor II is correct.

30. **B** Violation of a statute may establish the violator's negligence (or liability) in a particular case if the statute was designed to protect against the risk which led to the plaintiff's harm. Prill was hurt not because Drinker was drunk, but because Drinker had been poisoned. (Note that the facts indicate that Drinker was driving reasonably.) If the statute was not meant to protect against the risk of drinking poison, then its violation would not be relevant in the case of an injury which

resulted from drinking poison. Since poison could as easily be drunk in non-alcoholic drinks, it is unlikely that the statute in this case was designed to protect against drinking poison.

A is incorrect because the language of the statute appears to prohibit the sale of alcohol to a person who is already intoxicated, without regard to how he got intoxicated. **C** is based on an inaccurate statement. Conduct is a cause of harm if that harm would not have resulted without the conduct. Since Drinker's death and the resulting accident would not have occurred if Drinker did not drink the poisoned liquor, service of the liquor was a cause of Prill's injuries. **C** is, therefore, incorrect. If an intervening cause of harm was unforeseeable, it may be called a superseding cause and relieve a defendant of liability by resulting in the conclusion that his conduct was not a "legal" or "proximate" cause of the injury. Causes which existed or occurred prior to the defendant's conduct are not intervening causes, however, and, therefore, cannot be superseding causes of harm. **D** is incorrect because Fuller's conduct preceded Barr's service of liquor to Drinker.

ESSAY EXAM QUESTIONS & ANSWERS

The following questions were asked on various Harvard Law School First-Year Torts examinations. The questions are reproduced as they actually appeared, with only slight modifications. The sample answers are not "official" and represent merely one approach to handling the questions.

QUESTION 1

At points where a trail entered his property in a sparsely settled area, Farmer posted signs warning, "No trespassing. Snowmobilers and other unauthorized persons keep off. Violators assume all risks." Boisterous intruders continued to run snowmobiles through his property at night. Farmer then erected a barbed wire barrier across the trail at each edge of his property and again about 100 yards in from each edge. He piled brush over the two barbed wire barriers at the edges of the property, but left the barbed wire uncovered at the barriers farther in. Joyce, operating a snowmobile owned by Jimmy, her passenger, maneuvered around a barrier at the edge of Farmer's property, returned to the trail, and while proceeding at high speed, crashed into one of the inner barriers. Joyce, not having her seat belt fastened, was thrown off the snowmobile into a snowbank, unhurt. The snowmobile, uncontrolled, crashed into Farmer's barn, a quarter of a mile off the trail, and started a fire. Jimmy unfastened his seat belt and dragged himself away from the fire, severely injured. Farmer rushed out to the barn and tried to control the fire. Joyce appeared, discovered Jimmy's condition, and asked Farmer to take them to the nearest hospital, 40 miles away. When Farmer refused and continued his efforts to control the fire, Joyce, threatening Farmer with a knife, took Farmer's car keys and forced Farmer to help carry Jimmy to Farmer's car. Joyce then drove Jimmy to the hospital, where Jimmy was found to be suffering from exposure as well as the injuries from the crash. Farmer returned to the barn to fight the fire, but without success.

What torts? Explain.

ANSWER TO QUESTION 1

I will discuss the possible torts in the chronological order in which they occurred.

Trespass by Joyce and Jimmy: It seems clear that both Joyce and Jimmy have committed a trespass on Farmer's land. As trespassers, they are liable for virtually all consequences, probably including the burning of the barn (even if this was not foreseeable, and even if it was not the result of any negligence). Even though Jimmy was not the driver, he will almost certainly be held to have actively participated in the trespass, and he will be ***jointly and severally liable*** with Joyce for the barn-burning.

However, if Farmer is found to have committed a battery, this might constitute a superseding cause relieving Joyce and Jimmy of liability.

Nuisance by Joyce and Jimmy: Farmer could sue Joyce and Jimmy on a nuisance theory, since they (in combination with other snowmobilers) substantially interfered with his use and enjoyment of his property. However, in view of his trespass claim, it is unlikely that Farmer would bother to assert nuisance.

Battery by Farmer: The use of the barriers by Farmer might be a ***battery*** against Jimmy and Joyce, if they can show that Farmer either intended to cause the contact with their bodies or snowmobile, or knew that such a contact was substantially certain to follow. In trying to prove this, Joyce and Jimmy will want to point to the fact that the outer barriers were covered up, which indicates that Farmer was trying to hurt snowmobilers, not merely keep them out. On the other hand, Farmer could show that the barrier that was crashed into was uncovered, and could claim that he was just trying to keep people off the trail once they got onto the property.

In any event, Farmer is certainly likely to assert that he was ***privileged*** to erect the barriers, to prevent trespass. To sustain this privilege, he will have to show that he used no greater degree of forced than seemed reasonably necessary, and that this force was ***not deadly*** (i.e., not likely to cause death or serious bodily injury). Since Farmer knew that most of the snowmobiling took place at night, on what are presumably unlit trails, the use of such barriers does seem likely to cause serious harm. If so, the case would be similar to *Katko v. Briney*, and there would be no privilege, since Farmer's own safety, and the sanctity of his dwelling, were not in danger.

Even if Farmer succeeds in showing that the barrier should not be considered deadly force, he may lose his privilege by virtue of his failure to ***warn*** of the device's existence.

Negligence by Farmer in erecting barrier: Even if the erection of the barrier is not a battery by Farmer, it might be ***negligence*** on his part, if it constituted a failure to use ordinary care. However, the duty of care owed by a landowner to trespassers is limited.

Jimmy and Joyce might be found to have been "constant trespassers on a limited area" (the trail), in which case Farmer would have at least a duty to warn them of dangers they were unlikely to discover for themselves, of which the barrier is probably an instance. Alternatively, if Jimmy and Joyce are children (the question does not indicate whether they are), Farmer might have a duty of care towards them, if he knew that many of the snowmobilers typically were children.

Even if Farmer were found to have been negligent, Jimmy might be held to have assumed the risk, or to have been contributorily negligent. These defenses are discussed in the treatment of his suit against Joyce, below.

Negligence by Joyce towards Jimmy: Joyce's conduct in driving at high speeds was probably negligent as to Jimmy. However, she will be able to assert several defenses based on his own conduct. First, he may be held to have ***assumed the risk***. Normally one assumes the risk only as to ***particular*** risks that one is aware of; however, in this instance, Jimmy might be held to have assumed the risk of unknown dangers, especially ones that are incident to a dangerous activity like snowmobiling in the dark. However, even if Jimmy assumed the risk of a barrier, he did not necessarily assume the risk that Joyce would drive at high speeds; this would be a question of fact, turning on whether she had driven fast on other occasions with him, giving him reason to know that she was likely to do so again.

Alternatively, Jimmy may have been ***contributorily negligent*** in riding with Joyce. Again, this is likely to turn on whether he knew that she would drive too fast, or had an opportunity to get off when he saw that this was the case.

Lastly, there may be an ***automobile guest statute*** broad enough to include snowmobiles (e.g., a statute including "all motorized recreational vehicles), which would allow Jimmy to recover only if Joyce was "grossly" or "wantonly" negligent.

Assuming that Joyce is liable for negligence, she would certainly be liable for Jimmy's injuries from the collision. She may also be liable for his ***exposure*** injuries. She will argue that the exposure injuries are the direct result of Farmer's refusal to help, which should be treated as a superseding intervening cause. However, it seems probable that the exposure would be held to be reasonably foreseeable, even if Farmer's intransigence was not; the case would then fall under the rule that where the harm was foreseeable, and the manner of its occurrence not, there is liability.

Negligence by Farmer in his refusal to help Jimmy: Farmer's refusal to aid Jimmy might be negligence. The general rule is that one has no duty to rescue a stranger, even when this could be done at little danger to oneself. However, since Jimmy's injuries were the result of an instrument under Farmer's control, this would probably be enough to give rise to a duty on the part of Farmer to render reasonable assistance.

But even if Farmer had such a duty to give reasonable assistance, he may have been privileged not to so do because of his right to preserve his property (by fighting the fire). This question would depend on what a reasonable person would have done in the circumstances; normally human life is considered more important than property, but since Joyce was available to take Jimmy to the hospital, Farmer may have behaved reasonably. A court might also hold that Farmer's duty of care was lessened because of the fact that Jimmy was a trespasser (although this would contradict the rule that once a landowner discovers a particular trespasser on his property, he must behave with ordinary reasonable care towards him).

Assault by Joyce: Joyce's use of the knife to threaten Farmer is probably a prima facie case of ***assault***. Joyce's threat was a ***conditional*** one, but the general rule is that this is still an assault unless she had the legal right to make Farmer comply with the threat (by taking Jimmy to the hospital). She had such a right only if this fell within Farmer's duty of reasonable care, an open question as discussed above. In any case, even if she did have a legal right to compel him to take Jimmy, her use of a knife may have constituted an unreasonably violent way of accomplishing this result.

Conversion or trespass to chattels by Joyce: Joyce's use of Farmer's car to take Jimmy to the hospital may have been either conversion or trespass to chattels. It will be the latter rather than the former unless the inconvenience and harm to Farmer was substantial, which the question does not indicate it to have been.

Assuming that there was at most merely trespass to chattels, even this may fall within Joyce's privilege of ***private necessity***. This will be so if there was no better way of getting Jimmy to the hospital.

QUESTION 2

During his 63rd year, defendant D's wife died and he retired on his social security and a small pension. He moved out of the house he had lived in with his family for 35 years, into a smaller wood frame one in a residential neighborhood. About a year later, he became aware that an ailanthus tree was growing into the brick foundation. He consulted a friend who was a small time building contractor, and was told that unless he did something about the tree he would eventually have to replace that part of the foundation, at a cost of at least $50,000. He then called a local company that was in the business of pruning and removing trees. They told him that it would cost him about $10,000 to have the tree cut down and taken away.

$10,000 was his income for a month, so he decided to do the job himself. He was in good health. He owned a chain saw and some ropes, and he had often spent his lunch hour watching tree surgeons at work. The tree was about 30 feet high, but he knew that ailanthus wood is light and weak, being mainly water.

From his attic window, he tied a rope around an upper branch and then went outside and cut through about six of the 12 inches of the trunk. He pulled on the rope, in order to cause the tree to fall away from the street, along the side of his house, and into his back yard. What he didn't realize was that he had made the cut on the wrong side of the tree (only an expert would have known this) so that, given its angle and the distribution of its foliage, the natural direction of its fall was toward the street. The tree wouldn't budge, no matter how hard he pulled on the rope, and he found himself quickly out of breath and a little dizzy. He picked up the chain saw and cut further into the trunk, until he realized that the tree had begun to fall — toward the street! He tried to push it back and over into the right direction. He would probably have succeeded had he been a vigorous young man of 20. But he was too weak, and the tree fell into the street, severing an electric power line.

The power line had been put up twenty years before the accident by the Power Company, acting under technical specifications that had been approved by the state power regulatory commission. Two years before the accident, the regulatory commission had approved the Power Company's proposal to replace all old power lines with new ones. The new model is strong enough to withstand the impact and the weight of a tree like that which D cut down. But at the time of the accident the company had fallen six months behind in the implementation of the replacement program. Had it not been for the delay, a new wire would already have been installed on D's block.

It was a Sunday afternoon, and normally there would have been little if any traffic in D's street. But it happened that P, an out of town motorist who had gotten lost, came down the street just as the tree was falling. If he had been obeying the 20 m.p.h. speed limit, instead of going 25, it wouldn't have hit him, but it did. He was very frightened but unhurt by the impact. The roof of his car was dented. He slammed on the brakes and jumped out, stepping on the live power line and electrocuting himself.

His widow sues both D and the Power Company for the damage to her husband and to the car. Assume that she has the same rights her husband would have had if he had been injured instead of killed (i.e., there is no problem about interpreting a wrongful death statute in this case). Discuss the pros and cons of the issues that will arise in the case.

ANSWER TO QUESTION 2

(1) P vs. D: P can pursue two general lines of attack against D: negligence and strict liability. After discussing these two, I will discuss the proximate cause issues that are common to both. (I will treat the plaintiff as being P, rather than his widow, for simplicity).

Negligence suit against D: In order to establish a negligence cause of action against D, P must first show that D bore him a duty of care. This should not be hard to do, since a landowner's duty to persons outside the premises is generally one of reasonable care, at least where an activity, rather than a natural hazard, is concerned.

Assuming that D had the duty to behave as a reasonable person would, the principle issue is whether D should be held to the standard of care of persons habitually engaged in tree surgery (i.e., ***experts***), or the standard of care of a non-expert. (Disposition of this issue is obviously critical, since by cutting on the wrong side of the tree, D violated the former standard but not the latter)

In arguing for imposition of a "reasonable expert" standard, P can point out that the whole reason most tree surgery is done by experts is that it is a dangerous activity if not done correctly, and society has a strong interest in not being forced to run the risk of bungling amateurs. A person who performed medical surgery would certainly be held to the standard of a reasonable doctor, whether she had a license to practice medicine or not; similarly, a child who engages in dangerous activities usually pursued by adults will be held to an adult standard of care. P can make a strong argument that these principles should be extended to impose on D the standard of care which would be shown by a reasonable tree surgeon.

In response to this, D can argue that imposing a higher standard on him than that of a reasonable non-expert landowner would be grossly unfair. There was no way he himself could have met such a standard, since by definition it is one met only by experts. Nor did he behave unreasonably in not going to an expert, since to do so would have cost him a month's income, and the risk of accident did not seem to justify such a painful expenditure. Furthermore, D can contend, this situation is different from that of the unlicensed person holding herself out as a doctor; D has not represented to any one that he is an expert, and no one has relied on any indication of expertise.

Assuming that D is held to an ordinary reasonable person standard, and was therefore not negligent in the way he cut the tree, it could still be argued that he was negligent in not pushing the tree back in the right direction once it started to fall. Normally a person's physical attributes (in this case, his weakness and age) are taken into account, and not held against him, in determining what constitutes reasonable conduct. But the fact that D was weak, and not equipped to deal with an emergency, may be a factor indicating that it was not reasonable care on his part to start the cutting process in the first place; certain activities require an ability to react well in an emergency, and the actor will be negligent if he performs them without this capacity (e.g., a bus driver with slow reflexes).

Strict liability for abnormally dangerous activity: As a second line of attack, P can argue that tree surgery in this situation was an ***abnormally dangerous activity***, and that D should be strictly liable for the resulting accident. However, it is usually held that this kind of liability will apply only where the activity is such that substantial risk cannot be eliminated even by due care. Since a professional tree surgeon could probably have brought down the tree with almost no risk of this kind of accident, this condition seems not to be met.

Proximate cause: For each of these theories, P will have to establish that D's conduct was the proximate cause of his harm. To do this, he will have to overcome a number of hurdles.

First, D will contend that damage to the power lines was not a foreseeable result of his activity. But from the sound of things, given that P was negligent (or that the activity was abnormally dangerous), the risk of damaging power lines seems to be within the "cluster" of risks that made the conduct negligent or ultrahazardous.

But even if damage to the power lines was foreseeable, and thus a proximate result of D's conduct, it doesn't follow that the damage to P's car was also foreseeable. This was a sparsely travelled street, and there was very little danger that a motorist would happen to be passing by when the tree fell. D could plausibly argue that P was really in a *Palsgraf*-like position, an essentially "unforeseeable plaintiff." But P could convincingly argue that the Third Restatement's test should be applied: D will escape liability on proximate-cause grounds only if the harm was "different from the harms whose risk made [D's] conduct tortious." Here, the risks that make it negligent to cut a tree so that it falls onto the public road almost certainly include the risk that the tree will fall on a passing car, so D's negligence ought to be viewed as the proximate cause of the collision with P's car.

However, even assuming that D's act was the proximate cause of the damage to the car, it does not by any means follow that D is also the proximate cause of P's death. D will start by contending that he never imposed an unreasonable risk of bodily harm on P at all, and that P is in a *Palsgraf*-like position with respect to his personal injuries, even if he was not in such a position with respect to the damage to his car. However, D will probably lose with this *Palsgraf* argument; the court is likely to hold that once P was placed in danger for his personal property from a falling tree, he thus established himself as a foreseeable plaintiff, and any other harm arising to him in the same general episode would be D's responsibility. This result could be supported by analogy to those cases allowing recovery for negligent infliction of emotional distress to a parent who sees a child harmed, and who is himself within the "zone of danger" (i.e, put in risk of bodily harm).

Next, D has a string of several "superseding intervening cause" arguments. First, he can try to blame the whole accident on Power Co., for having delayed in putting in a power line that would have withstood the tree. But this contention is very unlikely to succeed; Power Co.'s negligence was almost certainly not "gross", and its ordinary negligence is unlikely to be considered a superseding cause. (The most this argument will get D is joint and several liability with Power Co.)

Then, D can claim that P's travelling above the speed limit was a superseding cause (or, alternatively, contributory negligence per se). But this argument is not likely to work either. P's fast driving did not increase the danger of the accident, at least as far as anyone observing from P's position before the accident would have been able to tell. (See the discussion of *Marshall v. Nugent.*)

Lastly, D can contend that P's leaving the car and stepping on a live power line was an irrational and bizarre act which should be superseding (or, alternatively, that it was contributory negligence). He could point to Illustration 2, §445 of the Second Restatement, which indicates that where a passenger, after being frightened by a near collision, panics, opens the door, and throws out her child, this is a superseding act for which the person who has caused the near-miss is not responsible. But P ought to be able to distinguish this example fairly easily, by stating that he merely got out of the car as a reasonable person would have, and didn't notice the power line. In any event, this was an emergency of sorts, and P should only have to live up to the standards of a reasonable person in such an emergency, which he probably did.

All in all, unless D succeeds in showing that he should be held to the standard of care of a reasonable non-expert, not a reasonable tree-surgeon, he is likely to be held liable for both the damage to the car and P's death.

(2) P vs. Power Co.: P may proceed against Power Co. under either a negligence or a strict products liability theory. And there is a remote possibility that he might succeed on a "strict liability for abnormally dangerous activities" theory.

Negligence: In order to establish that Power Co. was negligent, and that this negligence was a proximate cause of his damages, P will have many hurdles to overcome.

First, Power Co. will argue that the regulatory commission's approval of the technical specifications conclusively established that its conduct met the standard of reasonable care. While such compliance will probably not be conclusive on this issue, in the same way that a statutory violation would conclusively establish "negligence per se," the court might consider this compliance as ***evidence*** that Power Co. met reasonable standards of care. But it would do even this only on a showing that these technical specifications were drafted after consideration of safety needs imposed by possible storms, rotten trees, etc.

Even if Power Co.'s conduct was reasonably careful twenty years ago, however, this does not mean that it did not later become negligent by not replacing the power line. As stronger materials became available, the durability of the minimum reasonable installation surely increased; the question then becomes whether there is an obligation to go to the expense of substituting the newly-available materials. This question has generally been answered affirmatively in highway design cases, in which states have been held to be under an obligation to use newly-developed safe-design knowledge to remodel old roads now known to be unduly dangerous.

Even if Power Co.'s delayed installation of the new lines would not otherwise be negligence, it may have become "negligence per se" once the plan was approved by the regulatory commission, and then not followed. (This assumes that the commission approved not only the overall plan, but also the timetable, which was not met). Power Co. could counter this negligence per se argument by contending that its new program went far beyond the requirements of reasonable care, and that it should not be penalized for adopting an ambitious plan. Also, the court might hold that an administrative body's determination should not be accorded the same deference as the legislature's safety statutes.

Proximate cause: To show that Power Co.'s negligence (if established) was the proximate cause of the damage to the car, it will not be necessary for P to show that this particular accident (i.e., bad tree surgery) was reasonably foreseeable. The risk that trees might fall for other reasons (e.g., storms), was itself substantial, and this accident would probably be held to be an illustration of the principle that where a foreseeable kind of harm occurs in an unforeseeable manner, there will be liability. See, for instance, *Gibson v. Gar-*

cia, in which the defendant was held liable for a negligently maintained wooden pole next to the street, where it was knocked over by an unforeseeable car accident.

Power Co.'s next line of defense would be that even if it was negligent with respect to damage to the car, it was not negligent with respect to danger of electrocution. But again, danger of some sort of electrocution was probably one of the risks that made the conduct negligent in the first place, so the fact that this may have occurred in an unforeseeable manner (i.e., panic as the result of being hit by a tree) would not be enough to be a superseding cause.

Power Co. could try to blame the whole thing on D's negligence, arguing that his negligence contributed so much more directly to the accident that he should be the only one to be liable. But since Power Co.'s negligence was clearly a "but for" cause of the accident, and otherwise appears to have been a proximate cause of it, D's own negligence (surely not "gross" negligence) is unlikely to get it off the hook. The best that Power Co. can hope for from this argument is the right to ***contribution*** from D, according to an estimate of their relative degrees of fault; see the discussion of *Dole v. Dow Chemical*.

Lastly, Power Co. can, like D, argue that P's speeding was the superseding cause, since he wouldn't have been electrocuted if he had been within the speed limit (since he wouldn't have been hit by the tree, and therefore not have gotten out of the car). But this argument is no more likely to succeed for Power Co. than for D; P's speeding did not increase the perceivable risk of the electrocution, so it will not even be contributory negligence, let alone a superseding cause.

Strict products liability: P might try to argue that the Power Co. line was a "defective" product, and that Power Co. should have strict tort liability for it.

Normally, some kind of sale, rental or other transfer has been necessary for strict products liability. Here, since Power Co. has simply put up the power line for its own purposes, such a transaction seems to be missing. But D can argue that Power Co. was supplying a service (electricity) and should have strict liability for any physical product used in supplying that service. (He could analogize to *Newmark v. Gimbel's*, the beauty shop case). Then, the argument would continue, Power Co. would be liable to P as a "bystander", just as a car maker would be liable to a pedestrian injured by a defective car.

But even if a court were willing to extend strict products liability to this considerable extent, this probably wouldn't get P too far. He would still have to show that the product was "defective", and to do so, he would probably have to make the same kind of showing that the benefits of the new, stronger, lines outweighed their costs, that he would have to make in a negligence action. He might draw some support from the many cases holding that a design is defective if it doesn't meet a reasonable consumer's expectations as to safety; he might be able to show that the average driver or homeowner reasonably believed that a power line would withstand having a fairly light tree fall on it, or that it would go dead once severed.

Abnormally dangerous activity: Lastly, there is a very small chance that D might be able to establish that weak power lines constituted an abnormally dangerous activity, giving rise to strict liability. P could point to the *Lubin v. Iowa City* case, holding that a town which buries water mains and intentionally leaves them there till they start leaking has such strict liability. However, this case seems to be distinguishable on the grounds that it involved a danger which was almost certain to materialize, whereas the power lines were not at all certain to be hit by a falling tree.

QUESTION 3

In the early 2010s the Dow Drug Company developed a compound called XYZ, which its researchers hoped would prove effective in treating certain unusual blood diseases. By 2016, after experimentation with almost a thousand human subjects, the drug was approved by government authorities for distribution to only a few specially qualified physicians, who would themselves inject it into patients. Dr. Mary Jones, a specialist in blood diseases who practices in Ames City, is qualified to administer the drug. She became fully apprised of the drug's potentialities and side effects through the instructions sent to physicians by Dow with the drug. The instructions noted that short-term adverse side-effects were judged to be relatively slight — nausea, light-headedness, and blurring of vision, all normally expected to pass within five to ten hours after the drug was injected. The blurring of sight was related by experimenters to very slight hemorrhaging of the retina, and there was thought to be a theoretical possibility (not realized with any experimental subject) of more serious hemorrhaging and eye damage, particularly after repeated injections. Also, a handful of the experimental subjects reported continued nausea lasting on and off over a period of months, even from a single injection.

Early in 2018 Fred Smith, a 32-year-old construction worker, was referred to Dr. Jones by his family physician. Smith was afflicted with Price's syndrome, a rare condition of the blood for which no recognized treatment was available. Smith complained of characteristic symptoms of the Syndrome: a constant dull aching throughout his body and phases of debilitating listlessness which interfered with his work so much that he feared he might be fired.

After a thorough examination, Dr. Jones explained that there was no recognized treatment for his illness but added that a new drug just on the market might conceivably prove to be the answer, though no one could tell for sure. Smith, stating that he didn't want to spend the rest of his life feeling poorly and uncertain about employment, concluded that if the doctor thought this drug might work, he would try it. Dr. Jones replied that "on balance" she thought it worthwhile to go ahead. She injected Smith with the recommended dose of XYZ. Dr. Jones then said that, though the side-effects of the drug were apparently limited to "some mild discomfort that passes in a matter of hours," the drug still was "experimental", and therefore they should monitor its effects closely. Smith agreed to come back for a check-up the following week.

That night Smith was troubled by nausea, but he felt fine the next morning as he set out in his car to drive to the construction site where he worked. While on a little-travelled three-lane highway, Smith rounded a curve and saw that his lane was blocked by a stopped car about 50 yards ahead.

The car belonged to Elmer Brown, a senior official of the Ames City Health Department. Brown was to deliver the main address in one hour at a special state-wide meeting of health officers called to discuss the grave public health problems caused by recent heavy rains and flooding. His car's right rear tire had blown out. Brown's travelling companion had advised Brown to pull off the road before trying to change the tire, but Brown had rejoined that the side of the road was so muddy that they would probably get stuck there. As Smith approached, Brown was working furiously to change the tire, knowing that his chances of arriving on time for his lecture were decreasing.

When Smith saw the Brown car he maintained his speed but started to pull out into the middle lane to pass. There was no on-coming traffic. But at that moment Smith suddenly suffered serious retinal hemorrhaging and near total loss of vision. He hit the brakes but couldn't control direction or avoid a glancing collision with Brown's car.

Both cars were damaged in the collision, and both Smith and Brown were hospitalized with fractures. Tests showed that Smith's impairment of vision was irreversible.

Discuss the tort actions that Smith and Brown might bring. The State of Ames, where the relevant events occurred, is a common-law jurisdiction with respect to auto accidents; the Ames courts follow the rule of "pure" (not "partial") comparative negligence.

ANSWER TO QUESTION 3

Smith v. Dow Drug: Smith can bring a ***products liability*** claim against Dow Drug. Unless he can prove negligence in the testing procedures, he will have to proceed on either a strict liability or implied warranty cause of action. Because of possible privity problems with a warranty claim, this strict tort liability claim looks like his best bet, and this is what I will consider.

Smith will have to demonstrate that the product was ***"defective"***. Dow will undoubtedly argue that even if the product was dangerous, it was ***"unavoidably dangerous"***, since extensive experimentation failed to disclose the danger. The question is really whether the product's safety should be judged as of the state of medical knowledge at the time it was given to Dr. Jones, or as of the time of trial. Most courts would probably hold that the former is the time for evaluating the danger, and that the product was therefore unavoidably unsafe.

Dow can also point out that it was not engaged in mass distribution of the drug, but merely a new level of carefully supervised experimental testing. Particularly since this testing stage was approved by the government, Dow can make a powerful claim that it should not be held liable; otherwise, it would be impossible to test a drug sufficiently to market it. On the effect of government approval of the drug, Dow could assert a "regulatory compliance" defense, recognized by some courts, which would shield it from liability since XYZ was approved by an appropriate government agency.

Warning: Smith can also contend that even if the product was otherwise unavoidably unsafe, Dow at least bore the duty of giving an adequate warning of possible bad side effects. It is usually held that a drug manufacturer has no duty to warn of bad side effects of which it is unaware at the time of sale. But since Dow was aware of at least the theoretical possibility of retinal hemorrhaging, it might well be held that it had a duty to warn of this possibility. (I am assuming that severe retinal hemorrhaging was not mentioned to Dr. Jones as a possibility, although the question is unclear on this issue).

Smith may also contend that it was not enough that the warning was transmitted to Dr. Jones, and that Dow had an obligation to see that the patient himself received the warning. However, this argument is unlikely to prevail; it is usually held that a warning to the dispensing doctor is sufficient (the "learned intermediary" doctrine).

If Smith does make out his prima facie case that the product was defective, he will probably also be able to establish that the defect was a proximate cause of both his impairment of vision and the accident. As to the latter, even if the danger of severe hemorrhaging was only theoretical, there was a well-established danger of blurring vision; the accident would then fall within the principle that where the harm is foreseeable, but occurs in an unforeseeable manner, it is a proximate result. It is possible, however, that the court will apply a narrower standard of proximate cause in a case based upon strict liability than in the usual negligence case.

Smith v. Dr. Jones: Smith has two theoretical causes of action against Dr. Jones, one for products liability and the other for malpractice.

He is unlikely to be successful on his products liability claim. Such liability has almost never been imposed on ***professionals*** who supply a product in the course of rendering a service. See, e.g., the *Magrine* case.

Smith has a much stronger case against Dr. Jones for ***malpractice*** (i.e., professional negligence). Jones does not seem to have acted negligently in recommending the drug's use, since Smith appears to be the sort of candidate for whom its use was indicated. However, Smith has an excellent chance of showing that his ***informed consent*** was not obtained.

Prior to the injection, Smith was not informed of any of the possible side effects. Assuming that Dr. Jones was aware only of the minor side effects, and not of the possibility of severe hemorrhaging, she might be able to persuade the court that these side effects were so minor that a reasonable person in Smith's position would have taken the drug even had he known of them, and that they were therefore not material considerations required for informed consent. On the other hand, Jones' statement that "on balance" she thought the drug would be worth while seems to indicate that she did not regard these side effects as all that trivial, and should therefore have told Smith about them.

Assuming that Jones did not know about the risk of severe hemorrhaging, it seems very unlikely that communication of that risk to Smith was necessary for his informed consent. Informed consent is generally a matter of professional standards, and a professional could hardly be expected to warn of risks that he was not aware of. (Informed consent is not yet a matter of strict liability.) If my assumption that Jones did not know of the theoretical danger of severe hemorrhaging is incorrect, then it seems highly likely that she failed to gain Smith's informed consent. This would seem to be so even though the danger was only "theoretical", since a person in Smith's position, suffering a non-fatal disorder, might well decline to take the drug on account of this danger.

It may also have been negligent of Dr. Jones not to warn of the danger of on-and-off nausea for several months. Again, this is a factor that might well have been material to one in Smith's position. It seems probable that even though this particular risk never materialized in his case, its omission from Jones' description of the drug should be held against her for purposes of determining whether she was negligent. The question ought to be whether, taking all the undisclosed risks together, Smith was given enough information to make a reasonable choice.

If Dr. Jones is found to have been negligent in not obtaining Smith's informed consent, the court will then have to decide whether this negligence was the proximate cause of either the hemorrhaging or the auto accident. It seems likely that it will be a proximate cause of at least the hemorrhaging, since this was one of the risks (although theoretical) the non-disclosure of which was negligent. If this is so, then the car accident also ought to be a proximate result, since it is highly foreseeable that one who suffers a hemorrhage will do so while driving and get into an accident. Furthermore, since there was a danger of blurred vision anyway, the accident would, as noted, fall within the "foreseeable harm but unforeseeable manner" principle, as it would in Smith's case against Dow.

Brown v. Smith: Brown can try to maintain an ordinary negligence action against Smith. His biggest problem will be in showing that Smith was negligent, since there is no indication that Smith had any knowledge of the danger to his vision. Nor is there any indication that Smith was negligent in maintaining his speed when he moved to pass.

If Brown does somehow establish Smith's negligence, he would still be faced with a potent comparative negligence defense by Smith. Brown might be able to combat this by showing that it would have been unreasonable for him to have tried to change the tire at the side of the road, and risk getting stuck, particularly in view of the extreme social importance of his being on time for his speech. (In general, the value of the interest being pursued by the plaintiff will be taken into account in determining whether he was comparatively negligent.)

If there is found to have been comparative negligence, Brown's recovery will be reduced by the proportion which his negligence bears to the combined negligence of Smith and himself. If the jurisdiction is one in which ***last clear chance*** is still allowed as a defense despite comparative negligence, Brown might have a chance at having this doctrine applied. However, it doesn't seem that Smith, suffering as he was from a hemorrhage, really had a last clear chance to avoid the accident.

Brown v. Dow Drug: Brown might bring a strict tort liability claim against Dow. He would have to make the same showing as to defectiveness and lack of warning as Smith would. Beyond that, he would have to convince the court to extend the strict tort doctrine to cover him as a bystander. Most jurisdictions have been willing to make such an extension, particularly where the bystander is a pedestrian or motorist injured in a car accident. (However, most such cases have involved defective automobiles, where the risk of bystander injuries is probably greater than it is from a defective drug.) The proximate cause issue is likely to be resolved the same way as in Smith's suit against Dow for his fracture and the damage to his car.

Brown v. Dr. Jones: If Brown brought a negligence action against Dr. Jones, he would have to establish negligence on the same informed consent basis as would Smith. His biggest obstacle, however, would be in establishing that Dr. Jones bore him a ***duty of care***. A court might well hold that even assuming that there was a significant enough danger of hemorrhaging that Jones should have warned Smith of this, the danger to a passing motorist is slimmer, and the motorist might be in a *Palsgraf* position. On the other hand, Brown can point out the fact there was also a danger of an accident occurring through temporarily blurred vision, and that he was a foreseeable victim of such an accident.

Even apart from this, there remains the broader question of whether a doctor should ever be liable for injuries to third persons arising from side effects of a drug (whether or not there was informed consent). Suppose that Dr. Jones had made all required disclosure, and Smith elected to go ahead with the use of the drug; it would certainly seem unfair to hold Jones liable for Brown's injuries in this event. The old *Palsgraf* question arises again: why should Brown be able to take advantage of Jones' negligence (lack of informed consent) vis-à-vis Smith? All in all, it seems unlikely that a court would hold Dr. Jones liable.

QUESTION 4

Prime Textiles Corporation purchased a 30-year-old building in an industrial section of Amesville in late 2019 and converted its interior to a plant for the manufacture of brightly colored fabrics to be sold to dress manufacturers. Prime has been a successful innovator in designs and even in a year of recession shows a handsome profit. Its sales are at an annual rate of about $60 million, and it employs 400 workers and technicians at this, its only plant.

In early 2020, Dead-em Insecticides, Inc., constructed for $20 million a plant in the same industrial section of Amesville, five blocks (1/4 mile) distant from Prime. It employs 200 workers and technicians. Dead-em is a leading producer of insecticides for use against household pests — bees, roaches, etc. In 2021 it developed a new and commercially successful product, Strike, that has proved to be remarkably effective while meeting all safety requirements. The new process of manufacture necessarily involves the emission of gases and other by-products different in chemical composition from the by-products of the manufacture of the earlier type of insecticides.

By mid-2022, Prime began to receive complaints from its vendees that the colors on about 1/2 of its fabrics were not proving "true" or "fast". They faded after several months, and some took on a different tint. After investigation, Prime determined that the recent gaseous emissions from Dead-em had permeated its building and adversely affected certain of the dyes that it used for coloring fabrics.

Prime has retained your firm to advise it of what recourse it has against Dead-em. Your preliminary inquiry reveals the following additional information. (1) No other industrial producer in this section of Amesville has been adversely affected by these emissions. (2) The alternatives open to Prime, if it has no recourse against Dead-em, are to abandon a profitable and important part of its production involving certain standard, adversely affected dyes; to remove at great and perhaps prohibitive expense to another location; or to renovate its building (doors, windows, year-round air conditioning) to exclude the interfering gases. This last alternative would cost about $20 million, a serious expenditure that, in a competitive industry, would sharply reduce profits. (3) Prime's 2022 loss of profits (on many warranty claims from its vendees and then reduced sales) is estimated at $5 million.

The senior partner in your firm requests a memorandum outlining (a) the possible legal recourse against Dead-em, (b) your analysis of the difficulties in litigation and assessment of the chances of success, and (c) your recommendation of how Prime should proceed. No recent decision of the Supreme Court of Ames addresses this type of problem.

ANSWER TO QUESTION 4

Prime can proceed on either a trespass or a nuisance theory. On either of these theories, it can attempt to get compensatory damages for past and/or future harm, as well as an injunction against future wrongdoing by Dead-em.

Trespass: Prime should first try to show that the permeation of its plants by the Dead-em gases constituted a trespass. Until fairly recently, courts refused to recognize that gases and fine particles could constitute a trespassory invasion, and required a suit based on nuisance. But a number of courts now permit a trespass suit in this situation. For instance, in *Martin v. Reynolds Metals Co.*, a suit in trespass was allowed where gases and particles from an aluminum reducing plant ruined the plaintiff's farmland.

To maintain a trespass action, Prime will have to show that the gaseous invasion was "intentional". It will not have to show that Dead-em intended or knew that damage to the dyes would result, but it does have to show that Dead-em knew that the gases would enter the plant (i.e., that the trespassory contact was intentional). This may be difficult (at least prior to Prime's giving notice to Dead-em of the problem), since the two plants are some distance apart.

If the court accepts the argument that there has been a trespass, we should have no problem getting compensatory damages for the lost profits in 2022. Prime may also be able to get an injunction against future trespasses of this nature. It would have to show that permanent compensatory damages (i.e., an estimate of the harm caused in the future) would not be an adequate remedy. If the court is disinclined to give an injunction, there is a good chance that we could get it to award the $20 million required to gas-proof the plant.

Nuisance: If we fail to sustain the trespass theory (e.g., because the court won't recognizes gases as trespassory), we will have to resort to a private nuisance theory. We can certainly satisfy the basic requirement, a showing that Prime's use and enjoyment of its property has been substantially impaired.

We will also have to show that Dead-em's interference with Prime was either intentional, negligent, or abnormally dangerous. At at some point after Prime discovered the damage, I assume that it made a complaint to Dead-em. As to any damage occurring after this time, we would almost certainly be able to show that the nuisance should be treated as "intentional", since Dead-em knew that the gaseous invasion was occurring. But prior to our giving notice, I think we will have trouble showing that there was either negligence, intent or abnormal danger. We may simply have to write off the $5 million loss during 2022.

We face several additional hurdles in trying to get prospective damages or an injunction on a nuisance theory. First, Dead-em is almost certain to argue that Prime's manufacturing process constitutes an ***"abnormally sensitive activity"***, and that it should not be liable for this. Dead-em could cite *Rogers v. Elliott*, where a plaintiff who was sent into convulsions by the defendant's church bell was not allowed to recover for nuisance due to his abnormal sensitivity. On the other hand, what constitutes "abnormal" is determined in part by the plaintiff's location; since Prime is located in an industrial area, surely a suitable place in which to run a manufacturing and dying plant, its use might not be held to be abnormally sensitive.

An additional requirement that Prime will have to meet is a showing that Dead-em's interference was "unreasonable". Dead-em will be able to show not only that its plant employs a lot of people, and represents a large investment, but also that there is a substantial social good resulting from its product (i.e., freedom from bugs with safety).

Until recently, many courts would have simply determined whether the harm to Prime was greater or less than the social utility of Dead-em's product, and if the former was less than the latter, would have refused damages. Now, however, there is an increasing tendency to hold that even if the defendant's conduct has benefits outweighing the detriments to the plaintiff, the defendant must still pay for the harm he causes. This is the view of the Second Restatement. We would still have to show that requiring Dead-em to pay permanent compensatory damages (probably the $20 million required for gas-proofing) would not put it out of business, but I think we can make this showing.

I don't think we have much of a chance of getting an injunction on a nuisance theory. Here, the court will definitely balance the benefits of Dead-em's product against the harm to us, and I don't think we'll come out ahead. Even though we employ more people than Dead-em, the fact remains that we could keep the same employment merely by investing $20 million, whereas Dead-em would probably be put out of business, or at least have to slash a good portion of its working force (as well as giving up a socially useful product) if the injunction were granted. The court is likely to point to *Boomer v. Atlantic Cement* as authority for denying a permanent injunction.

Final recommendations: In summary, we might as well try both trespass and nuisance theories. We should try to develop facts which will push back as far as possible the date on which Dead-em knew or should have known of the invasion of the plant by its emissions, so that we will be able to get recovery for the 2022 lost profits. We should probably not devote too much of our resources to trying to get an injunction, since this seems futile; instead, we should try to recover the $20 million it would take to gas-proof Prime.

TABLE OF CASES

This table includes references to cases cited everywhere in this book, including in the various Exam Q&A sections.

SUBJECT MATTER INDEX

This index includes references to the Capsule Summary and to the Exam Tips, but not to Q&A or Flow Charts